T0339455

Consumer Behavior
and Advertising
Involvement

Consumer Behavior
and Advertising
Involvement

Selected Works of Herbert E. Krugman

EDWARD P. KRUGMAN

Routledge
Taylor & Francis Group

LONDON AND NEW YORK

First published 2008 by Routledge

2 Park Square, Milton Park, Abingdon, Oxfordshire OX14 4RN
711 Third Avenue, New York, NY 10017

Routledge is an imprint of the Taylor & Francis Group, an informa business

First issued in paperback 2018

ISBN-13: 978-0-8058-5788-7 (hbk)
ISBN-13: 978-1-138-38430-9 (pbk)

Library of Congress Cataloging-in-Publication Data

Krugman, Herbert.
    Consumer behavior and advertising involvement : selected works of Herbert Krugman / [edited] by Edward Krugman.
        p. cm. -- (Marketing and consumer psychology series)
    Includes bibliographical references and index.
        ISBN-13: 978-0-8058-5788-7
        ISBN-10: 0-8058-5788-5
        1. Advertising--Psychological aspects. 2. Consumer behavior. I. Krugman, Edward.
    II. Title.

HF5822.K78 2008
658.8'342--dc22   2008009298

EDITOR'S NOTE

It is impossible for a son to describe his father fairly to the rest of the world. One can be dry or maudlin; it is very difficult to find ground in between.

For the dry, consider the three short paragraphs of my Dad's official biography:

> From 1967 to his retirement in 1983, Herbert E. Krugman was manager of corporate public opinion research at the General Electric Company. He was previously research vice president for Marplan, for Ted Bates Advertising, and for the industrial design firm of Raymond Loewy.
>
> Dr. Krugman received his Ph.D. from Columbia University in 1952 and his B.S.S. from CCNY in 1942. He is a past-president of the American Association for Public Opinion Research, of the Division of Consumer Psychology of the American Psychological Association, and of the Market Research Council of New York.
>
> He has served on the faculties of Yale, Princeton and Columbia Universities and has been a trustee of the Marketing Science Institute in Cambridge, a director of the Advertising Research Foundation and chairman of the Research Policy Committee of the Association of National Advertisers.

For the maudlin—but, no. This is not the place to talk of dogs, horses, hockey, baseball, flying, shooting, sailing, kayaking, or being married sixty-five years to the same woman. Still less is it the place to talk of how blessed I feel to have the parents I do. Rather, this is the place to talk of a professional and intellectual life that has been second to none in its field. Professor Wells lays out that life in some detail in his Foreword, and his organization of the materials into four sections—Themes, Brain Waves, Corporate Advertising, and Methods and Observations—provides a remarkable perspective on a remarkable *oeuvre*.

This volume spans nearly half a century, from 1947 (Chapter 12) to 1994 (Chapter 49). Perhaps the most famous piece is the 1965 AAPOR Presidential Address, *The Impact of Television Advertising: Learning Without Involvement* (Chapter 6). It is significant, though, that the word "learning" appeared in the titles of three other articles in the few years leading up to that address. Herb Krugman is a student of learning, and this work could easily have been subtitled "Learning About Learning."

It is also significant that Dad was only forty-four when he delivered that Presidential Address, and but forty-six when he delivered the Presidential Address for the APA's Division of Consumer Psychology. His rise to the top of his profession as a relatively young man reflects broad recognition of the strength of his ideas. Such institutional positions are frequently segues into retirement, but not here: Herb Krugman had two decades of original and creative thought yet to come.

During the disgracefully long time it has taken me to complete this volume, I have had repeated opportunities to read and re-read both the articles in this volume and others that, because of their disparate subject matter, were not chosen for inclusion. I never failed to marvel at the intellectual power manifested in the pages before me. Dad's works combine insights from physiological and cognitive psychology, survey methodology, and other disciplines in ways that are uniquely his own. Each piece turns out to be just a little bit more interesting than the reader expected going in. The cumulative effect of those pleasant surprises is overpowering.

Enjoy.

CONTENTS

Section II: Brain Waves

Section III: Corporate Advertising

Section IV: Methods and Observations

SERIES FOREWORD

The Marketing and Consumer Psychology series serves as forum for the interaction of theory, basic research and practice. The publication of the lifetime works of Herbert Krugman in a single volume is a unique opportunity to see the evolution of work by a person who contributed so much to theory, research, and practice throughout his very productive and influential career.

In the foreword to the book, we are fortunate to have the perspectives of William D. Wells, another outstanding and longstanding contributor to the disciplines of consumer behavior, advertising, and marketing research.

Graduate students, new and established practitioners, and contem-porary researchers will benefit from an examination of how Herbert Krugman addressed fundamental issues associated with understanding, predicting, and influencing consumer behavior.

Curtis P. Haugtvedt
Ohio State
Marketing and Consumer Psychology Series Editor

FOREWORD

William D. Wells
University of Minnesota

SECTION I: THEMES

As he notes in Chapter 29 of this volume, the author of these papers began his research career as an aviation psychologist at Randolph Field, Texas. There he participated in a series of experiments intended to discover whether "critical flicker frequency," a little-known physiological phenomenon, could determine whether military aircrews were fit for duty.

These early experiments forecast major themes in his long and innovative research career. One theme is an enduring belief that social science research methods, including physiological responses measured in the laboratory, predict important behavior in the outside world. Another is an underlying assumption that academic social science theories, especially theories from academic psychology, provide useful guidance to managers who govern day-to-day events. Still another is unwillingness to accept conventional methods when something more sensitive, more reliable or more valid might be had.

Chapters 1, 2 and 3—"The Learning of Tastes," "The Learning of Consumer Preferences," and "An Application of Learning Theory to TV Copy Testing"—report early efforts to apply social science theories and methods in studies of consumer preferences. Here, theories of learning from academic psychology help explain relationships between liking and familiarity, and predict effects of repetition upon reactions to advertisements, packages, music and art.

Chapter 3 introduces another preoccupation. In quoting an 1885 essay called *Hints to Intending Advertisers*, the author initiates an enduring interest in one of advertising's most fundamental issues: How many exposures are enough? As following chapters will show, this question absorbed a large portion of his research effort, time and thought, and ultimately produced a counter-intuitive, radical and influential answer that is detailed in Chapter 16.

Chapters 4 and 5—"Some Applications of Pupil Measurement" and "A Comparison of Physical and Verbal Responses to Television Commercials"— introduce eye movements and pupil dilation as ways of delving into marketing communications. These reports initiate another theme. They express a growing conviction that physiological responses may be more sensitive, more reliable, and more valid than "conscious impressions verbally reported."

Although this conviction was never fully accepted by the advertising research community, and ultimately retracted by the author himself, the underlying theme remains. Chapters 4 and 5, and those that follow, continue to demonstrate unswerving dedication to the scientific method, restless dissatisfaction with the commonplace, and enduring commitment to finding new and better ways.

Chapter 6—"The Impact of Television Advertising: Learning Without Involvement"—pays off the work reported in Chapters 1 through 5 by calling attention to a fundamental difference between high-involvement persuasion and low-involvement persuasion. Its radical proposal to industry and academic researchers was (and is), "perhaps our model of the influence process is wrong." In Chapter 6, the author advances cogent reasons for considering this proposal, and delineates its implications for basic and applied research.

When Chapter 6 was written, the most usual way of thinking about persuasion was AIDA—Attention, Interest, Desire, and Action. In AIDA, the first duty of an advertisement is to attract Attention. The second duty is to arouse Interest in the product, service or issue being advertised. The third duty is to convert that Interest into Desire. The closing duty is to convert Desire into Action.

Underlying this dominant view is the key concept, attitude. Then as now, attitude theory held that consumers and voters learn enduring predispositions to behave in particular ways. According to AIDA, the role and duty of advertisements and other forms of persuasive communication is to revise these predispositions—these attitudes—and thereby alter the behavior they evoke.

As the author notes in Chapter 6, one shortcoming of AIDA is lack of confirming empirical evidence. Despite years of dedicated effort, neither academic nor applied researchers had accumulated a body of evidence that could have been said to demonstrate that the persuasion process invariably or even typically follows the AIDA route.

Even more telling, the author's own studies of the learning of preferences, and of consumers' responses to persuasive communications, had convinced him that AIDA was insufficient, especially when it comes to learning brand preferences from TV ads.

His radical resolution of this problem, outlined in Chapter 6, was to advance the notion that while AIDA may describe the process through which arguments influence important, well-thought-out decisions, it does not describe the process through which television commercials influence the many minor choices buyers make in supermarkets every day.

In these "low involvement" situations, he asserted, repeated exposures to television advertisements gradually shift the relative salience of vaguely apprehended brand impressions. At some point, in response to these shifts, and in response to whatever happens to have happened at the point of purchase, the buyer chooses then uses the brand. Then, and only then, a measurable change in attitude takes place.

This model is radically different from AIDA. It describes a different process, and it implies that advertising testing methods that are applied after exposure to the message but before purchase or use of the product or service are liable to overlook essential aspects of how low involvement advertising works.

This challenge to existing practice had major repercussions in two arenas. To advertisers and advertising researchers, it implied that while AIDA and the research methods based upon it may well be relevant to important, well-thought-out purchasing and political decisions, they are mostly irrelevant to low involvement choices among brands. To academic researchers, it implied that the conditions under which attitude change can be expected to follow rather than lead to behavior change would need to be systematically laid out.

Chapter 7—"The Measurement of Advertising Involvement"—picks up the major themes of Chapter 6, provides detailed instructions for measuring the personal connections that promote shifts in salience, describes a set of empirical findings based upon the low involvement model, and discusses implications for TV and print. The latter theme—television versus print—becomes increasingly important as the present volume unfolds.

Chapter 8—"Psychological Perspectives on Marketing Strategy"—now blends findings from Chapters 1, 2 and 3 with findings from more recent work on low involvement. The author summarizes this integration in this way: "with low involvement choices one might look for product or service adoption through gradual shifts in perceptual structure, aided by repetition, activated by behavioral choice situations, and followed at some time by attitude change. With high involvement product preference, one could look instead for the classic, more dramatic, more familiar conflict of ideas at the level of conscious opinion and attitude that precedes changes in overt behavior." This is the fundamental insight of this portion of his work.

Chapters 9 and 10—"Processes Underlying Exposure to Advertising" and "Television and Trust in Rationality"—report additional work on events within the respondent during attention to persuasive communications. Like previous chapters in this section, they draw real-world inferences from laboratory experiments, and favor covert responses over "conscious impressions verbally reported." They continue to contrast television advertising with print advertising, and they begin to speculate upon the broader implications of the thousands of hours American consumers spend with the tube.

At the time Chapters 9 and 10 were written, low involvement theory had attracted quite a lot of attention in the advertising and media worlds. To advertising researchers, low involvement theory meant that the most generally accepted advertising testing methods could not be trusted to assess the impact of television. To media researchers, it meant that cost per thousand viewers—the accepted metric for assessing media efficiency—could not provide a valid way to weigh TV against print.

Chapter 11, the only chapter in this volume not written by Krugman himself, reviews this controversy from an outside point of view. Originally a feature article in *Media Decisions*, a widely read industry periodical, it outlines Krugman's heretical views on low involvement advertising, describes his measurement proposals, and reports reactions to his theories from leading figures in advertising and media research. Not surprisingly, these evaluations are tentative and mixed. Even so, all agree that this reformation ranks among the industry's most interesting estimations of how persuasive communications work.

SECTION II: BRAIN WAVES

Chapter 12, written in 1947 on the basis of a study performed in the Army Air Forces in the Second World War, is a preview of the use of physiological methods that would characterize much of the author's work in the 1960s and 1970s. The development picks up in Chapter 13—"Passive Learning from Television"—which introduces a new element into the discussion of what goes on within the viewer's head during exposure to persuasive messages from print and television. Once again it rejects "one sided emphasis on verbal data and the measurement of comprehension, recall, attitudes and the like" in favor of more exacting analysis of the "animal, mechanical and physical properties, which define the limits, constraints, and conditions within which these verbal data function."

Here, the emphasis turns to measurement of electrical activity within the right and left hemispheres of the brain, sensitive indices that, according to the author, hold special promise for tracing differences between active, voluntary attention associated with print media, and relaxed attention associated with TV. While the method is distinctly different, the major themes remain: reservations about the sensitivity, reliability and validity of introspective copy testing methods, continuing conviction that the laboratory will yield externally valid findings of great practical importance, preoccupation with the processes that occur within the respondent during exposure to persuasive messages, and analysis of differences between TV and print.

Chapters 14 through 16—"Mass Media and Mental Maturity," "'Temporary' Effects of Communication," and "Brain Wave Measures of Media Involvement"—develop these themes by reporting experiments in which measurements of eye movements and brain activity lead to the expectation that "the response to print generally may come to be understood as active, and composed primarily of fast brain waves while the response to television might come to be understood as passive and composed primarily of slow brain waves." As the author notes, this premise may account for Marshall McLuhan's famous insight that print media are "hot" in the sense that they require effortful, active attention and participation, while electronic media are "cool" in the sense that they "effortlessly transmit into storage huge quantities of information not thought about at the time of exposure."

Chapter 17—"Why Three Exposures May Be Enough"—presents another challenge to conventional understanding of persuasive communication. In Chapter 3 of this volume, the author used *Hints to Intending Advertisers* and academic learning theories to launch a series of experiments on effects of repetition. In Chapter 17, he caps a decade of empirical investigation with a sensational conclusion: the first exposure to an advertisement stirs curiosity, the second prompts recognition, the third evokes decision, and further exposures yield nothing more than disengagement from a completed event.

To advertisers who were spending major resources on multiple exposures of the same advertisement, this conclusion, if deemed valid, would have most welcome impact on costly media plans. To the advertising industry, supported as it was by long-term, multi-repetition budgets, this conclusion—if accepted—would have devastating economic effects.

Chapters 17 through 29 are devoted to defending this point of view and developing its implications. They report empirical research intended to support the three-exposure proposition, continue to assert the superiority of physiological measurements over verbal measurements, and reemphasize the need to focus on processes that occur within the brain during exposure to persuasive communication.

Chapter 30, the last chapter in this section, is perhaps the most surprising. In a "personal retrospective" that reviews all this work, the author concludes, "Physiological research is not good at predicting success of advertising, and certainly not better than verbal data, although perhaps no worse." He then advocates a new measurement procedure in which physiological responses serve as cues that help direct depth interviews. Thus, after three decades of favoring physiological measurements over "conscious impressions verbally reported," he asserts that physiological responses are most instructive when they are analyzed in conjunction with, rather than instead of, meanings derived from words.

This revision stands as testimony to the author's unwavering devotion to the principles of scientific work. Instead of forcing findings to fit a long-standing conviction, he followed the data where they took him, and concluded that a blend of covert and overt responses can be expected to be more informative than covert responses alone.

SECTION III: CORPORATE ADVERTISING

At General Electric, the author managed a national survey that tracked social and economic issues of strategic importance to the firm. In the chapters that follow he describes the outcomes of this research program, with special focus on the effects of GE's corporate communications. As always, he reaches beyond the conventional to advocate new uses for established practices, and looks behind the obvious to gain new insights into how things work.

In Chapter 31—"Adapting Existing Survey Data Banks to Social Indicator Purposes"—he advocates a productive practice that is abysmally underused today. He says, "the opinion survey profession overvalues current and newsworthy data, rarely stops to look back or take stock," and shows how looking back and taking stock of long-term changes in attitudes and opinions can improve interpretation of unfolding events. In this context, the issues of most interest included public introductions of great technological innovations, news reports of corporate profits, and political reactions to the power "big" business exerts.

In the ensuing chapters the author reports experiments in which findings from this survey assess the impact of GE's corporate advertising. Here, he addresses interactions between spokespersons and advertisements, rethinks his earlier analysis of differences between TV and print, re-asks "how many exposures may be enough?" and evaluates the impact of GE Theatre dramas upon the commercials that they frame.

In these experiments, data from the survey data bank show that corporate advertisements can make corporate spokespersons more effective by making them more credible, that corporate advertisements can be every bit as thought-provoking on television as they are in print, that the answer to the exposure question may be "one," and that "interesting shows increase the effectiveness of interruptive but interesting commercials, and diminish the effectiveness of interruptive commercials of less interest."

At the time they were made, these conclusions were actionable answers to critical strategic questions. Now, like all insightful scientific findings, they invite exploitation in extensions of the work.

SECTION IV: METHODS AND OBSERVATIONS

In Chapter 4 of this volume, the author first expresses lack of confidence in the common questionnaire. There and in ensuing chapters he proposes a gallery of alternatives to asking direct questions and accepting direct answers. The first chapter of this last section advocates still another indirect method, the "draw a supermarket" technique. Instead of being asked about their attitudes toward the various departments of supermarkets, respondents are asked to draw a supermarket layout. Their drawings are then analyzed in conjunction with more conventional interviews to gain insights into customers' evaluations of supermarket planning and design.

The remaining chapters in this section are devoted to more general observations of the media landscape, additional evaluations of methods used to measure short term and long-term effects of advertising, and comments on history, present status and probable future of consumer research. These chapters repeat, organize and elaborate many of the anthems of the previous sections of this book. They discuss distinctions between the print media and the electronic media as instruments of mass communication. They lay new emphasis on the distinction between high involvement and low involvement responses to persuasion. They reiterate reservations as to the sensitivity, reliability and validity of conventional copy testing methods, and, from a "human factors" point of view, they speculate on the consequences of impending changes in the dimensions and capabilities of television sets.

Throughout these chapters the author maintains his interest in methodological innovation, his drive to draw insights from, as distinguished from merely reporting, the outcomes of surveys and experiments, and his fundamental premise that social science theories and social science methods can improve practical responses to real-world events.

CHAPTER 1

THE LEARNING OF TASTES

(with Eugene L. Hartley)

The subject of consumer taste has proved an elusive one for social scientists and businessmen alike. But while the latter energetically pursue the public on a day-to-day basis with ever new baubles and gadgets, the social sciences have for the most part confined their interest to a broad and distant view and only rarely descended to research on the specific processes of taste formation. For students of public opinion the particular process of familiarization has special relevance in view of their concern with the *new,* if not in products then certainly in ideas. Too often in the past, furthermore, explanations for public acceptance or rejection of the new have wandered without restraint between such commonplaces as "Repetition equals reputation," and "Familiarity breeds contempt," or "It's the novelty that attracts people," and "It's too new for the public."

All the social sciences have made at least some broad-gauged attempts to come to grips with the problem. Anthropologists like Kroeber and sociologists like Sorokin have made long-term historical analyses of changing styles in dress fashion and art, respectively.[1] Psychologists like Hurlock have studied personality factors in dress.[2] Social historians like Wector have traced the course of a broad variety of taste and style changes in upper-class American society.[3] A great deal of interest has been focused by sociologists on what is called "mass culture," or "popular culture," and here Rosenberg and White have brought together a wealth of material on the changing contents and functions of this culture.[4] Russell Lynes has written entertainingly about the differences between high-brow, middle-brow, and low-brow culture in America,[5] and Vance Packard has attempted to create a social issue out of the malevolent and omnipotent business forces which he sees as controlling the taste and buying habits of the general public.[6] What has not been dealt with, however, is the close study of the rise and/or fall of specific tastes. In a way, the sudden rise and often equally sudden fall of "fads" and fancies in the marketplace are treated as temporary aberrations not worthy of serious attention — perhaps in part because of the plainly trivial nature of some of the objects involved, for example, beanie caps,

Original Publication: *Public Opinion Quarterly*, Vol. 24, No. 4 (Winter 1960), pp. 621-631 hula-hoops, and beards. When perchance a fad or newly popular item becomes generalized into a broad acceptance for some new theme, *i.e.*, when a new "style" or "fashion" is born, then it is true there is talk of norms and mores and the social scientists may be interested. The question of how a fad turns into a style or fashion is necessarily unanswered, however, since the antecedent fad and the whole subject of fads have been left unexplored and un-understood. This applies equally to the new style or fashion which achieves a quiet and un-obtrusive acceptance without benefit of an antecedent and much-commented-upon fad.

The subject is important for several reasons. To the small businessman it represents a particularly tragic area of decision-making. How often a manufac-turer finds a sudden "hit" on his hands and borrows capital to expand plant and equipment, only to find in the midst of trebled production that the will-o'-the-wisp public has lost interest. At the other extreme, we have the manufacturer who is rightly convinced of the worth and potential of his new product, who miscalculates the time it will take for his product to catch on, and who closes his doors financially, unable to wait even in the face of mounting public interest.

For the social sciences, and especially for psychology, the subject is impor-tant because it concerns the question of how we *learn to like* objects or ideas. While there is a great deal of research and tested knowledge concerning our ability to learn new skills or solve new problems, we do not confidently know if the principles uncovered in those areas apply to the learning of likes or dislikes or, if not, what principles do apply.

To the market or consumer researcher, the subject is also unclear. Most tests of consumer likes and dislikes involve one-time exposure procedures, for example, "Madam how do you feel about this new product X (Like ...... dislike ...... or no opinion ......)?" No single-exposure procedure can allow for so many of the problems inherent in the learning process. Learning often implies time and repeated trials or exposures. What we like today may seem dull tomorrow. What seems uninteresting on first view may prove somewhat intriguing with a second look, etc. Indeed the market researchers' pre-testing of television and other programs on a single-exposure basis may in part be responsible for the low levels of taste in much of what is presented to the public. If repeated rather than single-exposure tests were made, it might be demonstrated that the audience could "develop a taste" for something new and different, and the sponsor might thereby be encouraged to forego the luxury of immediate popularity for his show.

When time is taken into account, and when it is determined how well an object or idea might wear ("Will it prove popular in the long run? Will it hold up?"), we encounter another equally significant part of the subject of consumer taste, the problem of familiarity. At the other extreme from faddism, yet theo-retically its blood brother, we find innumerable examples of manufacturers of-fering beautiful and superior new styles, fabrics, devices or packages to a strange market that seems perversely to prefer going along with the older but more familiar items. The psychologist's interest may be engaged here as he identifies a familiar problem, "resistance to social change." While it is a familiar problem in those terms, however, it may not be so familiar when linked with fads and fancies as one and the same problem. That problem concerns the beginning and the end points of *learning to like*. It is the problem of some new things becoming popular quickly and others slowly, of some dying out quickly and others slowly, of some fads broadening into fashions and some fashions persisting indefinitely, It concerns the question of when novelty is delightful and when familiarity outweighs all other considerations. Put simply and perhaps best, however, it is the question of how we learn to like, and what is the influence of the extent of familiarity on the degree of liking. We would like to know more, therefore, about familiarity and liking, about fads becoming fashions, and about the qualities that enable some individuals to "make" fashions or sense new ones in the making while others dismiss them as "only fads." The subject, it may be noted, involves not only the suddenly successful novelties known as fads but the liking or disliking, popularity or unpopularity, of any and all tastes and styles evoking different kinds and degrees of public comment and reaction.

BACKGROUND

The study of learning, especially in its relation to the phenomenon of memory, is perhaps the oldest of the classic interests of academic psychology. Indeed, it goes well back into the nineteenth century. Since that time the world of education has created enormous pressures and opportunities for psychologists to contribute to better understanding of the learning process in the classroom situation. Out of the vast body of research and literature produced to meet this challenge there developed several major and competing theories of learning, differing in important theoretical respects but similar in the factors or variables considered important to study, and similar also in many of the principles which later emerged as practical guides in the classroom.

The most widely accepted principles can be summarized thus: In learning new skills, repetition or practice is effective; active practice, or recitation, is more effective than passive practice; the learning of the task as a whole is more effective than learning it piece by piece; short practice sessions spread over a longer period of time are more effective than longer practice sessions crammed into a shorter period of time; when practice is continued beyond what is required for successful accomplishment of the task at hand, there is little forgetting of what has been learned even after long periods without practice.

Now the businessman may become interested and ask what implications there are here for how complete his advertisements should be in describing his product, how often and over how long a period his advertisements should be spaced, etc. To some extent practical implications do exist, but as far as we know only in terms of product awareness. We do not know but are now asking what implications there are in terms of product liking and disliking. One difficulty lies in the difference between classroom and marketplace. In the former we have motivated individuals actively coping with difficult problems, whereas in the latter we are much more involved with capturing the attention of a passive audience and creating likes for objects, forms, and ideas which, despite the manufacturers' pride, may be quite trivial in importance or consumer concern. These qualifications do not prevent us, however, from singling out the major factor in learning, *i.e.*, repetition, and putting it in terms of exposure and familiarity, to see where and how it can be linked to the development of likes and dislikes.

Two aspects of repetition and familiarity may be defined. One concerns what is called cognitive, or perceptual, learning, for example, how often do we have to look at an object or hear a theme before we recognize it as "familiar"? The second concerns what is called affective learning, for example, how often do we have to look or hear before we "like"? Both aspects will concern us, and the interrelationship of the two will be our particular focus.

THREE EXPERIMENTS

Familiarity may affect our attitudes toward a wide variety of items from everyday life. A pioneer attempt to study such variety in an experimental setting was made by Maslow.[7] He recruited fifteen students for a ten-day, two-hours-a-day experiment. During each session the students met in the same room and took the same seats. The room had large, bright pictures on the wall and a metronome ticking in the background. The sessions were devoted to looking at a series of paintings by fifteen well-known artists, trying to write down and spell correctly the names of Russian women read to them by the experimenter, copying out of a book those sentences that contained key words provided on a separate list, and marking true-false tests. Throughout the experiment the students wore smocks, used gray rubber bands, large paper clips, yellow blotters, unlined 3 x 5 cards, used copies of books, yellow paper, and pens. Cookies were available for refreshment. These conditions prevailed generally throughout the sessions until the last few, when periodically the students were offered something different, without warning, or asked to make a judgment of personal preference.

The students were offered a chance to change seats, to have the pictures on the wall removed, to have the metronome stopped; they were shown a matched series of paintings by the same fifteen artists and asked which in each matched pair was more beautiful; they were read a similar series of Russian women's names and asked which in each matched pair sounded nicer; they were offered the choice of copying significant parts rather than whole sentences, and of writing original sentences rather than copying; they were offered an easier test-marking system; in addition, they were offered a chance to remove their smocks and to use red rubber bands, small paper clips, orange blotters, lined 3 x 5 cards, new books, blue writing pads, pencils, and a new kind of cookie.

The results showed a general tendency to choose the "familiar," although some students were more likely to do this than others. More important, there was a great difference in what kinds of choice were affected by familiarity and what kinds were not.

Students did not care to change their seats and were no longer aware enough of the bright pictures on the wall or the metronome ticking in the background to care about these matters one way or another. These items were apparently peripheral to the tasks at hand and, while distracting at first, eventually disappeared into the background. Thus familiarity neutralized them to the point where no liking or disliking was involved, but only indifference.

Judgments of paintings and names were clearly affected by familiarity, that is, the more familiar were preferred as more beautiful. In addition, half or more of the students preferred the familiar ways of copying sentences or marking tests even though the new methods offered were easier. It is in these two areas that familiarity seemed to have its most positive effect. These represented, of course, the focus of the students' attention. In the case of paintings and names, however, it was more surely demonstrated that familiarity was responsible for preference of the original series by showing that another group of students, not previously exposed to the original series, split their preferences more evenly between the two.

Students did not, at first, care about removing their smocks, but half of them did so with further encouragement. No preference was shown for rubber bands or blotters of one or another color, or for large or small paper clips. There were some tendencies to prefer the familiar unlined 3 x 5 cards, old books, pens, and original cookies. In one case, that of blue writing pads versus yellow paper, the new item was preferred. However, results might have been different if single sheets of blue paper had been compared with the single sheets of yellow paper.

In all, this study is a challenging demonstration of the potent and yet varied influence of familiarity. Some items were affected greatly, others less, and still others not at all. We would understand more, perhaps, if we knew how repeated exposures affected the responses of those who initially liked a picture or name as opposed to those who initially disliked a picture or name. We would also like to know which kinds of familiarized preference stood up over a long period of time and which disappeared with time.

Most important, we would want to bring more directly into play the concept of the learning process. In Maslow's study he deals with items that are familiar and not familiar, on a cognitive level, rather than with items of a measured degree of more or less familiarity. Thus it would be instructive to know if the influence of repeated exposures upon preference for a picture or name was greater among those students who had learned to remember the pictures more vividly or to spell the names of Russian women more correctly.

A later study of Krugman attempts to control initial familiarity with the items used in the experiment, and also raises the question of generalization, that is, what happens to liking for the general category within which one may have learned for the first time to like a single item.[8] In his study he used "swing" and "classical" music as the categories and individual musical selections as the items. He first measured students' attitudes toward swing and classical music, then selected nine students, three each who were pro-swing, pro-classical, and indifferent to both. The three at each extreme were clearly prejudiced in their attitude and rarely listened to music of the other category.

A second step was to play classical music to the swing fans and to the in-different students, and to play swing music to the classical fans. For each student the items to be played were selected by playing a number of records until three were found which he neither liked nor disliked. From then on the same selections were played once a week for eight weeks. Degree of liking was rated by the student after every playing.

Results showed a general increase in liking from week to week, typically for at least two of the three selections per student, at least until the sixth week, when some flattening of the general upward trend appeared. At the end of the experiment all the students agreed that they could get to like some selections representing a category of music to which they had previously felt a marked prejudice. Furthermore, when the initial measure of attitudes toward categories of music was repeated, it was found that some had shifted in their attitudes toward the category as well as toward the individual items.

The questions posed by the Maslow study apply to this one as well. What would the results be if one started with items that were initially liked or disliked by the students? Which likes persist and which fade away? Do eight sessions or exposures constitute the same degree of learned familiarity and recognition for one student as they do for another? In addition, what is the difference between those students who learned to like the individual items but maintained their attitude toward the category and those who shifted in their attitude toward the category?

Perhaps the main contribution of this experiment was to suggest that the development of "new" likes for specific items is closely correlated with number of exposures, that the learning involves a gradual but regular process. A secondary contribution was to show that some students generalize from their experience with the new while others do not.

A third and more recent experiment by Hartley takes a closer look at the relationship between familiarity and liking for items and categories, and he does this for different types of categories, in an attempt to discover for what categories generalization from item to category is most and least likely.[9] In his study he used "Oriental," "modern," "portrait," "floral," and "landscape" as his categories, and individual paintings as his items.

Hartley had twenty-three students rate each of ten paintings on a five-point scale of familiarity, and then again on a five-point scale of liking. The ten paintings involved two each representing Oriental, modern, portrait, floral, and landscape subjects or styles. These he called the test paintings. A week later and five times during the three weeks thereafter the students were shown five other paintings, one for each of the categories above, and asked to study them carefully for twenty seconds. They then were asked to imagine the paintings and rate them for various aspects of clarity. These were called the familiarization paintings. After the five exposures were over and these exercises in imagery completed, the original test paintings were re-rated for familiarity and liking.

Comparison of the before and after ratings of the test paintings showed a general increase in familiarity for the ten items, but with different degrees of increase by category. Thus increases were greatest for Oriental, floral, modern, and landscape in that (decreasing) order, while portraits showed a decrease in familiarity, that is, exposure to portraits made them seem less familiar. Comparison also showed that there was no general change in liking for the categories but that moderns, especially, and portraits, slightly, were more liked, while florals were less liked.

In order to discover what these differential shifts implied for the relationship between items and categories, the question was raised as to the extent to which the two Orientals, moderns, portraits, florals, and landscapes were seen or treated as members of the same category. This was done by correlating the initial ratings of familiarity and of liking for each of the two paintings in the test series: did the two Orientals get similar or dissimilar ratings on familiarity and on liking?

Keeping the very rough (N=2) definition of category in mind, it may be reported nevertheless that all correlations on familiarity were significant and positive, and that this was especially true of portraits and florals; on a cognitive level these were all true categories or fell into accepted categories. As for liking, however, the correlations were both negative and positive, and only landscapes and moderns showed significant and positive correlations. In short, there were no prejudices or tendencies to like or dislike the items as a category except for landscapes and moderns. Furthermore, when familiarity and liking were correlated with each other by category, it was found that portraits and florals showed consistent and high negative correlations for the four items involved — the more familiar, the more disliked. Orientals showed a consistent positive correlation for the two items involved — the more familiar, the more liked.

What, then, are the implications of these initial reactions? First let us summarize the results as in Table 1.1 (with F = familiarity, L = liking, and D = disliking).

The Oriental paintings were seen as a category but were (predominantly) liked more on an item-by-item than on a category basis. Familiarity with the category increased more than any other, perhaps because the category is strange to Americans, but no increase in liking for the category took place.

Floral paintings were especially seen as a category but were (predominantly) disliked more on an item-by-item than a category basis. Familiarity with the category increased significantly and apparently produced dislike for the category as such.

Modern paintings were seen and liked or disliked as a category without much item-by-item sensitivity. Familiarity with the category increased moderately, while liking for the category increased significantly.

Landscape paintings were also seen and liked or disliked as a category without item-by-item sensitivity. Familiarity with the category increased, but liking for the category did not.

Portraits were especially seen as a category, but were (predominantly) disliked more on an item-by-item than a category basis. Familiarity with the category decreased, *i.e.*, began to be seen as different, and even produced some increase in liking for the category.

One might characterize the Oriental situation as "open"; individual items can be liked, but familiarity with the category still provides room for increase without any shift in liking for the category. Florals, on the other hand, could be characterized as a dead category, where further exposure and familiarity will only broaden the dislike for individual items into a dislike for the category as a whole. Moderns and landscapes are perhaps the most popular categories of those studied here, and further familiarity with the more popular moderns increases their popularity, while further familiarity with landscapes has no further effect on their popularity. Portraits, on the other hand, represent a dead category that apparently can be resurrected or re-appreciated.

In general, then, Hartley has shown that familiarity with and study of items (in this case, the exercises in imagery) for the most part increase familiarity with

TABLE 1.1

Category	Initial Test of F as a Category	Initial Test of L or D as a Category	Initial Relation of L and D as Items	Re-test Increase in F of the Category	Re-test Shifts in L of the Category
Oriental	Yes	No	Increased F=L	Most	None
Floral	Especially	No	Increased F=D	Second	Decrease
Modern	Yes	Yes	None	Third	Increase
Landscape	Yes	Yes	None	Fourth	None
Portraits	Especially	No	Increased F=D	Decrease	Increase (slight)

the category. What then happens to liking for the category may depend on what room for further familiarity still exists (as with Orientals), on the relationship between familiarity and liking for individual items (as with florals), on the popularity of the category (as with moderns), or possibly on other factors not involved in the categories used in this study. The case of the portraits suggests that the students learned to see the category differently. It would have been useful therefore to have had a direct measure of how successful or revealing the imagery exercises were. It would seem that something was learned there about portraits which would have been measurably larger than what was learned about other categories.

To sum up the three experiments discussed, it may be said that Maslow demonstrated that familiarity with items created liking for some items but not for others; Krugman demonstrated that when familiarity with items created liking for the items then some combination of familiarity and liking could create liking for the category; Hartley showed that familiarity with items created familiarity with the category, but that this might or might not create liking for the category depending upon a number of different factors.

Taken as a group these three experiments suggest what elements ought to be included in a more ideal experiment or series of experiments:

1. Measures of initial familiarity with, and liking for, items representing categories that are old and new, popular and unpopular, familiar and unfamiliar.
2. Measures of initial familiarity with, and liking for, each category, using more than two items as a basis for measurement, or using a more direct measure.
3. Measures of the individual's ability to learn, and to generalize from learning.
4. Repeated measures of liking for items.
5. Repeated measures of "true" familiarity (*i.e.*, cognitive learning) apart from judgments of "apparent" familiarity.
6. Comparison of results with different degrees of exposure or number of trials (*i.e.*, "assumed" familiarity).
7. Repeated but less frequent measures of familiarity with, and liking for, the category.
8. Comparisons between items that showed more and less change.
9. Comparisons between categories that showed more and less change.
10. Comparisons between people who showed more and less change.

The elements above may be used to conduct research on products, brands, tastes, styles, or ideas. It matters less what is actually studied than the fact that a real gap in our knowledge is represented here, a gap that should be a matter of concern to both the social scientist and the businessman.

[1] A.L. Kroeber, and J. Richardson, *Three Centuries of Women's Dress Fashions: A Quantitative Analysis,* Berkeley, Calif., University of California Press, 1940, and P. Sorokin, *Social* and Cultural *Dynamics, Vol. 1, Fluctuations in Forms of* Art, New York, American Book, 1941.

[2] E.B. Hurlock, *The Psychology of Dress: An Analysis of Fashion and Its Motive,* New York, Ronald, 1929.

[3] D. Wector, *The Saga of American Society,* New York, Scribner, 1937.

[4] B. Rosenberg, and D.M. White, *Mass Culture: The Popular Arts in America,* Glencoe, Ill., Free Press, 1957.

[5] R. Lynes, *The Tastemakers,* New York, Harper, 1954.

[6] V.O. Packard, *The Hidden Persuaders,* New York, McKay, 1957.

[7] A.H. Maslow, "The Influence of Familiarization on Preference," *Journal of Experimental Psychology,* Vol. 21, 1937, pp. 162-80.

[8] H.E. Krugman, "Affective Response to Music as a Function of Familiarity." *Journal of Abnormal and Social Psychology,* Vol. 38, 1943, pp. 338-392.

[9] E.L. Hartley, unpublished manuscript, February 1960.

CHAPTER 2

THE LEARNING OF CONSUMER PREFERENCE

Most consumer research is based on responses to single rather than repeated exposures to products, packaging, and advertising copy — despite an enormous body of evidence indicating that such responses change with experience and the passage of time.

Although there are real technical difficulties in directly measuring the effects of experience and time, it is sometimes possible to simulate repeated exposure. This article reports the results of one such attempt. In addition, it discusses a neglected theoretical orientation toward the nature of some of the changes which occur in consumer response through time.

A recent article on the learning of tastes (Chapter 1 above) points out that the vast literature on the psychology of learning new *skills* has produced a few general principles extensively applied in the world of education, but not yet exploited for their application to the understanding of *affective learning* (likes and dislikes).

The most widely accepted principles can be summarized thus:

- In learning new skills, repetition or practice is effective.

- Active practice, or recitation, is more effective than passive practice.

- The learning of the task as a whole is more effective than learning it piece by piece.

- Short practice sessions spread over a longer period of time are more effective than longer sessions crammed into a shorter period of time.

- When practice is continued beyond what is required for successful accomplishment of the task at hand, there is little forgetting of what has been learned even after long periods without practice.

When such principles are related to problems in the pretesting of new products, packaging, and advertising copy, two questions may be asked about the effects of repeated exposures. One question concerns perceptual learning, that is, how often do we have to look at an object or hear a theme before we recognize it as "familiar"? Question two concerns affective learning, that is, how

Original Publication: *Journal of Marketing*, Vol.26, No. 2 (April 1962), pp 31-33 often do we have to look at an object or hear a theme before we "like" it and later "dislike" it?

In the fields of taste, fashion, and consumer preferences in general there are three benefits to be obtained from increased emphasis on techniques of repeat exposures.

1. The first is to eliminate some of the errors that occur in the marketing of products. How often a manufacturer finds a sudden "hit" on his hands and borrows capital to expand plant and equipment, only to find in the midst of increased production that the will-o'-the-wisp public has lost interest. At the other extreme is the manufacturer who is rightly convinced of the worth and potential of his new product, but who miscalculates the time it will take for his product to "catch on."

2. The second benefit is to contribute to the social sciences a better understanding of *how we learn to like* objects or ideas. While there is a great deal of research and tested knowledge concerning our ability to learn new skills or solve new problems, we do not confidently know if the principles uncovered in those areas apply to the learning of likes or dislikes, or if not, what principles do apply.

3. The third benefit is to facilitate acceptance of innovation and creativity. If new and unusual products, copy, television shows, etc. require several exposures before liking begins to take place, there may be sponsors who would be willing, in the face of supporting pretest information, to sacrifice immediate popularity for a more slowly developing but longer-lived or more useful popularity.

In the article mentioned above, this approach to familiarization with and learning to like objects and ideas was illustrated by a number of experiments involving new (to the people used in the experiments) paintings, music, work materials, etc. The present study provides an illustration of how a marketing decision might be *reversed* when initial consumer reactions are compared with repeated reactions.

PRETESTING PACKAGES

Two sets of packages of a washday product were prepared for separate pretesting. Each set (ACD, BCD) was tested in an eastern, midwestern, and western location (New York, Memphis, Los Angeles). The testing procedure was as follows:

1. Pairs of 35 mm. color photographs of the packages were slide-projected onto a screen for an indication of preference individually from respondents. The projections were repeated five times tachistoscopically with exposure time in the first series at 1 second, in the second series at 1½ seconds, in the third at 2 seconds, in the fourth at 2½ seconds, and in the fifth at 3 seconds. For any one series, three pair choices were offered (A vs. C, C vs. D, A vs. D). Thus, each package could achieve a total preference "score" from 0 to 2 per series.

2. Between each series, respondents rated actual sample packages. After exposure to the first slide-preference series, they rated the packages on familiarity; after the second they rated them on appropriateness; after the third, on ease of use; and after the fourth, on relative size. The repeated attention given to the packages during the rating process, as well as the increasing exposure time allotted to the repeated slide-preference series was meant to simulate the process of familiarization to the new packages. That is, the respondents were exposed to the packages repeatedly for longer periods of time, and evaluated them from several different perspectives.

As a note of caution, it should be stated that techniques of simulation require validation before being put into standard use. The purpose of the simulation technique used here was to create the same kinds of changes (if any) which respondents would have experienced in the normal course of events with repeated exposure to the packages. The validity of the technique depends, therefore, on these and no other changes being produced. In the absence of such validation, the present study is offered more as an illustration of what may be a new and potentially useful approach, rather than as a conclusive evaluation of the packages under study.

RESULTS

One set of packages (ACD) showed a significant *reversal* of preferences with repeated exposures when tested in the western location, but not in the eastern or midwestern locations. The second set of packages (BCD) showed *reversal* of preferences in both western and midwestern locations but not in the eastern location. See Table 2.1.

Attention was focused on the rank order of preferences within each series (rows), rather than the series-by-series shifts for individual packages (columns) which led to the reordering of preferences.

That is, a marketer would tend to adopt the package achieving a first-rank position, if the difference between the first and second ranks were statistically significant. Accordingly, Chi Square values were computed for each series to test the proposition that differences in rank order as large as those which were obtained would have occurred on a chance basis.

In the first group in Table 2.1 (ACD, western location) differences within each series were significant at the 1 percent level. That is, differences of the magnitude indicated would have occurred on a chance basis only once in a hundred times. In this group, only two exposures were required to change the first ranking package from D to C. In this case a marketer would, on the basis of one exposure, have been justified in adopting package D. However, using the same statistical criteria he would, with a second exposure, change his selection to package C.

In the second group in Table 2.1 (BCD, western location) rank order differences within series were also significant at the 1 percent level. Again, two exposures were all that were required to change the first ranking package from D to C.

In the third group in Table 2.1 (BCD, midwestern location) differences in rank order were not significant within the first series, but increased with each series until the fifth where they attained significance at the 5 percent level. That is, differences of the magnitude indicated would have occurred on a chance basis only 5 times out of 100. Here, therefore, all five exposures were required to place package D clearly in first rank.

IMPLICATIONS

This study probably represents a minimal demonstration of the importance of repeated exposure.

TABLE 2.1

MEAN PREFERENCE SCORES FOR FIVE EXPOSURE SERIES
(Range 0.00 Low to 2.00 High)

Location	Series	A (N=60)	C (N=60)	D (N=60)
Western				
	1	.57	1.12	1.32
	2	.45	1.33	1.22
	3	.43	1.35	1.22
	4	.47	1.30	1.23
	5	.43	1.33	1.23

Location	Series	B (N=30)	C (N=30)	D (N=30)
Midwest				
	1	.60	1.13	1.27
	2	.57	1.50	.93
	3	.57	1.47	.97
	4	.50	1.47	1.03
	5	.57	1.53	.90

Location	Series	B (N=27)	C (N=27)	D (N=27)
Midwest				
	1	1.07	1.04	.89
	2	1.04	.78	1.19
	3	1.04	.78	1.19
	4	1.04	.74	1.22
	5	.93	.70	1.37

First, familiarization was only simulated, that is, the presumed effects of time and usage were "collapsed" into about half an hour of testing.

Second, none of the packages had any essentially new or unfamiliar elements per se; that is, they were only "new" for the brand.

Third, packaging generally does not represent a class of objects which the consumer approaches with anticipation of continual change, and readiness to accommodate to that change.

However, the study demonstrates that repeated exposures to a package can alter the rank order of consumer preference, and presumably a marketing decision as to which package to adopt.

It was noted that the influence of repeated exposures was manifest in some locations but not in others, thus suggesting a need to pretest in varied types of locations. Also, in two of the three cases where repetition did alter rank order of preference, two exposures of the packages were sufficient to bring about and stabilize an alteration in rank order, but more than two exposures were required in the third case.

CHAPTER 3

AN APPLICATION OF LEARNING THEORY TO TV COPY TESTING

Uncertainty about the true advertising effectiveness of television commercials is reflected in the variety of techniques purporting to measure it. These techniques include experimental-and-control group, before-and-after, and experimental-only designs. They encompass tests in mobile trailer, movie theater, and on-the-air situations. They deal with data on immediate retention, next-day recall, brand attitudes, and opinions about the uniqueness, importance, or credibility of copy points. They all provide helpful information. However, they do not tell us as much as we would like to know about the processes of copy impact. It is suggested that other equally useful techniques for evaluating TV copy may develop from an orientation which is not initially evaluative in purpose but which seeks instead to explore the usefulness of a particular theoretical approach for understanding those processes better.

One such approach is represented in the theory of learning, a body of systematic theory with roots going back well into the last century. It has enjoyed extensive application in educational practice throughout our school system, in terms of such widely accepted principles as these:

1. In learning new skills, repetition or practice is effective.
2. Active practice, or recitation, is more effective than passive practice.
3. The learning of the task as a whole is more effective than learning it piece by piece.
4. Short practice sessions spread out over a longer period of time are more effective than longer sessions crammed into a shorter period of time.
5. When practice is continued beyond what is required for successful accomplishment of the immediate task, there is little forgetting of what has been learned even after long periods without practice.

Such principles apply to the learning of skills and knowledge, but they may also apply to the market place in the competition for consumer preference, particularly the learning of likes and dislikes. Thus, it becomes important to determine the extent to which the principles of *skill* learning may also apply to

Original Publication: *Public Opinion Quarterly*, Vol. 26, No. 4 (Winter 1962), pp. 626-634 *affective* learning (that is, learning of likes and dislikes).[1] It will be the purpose of this paper to try to extend, perhaps heuristically overextend, some of the principles of learning theory to a few problems in connection with evaluating the effectiveness of television advertising.

EFFECTS OF REPETITION

To begin, we may consider the concept of the life cycle or the life span of copy impact. The following illustration is taken from Thomas Smith's *Hints to Intending Advertisers* published in London in 1885:

The first time a man looks at an advertisement, he does not see it.
The second time he does not notice it.
The third time he is conscious of its existence.
The fourth time he faintly remembers having seen it before.
The fifth time he reads it.
The sixth time he turns up his nose at it.
The seventh time he reads it through and says, "Oh bother"
The eighth time he says, "Here's that confounded thing again"
The ninth time he wonders if it amounts to anything.
The tenth time he thinks he will ask his neighbor if he has tried it.
The eleventh time he wonders how the advertiser makes it pay.
The twelfth time he thinks perhaps it may be worth something.
The thirteenth time he thinks it must be a good thing.
The fourteenth time he remembers that he has wanted such a thing for a
    long time.
The fifteenth time he is tantalized because he cannot afford to buy it.
The sixteenth time he thinks he will buy it some day.
The seventeenth time he makes a memorandum of it.
The eighteenth time he swears at his poverty.
The nineteenth time he counts his money carefully.
The twentieth time he sees it, he buys the article, or instructs his wife to
    do so.[2]

The early phases of the life cycle of copy impact include attention getting, interest attracting, and persuasion. Beyond this are such phases as reinforcement of the initial purchase decision, reminders to replace exhausted supplies of the product, and building resistance to competing claims for attention. Individual viewers may not experience all these phases, or several phases may be collapsed into one experience. However, we can speculate about the number of phases or jobs that can be handled by a new piece of copy, whether it has a potential for sequential effects, and whether it will have a life cycle marked by a gradual shift in the nature of its impact on the individual viewers.

On the simplest level, we ask whether repetition does anything at all for copy. Does copy become more familiar with repetition? How often must it be experienced before it is judged as "familiar"? Does it get better liked with repetition? How often must it be experienced, if more than once, to be liked? Is there any evidence at all of a life cycle or span of growth or decline?

The effect of repetition on affective learning seems to vary with the complexity of the class of objects involved. Twenty years ago the author conducted a study on liking for a variety of different kinds of music, and it seemed that on the average six to eight repetitions were required per respondent before growth in liking reached a plateau.[3] Last year another such study was conducted on a psychologically simpler class of objects, namely packages of a washday product (Chapter 2 above). Here, one repetition (*i.e.*, two exposures) seemed to be the common requirement for a stabilization of consumer preference among three different packages, although in one sample a growth in liking for one package did continue through four repetitions.

In television we may think of mood copy as more complex than hard-sell copy, and attended by greater learning and liking effects with repetition. Mood copy is purposely somewhat more vague in its message, and hopefully more interesting. With repeated exposures, its content affords the viewer the possibility of making a modest but personal effort to relate or associate mood effects to brand quality. Some individuals will increasingly like the copy only, and that is a danger; but some may also shift or generalize their good reactions to the brand.

Hard-sell copy is intended to be clear and direct in its message. Little is left to chance, to the viewer, or to changed meanings with repetition. If the message is right, fine; if not, not so fine. It is a more complete sales piece. When repeated, it may still be "right," but in its simplicity it may have a "nagging" quality that makes it less liked even as the nagging is acted upon as right or sound.

It should be stressed, however, that the effects of repetition need not be linear. In terms of Hartley's recent discussion of these effects, repetition may involve an indefinite or even an infinite series; there will be the original presentation, then repetition 1, 2, 3,.... n; the subjective processes differ at various points in the series.[4]

At the onset of the series, we contend with the affective significance of new stimuli, the pleasure of novelty or the gratification of curiosity. As we move into the mid-portion of the series of repetitions, the problem of what we mean by familiarization becomes important. The simplest case is that in which an object has been perceived only once and is recognized as the same when met a second time. It is accompanied by a "feeling" of familiarity, which is never present except when there is some degree of consciousness that the impression has been received before.

Apparently, it is in association with incomplete learnings that the familiarity feeling arises. In the repetitive approach, we may ask if there is any advantage in reducing this phase of familiarity feeling in order to get on with the message; or is it preferable to capitalize on it and its presumed positive effect in order to establish the proper attitude toward the product symbol — even in advance of precise comprehension of the message? This is the choice facing the proponents of hard- and soft-sell copy.

When we shift to the late stages in the series of repetitions, where the material is thoroughly familiar, we have an entirely different process. We usually think of the development of perceptions as involving three stages. The first is the primitive, gross, figure-ground organization of the stimulus material; the second is the progressive differentiation; and the third is the reorganization of the patterns. Presumably there is then reasonable stability. However, repetition of the stabilized pattern leads to a loss of associative power, a de-differentiation of perception, and boredom, satiation, or negative adaptation.

In short, the subjective processes attendant on repeated exposures are likely to be different at different points in the series. This kind of thinking was involved in the interpretation of a recently reported study, by Krugman and Hartley, of the effect of familiarization on the liking of different kinds of paintings (Chapter 1 above). With a sample of twenty-three college students exposed to five presentations of a painting reproduction over a three-week period, ratings of familiarity and liking for reproductions of similar paintings showed considerable variability.

For "Oriental" paintings, the repeated exposures caused considerable increase in rated familiarity but no increase in rated liking. For "modern" paintings, the repeated exposures caused moderate increase in familiarity and an increase in liking. For "floral" paintings, the repeated exposures created considerable increase in familiarity and a decrease in liking. The effects with landscapes and portraits were similarly different. Apparently, the same kind of repetition produced very different results with the various kinds of stimulus material, ranging from the esoteric Orientals, to the vaguely recognizable moderns, through the almost banal florals, landscapes, and portraits.

We have, then, the following three propositions: (1) phased effects of repetition include the opportunity to like the impression of novelty and (to a point) the feeling of familiarity; (2) the amount of repetition that exhausts the potential for such effects varies with the type of experience, object, or class of objects (music, paintings, packages, copy); and (3) the extent to which increased liking for the experience of the object generalizes into liking for associated objects or the class itself also varies.

THE U-CURVE PHENOMENON

Using TV copy now as a test case, we ask whether one commercial can be learned more readily than another; whether one commercial will be liked more readily than another; and, most important, whether the processes of affective learning involved in these two dimensions accords with what we know about processes of skill learning.

Let us take so classical an experiment in the history of skill learning as Ebbinghaus's original study of the effect of serial order on difficulty in memorizing.[5] In this study he found that when subjects were asked to memorize ten units they learned the first and last units most easily, thereby producing a U-shaped curve. In later years, the phenomena evident at the two extremes of this curve came to be called the principles of "primacy" and "recency."

Now picture four commercials presented to 240 women in a copy-testing trailer parked at a shopping center. The commercials involved margarine, floor wax, a deodorant, and a hand soap. Each of four groups of sixty respondents, matched on age, income, education, product use, viewed the commercials in a different order, so that the various measures of copy impact could be related to the serial order of presentation, from 1 to 4. Four items constitute a very brief series indeed — less than the number of commercials average viewers see on a TV evening at home, and less than the ten items used by Ebbinghaus. There was some doubt, then, that any U curve could be obtained from this experiment.

First, let us look at the order in which the commercials were spontaneously written down and described when our respondents were asked to write everything they remembered having seen or heard. That is, of which commercial were they, in retrospect, more aware?

For the margarine commercial presented in first position 40 Out Of 6o recalled or wrote about it first, in second position 13 out of 6o recalled it first, in third position 8 out of 60 recalled it first, and in fourth position 21 out of 60 recalled it first. Obviously, we have here a very clear U curve. And so it goes, with one exception, for the other commercials. For the floor wax, the numbers of first recalls by position were 25, 5, 7, 17; for the deodorant, 29, 4, 7, 9; for the hand soap, 31, 6, 10, 8.

Some of the commercials produce a distinct U curve while others do not, as is more apparent when order of presentation is related to the extent to which each of the four commercials was "liked best." For the margarine commercial presented in first position 28 out of 60 liked it best, in second position 18 out of 60 liked it best, in third position 21 out of 60 liked it best, and in fourth position 22 out of 60 liked it best. For the floor wax the number of "liked bests" by position was 17, 4, 6, 12; for the deodorant 9, 2, 8, 4; for the hand soap 27, 16, 22, 19.

With such evidence of a U-curve phenomenon, we can probably say that awareness of, and liking for, TV copy is learned according to some of the same processes with which skill or knowledge is learned.[6] From a practical standpoint, however, we note that some copy produces, or is more susceptible to, a U-curve phenomenon than others. For example, the floor wax copy produces a more marked U curve on both awareness and liking.

The effects of order of presentation, furthermore, while correlated with awareness and with liking, do not correlate with other measures of copy impact, including retention, obtained in this study. There is no correlation between order of presentation and increase in favorable attitudes toward the brand, measured on a before and after basis; nor is there any correlation between increases in brand rating and awareness or liking for the commercial. Is this, then, just another demonstration of the unimportance of awareness or liking for impact on attitudes, or does it suggest a new measure with different kinds of implications for the evaluation of copy effectiveness?

It is suggested that the extent to which copy produces a U-curve phenomenon in the experiment described is a measure of its durability, wearability, or potential for further awareness and liking with repetition, and that as the copy wears out, as full awareness and liking are achieved, the U curve will belly upward to form a more or less straight line. This is not to say that it is a better commercial or a more effective commercial, but only that as a commercial more subject to positional effects at the time tested it has more learning potential left in it for whatever there is in the commercial that creates awareness and liking.[7] If the floor wax commercial is on other measures found to be effective, we might then say that no impairment of effectiveness can be anticipated with heavier and longer exposure. Although this is a secondary criterion of copy effectiveness, there are many cases where the same copy will be run, either unchanged or in slightly modified versions, year in and year out. Any desire or decision to change copy is then attended by much conflict. These conflicts have been vividly dramatized in Rosser Reeves' *Reality in Advertising.*[8]

Speaking more broadly now, we are in effect proposing that measures of the effects of serial order on affective learning can be substituted for the more administratively awkward job of studying effects of repetition per se.[9] That affective learning processes may be studied via serial order is not only a concession to administrative convenience but also a gesture toward the reality of the television experience, which is a serial phenomenon. For example, we may look back on our little experiment and, U curve or no U curve, note that first and last positions tend to be best. We note that serial order seems important, and that the principles of primacy and recency are at work. On the grounds, therefore, that an often-repeated commercial is more likely than others to be seen first and/or last in one evening's viewing, repetition is good. That is, apart from repetitive effects of commercials per se or even the effects of placement of commercials within programs, a heavy exposure budget entails serial-order effects. The two acts of the viewer, in one evening's viewing, that are considered here as generally most relevant to serial order effects are (1) turning the set on — and what comes after this act; and (2) turning the set off — and what comes before this act.[10]

The reality of television includes not only serial phenomena but advertising copy that is typically of very little importance to the viewer. In his studies on the subject, Hovland concluded that "Order of presentation is a more significant factor in influencing opinion for subjects with relatively weak desires for understanding, than for those with high 'cognitive needs.'"[11] Although Hovland studied only a two-position series, one should nevertheless beware of assuming that serial effects on the impact of TV copy would be matched by similar effects on more serious television content. Despite this caution, it is provocative to recall audience interest in the Kennedy-Nixon television debates at the height of the 1960 presidential campaign. The audience, which had been highest for the first debate and dropped off slightly for the second and third, returned on the last debate almost to the total of the first.

CONCLUSION

In closing, let us consider again the long series of equivocal research findings concerning the relationship between the liking and disliking of advertising copy and its persuasiveness. It is suggested that these involve psychologically different processes, that liking or disliking involves a physical, or motor, response while persuasion involves perceptual, or cognitive, restructuring. The two processes as such are independent of one another. However, the practical consequences of learned liking (or disliking) in combination with learned awareness or familiarity are revealed in an increase in spontaneous attention and recall. This may be illustrated in part by Schwerin's study of memory for extremely well-liked or disliked radio commercials.[12] The specific aim of this paper is to suggest a method for identifying the point at which this increased attention and recall are no longer reinforced by further exposure to copy, but the more general aim is to suggest the usefulness of affective learning theory as a tool for better understanding the processes of copy impact. This includes persuasion, at least to the extent that familiarity, which like persuasion also involves cognitive restructuring, is involved. Seeking evidence, then, for a U curve in this area, we may turn to a Schwerin report on the effect of variations in test conditions on the reliability of the competitive preference technique.[13] In this study, the effects of five variables, including order of presentation, were evaluated. Using thirty-four commercials spanning seven product classes, to provide a total of forty-nine cases in which commercials had been tested two or more times, Schwerin concluded that none of the variables had a significant effect on the reliability of increment scores. However, this conclusion reflects only a failure of critical differences to attain 90 percent confidence limits on individual cases, and gives no indication of descriptive trends or cumulative probabilities within the data. When the data are re-analyzed, it appears that the eleven commercials tested in first position achieved an average increment score of 11.04, the ten commercials tested in second position an average increment score of 7.35, and the thirteen commercials tested in third position an average increment score of 8.97. We thus have a recognizable U curve even though the series contains only three units.[14] We close, therefore, with some hope that our use of a serial order to simulate effects of repetition provides a means for measuring durability of TV copy not only in terms of awareness and liking, but in terms of persuasion as well.

[1] While it is evident that the process of "learning to like" operates between individuals, and that repetition plays a role in the development of human friendships, such sharply defined hypotheses as those of George Homans on the relationship between frequency of interaction and degree of liking (*The Human Group,* New York, Harcourt, Brace, 1950, especially pp. 108-113) have yet to be fully explored. This applies as well to Freud's hypotheses on fixation and object cathexis.

[2] Thomas Smith, *Hints to Intending Advertisers,* London, 1885. Quoted by James Playsted Wood, in *The Story of Advertising,* New York, Ronald, 1958, p. 241.

[3] H.E. Krugman, "Affective Response to Music as a Function of Familiarity," *Journal of Abnormal and Social Psychology,* vol. 3 (1943), pp. 388-392.

[4] E.L. Hartley, "The Influence of Repetition and Familiarization on Consumer Preferences," paper presented at the Convention of the American Psychological Association, Sept. 6, 1961.

[5] H. Ebbinghaus, *Grundzuge der Psychologie,* Leipzig, Germany, Veit & Co., 1902.

[6] The study design was partially replicated in a three-position series with toothpaste, laxative, and candy commercials presented to 100 men and women. The U-curve phenomenon was, as expected, less clear. For example, the numbers of first recalls (with a third of the presentations each in positions 1, 2, 3) were as follows: toothpaste 19, 10, 6; laxative 16, 1, 4; candy 20, 11, 12.

[7] An example of the U-curve hypothesis may be taken from the field of romance, with "first love" characterizing one tip of the U, and the other tip characterized by a popular song that goes, "When I'm not near the girl I love, I love the girl I'm near." In these terms, the wearability hypothesis may be expressed as follows: When a man who has had four loves gets to the point where the first and fourth no longer exceed the second and third in his reminiscence and affection, it's time to seek a fifth.

[8] Rosser Reeves, *Reality in Advertising,* New York, Knopf, 1961.

[9] To follow up on the U-curve demonstration, one could test new copy vs. competitive copy. If done with two pairs of such copy to provide four rotated positions, one could measure the extent to which awareness and liking of a piece of copy would be "competitively" enhanced or diminished by the effects of serial order. In addition, one would obtain measures of the direction of contamination or perceptual dominance similar to that obtained by National Analysts and others in measures of binocular rivalry of print ads.

[10] The serial nature of television (commercial-entertainment-commercial-etc.) also seems to inhibit an action response to television copy. That is, copy tells the viewer to buy product X, but what does the viewer do? Nothing! He sits tight — for he has learned that if he stays in his chair and does not get too involved with the copy, he will soon be rewarded with the rest of the entertainment program. From this point of view the hard-sell commercials that say "Make a note" or "Call now" make good sense. From this point of view also, any soft-sell commercial that can bear extra repetition is more likely to profit from prime and recent exposure situations.

[11] C.I. Hovland *et al., The Order of Presentation in Persuasion,* New Haven, Yale University Press, 1957, p. 136.

[12] *How You Can Get More Out of Your Radio Dollar,* Schwerin Research Corp., 1947.

[13] *Technical and Analytical Review,* Schwerin Research Corp., Winter 1959-60, No. 3.

[14] There is an obvious contrast here between Schwerin's findings and our own, the latter involving no correlation between attitude shift and awareness or liking. The explanation may lie in Schwerin's use of an award of merchandise, made on the basis of a lottery

drawing and used to elicit the before and after brand preferences that provide increment scores. That is, some psychologists have suggested that the results of latent learning are discernible only at a point of reward. It may also be significant that Schwerin places his three test commercials in a half-hour entertainment program, whereas in our test the four commercials were presented alone.

CHAPTER 4

SOME APPLICATIONS OF PUPIL MEASUREMENT

In 1960, Hess and Polt[1] reported finding a relationship between pupil dilation and the interest value of visual stimuli. Since then, over seventy studies utilizing measurement of changes in pupil diameter have been conducted by Marplan personnel on problems involving the evaluation of advertising materials, packages and products. These studies have led to a growing conviction that in many areas of human behavior one might make better predictions of behavior from pupil responses than from verbal or opinion data. The purpose of this report is to provide a brief review of the concepts involved, method of measurement, measurement goals, problems of data collection, two recently completed validation studies, and some objectives for the future.

CONCEPT

Hess and Polt reported that "Increases in the size of the pupil of the eye have been found to accompany the viewing of emotionally toned or interesting visual stimuli." A technique for recording such changes was developed so that the factor of adjustment to light was eliminated as a measurement problem. While the pupil is capable of changes from about 2mm to 8mm. in response to light, or an areal increase of 16-fold, the variation in pupil diameters involved in studies of interest is usually well within ±10 percent and often within ±2 percent.

The "plus or minus" quality referred to here is an operational function of the method of measurement (to be described). However, it does raise the question of what kinds of stimuli create measurable dilations and what kinds create measurable contractions.

Apparently there are two broad categories of affect-arousing or interest-producing stimuli that create dilations. The first category involves pleasant stimuli; the second involves stimuli that evoke fear, anxiety or shock. Contractions, on the other hand, are associated with stimuli that lack the power to interest or arouse the viewer. While stimuli that evoke fear, anxiety or shock are usually absent in commercial objects and symbols, the meaning of stimuli must be considered before one can infer that a dilation indicates pleasurably toned interest.[2] Airline, insurance, and drug advertising, for example, might be ruled

Original Publication: *Journal of Marketing Research* (November 1964)

ineligible for measurement of pupil response because a dilation might represent anxiety rather than pleasurably toned interest. In the case of such questionable stimuli one might have to consider the circumstances, inquire of the respondents, and exercise a degree of judgment before deciding that dilation represented a favorable response. While such problems are in fact quite rare in the commercial environment, their possibility must be noted.

METHOD

To conduct pupil dilation studies in the manner developed by Hess and Polt, three work stages are required.[3] First, the material to be tested is prepared in 35mm. slide form and each stimulus slide is matched for reflected illumination with a neutral control slide containing nothing but the Numbers one through five. Each study usually accommodates ten stimuli, or a total of ten pairs of stimulus and control slides.

In preparing stimulus slides it may be necessary to reduce light/dark contrasts within a picture. Modification of the stimulus to reduce light/dark contrasts may diminish somewhat the aesthetic value of pictures, but this has not yet seemed to present a problem.

The subject looks at each slide for ten seconds while his left eye is photographed at the rate of two photographs per second. While looking at each control slide, the pupil diameter is primarily a function of the light value of the slide.[4] As the matched (for light value) stimulus slide comes on, the pupil diameter may increase (as a function of greater interest) or it may decrease (as a function of lesser interest). It is this increase or decrease which is measured for each pair of control and stimulus slides.

The films are developed and each negative is projected onto a special scoring table large enough for the pupil to be measured with a ruler. The basic measure is the percent increase or decrease in the average pupil diameter for the twenty photographs taken while viewing a stimulus slide, in comparison with the average pupil diameter for the twenty photographs taken while viewing the control slide.

MEASUREMENT GOALS

Early studies were concerned primarily with measuring the pleasurably toned interest or "appeal" of individual ads, packages or product designs.[5] To this was added before-and-after measurement in which responses to a photo of the product were measured twice. Between exposures to the photo of the product, different respondents were exposed to different information (*i.e.*, different ads, paragraphs of copy, etc.) to see which information was more persuasive or which added more appeal to the product (which, along with awareness, is the goal of advertising).[6]

Television commercials have also been inserted as "in-between" stimuli for before-and-after studies. In this indirect manner, animate stimuli were evaluated for the first time. Equipment has since been developed to take direct measures of response to animate stimuli, so that pre-testing of television commercials, television programs and motion pictures can be considered as possible applications of pupil research.

DATA COLLECTION

Conventional measures usually require the subject, as he views stimuli, (1) to decide whether he likes or dislikes the stimuli, (2) to decide how he will tell this, and (3) to tell it. These three operations or units of response are absent in pupil measurement. Pupil measurement therefore circumvents language and translation problems in cross-cultural opinion and attitude surveys.

Subjects who participate in pupil measurement studies look at slides with the assumption that questions will be asked when the slides have all been shown. To fulfill this expectation, and also to interrelate pupil with verbal data, an interview is always conducted. The camera is quiet though visible and few subjects comment about it. Those who ask are answered frankly.

VALIDATION

A number of studies suggested the usefulness of pupil measurement as a predictor of behavior. In the case of products, pupil response was found to be related to sales data for watches, while in the case of ads, pupil response was found to be related to (split-run) coupons returns.[7] These studies, however, were confined to pairs of stimuli. To evaluate the extent of the relationship, or to determine whether pupil response was perhaps more predictive of sales than were other measures, it became desirable to compare an array of pupil responses and an array of verbal responses (*e.g.*, ratings) from the same subjects against a similar array of sales data. Two such studies were conducted and are reported here. They involved greeting cards and sterling silver patterns.

Greeting Cards

Ten humorous greeting cards (four friendship and six birthday) were chosen by a cooperating manufacturer to represent wide ranges in sales performance. Each card was photographed with the first and third slides of the four-sided (foldover) card showing on the slide. This eliminated the surprise element of "turning the page" and, in one card, of a mechanical pop-out device. More recently developed equipment permits a film presentation of realistic card handling and card opening.

Camera equipment was installed in a rented store in the Roosevelt Field Shopping Center (Garden City, Long Island) during January 1964, and twenty-three male and twenty-six female subjects were recruited from among passing shoppers.[8] Immediately after pupil measurement, interview data were obtained on order of recall, and then with the actual cards shown, on "card liked best" and "card liked least." The data were given to the manufacturer who then provided rank order information on sales. Results are shown in Table 4.1.

Although the pupil response correlated approximately +.4 for both sets of cards, because of the small number of cases neither correlation is statistically significant. The correlation of pupil response with sales rank would possibly have been higher if the testing procedure had not required removal of the pop-out spring from "Hi!" before photographing.

It may also be worth noting that, in the case of the larger group (birthday cards), the correlation between pupil response and sales was numerically larger than that between verbal rank and sales, but also that pupil response was *negatively* correlated with verbal rank ($R = -.60$).[9]

Sterling Silver Patterns

A cooperating retailer (Georg Jensen, Inc.) selected ten sterling silver patterns to represent a wide range in sales performance. These patterns are an exclusive line identified with the retailer. Each pattern was represented by a single place setting consisting of knife, fork, and spoon, and was photographed on a blue velvet background.

TABLE 4.1

COMPARISON OF SALES, PUPIL RESPONSES, AND VERBAL
RATINGS FOR GREETING CARDS

Title of Card	*Sales rank*	*Pupil Response*		*Verbal Rank*
		Rank	*Percent Change*	
(Friendship)[a]				
Hi!	1	3	− 0.1	2
Awkward Age	2	1	+ 1.7	3
Dolce Vita	3	2	+ 1.0	1
You're Nice	4	4	− 0.2	4
(Birthday)[b]				
Old as Hills	1	1	+ 2.9	4
Elephant	2	6	− 0.1	2
Swiss Cheese	3	2	+ 2.7	5
Cane	4	4	+ 1.7	1
Witch	5	3	+ 1.8	6
Horn	6	5	+ 0.4	3

[a] Rank order coefficient:	Sales rank with Pupil rank =	+.4
	Sales rank with Verbal rank =	+.4
	Neither value is significant	
[b] Rank order coefficient:	Sales rank with Pupil rank =	+.37
	Sales rank with Verbal rank =	+.09
	Neither value is significant	

Camera equipment was installed in an alcove at the rear of Jensen's Fifth Avenue store during February 1964, and thirty-nine female subjects were recruited from among those shoppers entering the silverware section to examine this category of merchandise. Immediately after pupil measurement, respondents were shown the ten actual place settings and were asked to rank them in order of liking, *i.e.*, 1 high to 10 low. As it happened, the thirty-nine subjects included thirteen who reported that they were actually shopping for sterling and twenty-six who were only browsing. The data were given to the retailer who then provided retail sales data for the completed year of 1962. It must be noted, however, that these 1962 data represent a combination of sales of flatware (primarily) and serving pieces and are not available on a separate basis. However, to supplement these data, Table 4.2 includes some retailer comments which appear relevant.

For both the shoppers and the browsers, the correlation between sales history and pupil response was numerically larger than the correlation between sales and verbal ratings (the difference was not statistically significant, however).[10]

It is interesting to note that the pupil response and verbal rating differed sharply for "Pyramid," with the pupil response in "agreement" with sales. "Pyramid" received the highest verbal rating from both shoppers and browsers, but ranked tenth and eighth, respectively, in pupil response. Apparently the public showed better taste than their verbal ratings would indicate.

Logically, we would expect that shoppers (who are actually planning to purchase silver) would be more "interested" in sterling than browsers. The results of the pupil response, *i.e.*, shoppers having larger percent increases and smaller percent decreases in pupil size, support this expectation. This finding, which was statistically significant, adds suggestive, though not definitive, indication of validity.

RELIABILITY

The results of the studies reported in this paper, as well as the accumulating results from a variety of similar studies, encourage the belief that pupil response is a promising new tool for study of consumer behavior.

However, because the magnitudes of changes in pupil diameter are relatively small, the question of reliability of measurement becomes important. For example, in view of the relatively small range of pupil response (from approximately −2 percent to +3 percent in the studies reported in this paper), are the responses to these stimuli really significantly different, or are they simply within the range of random fluctuation? Furthermore, is there any real agreement from subject to subject? We shall present what data are available bearing on these two questions.

SIGNIFICANCE OF STIMULUS EFFECTS

An analysis of variance was performed at the time the pupil response data were collected for the greeting cards. This analysis was designed to evaluate the effects attributable to sex stimuli (the greeting cards), and interaction of sex and stimuli. The results are presented in Table 4.3.

TABLE 4.2

COMPARISON OF SALES, PUPIL RESPONSES AND
VERBAL RATINGS FOR SILVERWARE

Pattern[c]	Shoppers[b]				Browsers		
	Sales rank[a]	Pupil rank	Percent change	Verbal rank	Pupil rank	Percent change	Verbal rank
Acorn	1	5	+0.5	8	1	+ 1.0	2
Acanthus	2	1	+2.3	6.5	3	+ 0.2	4.5
Cactus	3	7	−0.9	3	6	− 0.1	3
Cypress	4	3	+1.7	4	5	0.0	7
Continental	5	2	+2.1	2	2	+ 0.6	4.5
Pyramid	6	10	−2.6	1	8	−1.4	1
Blossom	7	9	−2.2	10	10	−3.7	10
Caravel	8	4	+0.8	9	4	+ 0.1	9
Argo	9.5	6	−0.1	6.5	7	− 0.9	8
Nordic	9.5	8	−1.4	5	9	−2.2	6

[a] The following rank-order correlations were obtained:
    Sales rank with shoppers' pupil rank=+.43
    Sales rank with shoppers' verbal rank=+.14
    Sales rank with browsers' pupil rank = +.66 (p = .05)
    Sales rank with browsers' verbal rank = +.60 (p =.05)

[b] The shoppers' percent change in pupil dilation was more favorable than the browsers', i.e., larger +% or smaller −%, for seven of the ten patterns, suggesting greater interest in silverware in general on the part of the shoppers. A one-tail test of this hypothesis shows that $f = 1.84$, df = 9, p = .05.

[c]   Retailer's comments:

     Acorn   "This gets the bulk of our advertising by far"
     Acanthus
     Cactus
     Cypress   "Sells better out of town"
     Continental   "Only pattern that doubled its volume in recent
            years—will be advertised next year"
     Pyramid   "What the public thinks is tasteful but isn't"
     Blossom
     Caravel   "A 'designer's design'—not expected to sell in the
            USA"
     Argo   "Introduced in 1963 and not doing well"
     Nordic   "Discontinued years ago — didn't sell"

TABLE 4.3

ANALYSIS OF VARIANCE SUMMARY

Source of variation	Sum of squares	d.f.	Mean square	F
Sex	17,987.72	1	17,987.72	2.78
Error I	304,064.39	47	6,469.46	
Greeting cards	57,157.72	9	6,350.86	5.29[a]
Sex x cards	46,848.62	9	5,205.40	4.33[a]
Error II	508,264.86	423	1,201.57	

[a] p=.01

The results presented in Table 4.3 may be interpreted as follows:
1. On the whole, male and female subjects do not differ significantly in their pupil responses to greeting cards.
2. The various greeting cards do evoke significantly different pupil responses.
3. Male and female subjects do differ significantly in their pupil responses to certain greeting cards.

In other words, the differences in pupil response, though numerically small, are real.

INTERSUBJECT CONSISTENCY

In Tables 4.1 and 4.2, pupil responses were averaged for all subjects, then ranked for comparison with sales rank data. The question remains, to what extent do pupil response rankings agree from subject to subject? To answer this question, Kendall's coefficient of concordance (W) was computed with the results shown in Table 4.4.

For each of the groups, the odds are better than a thousand to one that the consistency of pupil response ranking was not due simply to chance. In short, the answer to the question is that pupil response rankings do agree significantly from subject to subject. Furthermore, in the case of the greeting card study, the average pupil response rank of cards for male subjects correlated +.77 (p = .01) with the average pupil response rank of cards for female subjects. For shoppers and browsers in the sterling silver study, the correlation was +.81 (p = .01).

TABLE 4.4

INTERSUBJECT CONSISTENCY

Stimulus	Shoppers	W	P
Greeting cards	Total (49)	.11	<.001
Sterling silver	Shoppers (13)	.19	<.01
Sterling silver	Browsers (26)	.11	<.005

THE FUTURE

In general, the results of our experience with measurement of pupil response indicate that this is a sensitive and reliable technique with considerable promise for study of the interest-arousing characteristics of visual stimuli. The impact of the environment is often difficult to determine from conscious impressions verbally reported. For a variety of reasons, people may not be practiced or competent to accurately verbalize their feeling in certain areas of living. Pupil measurement seems to provide a powerful new tool for the study of these areas.

ACKNOWLEDGMENTS

The basic design for the equipment and data handling procedures were developed by Dr. Eckhard Hess and Mr. James Polt, both of the University of Chicago, under a grant from Marplan.

Grateful appreciation is extended to the management, and particularly to Mr. Just Lunning, President of Georg Jensen, Inc., for providing the opportunity to collect and report the sterling silver data presented in this article.

---

[1] E.H. Hess and J.M. Polt, "Pupil Size as Related to Interest Value of Visual Stimuli," 132, *Science* (1960), 349-350.

[2] Presumably we are concerned here with the parasympathetic branch of the autonomic nervous system (vegetative functions) whereby the pupil may be dilated via inhibition (the lay term might be "relaxation") of that system and a weakening of control of the sphincter muscle in the iris; one would hope to eliminate the role of the sympathetic branch (fight, flight, *etc.*) whereby the pupil may be dilated via stimulation of the system and a contraction of the dilator muscle in the iris.

[3] For further details of the method, see E.H. Hess and J.M. Polt, "Pupil Size in Relation to Mental Activity During Simple Problem Solving," 143, *Science* (1964), 1190-1192.

[4] The control slide probably has some interest in its own right or as a signal to anticipate something of interest. Contraction may involve disappointment. Rotation of stimuli is, therefore, quite important.

[5] By-product data obtainable from pupil photographs include where subjects are looking during the period of exposure. Thus, dilation or contraction can be traced approximately to parts of a stimulus. In addition, a persistently ascending or descending response can be identified, if such occurs during the period of exposure.

[6] This may circumvent the problem of an anxious response to airline, insurance, or drug advertising, *i.e.,* instead of measuring response to the ad itself the emphasis is on shifts in the non-anxious product appeal.

[7] Conducted and to be published by F.J. Van Bortel of the Chicago office of Marplan.

[8] Actually, a total of 57 subjects were tested, but records for eight had to be discarded because of incomplete or blurred photographic plates.

[9] The agreement between sales and pupil response is relatively independent of the influence of verbal rating, as determined by the Kendall partial rank correlation coefficient. With verbal rating partialled out, the Kendall coefficient increased +.04, a negligible change. (See S. Siegel, *Nonparametric Statistics*, New York: McGraw-Hill, 1956, 223-229, for details of this test.)

[10] A more precise test of interpretations of this order might be to compare the predictive power of pupil and verbal data against the later sales behavior of the same group, *i.e.*, even though it may be practical to use pupil data on small groups to predict something about larger groups, the interpretations underlying these predictions would in most cases require special testing.

CHAPTER 5

A COMPARISON OF PHYSICAL AND VERBAL RESPONSES TO TELEVISION COMMERCIALS

Judging respondent interest by measuring the diameter of the pupil of his eye is a new method for pre-testing television commercials.[1] The procedure currently in use involves exposure of a test commercial and a competitive commercial as a pair. Every half-second the camera records the diameter of the respondent's left eye.

THE STUDY

A comparison of data was obtained for two orders of presentation, test commercial (TC) followed by competitor commercial (CC) and competitor commercial followed by test commercial. The sample comprised seventy-four women tested at a shopping center in the New York area. All were users of a particular laundry product but not of the two brands represented. As each respondent viewed the two commercials, her left eye was photographed. Prior to the commercials a relatively "empty" (except for numbers 1 to 5) strip of leader film of the same brightness was shown. Average pupil diameters in response to the commercials were compared with average response to the neutral leader film as an overall measure of interest in the commercial. The results are given in Table 5.1.

TABLE 5.1

PERCENTAGE CHANGE IN PUPIL DIAMETERS IN RESPONSE TO TWO COMMERCIALS

Order of Presentation	TC Pupil Response	CC Pupil Response
First	+ 7.3	+5.1
Second	+11.5	− .1
Average	+ 9.4	+2.5

Original Publication: *Public Opinion Quarterly*, Vol. 29, No. 2 (Summer 1965)

In order to compare immediate physical response with later verbal response, verbal data of two kinds were obtained after the viewing. Half the respondents within each order of presentation were asked which commercial they would most like to see again, while the other half were asked which they found most convincing (Table 5.2).

TABLE 5.2

EXPRESSED INTEREST AND CONVICTION IN RESPONSE TO
TWO COMMERCIALS

Order of Presentation	"See Again?"		"Most Convincing?"	
	TC	CC	TC	CC
First	6	6	9	10
Second	14	12	7	10
Total	20	18	16	20

From these tables we observe the following:

1. The interest expressed in seeing the two commercials again was approximately equal within each order of presentation (Table 5.2).
2. Verbal expressions of conviction were approximately equal (Table 5.2).
3. Despite (1) and (2) above, interest expressed in seeing the commercial again was highly related to order of presentation, while expressions of conviction were not.
4. Despite (1) and (2) above, pupil response was greater to the test commercial than to the competitor commercial, particularly when presented in second position.

DISCUSSION

The data show that, although respondents expressed approximately equal interest in and conviction about the two commercials, nevertheless, one commercial was of more immediate interest, as measured by pupil response, than the other. In particular, verbal measures of interest were less reliable than verbal measures of conviction. The former were much influenced by order of presentation; each commercial was favored by later exposure, so that differences between the two commercials were obscured.[2] Physical measurement of interest also showed the effect of order of presentation, but with later exposure highlighting the differences between the two commercials.

For purposes of pre-testing television commercials, these observations raise serious questions about the reliability of verbal expressions of interest obtained after viewing, in spite of the small cell numbers in this test. Those doubts apply not only to a pair or series of exposed commercials but even to a singly exposed commercial, since even one commercial is a sequential phenomenon with a beginning and an ending, *i.e.*, with early and later effects within the sixty seconds. Pupil measurement on the other hand, while it may possibly exaggerate differences between compared commercials on the basis of contrast effects, would involve no parallel problem of response within a commercial.

These data suggest that in measuring liking for, or interest in, television commercials the use of an immediate physical response such as pupil size involves less bias than a later verbal response. Verbal measures of conviction are unrelated to measures of liking and do not appear to have the same shortcomings.[3]

---

[1] See Chapter 4 above and "Eye Camera," *Sponsor*, Dec. 28, 1964, pp. 25-29. For the original research from which applications were developed, see E.H. Hess and J.M. Polt, "Pupil Size as Related to Interest Value of Visual Stimuli," *Science*, Vol. 132, 1960, pp. 349-350.

[2] It should be noted, however, that the *extent* of these order-of-presentation effects may provide useful diagnostic information on the impact of commercials (see Chapter 3 above).

[3] These findings are in agreement with distinctions between liking and conviction (or persuasion) which define the former primarily in terms of physical processes and the latter primarily in terms of cognitive processes.

CHAPTER 6

THE IMPACT OF TELEVISION ADVERTISING: LEARNING WITHOUT INVOLVEMENT

Among the wonders of the twentieth century has been the ability of the mass media repeatedly to expose audiences numbered in millions to campaigns of coordinated messages. In the post-World War I years it was assumed that exposure equaled persuasion and that media content therefore was the all-important object of study or censure. Now we believe that the powers of the mass media are limited. No one has done more to bring about a counterbalancing perspective than ex-AAPOR president Joseph Klapper, with his well-known book *The Effects of Mass Media*,[1] and the new AAPOR president Raymond Bauer, with such articles as "The Limits of Persuasion."[2]

It has been acknowledged, however, that this more carefully delimited view of mass media influence is based upon analysis of largely noncommercial cases and data. We have all wondered how many of these limitations apply also to the world of commerce, specifically advertising. These limitations will be discussed here as they apply to television advertising only, since the other media include stimuli and responses of a different psychological nature, which play a perhaps different role in the steps leading to a purchasing decision.

The tendency is to say that the accepted limitations of mass media do apply, that advertising's use of the television medium has limited impact. We tend to feel this way, I think, because (1) we rarely feel converted or greatly persuaded by a particular TV campaign, and (2) so much of TV advertising content is trivial and sometimes even silly. Nevertheless, trivia have their own special qualities, and some of these may be important to our understanding of the commercial or the noncommercial use and impact of mass media.

To begin, let us go back to Neil Borden's classic Harvard Business School evaluation of the economic effects of advertising.[3] Published in 1942, it concluded that advertising (1) accelerates growing demand or retards falling demand, *i.e.* it quickens the pulse of the market, and (2) encourages price rigidity but increases quality and choice of products. The study warned, however, that

Original Publication: *Public Opinion Quarterly*, Vol. 29, No. 3 (Fall 1965), pp. 349-356; Presidential Address, American Association of Public Opinion Research, May 15, 1965 companies had been led to overlook price strategies and the elasticity of consumer demand. This was borne out after World War II by the rise of the discounters!

The end of World War II also brought mass television and an increased barrage of advertising messages. How much could the public take? Not only were early TV commercials often irritating, but one wondered whether all the competition would not end in a great big buzzing confusion. Apparently not! Trend studies of advertising penetration have shown that the public is able to "hold in memory," as we would say of a computer, a very large number of TV campaign themes correctly related to brands. The fact that huge sums and energies were expended to achieve retention of these many little bits of information should not deter us from acknowledging the success of the overall effort.

It is true that in some categories of products the sharpness of brand differentiation is slipping, as advertising themes and appeals grow more similar. Here the data look, as one colleague put it, "mushy." In such categories the product is well on its way toward becoming a commodity; even while brand advertising continues, the real competition is more and more one of price and distribution. But prices, too, are advertised, although in different media, and recalled.

What is lacking in the required "evaluation" of TV advertising is any significant body of research specifically relating advertising to attitudes, and these in turn to purchasing behavior or sales. That is, we have had in mind a model of the correct and effective influence process which has not yet been verified. This is the bugaboo that has been the hope and the despair of research people within the industry. Always there looms that famous pie in the sky: If the client will put up enough money, if he will be understanding enough to cooperate in blacking out certain cities or areas to permit a controlled experiment, if the cities or areas under study will be correctly matched, if the panels of consumers to be studied will not melt away in later not-at-homes, refusals, or changes of residence, if the sales data will be "clean" enough to serve as adequate criteria — *then surely* one can truly assess the impact of a particular ad campaign. Some advertisers, too, are learning to ask about this type of evaluation, while the advertising agencies are ambivalent and unsure of their strength.

This seems to be where we are today. The economic impact of TV advertising is substantial and documented. Its messages have been learned by the public. Only the lack of specific case histories relating advertising to attitudes to sales keeps researchers from concluding that the commercial use of the medium is a success. We are faced then with the odd situation of knowing that advertising works but being unable to say much about why.

Perhaps our model of the influence process is wrong. Perhaps it is incompletely understood. Back in 1959 Herbert Zielske, in "The Remembering and Forgetting of Advertising," demonstrated that advertising will be quickly forgotten if not continuously exposed.[4] Why such need for constant reinforcement? Why so easy-in and easy-out of short-term memory? One answer is that much of advertising content is learned as meaningless nonsense material. Therefore, let us ask about the nature of such learning.

An important distinction between the learning of sense and nonsense was laid down by Ebbinghaus in1902 when he identified the greater effects of order of presentation of stimuli on the learning of nonsense material. He demonstrated a U curve of recall, with first and last items in a series best remembered, thus giving rise also to the principles of primacy and recency.[5]

In 1957, many years later, Carl Hovland reported that in studying persuasion he found the effects of primacy and recency greater when dealing with material of lesser ego-involvement. He wrote, "Order of presentation is a more significant factor in influencing opinions for subjects with relatively weak desires for understanding, than for those with high 'cognitive needs'."[6] It seems, therefore, that the nonsensical à la Ebbinghaus; and the unimportant à la Hovland work alike.

At the 1962 AAPOR meetings I had the pleasure of reading a paper on some applications of learning theory to copy testing. Here it was reported that the spontaneous recall of TV commercials presented four in a row formed a distinct U curve. In the same paper a re-analysis of increment scores of fifty-seven commercials tested in a three-position series by the Schwerin television testing method also showed a distinct U curve, despite the earlier contentions of the Schwerin organization. That real advertising materials presented in so short a series could produce distinct U curves seemed to confirm that the learning of advertising was similar to the learning of the nonsensical or the unimportant (Chapter 3 above).

What is common to the learning of the nonsensical and the unimportant is lack of involvement. We seem to be saying, then, that much of the impact of television advertising is in the form of learning without involvement, or what Hartley calls "un-anchored learning."[7] If this is so, is it a source of weakness or of strength to the advertising industry? Is it good or bad for our society? What are the implications for research on advertising effectiveness?

Let us consider some qualities of sensory perception with and without involvement. Last October I participated along with Ray Bauer, Elihu Katz, and Nat Maccoby in a Gould House seminar sponsored by the Foundation for Research on Human Behavior. Nat reported some studies conducted with Leon Festinger in which fraternity members learned a TV message better when hearing the audio and watching unrelated video than when they watched the speaker giving them the message directly, *i.e.* video and audio together.[8] Apparently, the distraction of watching something unrelated to the audio message lowered whatever resistance there might have been to the message.

As Nat put it, "Comprehension equals persuasion": Any disagreement ("Oh no! That can't be true!") with any message must come after some real interval, however minute. Ray asked Nat if he would accept a statement of this point as "Perception precedes perceptual defense," and Nat agreed. The initial development of this view goes back before World War II to the psychologist W. E. Guthrie.[9] It receives more recent support from British research on perception and communication, specifically that of D. E. Broadbent, who has noted the usefulness of defining perception as "immediate memory."[10]

The historical importance of the Maccoby view, however, is that it takes us almost all the way back to our older view of the potent propaganda content of World War 1, that exposure to mass media content is persuasive per se! What is implied here is that in cases of involvement with mass media content perceptual defense is very briefly postponed, while in cases of noninvolvement perceptual defense may be absent.

Does this suggest that if television bombards us with enough trivia about a product we may be persuaded to believe it? On the contrary, it suggests that persuasion as such, *i.e.* overcoming a resistant attitude, is not involved at all and that it is a mistake to look for it in our personal lives as a test of television's advertising impact. Instead, as trivia are repeatedly learned and repeatedly forgotten and then repeatedly learned a little more, it is probable that two things will happen: (1) more simply, that so-called "overlearning" will move some information out of short-term and into long-term memory systems, and (2) more complexly, that we will permit significant alterations in the *structure* of our perception of a brand or product, but in ways which may fall short of persuasion or of attitude change. One way we may do this is by shifting the relative salience of attributes suggested to us by advertising as we organize our perception of brands and products.

Thanks to Sherif we have long used the term "frame of reference," and Osgood in particular has impressed us with the fact that the meaning of an object may be perceived along many separate dimensions. Let us say that a number of frames of reference are available as the primary anchor for the percept in question. We may then alter the psychological salience of these frames or dimensions and shift a product seen primarily as "reliable" to one seen primarily as "modern."[11] The product is still seen as reliable and perhaps no *less* reliable than before, but this quality no longer provides the primary perceptual emphasis. Similarly, the product was perhaps previously seen as modern, and perhaps no *more* modern now — yet exposure to new or repeated messages may give modernity the primary role in the organization of the percept.

There is no reason to believe that such shifts are completely limited to trivia. In fact, when Hartley first introduced the concept of psychological salience, he illustrated it with a suggestion that Hitler did not so much increase anti-Semitic attitudes in Germany as bring already existing anti-Semitic attitudes into more prominent use for defining the everyday world.[12] This, of course, increased the probability of anti-Semitic behavior. While the shift in salience does not tell the whole story, it seems to be one of the dynamics operating in response to massive repetition. Although a rather simple dynamic, it may be a major one when there is no cause for resistance, or when uninvolved consumers do not provide their own perceptual emphases or anchors.

It may be painful to reject as incomplete a model of the influence process of television advertising that requires changes in attitude *prior* to changes in behavior. It may be difficult to see how the viewer of television can go from perceptual impact directly to behavioral impact, unless *the full perceptual impact is delayed.* This would not mean going into unexplored areas. Sociologists have met "sleeper effects" before, and some psychologists have long asserted that the effects of "latent" learning are only or most noticeable at the point of reward. In this case, it would be at the behavioral level involved in product purchases rather than at some intervening point along the way. That is, the purchase situation is the catalyst that reassembles or brings out all the potentials for shifts in salience that have accumulated up to that point. The product or package is then suddenly seen in a new, "somehow different" light although nothing verbalizable may have changed *up to that point.* What we ordinarily call "change of attitude" may then occur after some real interval, however minute. Such change of attitude after product purchase is *not,* as has sometimes been said, in "rationalization" of the purchase but is an emergent response aspect of the previously changed perception. We would perhaps see it more often if products always lived up to expectations and did not sometimes create negative interference with the emerging response.

I have tried to say that the public lets down its guard to the repetitive commercial use of the television medium and that it easily changes its ways of perceiving products and brands and its purchasing behavior without thinking very much about it at the time of TV exposure or at any time prior to purchase, and without up to then changing verbalized attitudes. This adds up, I think, to an understandable success story for advertising's use of the television medium. Furthermore, this success seems to be based on a left-handed kind of public trust that sees no great importance in the matter.

But now I wonder about those so-called "limits of effectiveness" of the noncommercial use of the mass media. I wonder if we were not overusing attitudes and attitude changes as our primary criterion of effectiveness? In looking for behavioral changes, did we sometimes despair too soon simply because we did not find earlier attitude changes? I wonder if we projected our own attitudes and values too much onto the audiences studied and assumed that they, too, would treat information about such matters as the United Nations as serious and involving? I wonder also how many of those public-spirited campaigns ever asked their audiences to do something, *i.e.* asked for the kind of concrete behavior that at some point triggers whatever real potentials may have developed for an attitude change to begin or perhaps to complete its work.

I would like to suggest, therefore, that the distinction between the commercial and the noncommercial use of the mass media, as well as the distinction between "commercial" and "academic" research, has blinded us to the existence of two entirely different ways of experiencing and being influenced by mass media. One way is characterized by lack of personal involvement, which, while perhaps more common in response to commercial subject matter, is by no means limited to it. The second is characterized by a high degree of personal involvement. By this we do *not* mean attention, interest, or excitement but the number of conscious "bridging experiences," connections, or personal references per minute that the viewer makes between his own life and the stimulus. This may vary from none to many.

The significance of conditions of low or high involvement is not that one is better than the other, but that the processes of communication impact are different. That is, there is a difference in the change processes that are at work. Thus, with low involvement one might look for gradual shifts in perceptual structure, aided by repetition, activated by behavioral-choice situations, and *followed* at some time by attitude change. With high involvement one would look for the classic, more dramatic, and more familiar conflict of ideas at the level of conscious opinion and attitude that precedes changes in overt behavior.

I think now we can appreciate again why Madison Avenue may be of little use in the Cold War or even in a medium-hot presidential campaign. The more common skills of Madison Avenue concern the change processes associated with low involvement, while the very different skills required for high-involvement campaigns are usually found elsewhere. However, although Madison Avenue generally seems to know its limitations, the advertising researchers tend to be less clear about theirs. For example, from New York to Los Angeles researchers in television advertising are daily exacting "attitude change" or "persuasion" scores from captive audiences, these scores based on questionnaires and methods which, though plausible, have no demonstrated predictive validity. The plausibility of these methods rests on the presence of a more or less explicit model of communication effectiveness. Unfortunately, the model in use is the familiar one that assumes high involvement. Perhaps it is the questionnaires and the research procedures themselves that are responsible for creating what high involvement is present, which would not otherwise exist. The wiser or more cautious researchers meanwhile retreat to the possibilities of impersonal exactness in controlled field experiments and behavioral criteria. What has been left out, unfortunately, is the development of a low-involvement model, and the pretest measures based on such a model. The further development of this model is an important next step, not only for the perhaps trivial world of television advertising but for the better understanding of all those areas of public opinion and education which, socially important as they may be, may simply not be very involving to significant segments of the audience.

In time we may come to understand the effectiveness of mass media primarily in terms of the *consistency* with which a given campaign, commercial or noncommercial, employs talent and research sensitively attuned to the real level of audience involvement. In time, also, we may come to understand that behavior, that is, verbal behavior and overt behavior, is always consistent provided we do not impose premature and narrowly conceived rules as to which must precede, or where, when, and how it must be measured. [13]

---

[1] Joseph Klapper, *The Effects of Mass Media* (Glencoe, Ill.: Free Press, 1960).

[2] Raymond Bauer, "The Limits of Persuasion," *Harvard Business Review,* September-October 1958, pp. 105-110.

[3] Neil Borden, *The Economic Effects of Advertising* (Chicago: Irwin, 1942).

[4] H.A. Zielske, "The Remembering and Forgetting of Advertising," *Journal of Marketing,* January 1959, pp. 239-243.

[5] H. Ebbinghaus, *Grundzuge der Psychologie* (Leipzig, Germany: Veit, 1902).

[6] C.T. Hovland et *al., The Order of Presentation in Persuasion* (New Haven, Yale University Press, 1957), p. 136.

[7] This is the title of a working manuscript distributed privately by E.L. Hartley in 1964, which concerns his experimentation with new methods of health education in the Philippine Islands.

[8] L. Festinger and N. Maccoby, "On Resistance to Persuasive Communications," *Journal of Abnormal and Social Psychology,* vol. 68, no. 4, (1964), pp. 359-366.

[9] E.R. Guthrie, *The Psychology of Learning* (New York: Harper, 1935), p. 26.

[10] D.E. Broadbent, *Perception and Communication* (London: Pergamon Press, 1958), Chap. 9.

[11] Psychological salience was first discussed in this manner by E.L. Hartley, *Problems in Prejudice* (New York: Kings Crown Press, 1946), pp. 107-115.

[12] *Ibid,* p. 97.

[13] The consistency of verbal and overt behavior has also been reasserted by Hovland, who attributes pseudo-differences to those *research designs* which carelessly compare results of laboratory experiments with results of field surveys (C.I. Hovland, "Reconciling Conflicting Results Derived from Experimental and Survey Studies of Attitude Change," *American Psychologist,* Vol. 14, 1959, pp. 8-17); by Campbell, who attributes pseudo-differences to the fact that verbal and overt behaviors have different situational thresholds (D.T. Campbell, "Social Attitudes and Other Acquired Behavioral Dispositions," in S. Koch, ed., *Psychology: A Study of a Science,* Vol. 6, McGraw-Hill, 1963, pp. 94-172); and by Rokeach, who attributes pseudo-differences to the fact that overt behavior is the result of interaction between *two* sets of attitudes, one toward the object and one toward the situation, and that most research leaves one of the two attitudes unstudied (M. Rokeach, "Attitude Change and Behavior Change," paper presented at the annual conference of the World Association for Public Opinion Research, Dublin, Ireland, Sept. 9, 1965).

CHAPTER 7

THE MEASUREMENT OF ADVERTISING INVOLVEMENT

The study of involvement has a long and impressive history culminating in the recent classic by the Sherifs and Nebergall.[1] However, all the recent history concerns involvement with issues or topics, and not with particular and specific persuasive stimuli. While topic or issue involvement does hold implications for the level of stimulus involvement that a subject is predisposed to bring into the stimulus situation, it is demonstrably inadequate as a measure of stimulus (*e.g.*, advertising) differences on the same topic (*e.g.*, product or brand).

The main difference between involvement predispositions associated with topics and the actual involvement in exposure to persuasive stimuli concerns the factor of *direct personal experience*. In the United States the study of experience, or what is usually called "subjective" experience, has had a peculiar history. Since the death of Edward Titchener in 1927, and the ultimate triumph of the then rising tide of behaviorism, there has been little concern with introspection or with immediate experience. Titchener and other students of Wundt declined in prestige to such an extent that by the middle thirties no major department of psychology in the United States was visibly active in this area of study. Then came Freudian psychology, without competition then and without competition today. That is, only the psychoanalysts seem interested specifically in what went through one's mind, what one thought at a given moment in time, what was one's immediate subjective experience of some particular event or stimulus.

Our definition of involvement is the number of "connections," conscious bridging experiences or personal references per minute, that the subject makes between the content of the persuasive stimulus and the content of his own life. This definition necessitates a report of immediate experience or conscious reaction to a stimulus. "Connections" must be identified and counted in the protocols. Manuals must be prepared for coders. The requirements take us back, therefore, to Titchener to pick up what he learned of the errors of objective reference and to carry on from there.[2] This paper will report three small studies which applied the measurement of connections to various mass media stimuli.[3]

Original Publication: *Public Opinion Quarterly*, Vol. 30, No. 3 (1966), pp. 583-596

COMPARISONS ACROSS MEDIA

In the earlier model development (Chapter 6 above), only the television medium was discussed, because it was in the attempt to understand the impact of television that the low involvement model was developed. In the present paper, we hypothesize that the special quality of television advertising impact is low involvement, as compared with higher involvement for magazine advertising.[4] Therefore, to illustrate differences between the low and high involvement models we propose here to formally compare the television and magazine media.

TELEVISION VERSION OF
LOW INVOLVEMENT MODEL

1. The quality of the stimulus is animate while the observer is inanimate. With the pace of the experience or rate of stimulation out of the individual's control, there is relatively low opportunity for connections, for dwelling upon a point of advertising.

2. The change processes require:

    a. Stimulus repetition to build a potential for alteration in perceptual structure of advertised brands, *i.e.*, a gradual development of the ability to see the brand differently without being specifically aware of any change.

    b. A behavioral opportunity, such as in-store shopping, to trigger the potential for shift in perceptual structure, *i.e.*, suddenly to see the brand in the new manner when confronted by it on the supermarket shelf.

    c. Behavioral completion to release appropriate attitudes supportive and consistent with the shift in perceptual structure, *i.e.*, if the brand is then purchased the new way of seeing it may then for the first time be expressed in words, for example, to "explain" why it was selected.

3. The role of behavior is as part of the change process, which continues beyond the store. Unless behavior completion, or purchase, occurs, there ensues an unstable condition characterized by a shift in perceptual structure without a corresponding shift in attitudinal structure. Without behavioral completion, therefore, the impact of a behavior opportunity is temporary only and perceptual structure reverts to its initial condition, though still carrying the potential for shift on other occasions. For example, a housewife may be repeatedly struck by some new (advertised) brand attribute each time she confronts it on the store shelf, and yet never retain this impression long enough to put into words, until one day the actual purchase is made.

MAGAZINE VERSION OF
HIGH INVOLVEMENT MODEL

1. The quality of the stimulus is inanimate, while the observer is animate. With the pace of the experience, or rate of stimulation, under the individual's control, there is relatively high opportunity for connections, for dwelling upon a point of advertising.

2. The change processes require transmission of specific news, new information, or new ideas which represent a way of looking at a topic that is in conflict with or different from that represented in older information or ideas, and which may lead to resolution of the difference through new decisionmaking.[5]

3. The role of behavior is as a consequence of new decisions, and is not part of the change process itself, *i.e.*, the change process may be over before the subject enters the store.[6]

Before field studies, we wanted to create various degrees and conditions of involvement with advertising in order to become familiar with whatever problems of measurement might arise. To this end, an experimental laboratory exercise was conducted.

1. To create variety of involvement with advertising it was decided to manipulate (a) medium, (b) expensiveness of product or service advertised, (c) interest value of editorial environment of ad, and (d) instructional "set" given to respondents.

    a. Medium

        Magazine – A.M.O. portfolio[7]

        Television – Fairchild #400 rear projector, 8 x 10 inch screen

    b. Product or service advertised

        Airline   { Similar television and print versions of
        Margarine   { brand and ad theme; airline roughly similar but margarine almost identical

    c. Editorial environment

        Magazine:

           "Personalities":

               Two-page article, "England's Firebrand Princess," with five photos of Princess Anne

               ADVERTISEMENT

               Two-page article, "Some Poignant and Memorable Personal Reflections, What Prayer Means to Me," with nine photos of various entertainment and political personalities and their comments about prayer.

           "Dollars":

               Two-page article, "Stanching the Dollar Outflow," with one illustration, no photos

               ADVERTISEMENT

Two-page article, "Riches for a New Region — Harnessing the Arkansas River," with three photos, one map

Television:

"Variety show":

2'25" of a visit with James Bond (Sean Connery); sequence from a popular variety show

COMMERCIAL

2'02" of an Edie Gormé song from same variety show

"Press interview":

1'06" of a translated interview between a group of reporters and a Dominican political leader

- COMMERCIAL

3'00" of same interview

d. Instructions

Editorial set: "We're doing a study of magazine topics and I'd like you to spend a few minutes looking at some stories that appeared recently."

Advertising set: "We're doing a study of magazine advertising and I'd like you to spend a few minutes looking at a particular ad and also the stories that appeared next to it."

Combinations of the above four variables provided sixteen experimental conditions for observation (Table 7.1):

The definition of involvement required that conscious connections occur

	Magazine		Television	
Editorial	P$P	P¢P	V$V	V¢V
set	D$D	D¢D	I$I	I¢I
Advertising	P$P	P¢P	V$V	V¢V
set	D$D	D¢D	I$I	I¢I

TABLE 7.1

NOTE: P = personalities and D = dollars; V = variety show and I = press interview; $ = airline and ¢ = margarine

Testing was conducted at various times during the day with a variety of women recruited at a regional shopping center in New Jersey. Respondents were unpaid. The test environment was a rented store which has been regularly used as a research center within the shopping center area.

between the persuasive stimulus and something in the respondent's life. This differs from the more general definition of involvement phrased in terms of the importance of issues or of opinions or positions taken about issues, *i.e.*, definitions oriented to topic rather than to stimulus material. The interview situation is also somewhat different in that, rather than information, opinions, or attitudes, respondents are asked to recall and report what they were thinking at the (earlier) time they viewed an advertisement, *i.e.,* they are asked to report mental incidents.

The method of questioning included a few questions on likes and dislikes of the editorial material followed by, "What about the advertisement — what thoughts came to mind while you looked at it?" with such probes as, "Can you remember all your thoughts about the ad?" and "Try to think back to everything that went through your mind as you looked at it." The major problem in this type of interview is that the respondent may occasionally switch from past to present tense in reporting, suggesting that she may be reporting a connection of the moment rather than one that occurred while viewing the ad. This was checked with, "I'm going to read back to you each of the thoughts you have mentioned. For each one I'd like you to tell me whether you had this thought *while* you were looking at the advertisement or *while* you were talking to me." This probe finally became shortened to the vernacular "Then or now?"

Some examples of single connections per protocol:

- It made me think of traveling there myself
- It made me feel as if I would like to go on my vacation

Some examples of double connections per protocol:

- My husband flies all the time. . . . I think wouldn't it be great to go
- I thought I'd like to go. . . . You'll think I'm crazy [in response to probe]; my niece is getting married and going to Europe to live.

When connections go above three or four, they may require the careful checking of inconsistencies in tense.

- I recognized the brand name though I don't really use margarine. My husband is a strict believer in butter or oil. I have tried using it but they prefer the flavor of butter. . . . It's interesting to know that you can buy margarine which doesn't burn. With butter you have to be careful. I may even try this. . . . The main thing is the burnt egg [in ad illustration]. If there's anything I detest it's burnt egg. We like our eggs soft and juicy. . . . I was just thinking I bought some [brand] oil this morning. I had a recipe for fruit bread. It turned out so nice. I made two fruit breads. I'm not interested in margarine. . . . I may try it now that I know it doesn't burn at high heat. . . . I had one thought here. This was the main thought. I don't cook with high heat unless I'm searing. Particularly I cook eggs on a low heat. . . . Margarine is neither good nor bad. Some people like to cook with less heat that has nothing to do with margarine.

The checking question on connections during exposure vs. connections during interview suggested a fifty-fifty split. Thus, if half are spontaneous in response to test stimuli and half are liberated by the interview, we have here a crude and quite tentative indication that some pre-test research procedures may double the apparent involvement of respondents with the advertising copy being tested.

A structured scale administered at the end of the interview was pre-tested to see if respondents themselves could differentiate between those of their responses which were only stimulus-oriented and those which made a connection to their own lives.[8] Results indicated that they could not do this reliably (*i.e.,* in agreement with the taped interview protocol) on the scale in question, and that coding of unstructured interview response was essential. The major problem in coding individual protocols was to identify separate thought sequences, usually in terms of temporally different incidents or interpersonal situations mentioned. There are, however, some types of connections that deserve special comment. These appeared in response to the advertising "set," and concern connections to the interview or to other occasions when the ad was seen.

- I thought you would want to know what attracted me.
- I was wondering if this was the ad you wanted my opinion on.
- I thought here's another ad. I hope it doesn't take too long.
- I've seen this on TV.
- I've seen the ad before. It's not convincing.

It may be noted, as in the last above, that a few connections are unfavorable and are so tallied. It may also be noted that, while connections to other advertising could reasonably be expected to occur quite often, they appeared in the experiment only in response to the advertising set. Again, therefore, one must indicate concern about conventional pre-test research procedures, in this case because of their apparent tendency to create irrelevant connections.

Use of the experimental materials produced two surprises. One was that Princess Anne and the prayers of famous personalities were less interesting than the dollar gap and hydroelectric resources. Most seemed obliged to read the "serious" material more carefully. A second surprise was that the airline advertisement was only slightly more involving than the margarine advertisement.

TABLE 7.2

NUMBER OF CONNECTIONS PER SECOND AND EXPOSURE TIME FOR MAGAZINE
AND TV COMMERCIALS, BY EDITORIAL OR ADVERTISING SET, EDITORIAL
ENVIRONMENT, AND PRODUCT ADVERTISED

| | *Magazine* | | | | *TV* | |
	(*N*)	*Seconds per Ad*	*Number Conn.*	*Seconds per Conn.*	(*N*)	*Average Conn.*
Set:						
Editorial	(14)	17.6	1.9	9.14	20	.75
Advertising	(15)	24.3	1.2	20.25	21	.43
Editorial environment:						
Serious/news	(15)	21.9	1.8	12.14	26	.65
Light/entertainment	(14)	19.6	1.3	15.23	15	.47
Product advertised:						
Airline	(15)	24.2	1.8	13.48	9	.67
Margarine	(14)	16.6	1.3	12.90	32	.56

The largest difference in involvement was produced by the variation in instructions, or perceptual set.

Twenty-nine female respondents spent an average of 21.0 seconds per page on the seven pages over all, and an average of 19.4 seconds on the advertising page itself. To the advertisement they produced an average of 1.55 connections. While ten respondents "read" the material and spent over 150 seconds over all, and nineteen respondents "browsed" over the material in less than 150 seconds over all, each of these groups produced an average of 1.5 connections per advertisement.

Table 7.2 suggests that direct attention to advertising materials produces fewer and slower connections than when attention is focused on something else, in this case the more natural focus on editorial matter.[9] One may re-appreciate the psychoanalyst's persistent view that peripheral thoughts obtained under real-life conditions or under conditions of relaxed association may have as much value for the understanding and prediction of behavior as do responses to direct questions.[10]

In the television materials, the more serious press interview unexpectedly aroused much closer attention and interest than the variety show material. Another surprise was the frequency of unfavorable remarks about television commercials, occurring in a third of all television interviews.

Forty-one female respondents produced an average of .59 connections in response to the commercials, contrasting markedly with the 1.55 for print advertisements.[11] In other respects, the results paralleled the print data. That is, there were more connections in response to an editorial than to an advertising set, more connections when the editorial matter was serious, more connections to airline than to margarine advertising.

Within the context of the laboratory exercise, it would seem that the magazine advertising was indeed more involving than the television advertising. A 2– or 3–to–1 ratio is suggested by the contrast between one-and-a-half connections in twenty seconds and a half connection in sixty seconds. Of course, these figures are products of a small piece of research and one that has itself provided fresh grounds for questioning the predictive ability of laboratory evaluations of advertising.[12]

COMPARISONS ACROSS TESTING SITUATIONS

The field work of the laboratory study was conducted with women respondents in a rented store in Paramus, New Jersey, in July 1965. A second study was conducted in Cleveland, Ohio, in November of the same year, but on a home-interview basis, and with a fresh selection of materials. This time 156 women were tested, 53 on print, 56 on a sixty-second television version of the same ad, and 47 on a twenty-second version. The subject of the advertising was an electric broiler that cooked both sides of a steak simultaneously.

During the same period, 144 men were tested, 44 on print, 56 on a sixty-second television version of the same ad, and 44 on a twenty-second version. The subject of the advertising was a small cigar currently in competition with cigarettes.

Editorial matter for both men and women consisted of the following:

Magazine:

> Cover plus one page of article "Modern Living — The Best Resorts," with one photograph

> ADVERTISEMENT

> Two pages of continued article with two photographs

Television (same for 60" and 20" commercials):

> 6'19" of an Alan King comedy sequence from a popular variety show

> COMMERCIAL

> 2'01" of continued King sequence.

Only an editorial set was used in the instructions to the respondent, since this seemed more "natural" as well as more involving. The average number of connections per female respondent was 1.00 for print, .86 for 60" TV, and .72 for 20" TV. Connections per male respondent were .34 for print, .37 for 60" TV, and .30 for 20" TV. The low level of male involvement was a surprise. Apparently, the "entertaining" aspects of the advertisement were responded to more than those related to smoking or to the product. An overall comparison with results of the first study is presented in Table 7.3.

The evidence presented in Table 7.3 of a decrease in print connections from about 1.8 for airlines to less than parity for cigars suggested that an "advantage" in involvement for magazines may hold true only with higher in-

TABLE 7.3

NUMBER OF CONNECTIONS PER SECOND AND EXPOSURE TIME FOR MAGAZINE AND TV COMMERCIALS, LABORATORY AND HOME SETTINGS COMPARED

	20" TV		60" TV		Print		
	No. Conn.	*(N)*	*No. Conn.*	*(N)*	*No. Conn.*	*Seconds per Ad*	*(N)*
Laboratory (half editorial set, half advertising set):							
Airline			.67	(9)	1.8	24.2	(15)
Margarine			.56	(32)	1.3	16.6	(14)
Home (editorial set):							
Range	.72	(47)	.86	(56)	1.0	18.9	(53)
Cigar	.30	(44)	.37	(56)	0.3	14.7	(44)

volvement topics, products, or advertisements. It should be emphasized, however, that the data in this report are presented only as suggestive aids in the refinement of hypotheses.

COMPARISONS ACROSS ADVERTISEMENTS

Fifteen pairs of print ads were selected for study. Each pair contained a high and a low Starch ("Noting") advertisement for the same product and brand (H and L in Table 7.4).[13] The fifteen pairs were then separated into three groups. Within each group each respondent was exposed to one ad from each pair. Half the respondents saw three high- and two low-Starch ads (HLHLH) and half saw two high- and three low-Starch ads (LHLHL). Each of the two sequences was rotated through five subgroups of six respondents each. Presentation of the ads was made in the A.M.O. book with exposure time recorded. Respondents for the February and March groups were again recruited at the Paramus, New Jersey, shopping center, while the April group was recruited at a shopping center in Ridgewood, New Jersey, and screened for management or technical positions earning over $10,000. No editorial matter was used in testing these three groups:

The results of the February test of connections to the first group of advertisements are shown in Table 7.5.

Several observations can be made from Table 7.5.

(1) The general level of involvement (*i.e.,* under .5) is significantly less than under previous conditions of testing, presumably because of concentration of ads without editorial relief.

(2) The range of involvement across categories (.35/.22) is less than 2-to-1 and frequently less than the range within categories (.43/.13, .37/.13, .30/.13), which over all tends to be more than 2-to-1.

(3) There appears to be no relationship between involvement and Starch noting, and no relationship between involvement and exposure time.

TABLE 7.4						
For February 1966 Testing with Women		*For March Testing with Men and Women*			*For April Testing with Managers*	
Women H/L	Product Advertised	Men H/L	Women H/L	Product Advertised	Men H/L	Product Advertised
67/41	Hair coloring	47/22	45/20	Cigarette	62/43	Automobile
54/26	Canned corn	57/27	43/23	Organ	59/30	Industrial glass
65/41	Refrigerator	52/25	47/39	Insurance	30/19	Insurance
68/33	Carpeting	59/30	57/30	Travel	57/25	Bus. machines
37/27	Analgesic	39/22	60/45	Scotch	61/14	Corporate (fuel)

TABLE 7.5

AVERAGE NUMBER OF CONNECTIONS AND EXPOSURE TIME TO
HIGH- AND LOW-STARCH WOMEN'S PRINT ADS, WOMEN ONLY

Product Advertised	*Average No. Connections*			*Average No. Seconds*		
	Total (60)	*High Starch (30)*	*Low Starch (30)*	*Total (60)*	*High Starch (30)*	*Low Starch (30)*
Refrigerator	.35	.43	.30	17.5	12.3	22.7
Hair coloring	.28	.13	.43	12.7	13.5	11.8
Carpeting	.27	.20	.33	14.5	16.4	12.6
Analgesic	.25	.13	.37	14.7	17.4	12.1
Canned corn	.22	.30	.13	12.8	10.5	15.0

(4) The +2-to-1 range of involvement within categories is greater than the Starch range within categories, which over all tends to be slightly under 2-to-1.

(5) The +2-to-1 range of involvement within categories is greater than the range of exposure time within categories, which tends over all to be less than 2-to-1.

In short, the involvement variable seemed more sensitive than Starch "Noting" or exposure (dwell) time, and is independent of them. Most important, it needed to be examined on a specific stimulus basis and not solely in terms of categories. These observations were then reconsidered in the light of the next group of ads.

It is apparent from Table 7.6, which gives the results of the March test, that the overall level of involvement of men is about half that of women. Furthermore, the sensitivity of the involvement variable among the relatively less involved men is consistent with the findings of the February group, *i.e.,* the more than 2-to-1 range of involvement within categories is greater than across categories and greater than the variation of Starch "Noting" (or exposure time, not shown) within categories.

It had been noted earlier (Table 7.3) that the level of involvement of men was half or less than that of women. At the time it was considered to be a reflection of the particular ads used, rather than a possibly general difference between men and women. It should also be noted that the lowered stimulus sensitivity of the involvement variable among the relatively more involved women in the March group should be seen along with the greater stimulus sensitivity and lower involvement of the women of the February group. Thus, apart from questions of differences between the sexes, we have here two cases where stimulus sensitivity varied with the general level of topic involvement. This suggests a possible postscript to the work of Gutman, Hovland, Sherif, *et al.*, which treats issue or topic involvement but tends to ignore stimulus involvement as an important variable in attitude change. It is suggested that at some point of (decreasing) involvement, the stimulus involvement within issues or topics may be just as varied and important, if not more so, than involvement across issues or topics. Coupled with this suggestion is the observation that for women this "point" is represented in the present data, *i.e.,* the women of the February group represent a level of involvement in which stimulus supersedes topic, whereas the women of the March group represent a higher level of involvement in which topic involvement (especially travel) supersedes stimulus involvement.

TABLE 7.6

AVERAGE NUMBER OF CONNECTIONS AND EXPOSURE TIME
TO HIGH- AND LOW-STARCH GENERAL PRINT ADS
MEN AND WOMEN SEPARATELY
(Minus signs indicate unfavorable connections)

	Men			*Women*		
Product Advertised	*Total (30)*	*High Starch (15)*	*Low Starch (15)*	*Total (30)*	*High Starch (15)*	*Low Starch (15)*
Travel	.33	.53	.13	.70	.60	.80
Organ	.37	.20	.53	.57	.33	.80
Insurance	.17	.27	.07	.33	.33	.33
Cigarette	−.13	.00	−.27	−.30	−.33	−.27
Scotch	.20	.20	.20	.20	.20	.20

The final group of ads, tested on male managers, tended to cast some doubt on the generality of a sex difference in involvement (Table 7.7). While the average number of connections is not high, it is not lower than that of the women responding to women's ads (Table 7.5). It does, however, include a higher number of unfavorable connections, and it does include such interesting topics as automobiles and dogs (glass advertisement).

Table 7.7 shows more variation across topics than within. The data were then split into lower vs. higher income (age-related) subgroups. In Table 7.8 it is shown that the less affluent but younger respondents are much more involved, especially with automobiles and the glass advertisement (showing the head of a strikingly handsome collie dog), than the more affluent older respondents. While variation in stimulus involvement increases to 2-to-1 as topical involvement declines, this is evident only within the younger group.

TABLE 7.7

AVERAGE NUMBER OF CONNECTIONS AND EXPOSURE TIME TO
HIGH- AND LOW-STARCH MEN'S PRINT ADS, MALE MANAGERS ONLY

Product Advertised	*Average No. Connections*			*Average No. Seconds*		
	Total (60)	High Starch (30)	Low Starch (30)	Total (60)	High Starch (30)	Low Starch (30)
Automobile	.38	.33	±.43[a]	12.0	11.6	12.4
Insurance	.30	±.30[b]	.30	12.4	12.2	12.6
Industrial glass	.28	.30	.27	14.5	12.9	16.0
Business machines	.28	.27	.30	11.6	10.7	12.6
Corporate (fuel)	.18	.30	.27	13.3	12.1	14.4

[a] Six of thirteen connections unfavorable
[b] Four of nine connections unfavorable

CONCLUSIONS

The series of small studies described in this report point to certain hypotheses about the nature of involvement with advertising, and to some degree with media messages in general. These hypotheses are as follows:

1. Involvement with advertising in magazines or television tends to be highest when attention is directed to the editorial environment, less when it is directed to the advertising, and least when advertising is presented alone.

2. Involvement with advertising tends to be consistent with interests in the editorial environment, *i.e.,* greater interest "carries over" to produce higher in-

TABLE 7.8

AVERAGE NUMBER OF CONNECTIONS IN RESPONSE TO HIGH- AND LOW-STARCH
MEN'S PRINT ADS, MALE MANAGERS BY LOW AND HIGH INCOME

Product Advertised	*Incomes $10,000-14,999*[a]			*Incomes $15,000 and Up*		
	Total (22)	High Starch (11)	Low Starch (11)	Total (38)	High Starch (19)	Low Starch (19)
Automobile	±.64[b]	±.64[b]	±.64[b]	.24	.16	.32
Insurance	.45	.55	.36	.18	.16	.21
Industrial glass	.36	.27	.45	.26	.32	.21
Business machines	.27	.36	.18	.29	.21	.37
Corporate (fuel)	.14	.18	.09	.21	.10	.32

volvement.

3. Involvement with advertising tends to be higher for magazines than for television with high involvement products, but no different with low involvement products.

4. Involvement, as measured by number of "connections" per minute, tends to be more sensitive than, and independent of, two other measures (a) Starch Noting scores, and (b) seconds of stimulus exposure.

5. Involvement with specific stimuli tends to be more varied and consequently less predictable with products of intrinsically low involvement, while stimuli representing a high involvement product more often tend to share the same level of involvement.

A final and equally tentative hypothesis may apply only to advertising and not to media messages in general. This is the hypothesis that women tend toward higher or more favorable involvement than men. The difference may be viewed in terms of the woman's role as family "purchasing agent" in American society. Moreover, in terms of our general theory of involvement, which relates low involvement impact to conditions in which behavioral changes precede attitude changes, it supposes that the less highly involved men are more likely to be "impulse" buyers, while the more highly involved women are more likely to be "planful" buyers of advertised goods and services.

A next step in research will be to attempt to relate involvement measures to the purchasing consequences of advertising exposure

.

---

[1] Carolyn W. Sherif, Muzafer Sherif, and Roger E. Nebergall, *Attitude and Attitude Change: The Social Judgment-Involvement Approach* (Philadelphia: Saunders, 1965).

[2] Summaries of Titchener's relevant methodological contributions appear in Robert S. Woodworth, *Contemporary Schools of Psychology* (New York: Ronald, 1931), pp. 40-41, and in Edna Heidbreder, *Seven Psychologies* (New York: Appleton-Century, 1933), p. 129.

[3] The studies reported here were sponsored by *Time* Magazine. For those who may be interested, a manual that discusses rules for scoring of connections is available from the author.

[4] It is relevant that the Sherifs did find that highly involved and less involved persons appraise communications differently *(op. cit.,* Chap. V).

[5] The concept of motivation is excluded from the model because its arousal is often so general as to permit a large and unpredictable number of resolutions, including, commercially, the purchase of a competitor's brand.

[6] The point here is that the magazine itself is a store (like a catalogue) where "browsing," shopping, and purchase decisions may occur.

[7] The *Appareil à Mésure d'Observation* (Instrument for Measuring Observation), designed at the Marplan Perception Laboratory in Paris, France, is a fourteen-page hardcover portfolio that contains seven stopwatches within the back cover of the portfolio. A complex of unseen pulleys permits the opening and closing of seven of the pages to be precisely timed.

[8] Please check those statements that best describe the kinds of thoughts that came to mind while you looked at the advertisement.

    ___The advertisement held my attention but no particular thought came to mind.

    ___I had at least one thought but it had nothing to do with the main idea of the advertisement.

    ___I had at least one thought about the advertisement but it had nothing to do with me personally.

    ___I had at least one thought which tied in something about the main idea of the advertisement to something about me personally.

[9] In terms of distraction theory, these data are consistent with earlier findings by L. Festinger and N. Maccoby, "On Resistance to Persuasive Communications," *Journal of Abnormal and Social Psychology,* vol. 68, no. 4 (1964), pp. 359-366.

[10] The quality of relaxation in viewing assumed unexpected importance when an attempt was made to interrupt and terminate the viewing procedure immediately after the third, or advertising, page, without removing the following two pages. This unsuccessful experiment in interview economy was attempted with an additional twenty-four respondents, almost all of whom indicated some degree of suspicion or complaint about not being allowed to finish the "book" and then showed what seemed like a constricted response. Thus, the average number of reported connections dropped to .6, and the average number of words of comment about the *advertising* dropped from 120 to 86.

[11] It should be noted, however, that the transmission quality of the commercials seemed inferior to that on home television receivers. This should be corrected in future tests

[12] One implication here for modification of laboratory research procedures is to *depersonalize* the researcher and his influence on the respondent. At the least, he might be out of the room when copy is viewed and questionnaires completed; "obviously" recorded (voice) instructions might represent a further step; one ultimate procedural goal might be described as self-service research. For a broader discussion of this problem, see M.T. Orne, "On the Social Psychology of the Psychological Experiment: With Particular Reference to Demand Characteristics and Their Implications," *American Psychologist,* vol. 17 ()1962, pp. 776-783.

[13] Starch Noting scores are the percentage of readers of magazine issues who at least noticed high- and low-scoring advertisements, as reported by the Daniel Starch organization.

CHAPTER 8

PSYCHOLOGICAL PERSPECTIVES IN MARKETING STRATEGY

A consumer psychologist might view questions of marketing strategy from three particular perspectives. One is to acknowledge that purchasing decisions are based on learned behavior, and that learning is based on repeated exposures to stimuli, *i.e.*, to advertisements, to products, to stores. While a great deal is known about classroom learning, its counterpart in the marketplace is not often noted.

The second perspective is a concern for *what* is learned. Some products or brands elicit strong loyalties based on liking or belief, while other products are bought only as a matter of habit and can be substituted for without care. This range of response to products represents *different* behaviors, each of which is also learned differently. That is, there is a different learning process for emotional likes, for rational preferences, and for simple or habitual choices.

The third perspective is to try to relate the kind of learning which may be most common within a particular market to the allocation of marketing dollars among such activities as sampling, research and development and to types of advertising campaigns.

Advertisers have long been aware that some kind of learning process is at work in the marketplace. The question is what kind or kinds, and what are the practical implications, if any? Consider this charming illustration taken from Thomas Smith's *Hints to Intending Advertisers*, published in London in 1885:

> The first time a man looks at an advertisement, he does not see it.
>
> The second time he does not notice it.
>
> The third time he is conscious of its existence.
>
> The fourth time he faintly remembers having seen it before.
>
> The fifth time he reads it.
>
> The sixth time he turns up his nose at it.
>
> The seventh time he reads it through and says, "Oh bother!"
>
> The eighth time he says "Here's that confounded thing again!"

Adapted from an Address to The Association of National Advertisers, 1966 National Conference, Colorado Springs, October 24, 1966.

The ninth time he wonders if it amounts to anything.

The tenth time he thinks he will ask his neighbor if he has tried it.

The eleventh time he wonders how the advertiser makes it pay.

The twelfth time he thinks perhaps it may be worth something.

The thirteenth time he thinks it must be a good thing.

The fourteenth time he remembers that he has wanted such a thing for a long time.

The fifteenth time he is tantalized because he cannot afford to buy it.

The sixteenth time he thinks he will buy it some day.

The seventeenth time he makes a memorandum of it.

The eighteenth time he swears at his poverty.

The nineteenth time he counts his money carefully.

The twentieth time he sees it, he buys the article or instructs his wife to do so. [1]

That was eighty-five years ago. Perhaps Mr. Smith was a bit ahead of his time; the questions remain.

THE LEARNING OF SKILLS

The study of learning, especially in its relation to the phenomenon of memory, is perhaps the oldest of the classic interests of academic psychology. Indeed, it goes well back into the nineteenth century. Mr. Smith was not really too far ahead of his time. However, since that time the world of education has created enormous pressures and opportunities for psychologists to contribute to better understanding of the learning process in the classroom situation. Out of the vast body of research and literature produced to meet this challenge, there developed several major and competing theories of learning, differing in important theoretical respects but similar in the factors or variables considered important to study, and similar also in many of the principles which later emerged as practical guides in the classroom.

The most widely accepted principles can be summarized thus: In learning new *skills*, repetition or practice is effective; active practice, or recitation, is more effective than passive practice; the learning of the task as a whole is more effective than learning it piece by piece; short practice sessions spread over a longer period of time are more effective than longer practice sessions crammed into a shorter period of time; when practice is continued beyond what is required for successful accomplishment of the task at hand, there is little forgetting of what has been learned even after long periods without practice.

This is what we are accustomed to hearing about the learning of new skills, but what about new likes, beliefs, or choices?

THE LEARNING OF LIKES

Likes involve affective tone or pleasure, some of which is evident and sometimes growing or developing from learning exposure to learning exposure. Because pleasure is basically physical in nature, it has been suggested that learning to like involves the satisfaction by a specific stimulus of some general need. Repetition of the specific "solution" to the general need, so to speak, progressively increases response to the stimulus. Some have called this process channelization or *canalization* to distinguish it from the process of conditioning. In canalization the stimulus *itself* is satisfactory and is not becoming liked simply because it may be presented in the presence of some already liked object. The classic example of conditioning is the case of Pavlov's dog who was taught to salivate whenever he heard a bell, *i.e.*, his salivating response to the appearance or expectation of dinner was transferred to the dinner bell itself. It is also contended that canalized likes, though they may wax and wane with temporary satiation, are never completely extinguished, *e.g.*, having once acquired a taste for olives or for beautiful paintings it always remains.[2]

From this point of view the marketer has reason to prize consumer liking of his brand or product, since the developed loyalty may withstand counterargument from competitors quite easily. "Argument" or rationality may have nothing to do with the matter. The likes, having been built upon repeated satisfaction, stand by themselves.

In the market place it is the *generic* product likes that are usually of this nature. Once the market has been so established for, let us say olives, it is then up to the brands to compete for preference or choice. Occasionally a marketer is lucky enough to have his brand identified with the generic category, as in the case with consumers who grew up on only one brand. More often than not, however, deep-seated likes are reserved for the category and not the item. Thus, market researchers, especially motivation researchers can discuss product likes and dislikes with consumers and quickly tap the important attitudes towards the generic class of product. The question of individual brands or companies, however, is harder to discuss in a reliable and meaningful way.

Much of new product development or service research attempts to identify unsatisfied needs which may now be satisfied. It is a kind of research which is very satisfying to the researchers themselves because of the "real" contribution they are making to consumers, and because of the sincerely enthusiastic feedback which may be achieved from consumers. In this connection it should be noted that the progressive satisfaction of needs and the associated learning to like is a fairly conscious phenomenon on which consumers can report. In every way the situation is made easy for research — provided there are good new products or services to research.

The determined psychologist may pass up the enthusiasms of new product research for something more complex and more common — for, after all, the really new mousetrap is a rarity. The everyday marketplace situation is more aptly described as one of a hundred better mousetraps with some better (in sales) than others. How to account for clear differences in preference or choice when unrelated to true liking or perhaps even to tangible product-to-product differences? Here we move into kinds of learning which are more subtle. Here we take more account of the process of *influence* by other factors than the product or service itself. This may be contrasted with learning to like wherein response is based more directly on the product experience itself.

THE LEARNING OF PREFERENCES AND CHOICES

Preferences are defined here as consumer decisions based on belief in the superiority of one's own (selected) item over others. It is a matter then of the many better mousetraps, and of the need to say so or claim so.

Marketers would like to think that their products or services were indeed better and/or that consumers believed them to be better. What is often the unrecognized case, however, is that their products or services are neither liked, nor considered better, but chosen only because they are adequately "good" *and* for the pleasure of their recognition, *i.e.,* sheer familiarity.

Just as new product research and true consumer liking may be more exciting to marketers and researchers, so is brand competition to be "better" more exciting merely than to be the familiar and routine choice. Nevertheless the determined psychologist will pass up research on being better to the still more complex and common situation of research on being chosen — chosen without liking or reason. Most provocatively, to the researcher, is the fact that choices of the latter sort cannot be "explained" to the inquiring researchers and may look deceptively like random behavior.

Most of what currently passes for consumer research in popular theorizing about consumer behavior is based on the "better product" type of thinking. Thus, many advertising agencies' managements try to identify prior to campaigns some one unique selling proposition, purchase proposition, persuasion proposition, etc. that communicates that their brand has a reason to offer the consumer for his preference. Those who actually produce the advertising materials may inject other strategies, but industry and client thinking tends to emphasize the "better" approach, even in the face of categories and markets where no brand loyalty can be found or in markets where loyalty persists in the face of "better" type claims.

This is not to say that "better" type advertising and its rational, conscious learning by consumers is inappropriate or wrong. It is indeed, however, what marketing men know best, know too well in fact, so that other equally common types of learning are not distinguished as requiring different treatment.

To redress this imbalance it may be helpful to highlight the processes of consumer choice and the nature of the learning or advertising influences which distinguishes it from the processes of consumer preference.

The learning of consumer preference is represented by acceptance of a "better" type of claim or belief. The change processes *minimally* require one-time transmission of specific new information which represents a way of looking at the product or service which is in *conflict* with or different from that represented in older information, and which may lead to resolution of the difference through new decision-making. While changed behavior may result as a consequence of new decisions, the behavior is not necessarily a part of the change process, *i.e.*, the change process itself may be over before the customer heads for the store, shopping list in hand.

The learning of consumer choice is quite different. It requires repeated exposure to information which the consumer recognizes as present but to which he makes no personally relevant connections, *i.e.*, he remains uninvolved. Such repeated exposure can, however, build a potential for the ability to see a product or service differently. What is required to release or trigger this potential is a behavioral opportunity such as in-store shopping, *i.e.*, to suddenly see the product in the new manner when confronted by it on the supermarket shelf. This may also be described as recognizing the previously unconnected exposures as familiar, *i.e.*, known. What is *also* required is behavioral completion to release appropriate attitudes supportive and consistent with the shift in perceptual structure, *i.e.*, if the product is then purchased the new way of seeing it may then for the first time be expressed in words, for example, to "explain" why it was selected.

The role of behavior in consumer choice then is as part of the change process, which continues beyond the store. Unless behavior completion or purchase occurs, there entails an unstable condition characterized by a shift in perceptual structure without a corresponding shift in attitudinal structure. Without behavioral completion, therefore, the structure reverts to its initial condition, though still carrying the potential for shift on other occasions. For example, a housewife may be repeatedly struck by some new (advertised) brand attribute each time she confronts it on the store shelf, and yet never retain this impression long enough to put into words until one day the actual purchase is made.

In short, with low involvement choices one might look for product or service adoption through gradual shifts in perceptual structure, aided by repetition, activated by behavioral choice situations, and *followed* at some time by attitude change. With high involvement product preference, one could look instead for the classic, more dramatic, and more familiar conflict of ideas at the level of conscious opinion and attitude that precedes changes in overt behavior.[3]

The overall model inherent in the theory of involvement differs pointedly from past models of communication effectiveness. For example, past models of advertising impact have tended to assume that somewhere between initial awareness and later action there occurred a rational decision-making process usually called "evaluation." This was supposed to take place just before what was called "trial," as in Awareness*Interest*Evaluation*Trial*and finally Adoption. There was also a tendency to assume that the models of the day applied equally to *all* advertising.

Since those days motivation research has sharply challenged the assumption that decision-making or evaluation was always "rational." Now involvement theory challenges the assumption that all advertising can be treated equally. It asserts two models of impact, one each for high and low involvement advertising. It asserts that with low involvement the decision process is skipped altogether and that the sales impact of repeated advertising exposure occurs in the form of very special kinds of impulse behavior.

There is a problem in client acceptance of involvement theory, because each would like to think that his product or service is a high involvement product, and that high involvement is somehow better than low involvement. By implication it also suggests a client acceptance problem of advertising itself, since it is in relation to low involvement consumer response that frequency of advertising exposure is most critical.

Involvement is defined as the number of connections, conscious bridging experiences or personal references per minute that the viewer makes between the content of the persuasive stimulus and the content of his or her own life. This may vary from none to many.

To measure involvement, therefore, one has to ask respondents, "What thoughts came to mind *while* you looked at the advertisement?" The respondent is not asked for an opinion or for a judgment but for a report of the occurrence or non-occurrence of certain mental *events*. For example, a housewife might say "The recipe at the bottom of the ad made me think of what I was going to serve the family for dinner." The object of study then is the immediate experience of advertising, *i.e.*, what happens during exposure?

High involvement products or services may be tentatively described as those whose ads average 1.0 or more connections per exposure, and low involvement products or services as those whose ads average 0.5 or fewer connections per exposure. A middle group would include those over 0.5 and under 1.0.[4]

Other measures of advertising impact concern viewers opinions about impact, later reactions such as recall, or attempts (difficult) to measure effects on behavior. All these other measures have value but the significance of involvement has been overlooked.

THE MOSAIC OF THE MARKET

The learning of likes is based on satisfying experience, preferences on ideas of superiority, choices on recognition of influences made familiar by repeated exposure. All three types co-mingle, sometimes vis-à-vis a single brand. Sometimes there develops a sequence of choice first, then of preference, and finally of liking, but none need necessarily develop.

It does seem important for a given market to find out how people are coming into and staying in that market, or how many are coming in in each way. The learning of liking can be furthered by investments in forced exposure, *i.e.*, sampling, free trials, etc. The learning of preference can be furthered by investment in research and development to make completely better products and in advertising with targeted reach but not necessarily high frequency of exposure. The learning of choice can be furthered by investments in high frequency advertising to make the sales effort very familiar to those who are exposed. Each of these investment strategies may have natural proponents in the form of merchandisers, designers and advertising personnel. The strategy for a particular market, however, should rather be based on good information about the consumer himself. If the pitfalls of terminology are avoided, and if research based on rigorous definition of the consumer behaviors involved, this would seem to be a practical and profitable policy.

---

[1] Thomas Smith, *Hints to Intending Advertisers* (London, 1885). Quoted by James Playsted Wood in *The Story of Advertising* (New York: Ronald, 1958), p. 241

[2] For a review and discussion of research on learning to like, see Chapter 1 above.

[3] The particular mechanisms of low involvement learning are discussed in more detail in Chapter 6 above.

[4] Measurement procedures are described in Chapter 7 above.

CHAPTER 9

PROCESSES UNDERLYING EXPOSURE TO ADVERTISING

We are somewhat the prisoners of our environment, and this blinds us to certain things, especially the elemental things. We are in this respect like the fish in the sea. The last thing the fish would be aware of is water. In advertising research the environment is one of thinking up, promoting and applying a variety of partial measures of advertising effect. Rarely do we ask how people really respond to advertising, or how to explore the natural dimensions of the advertising experience.

I refer here to direct response, that is, the experience of being exposed to advertising. For the most part it has not been studied. We can blame this omission on J.B. Watson and the behaviorist tradition in American psychology, on such accepted symbols of the "researcher's" trade as the before-and-after questionnaire, on a practical businessman's concern for the subsequent or net effects of advertising, or somewhat belatedly on the technical difficulty of studying what actually goes on during the moments of advertising exposure. Nevertheless, we are strange students of advertising indeed to be so concerned with the after-the-fact recall, comprehension, believability and motivational effects of advertising and yet know so little about what happens during the event.

By response to advertising I mean to ask what people are actually thinking, I mean to ask what are they looking at, I mean to ask what they are feeling during the moments of exposure.

I will report and discuss some results of research on the three processes of thinking, looking and feeling defined as follows:

1. *Thinking* will be defined in terms of thoughts which came spontaneously to mind while an ad was being viewed. The report of such thoughts is based on an interview shortly after exposure, in which the respondent is reminded of the ad, sometimes shown the ad again, and asked to report on the earlier mental events.

For other purposes, for example, to develop a measure of involvement with advertising, these thoughts have been examined for the

Original Publication: Advertising Research Foundation Proceedings of the 14th Annual Conference New York Hilton, October 15, 1968. Adapted from the Presidential Address to the Division of Consumer Psychology, American Psychological Association, Washington, D.C., September 5, 1967 (*American Psychologist*, Vol. 23, No. 4, April 1968, pp. 245-253.)

number of "connections" which they contain. Connections are those thoughts which link some content of the ad to some content in the personal life of the respondent. While research on connections was reported in the Chapter 7 above, I will refer in this paper to all thoughts, whether connected or not.

2. *Looking* will be defined in terms of the capabilities and limitations of the Mackworth stand mounted eye movement recorder in which the respondent's head is rendered immobile with the aid of a bite-plate and a 6 x 8 inch picture is viewed at a distance of 18 inches.[1] Eye movements are recorded to produce a developed motion picture film of the viewed scene and a superimposed white spot or marker indicates the path of eye movements. Ten-second exposures are recorded, and from the developed film a plot is made of location of eye fixations, duration or dwell time, and shifts to new fixations. The type of equipment is described in the August 1968 cover story of *Scientific American* Magazine.

3. *Feeling* will be defined in a fairly strict physical sense, *i.e.*, intensity of response, sometimes called arousal. Change in pupil size is used as a measure of intensity not because it is superior in any way to such measures as changes in heart rate, skin temperature or other indicators, but because the Hess apparatus has the advantage of measurement of pupil size during viewing without attachment of any equipment to the body of the respondent. The respondent is consequently less involved with the process of measurement *per se.* See Chapter 4 above. The term intensity of response is used in part because the more common terms such as excitement or interest carry at least slight positive meanings which I do not necessarily intend.

The pupil data consist of measurements of pupil diameters from motion picture films of the left eye. The stimuli are treated to eliminate internal high and low points of brightness, and each experimental stimulus is preceded by a base line control stimulus of the equivalent amount of white light empty of pictorial content. Changes in pupil size are obtained therefore with the influence of light removed. The type of equipment is described in the April 1965 cover story of *Scientific American* magazine.

THINKING

The last published study by the late Gary Steiner of the University of Chicago employed 325 college students from the University of Chicago to surreptitiously observe the television commercial viewing of behavior of another member of their own family in their own homes over the nine-day period from Saturday morning May 16, 1964 through Sunday evening May 24.[2] Each selected one other member of the household (usually a parent or spouse) and was to make as many observations as possible within the nine-day period, though a twenty-five-observation-hour limit was imposed to keep some control of the quality. A total of 6,460 observation hours produced over 80,000 separate observations.

To summarize the results, "Most people are paying attention just before a commercial comes on; over 80 percent sit through the commercial; only 5 percent show any signs of annoyance at outset; and during the commercial itself, more people have something good to say than something bad."

When one considers that college families are generally more critical and less addicted to television to begin with, or the popular impression that all viewers use station break and commercial time to go to the bathroom, this summary provides a startling picture of faithful attention to commercials. At least on the level of overt behavior, viewers, even in college families, stay with their commercials. To me such stark data on overt attention underscores the importance of describing more intimately what else is going on, even if one must turn initially to research under less than natural viewing conditions.

To begin with thinking, I shall refer to a series of studies of television and print advertising in which advertising was shown in the home with rear view projectors or with portfolios and magazines. Some advertising was shown within an editorial context and some not. After exposure the respondent was asked what thoughts came to mind during exposure. Careful checks were made to separate thoughts during exposure from thoughts which occurred later, *i.e.*, during the interview.

The first point to make is that thinking is present, that mental activity is taking place. The overall average of connections per respondent for all our ads and studies taken together is over .5 per ad exposure, and this is just for connections. Since connections are stringently defined as linking some content of the ad to some content of the personal life of the respondent one can imagine that less stringently defined thoughts are even more common. Other thoughts not qualifying as connections are two to three times as numerous.

One might suppose that the artificiality of the research situation might inflate thinking during exposure. However, experimentation with different response sets and degrees of artificiality consistently shows more connections in the more natural settings. Thus, we are inclined to conclude that advertising not only holds its audience physically as Steiner indicates, but that when it does, it elicits much subjective response.

This subjective response is greater than the overt behavioral response. For example, Steiner's data suggest that five percent of all viewers make negative comments about television commercials; our data suggest that a *third* of all viewers have negative thoughts about television commercials. Similar negative thoughts were absent in response to print advertising, with the exception of advertising having to do with cigarettes, which was the sole product category to evoke more negative than positive thoughts.

Turning generally to the *content* of thinking during advertising exposure it seems that thought content is quite naturally a function of advertising content. But let us look closely. Let us take 90 respondents and show them three ads varying in differentiation or structure. The most specific is an ad for Timex watches, the page almost entirely taken up by two watches. Next is an ad for Opel automobiles showing a dozen different models of the automobile parked in various positions on a dock right next to a cargo ship. The third is an ad by Pan American Airways showing a picturesque fishing village in Southern Europe.

It is clear that the Timex ad is about watches and nothing else. The Opel ad has something to do about cars landed by a ship. The Pan Am ad is most ambiguous until one reads the travel-oriented paragraph at the bottom of the page. It is the Pan Am ad with the least structure that elicits the most thoughts per respondent, and the Timex ad with the most structure that elicits the least number of thoughts (Pan Am 1.5, Opel 1.1, Timex 1.0 per respondent). It is the Pan Am ad with the least structure that elicits the widest variety of thoughts, and the Timex ad which elicits the narrowest range of thoughts, that is, thoughts confined to the product or service represented (Pan Am 26 percent, Opel 32 percent, Times 36 percent of thoughts per ad). Finally, and despite the wider range of thoughts for the Pan Am ad, it is the Pan Am ad which elicits the most thoughts expressing desire for the product and service, and the Timex ad which, though it elicits the most product-oriented thoughts, elicits the least number of thoughts expressing desire for the product (Pan Am 20 percent, Opel 3 percent, Timex 1 percent of thoughts per ad).

The point illustrated is simply that structure in the stimulus elicits structure in the response. This is better than saying that the content of advertising or of propaganda "controls" the content of response because it permits the observation that there may be more or less content *per se*. It also permits the observation that a highly structured or controlled stimulus, while it may be most communicative or informative, may be least motivating or persuasive. Thus, *information is not simply persuasive, and control is not simply manipulative.*

Thought activity in response to advertising is also a function of the quality of the advertising context. For example, interest in editorial matter, (*i.e.*, in magazine stories or TV shows) seems to carry over to heighten response to the advertising. Thus, interest itself is a set, a set or expectation of further interest - In this way the first ad or commercial after interesting editorial matter has an advantage over the second or third ad.

We will have more to say about the sheer levels of response intensity and feelings later on, but let us shift first to the matter of eye movements and looking.

LOOKING

In and of itself, looking is of little concern to us in the particular research described since we start with the premise that our respondents are looking at our ads. Our concern is with how they are looking, how they are looking when communication or learning is taking place as compared with how they are looking when communication is not taking place, *i.e.*, what are the response qualities of looking-with-learning?

Of parallel concern are the stimuli themselves. How are easily learned ads looked at as compared with ads which are difficult to learn, *i.e.*, what are the stimulus qualities of looking-with-learning?

The respondents in such studies were brought to a laboratory, exposed to different ads for ten seconds each via the Mackworth Optiscan, and then interviewed for recall of the ads. Recall therefore was the criterion of learning. Additional respondents were brought back once a week for three weeks, without verbal interviewing, just to note the effects of repeated exposures on looking.

Of various scoring methods the one of most interest concerned looking in only one place vs. looking all over, or "bunched up" vs. "spread-out" looking. Ms was finally called focusing and scanning and was scored by dividing the total area of each advertisement into I" x V cells and counting the number of different cells which were "looked into."

Initial findings presented an interesting paradox. On a respondent basis, scanning represents looking-with-learning, *i.e.*, the respondents who scanned more recalled more. However, on a stimulus basis, focusing represents looking-with-learning, *i.e.*, the ads which were scanned less were better recalled.

The resolution of the paradox is apparently this: ads which are easily learned require very little of the respondent, they communicate with little work on his part. But ads which do not learn easily do require the respondent to be more active, to look around, to scan.

So we have here a situation where at one extreme the work of communication must be done by the communicator via creation of an easily learnable ad or communiqué, or on the other hand where the work of communication may be done by the respondent or communicant via an ability to learn difficult communiqués.

Now then what is best for advertising? There is no question that some public messages must communicate easily or immediately for even the poorest learners, e.g., a highway STOP sign. There is no question that an outdoor poster must communicate more easily and more quickly than a newspaper ad. When there is time or the opportunity for repeat exposures, however, what then is best? Should an ad do all the work, or should some be done by the viewer?

I would approach this question first with another question which is "How much work is there to be done?" The data from our experiments on repeat viewings provide a clue; this in the form of a consistently narrowing range of scanning from respondent to respondent as they view the same ads over three separate occasions. This means that those who scan more on the first trial scan less on the second, that those who scan less on the first scan more on the second; that those who scan more on the first and second trials combined scan less on the third, and that those who scan less on the first and second trials combined scan more on the third. For example, the range of respondent differences in average number of cells scanned for three trials was in one study 5.5, 3.6, and 1.8. Thus, there are those respondents who learn more quickly and those who learn less quickly. That differences in the amount of learning dwindles to zero, however, implies that for each advertisement studied there is a finite amount to be learned, a finite amount of work to be done.

If there is a finite and measurable amount of work in an ad, what becomes the role of the ad when this initial work is done, completed? Presumably, when it is well learned and even over-learned, the ad may begin to undergo a process of de-differentiation, but this will have to be checked by experiments which carry the learning process to that possible point.[3] Meanwhile, it seems sufficient to infer that a finite amount of work has implications for a finite number of exposures, that *it should be possible to say how many exposures are required to learn a particular ad, and that the number of required exposures will vary greatly from ad to ad,* this perhaps as a reflection of the degree of structure in ad content as discussed under thinking.

If we are going to be able to specify exposure requirements for different ads and for different types of ads, we will close somewhat the currently large gap existing between the advertising agency creative department and the media planning department. As it is now, the media people decide how to spend an advertising budget without great regard for the type of ad produced. Since none of the ad pre-test procedures are able to tell the agency about exposure requirements, it is quite natural that this factor should not be taken into account. However, the fact is that there are multi-million dollar campaigns so planned that many people will be exposed to an ad only a few times, and also multi-million dollar campaigns planned so that few people will be exposed to an ad many times. Neither plan seriously takes into account how many exposures are required to do what to whom.

In time we will test and then provide some form of general typology which may include such generalizations as that *high structure transmits information via focusing and requires few exposures while low structure permits repeated motivational effects via repeated scanning. More* important, however, would be to indicate the distribution of effects to include an evaluation of the results of unavoidable under and over exposure of each type of ad both within and independent of editorial contexts.

FEELINGS

Turning to the subject of feelings or intensity of response one may wonder what new functions can be attributed here. Up to now we have talked about such mechanical sounding concepts as structure, scanning, and repetition. In general we have made communication sound like a job of work to be done. How does intensity fit in?

First, intensity is energy. It indicates the extent of bodily mobilization for the task at hand. If eye movements indicate the direction of that energy, and thoughts the conscious product, then intensity as measured by pupil response (perhaps correlating with eye movement scanning) indicates the sheer amount.

If we can accept the term arousal instead of intensity we are fortunate in that Elizabeth Duffy, who has made the topic an object of life-long study, has published a summary under the book title *Activation and Behavior* (John Wiley, 1962). Her most generalized conclusion is that learning is enhanced in the presence of some arousal, but is hindered by its absence or by its abundance. I would link this conclusion to certain observations about the difference between products, packages and ads that get no or low pupil response and products, packages and ads that get high pupil response. Here one can make at least the one generalization that familiar items get low responses. While a peek at next year's automobile styles may elicit a five to ten percent response, last year's styles will elicit only a one percent response. Proposed designs for a new type of malt beer may elicit from two to five percent, but established brands will elicit only one to two percent. Non-users of a particular stomach remedy will usually respond more to a novel television commercial than will users of the brand.

So here is our old research problem of the familiar vs. the novel and how to test it. Both package and product researchers have long coped with this problem and advertising research people are now also involved. It is easy to compare one new package, product or TV commercial with another new package, product or TV commercial, but how can you then fairly compare the winner with the old package, old product or old TV commercial currently in use?

I would like to suggest a redefinition of this problem, and a generalized solution. The redefinition is suggested by such studies as that of Hutchinson on the role of frustration in creative endeavor, by Hess and Polt on mental activity during problem solving, by Kahneman and Beatty on a replication and confirmation of the Hess and Polt findings, and by Buckhout on changes in heart rate accompanying attitude change.[4] Taken together these studies seem to suggest, whether you call the phenomenon insight or solution or learning, that "it" takes place in conjunction with arousal, "it" occurs at or just after the peak of arousal, "it" occurs on the ebb tide so to speak, or at some point immediately followed by a dramatic ebb tide or off-loading. The final state in the process is back to rest, homeostasis.

If this picture of the work of learning is applied in a communications context to the problem of familiar vs. novel stimuli we may say that *familiar stimuli are not arousing simply because they have already been learned, that there is no further work to be done.* Novel stimuli, however, represent problems. One must respond at least with an automatic cognitive "What *is* it?" and perhaps later even with an intellectual "What of it?" type of response.

It is therefore of no very great credit to a novel stimulus that it is more arousing or exciting than a familiar stimulus, and no discredit to the familiar stimulus that it makes little impression. Most of the familiar tools of life all around us, the very chairs in this room are so dull that they are taken for granted.

Therefore we introduce another question about the work of communication. We have already proposed the question "How much work is there to be done?" and answered by saying that there was a finite and measurable amount of work to be done. Now, we propose to ask, "How will we know when the work is done, *i.e.*, completed?" The proposed answer follows: when the stimulus has lost excitement, when the response has returned to rest or to some form of plateau.

This question about the work of learning refers to more than mere recall. The answer implies that even if the cognitive aspects of advertising are learned perfectly on one exposure some other learnings (e.g., affective) are taking place so long as intensity is left in the response. What we propose here is a way to identify cessation of the cognitive as well as these other effects. This also recognizes the possibility of identifying more truly the absence of such effects, as in the case of the highly structured stimulus which in one exposure easily communicates a familiar and memorable message limited in purpose, e.g., the "reminder" advertisement.

With such distinctions we can re-approach the question of when to measure the so-called "effects" of particular advertising. These effects are really supposed to be aftereffects, at least in the client's mind. Yet laboratory measurement today is based on before-and-after single exposures. The question is: has the effect process begun, is it midway, is it concluded — after a single exposure?

The repugnant alternative to single exposures in the laboratory has been repeat exposures, but this has been considered unwieldy, expensive, and contaminated by the repetition of questions to the respondent along with repetition of the stimulus. These objections may no longer hold.

If we accept that the work of communication is finite, and that its completion can be identified, then there is no reason to commit oneself to a fixed or to a large number of exposure trials. Instead the number of trials would itself be a datum. Each individual would be exposed sufficient times for response to cease, and then undergo the "after" part of his before-and-after verbal interviewing. The statistical distribution of trials required would incidentally tell the media planners something about the kind of reach/frequency ratio to build into their media plan.

What we have here now is the very real possibility of simulating campaign effects in the laboratory, rather than just the effects of a single exposure. We also have the opportunity to explore other response processes which go on in between rather than during exposure trials.[5] Insight, solution, a tipping point of perceptual restructuring or of attitude shift, the so-called "sleeper effects," can occur in between exposures. It is therefore hard to predict from trial to trial whether the respondent will have stopped or will continue to work on our piece of communication. Because we can measure the stopping point, however, we can be fairly confident of including these other processes and effects into our system.

It is not always necessary to measure response to the total communication. For example, somewhere between four and ten seconds after the onset of a 60-second television commercial there occurs a peak pupil response (*i.e.*, peak *within* the first ten seconds) which on a sample of 160 commercials correlated .83 linear or .85 curvilinear with the average response for the total of 60 seconds. This localizes in fairly specific time what appears to be an evaluative event accompanied by commitment of a specific degree of energy to the ensuing experience. That the total amount of work can be so well determined at so early and specific an intervening period is an encouraging indication of how much there is to be learned about intervening processes generally.

Finally, we will give some attention to the problem of feasibility. Are we proposing a methodology which requires an unwieldy or endless number of repetitions for significant numbers of respondents to complete their response? Let us again ask, "How much work is there to be done?" but this time let us go beyond the proposition that the work is finite, and ask "How much, *i.e.*, how many trials to completion?" Shall we expect hundreds of trials as if we were counting therapeutic hours in the fife of a patient being psychoanalyzed? Or shall we draw a parallel with the six dance lessons from Madame Lazonga - for those who are old enough to remember the song. It seems from our experience that six trials are more than enough.

I previously cited an eye movement study in which the range of respondent differences in average number of cells scanned for three trials was 5.5, 3.6 and 1.8. This would imply general completion by a fourth trial. Now if we look at pupil data where we have three or more exposures, we find this sort of thing on some samples of 25 respondents each: that average response may go up dramatically on second exposure and down dramatically on third, may go up on second exposure and then plateau, may go up slightly on second exposure and up slightly on third, and also may go down on second exposure and stay down. What I should like to emphasize is twofold: first, that there were no cases of dramatic increase followed by dramatic increase, and second, that in two thirds to three fourths of the cases the third response was down, *i.e.*, lower than the second response.

Thus, the work of communication may not only be finite on the part of the respondent, but finite and feasible for study by the research psychologist as well.

CONCLUSION

In conclusion, what has been proposed here is that the processes of communication response are feasible to study, that they involve a finite and measurable amount of work to be completed, that the distribution of that work among communicator and communicant can be measured in terms of number and frequency of exposures to "learn" (*i.e.*, cognitive and affective), and that one can also identify the starting and finishing points of the learning or work process, the whole process completed in most cases well within a half dozen trials.

If these propositions are borne out then the tactics of the before-and-after experiment in communications research and evaluation will be capable of individualization. We will be able to go on from the before-and-after study of single or first exposure effects, which often means a premature finding of no effect, to the study of effects before and after the learning processes inherent in individual response have been completed. That is, we propose a laboratory to study the effects of *completed* communication.

Such completed communication may be "complete" because respondents have stopped only when all learnable (cognitive, affective, etc.,) aspects of the stimulus content have been exhausted and there were no barriers or resistances to any such learnings. This may be called a stimulus type of completion. Other completed communication may be considered to be complete because respondents have gone so far and no more - possibly stopped far short of where other respondents have gone, but truly stopped nonetheless. This may be called a respondent type of completion.

This approach may re-open general questions of evaluating the effects of advertising and of the impact of the mass media. It may be fruitful again to ask, "What are the real aftereffects of advertising?" and consequently "What is the true power of the mass media?"

Further Considerations

The approach may also raise many more specific questions. For example, the aftereffects of new campaigns of advertising are usually considered as the effects on the respondents, *i.e.*, how they are different from what they were before for having been exposed to the advertising. There is, however, another kind of aftereffect and this concerns the advertising, *i.e.*, how is it now different for having completed its job of providing new information, for having become familiar and well learned? Our communication environment is primarily composed of familiar and well-learned communiqués. We live in a world of STOP and GO signs, posters, chairs, roadways and symbols which require no work in order to communicate their necessary and sufficient meanings. These communiqués do not even require a flicker of interest to do their daily jobs.

Therefore it should not be assumed that after the work of responding to a new communication has been completed, that the communiqué is ready to be discarded. On the contrary, the communiqué may only be ready to take its undramatic place in the environment, to be available when and if needed by the selective and searching ideas of the occasional beholder. So-called "reminder" advertising, while it does not carry large information burdens at any one time, is available to repeatedly communicate its modest message over long periods of time. These communiqués can also be re-evaluated to see if they are in fact still performing their more modest roles, even if the indicators of communication do not involve all three aspects of thinking, looking and feeling.

---

[1] Norman H. Mackworth, "A Stand Camera for Line-of-Sight Recording," *Perception and Psychophysics,* March 1967.

[2] Gary A. Steiner, "The People Look at Commercials: A Study of Audience Behavior," *Journal of Business,* Vol. 39, No. 2, April 1966, pp. 272-304.

[3] For an earlier development of this point see Chapter 3 above.

[4] E.D. Hutchinson, "The Period of Frustration in Creative Endeavor," *Psychiatry,* 1940, 3, pp. 351-360.

Eckhard H. Hess and James M. Poll, "Pupil Size in Relation to Mental Activity During Simple Problem Solving," *Science,* vol. 143, no. 3611 (March 13, 1964), pp. 1190-1192.

Daniel Kahneman and Jackson Beatty, "Pupil Diameter and Load on Memory," *Science,* vol. 154, no. 3756 (December 23, 1966), pp. 1583-1585.

Robert Buckhout, "Changes in Heart Rate Accompanying Attitude Change," *Journal of Personality and Social Psychology,* vol. 4, no. 6 (1966), pp. 695-699.

[5] For a discussion of learning, see Herbert E. Krugman, "The role of resistance in propaganda," *International Journal of Opinion and Attitude Research,* vol. 3, no.2 (1949), pp. 235-250.

CHAPTER 10

TELEVISION AND TRUST IN RATIONALITY

The problem of TV *versus* print is still with us, as the commercial media debate which is more memorable. It should have been granted long ago that this was not television's prime virtue and that its advertising is not memorable, at least not without much repetition and reinforcement. The Gallup Total Prime Time measurement service set up some years ago in Philadelphia to report next-day recall of TV commercials went out of business, in part because advertisers could not, presumably did not want to, believe the reported low levels of commercial recall, *i.e.*, of commercials which were known to have been seen by the viewer. Memorability or recall *is* an appropriate criterion for a thought-provoking medium like print, but not for TV, which is a medium that importantly provokes something else of equal value. Rather than force the use of common criteria we must first acknowledge that each medium requires its own research procedures. This is a critical way for the research to acknowledge that the media *do* perform different jobs.

The situation in the print media is that the individual member of the audience actually interacts with the message. He comprehends, thinks, forms intentions, remembers. In television, however, usually nothing happens except that a faint imprint of the message is left behind, and it may with repetition and reinforcement some day become well fixed. For example, it is a delight, at first, to *recognize* (not remember) a previously liked TV commercial. Children may go so far as to actually "learn" the commercial and sing it about the house. The trick here is not memorability, however, but the pleasure and surprise inherent in simple recognition.

You can recognize hundreds of TV commercials you can't remember. You can also recognize hundreds of print ads too but it doesn't give you pleasure to do so. You don't need to recognize print ads because you finished with them, more or less, at the time of exposure. You thought about the message, decided something or other, and that was that! So it takes a lot of input, much of it finished, to be able to recall, but it takes very little input to be recognized. People don't do much with TV commercials at time of exposure, because they are not finished with them, and they may never finish with them, *i.e.*, until a relevant act triggers what they have absorbed from them.

Undated manuscript, ca. 1970

Life is full of unexpected triggers, unanticipated needs to decide, to act in situations where an at least faintly imprinted TV input provides the sole personal input which the individual may bring to an otherwise "don't know" situation, the tie-breaking input in an otherwise "undecided" situation, the most familiar input in an otherwise strange or challenging situation. Thus, the impact of television is rarely seen until it is unexpectedly triggered into life, full-blown and all at once.

The most obvious area of television's commercial success is the self-service supermarket. Every aisle is full of triggers. Other things being equal, advertising recall and intentions to buy are better criteria of print advertising effectiveness, while actual sales are a better criterion of television advertising effectiveness.

Two points must be emphasized here. One is that the "obvious" impact of television on supermarket behavior is paralleled by a "not so obvious" impact on many other areas of life. Second is that the impact of television is more likely to be seen in changes of behavior rather than, *and not preceded by*, changes in attitude.

The assertion that behavior change is not necessarily preceded by attitude change has come up as an issue time after time in recent years. It might be left alone except that it now appears to be central to the understanding of the television experience and the impact of television.

Times have changed since Leon Festinger made the attitude/behavior issue controversial within *Public Opinion Quarterly*. While communication research has left the issue unattended, the profession of psychology has undergone a related upheaval which gets much publicity in the mass media. How is it that communication research has not recognized what is happening?

Large numbers of psychologists, patients and other clients have been indulging in behavior-therapy and/or encounter sessions. The idea is that new physical experience and new acts of behavior will pave the way for other behavior changes *and* attitude changes. This is the big new thing in psychology today: behavior first, attitudes second. A new generation is pushing forward into new experiences *in search of* attitudes. Is it rational? Shouldn't one think things through first?

Our rational, verbal and print biases are very strong. However, we've been warned of this almost a hundred years before McLuhan's *Understanding* Media. We were warned very mildly in the 1920's and 1930's by psychologists such as Gordon Allport, who declined even to define attitudes in terms of verbal referents but more broadly in terms of a "readiness to respond." If we use this approach to attitudes there is no problem of verbal *vs.* behavioral. However, we would have to admit that we had been taking the easier and less expensive course in concentrating on verbal measures. Then we would have to go on to untangling the question of when a verbal expression of attitude was a proper focus or objective and when a behavioral expression was the proper focus or objective, and when verbal and behavioral expressions of an attitude were inconsistent we might be more ready to question whether there was an attitude present at all.

This is one way to go, *i.e.*, to put attitudes and behavior in the same pot without saying they are different and without saying that one causes the other. The other way to go is to say that they are very different indeed, but still without saying that one causes the other. Granted that there are many cases where one does cause the other but those are the only kind we have let ourselves see. We must see the rest of it.

To find warnings that attitudes and behavior are very different indeed, to go beyond the milder caution of Gordon Allport, we have to go back to the turn of the century to the master, Freud himself. Freud brooded very ominously from time to time about the basic nature of mankind. He tried to remind us of man's animal nature, predicted the discovery of the biological foundation of personality, and was clearly no champion of man's rational or good will.

There was a student of Freud who bridged the gap between this view and Allport's milder view, *i.e.*, Freud's view that (verbal) attitudes and (instinctual) physical drives were different and at war, and Allport's view that all behavior, verbal and otherwise was a manifestation of more broadly defined and learned ways of responding to the world. Freud's student suggested that at times the verbal and the physical were interchangeable and *could be* interchanged.

Freud had many eminent students — most of whom rebelled and went on to make independently important contributions. None was more rebellious than Wilhelm Reich, of all Freud's students the one most notorious for emphasis on the explicitly sexual aspects of psychoanalytic theory, the one most radical politically, the one most quick to assert a relationship between sexual freedom and political freedom. He had the distinction, among students of Freud, of being at one time or another jailed, deported, and head of a commune (in Maine), and was altogether in the thirties and forties a premature embodiment of today's humanistic radical.

More importantly Reich was the first and only student of Freud to write a textbook on *how to do psychoanalytic therapy* as opposed to writing books about psychoanalytic theory. The book was entitled *Character Analysis*. This was followed by a bizarre and exciting book called the *Discovery of the Orgone*, which among other things developed a then-new therapeutic principle relevant to the present discussion. This is that when a patient is verbally blocked, when his resistances are so strong that further verbal or attitudinal progress comes to a halt, the therapist should switch attention to the tense musculature, somehow force a change in the body (the "muscular armor" as Reich calls it), and the verbal resistance will weaken or collapse. Then when further work on the body brings *it* to a resistant halt, switch back to the verbal.

The reverberations of this view written in the 1930's (imagine the therapist touching the patient!) are coming into fruition right now. Almost all the new therapies acknowledge that the patient has a body, that it too can have an active part in therapy, and that physical actions or "behavior" sometimes must come into play first in order to revise old or even to create new attitudes.

Perhaps those who know most about how to change people are not teachers or psychotherapists, both of who have usually been limited to verbal interactions with pupils or patients, but revolutionaries — for none have such urgent needs to recruit, convert and discipline new members for the performance of daring *deeds*. Some of that wisdom has been set down in writing and published to be read. It is best appreciated by scholars of and within the Church which has its own sophistication in matters of conversion and of the powerful potentials of significant *acts* of faith. Meanwhile, the twentieth century experts in the changing of individual personality and behavior include such as V.I. Lenin and Dr. Franz Fanon.

To an American, this side of Lenin is perhaps best appreciated via Lenin's disciple "Pop" Mindel, for twenty years the director of the U.S. Communist Party's National Training School. A study of such training was written by Frank Meyer for the Rand Corporation. The Lenin or Mindel tactic was to direct an individual to do something "bad" to test his discipline. It could be to curse the boss, rat on a friend, break a law. The idea was to give one the feeling that he couldn't turn back, could not defect, for so long as he was loyal he had a reason for having done the bad thing, whereas as a defector he would have to contend with the guilt. This principle, carried out in varied forms and increasing degrees, developed increasing ruthlessness, commitment and cynicism. It finally produced people who valued and lived for and by power alone.

Psychologists may recognize the specific technique, however, as a variant of those used in dissonance research, which is very much oriented to placing people in unusual action situations, where they are sometimes made to do things they would prefer not to. Of course, it can only be accomplished experimentally or in a training session in which one has control of the individual.

Dr. Franz Fanon took the Lenin tactic a great step forward, and changed it from being an essentially unpleasant to a finally pleasant and rewarding experience. Dr. Fanon was a black West Indian psychiatrist active in the Algerian revolution and the master of the tactic of confrontation. Recently deceased, his best known book is *The Wretched of the Earth*. An example of the Fanon tactic might involve a black who feels inferior to whites. He would then be made to go up to very powerful and important white and shout obscene curses. The black would expect the earth to open up and swallow him, but surprise — nothing happens, he is still alive. Can it be that he was mistaken, that the white man is not so powerful? A few more confrontations and his sense of inferiority has disappeared.

Now there are educators, psychotherapists and attitude-change people who have ready classifications for this bit of behavior, but it does represent a line going back from Fanon (or facetiously Festinger) to Reich, or perhaps Moreno, to Freud and to the Church, and it will be increasingly applied in education, psychotherapy and in attitude-change research as well.

Some of the new freedoms experienced by individuals via this type of action rather than via deliberate verbal procedures will necessarily be accompanied by a lessening trust of rationality and an increasing interest in what is essentially religious behavior or acts. We may expect some new religions.

So at the same time as we rediscover the great reservoir of intellectual energy potentially available to this planet, we will also be discovering new anti- or non-intellectual energies. Much of this development is perhaps attributable to the unique quality of the television experience, a communication or learning experience requiring almost no energy itself but building up an enormous potential for later releases of energy.

CHAPTER 11

WHAT'S A KRUGMAN CONNECTION?

Although it's not usually realized, advertising is a two-way street between the communicator and the audience. Too often advertising is thought of — particularly by its detractors — as a form of brainwashing or hidden persuasion, possibly sinister, usually self-seeking and, certainly effective, with a strictly one-way message wherein the communicator, *i.e.*, advertiser, is in full control. The customer is not supposed to talk back and, even if he were so minded, there would be no way to record his thoughts.

One scientist who knows this is not true is Dr. Herbert Krugman, now head of communications research at General Electric, formerly Vice President and Research Director of MARPLAN (Interpublic), and an indefatigable life-long pursuer of his own unique theories on advertising involvement. Krugman knows that people do "talk back" to advertising and he has found a way to listen to them.

Herb Krugman evaluates the dialogue in terms of what he calls "connections." And the number of connections that a respondent makes with an individual ad denotes his/her "involvement" in that ad. The official definitions (which Krugman has been spelling out for several years now in learned articles for such journals as the *Public Opinion Quarterly,* and in speeches delivered before such prestigious organizations as the Advertising Research Foundation) go as follows:

"Involvement is defined as the number of connections, conscious bridging experiences or personal references per minute that the viewer makes between the content of the persuasive stimulus and the content of his or her own life. The number of connections may vary from none to many."

Original Publication: Media Decisions, *November 1968*

Editor's Note: Alone among the articles in this compilation, this piece is not *by* Herb Krugman but is rather *about* him. It comes three years after his AAPOR Presidential address (Chapter 6 above) and a year after his APA Division 23 Presidential address (Chapter 9 above). It fairly reflects a man who has reached the top of the professional ladder. In the Krugman household, however, the article raised an issue that we have wrestled with for more than three decades: Who, we all wondered, would be the one to tell Leo Bogart that you don't shoot skeet with a rifle? Leo's passing in 2005 not only deprived us all of a good man, a good mind, and a good friend; it also put an additional entry onto the list of questions that will never be answered.

Whether or not this definition seems forbidding, what about the next step? What about methodology? How can these connections (responses) be scientifically determined? Some day soon we may be able to attach a machine with penetrating electrodes to the respondent's head, and thus have a handy do-it-yourself method of finding out what we want to know about the cerebral convolutions of our respondent's mind. But this day is not yet.

So a more simple method is used. Just listen to Krugman. "To measure involvement, you merely ask the respondents, 'What thought came to mind while you looked at the advertisement?' But there is no other aid to his recall, no loaded questions. The respondent is not asked for an opinion or for a judgment, but for a report of the occurrence or non-occurrence of certain mental *events*. For example, a housewife might say, 'The recipe at the bottom of the ad made me think of what I was going to serve the family for dinner.'"

According to Krugman, the answers to this general question have so far proved to be satisfactory and most illuminating. What is more difficult is the interpreting of the answers and deciding what is and what is not a connection. (See Rules for Scoring of Connections, reprinted at the end of this article.)

It is also vital that the respondents be questioned *immediately* after their viewing of the ads under study because, according to Krugman, "What we are testing is the immediate experience of advertising, that is, what happens during exposure. Other measures of advertising impact concern viewers' opinions about impact, later reactions such as recall, or attempts — difficult as they are — to measure effects on behavior. All of these measures have value, but involvement has been overlooked."

Krugman makes a big point of drawing a line between, and treating differently, ads and products that create high reader involvement and those that engender low involvement. But the line that he draws is purely arbitrary. If the ad in question produces 1.0 more connections, it is counted as high involvement. If .5 or less, it's low involvement. For purposes of simplification, Krugman more or less ignores, and fails to draw any significance from, the gray area between .5 and 1.0. The table on the next page lists tested ads numerically according to the number of connections:

It is not necessary that you have a product of high involvement to make sales and show a profit. For example, Ted Bates, where Krugman was once director of research (1961-62), made its reputation on package-good products selling for less than a dollar (usually low-involvement products) and then pushing them on TV with hard-sell commercials at great frequency. But regardless of the nature of the product, it is important to create and use the highest-involvement ad/commercial possible and to pick the appropriate media. And this is where much research remains to be done.

Even Krugman does not yet know all the answers down to the crossing of every "t" but, if he doesn't, it's not for lack of trying. He has long recognized the need for this type of research and, almost as long as he can remember, has been thinking about and developing his theories. Pieces of his plan began to emerge back in 1941 when he was a psychology student at City College, at which time he published his first article on the effects of repetition on attitude change. During subsequent years when he was a wartime Air Force psychologist, a vice president and research director of Ted Bates (and the same at MARPLAN), and now a research executive of General Electric in New York, he has published 40 professional articles, some half-dozen of which have concerned themselves with advertising involvement in one way or another.

He seems surprised to have been such a lonely pioneer all these years. He

Involvement: Average number of connections	Subject of advertisement	Presented in editorial environment?	Television or print?	n	Sex
	How Some Ads Rated on the "Connections" Barometer				
1.80	Airline	Yes	P	15	F
1.30	Margarine	Yes	P	14	F
1.00	Electric range	Yes	P	53	F
.86	Electric range	Yes	TV	56	F
.70	Travel	No	P	30	F
.67	Airline	Yes	TV	9	F
.57	Electric organ	No	P	30	F
.56	Margarine	Yes	TV	32	F
.38	Automobile	No	P	60	M
.37	Small cigar	Yes	TV	56	M
.37	Electric organ	No	P	30	M
.35	Refrigerator	No	P	60	F
.33	Travel	No	P	30	M
.33	Insurance	No	P	30	F
.30	Insurance	No	P	60	M
.30	Small cigar	Yes	P	44	M
.30	Cigarette	No	P	30	F
.28	Bus. machines	No	P	60	M
.28	Industrial glass	No	P	60	M
.27	Carpeting	No	P	60	F
.28	Hair coloring	No	P	60	F
.25	Analgesic	No	P	60	F
.22	Canned corn	No	P	60	F
.20	Scotch	No	P	30	M
.20	Scotch	No	P	30	F
.18	Corporate (fuel)	No	P	60	M
.17	Insurance	No	P	30	M
.13	Cigarette	No	P	30	M

Five 1966-67 pilot studies conducted by Krugman for Time Magazine has virtually single-handedly established a new kind of dialogue between advertiser and respondent. He has been a Lindbergh, if you will, in this particular kind of flight beyond the demographics.

But now he is less alone. Others are following in his footsteps using his methods and ideas, and in some cases improvising on them. Research practitioners who acknowledge Krugman's leadership in this area, and who have used his ideas in whole or in part, include Leo Bogart, executive VP of the Bureau of Advertising; Benjamin Lipstein, senior VP for research at SSC&B, New York; and Clark Leavitt, head of research at Leo Burnett, Chicago. Furthermore, Krugman's involvement theories are taught at Harvard (School of Business Administration), Lafayette, Purdue and Boston University. He receives over 100 requests a year for elucidation of his theories and methods (and will no doubt receive more after the appearance of this article).

Amazingly enough, Krugman has developed his involvement techniques as a sideline to his regular work. He has, in effect, kept one eye on the future while still attending to his workaday operations. Still more amazing, the sideline has been a labor of love and he is not making, nor does he intend to make, a financial profit on the use of or proliferation of his ideas. He says sternly, "When you start being a businessman, you stop being a psychologist." Or as Bogart puts it, "This man has great integrity in addition to being one of the most stimulating theorists and practitioners in the advertising field today." He could have added, "Krugman doesn't need the money."

Be that as it may, the only financial support enjoyed by Herbert Krugman has been subsidization by *Time* Magazine of five pilot studies during the past two years in Paramus, N.J., Ridgewood, N.J. and Cleveland, Ohio.

Dick Vincent, Time's manager of research development, feels that the pilot studies show the markedly greater impact of print ads over TV commercials in certain situations. As far as *Time* is concerned, it is already sufficiently interested to have developed an experimental sales presentation based on Krugman's findings. There is the further possibility that experimental studies will be continued, a consummation devoutly to be wished by Krugman even though his function in such a study would be largely advisory without financial reward.

As for the five pilot studies already undertaken, the results have been tabulated and combined into one table for the purpose of this article. Every attempt was made to keep the factors constant. Although the tests for men and women were done separately, the same products and the same ads were used on both groups. Where there is a media comparison between magazines and television, the commercials matched the print (as far as possible) in copy theme, sales points, headlines and illustrations. Television was used only four times because of the higher cost entailed in the renting of rear-view projectors. The TV commercials were in black and white. It may be of interest to show the results of these studies as summarized by Krugman:

1. Involvement with advertising in magazines or television tends to be highest when attention is directed to the editorial environment, less when it is directed to the advertising, and least when advertising is present alone.

2. Involvement with advertising tends to be consistent with interest in the editorial environment, i.e., greater interest "carries over" to produce higher involvement.

3. Involvement with advertising tends to be higher for magazines than television with high-involvement products, but no different with low-involvement products.

4. Involvement tends to be more sensitive than, and independent of, two other measures: (a) Starch "Noting" scores, and (b) seconds, of stimulus exposure.

5. Involvement with specific stimuli tends to be more varied and consequently less predictable with products of intrinsically low involvement, while stimuli representing a high-involvement product tend more often to share the same level of involvement.

6. Women tend toward higher or more favorable involvement with advertising than do men.

Krugman was asked about the comparative effectiveness of TV vs. print. Isn't it true that TV has the advantages of sight, sound and motion and thus creates an emotional impact that works automatically toward higher involvement?

"Not necessarily true," he said. "You have to balance that against the fact that the TV commercial is off the air before you know it, before you can really take in its message. Whereas with a print ad you can read it at your own rate of speed, at your own leisure, and at the time that you select. Let's put it another way. When the product involvement is low, as with a cereal, no one gets very excited about a choice of cereals—then the choice of medium is less important and is based on factors unrelated to involvement such as reach, frequency and cost. But when product involvement is high — that is, where the readers cares about the product and is having a struggle making a choice — then print seems superior. Note that a print ad is inanimate but the reader is active, whereas in TV it's the opposite, that is, the commercial moves and the viewer is more or less inanimate. They are actually two quite different media, each with its own rules."

It is generally agreed in the media research world that more facts are needed but that Krugman is on the right track. Some agencies are using his methods but with refinement and extensions of their own, e.g., Leo Burnett in Chicago under the leadership of research director Clark Leavitt.

Some agencies seem fascinated by his approach, find no fault with it but do not judge his methods practical as yet. Dick Jones of JWT says, "I would like to see Krugman's involvement theory pursued further. 1 had lunch with him recently and found the whole idea most provocative. But there's nothing that we can use as yet."

Sam Vitt of Bates provides an echo: "It has great potential in my opinion. It's along the road that advertising must take. But we don't usually go for projects that are not operable at the moment. We're working in the salt mines here at Bates, but we can't get the salt out of this one as yet. We applaud the effort and we're watching the next step."

Still other agencies use Krugman as a launching pad to go off on individual tangents. Ben Lipstein of Sullivan, Stauffer, Colwell & Bayles says, "The great thing about Krugman is that he challenges existing points of view. But I don't agree with everything he says. You might put me down as a critical admirer, I have to admit that if it had not been for Krugman's studies, I never would have written my own paper which I delivered last fall at the Attitude Research Council of the American Marketing Association."

Perhaps some of the print media are even more interested than the agencies. Dick Vincent of *Time* is all aglow: "Advertising involvement is the new wave of media research. My strong belief in it is shared now by many leaders in the advertising industry. Krugman's idea is a working definition, and subsequent validity tests reveal it to be more than just a blue-sky definition."

Leo Bogart of the American Newspaper Publishers' Association concludes: "Krugman's intriguing hypothesis continues to stimulate new research, including my own. The Bureau of Advertising here has just sponsored a series of eye-movement studies based on Krugman's ideas. He's certainly one of our leading theorists in consumer psychology."

Bogart laughed, then added, "You want to know what this man Krugman *is really* like? He's the greatest rifleman I know."

"Rifleman?" we asked.

"Yes," said Bogart. "The only thing I have against him is his cruelty to skeets. Also he's quite a sailor. He's got more damn small boats. He and his family, you know, they're always out sailing, his wife and two children . . .

"We're glad to hear it," we said. "We're glad he's involved and so well connected."

Rules for Scoring of Krugman Reader/Viewer Connections

Any statement that relates the content of the ad to specific incidents or events (or ongoing events) in a person's life is a connection. Mention of other people or relationships usually includes a series of ongoing events.

1. **Motivational statements**

    a.   General motivational

Generalized motivational statements by themselves are not connections unless they are qualified by references to specific times, places, or people in the respondent's personal life.

Not a connection

I would like to have that car.
I wish I could go on a cruise.

A connection

I would like to have . . . for my *daughter*
I wish I could . . . because I enjoyed it *last* time.

b. Personal situations

A motivational statement which involves a whole complex of evaluations of a personal situation in order to make a decision is a connection.

A connection

I would like to go on a cruise but I *can't afford it.*
I don't have the time to learn to play the organ.

c.   Wants and desires

If the ad brought to mind a want or desire that was in existence before the respondent was exposed to the ad, it is a connection.

If there is any doubt as to the pre-existence of a stated want or desire it is not to be scored as a connection.

Not a connection

It made me think that I would like to go on a cruise.
It made me think that I would like to go swimming.

A connection

It made me think that I have always wanted to go on a cruise.
It made me think that I have had an urge to go swimming for the past week.

d. If intent designates a specific or relatively specific time for occurrence,

it is a connection. It is also a connection if it derives from a pre-

existing plan. If it is just general intent it is not a connection.

Not a connection

I like Delmonte corn and I'm going to buy some.
I'll go on a cruise sometime 'within 20 years.

A connection

I like Delmonte corn and I'm going to buy some *tonight.*
I will plan a trip for the *near future.*
I have *already planned* to go on a cruise within the next 20 years.

2. **Attitudinal statements**
    a.   General attitudinal statements

Attitudinal statements by themselves are not connections unless they are qualified by references to personal experiences.

Not a connection

I think General Electric is a good company.
I like that brand.

A connection

I think General Electric makes a good refrigerator *because I have one
at home* which is excellent.
I like that brand *because we used it at home last night.*

b. Personal pre-existing attitudes

If the ad brings to mind a personal pre-existing attitude which is
not used as a positioning statement it is a connection.

Not a connection

I don't like cats so I'm not interested in the ad.
I'm afraid of water so I'm not interested in the ad.

A connection

It makes me think how *fond I am of cats.*
It makes me think *how afraid I am of the water.*

c.   Preference statements

If a statement makes a comparison between the advertised product
and another like product we must infer that it is based on a pre-existing
attitude and consequently call it a connection.

A connection

I see it is for a Westinghouse refrigerator. I *prefer* General Electric.
I see it is for a Baldwin Organ. My *preference* would be for a piano.

Above are listed two of a total of 10 categories of guidelines that are used
in deciding what is and what is not a connection. For a full (and gratis) exposition of Dr. Krugman's scoring methods, write him direct at General Electric,
570 Lexington Avenue, New York, New York 10022.

CHAPTER 12

FLICKER FUSION FREQUENCY AS A FUNCTION OF ANXIETY REACTION: AN EXPLORATORY STUDY

The ability to perceive a certain number of visual stimuli per unit of time has been found to differ significantly between hypothyroid patients and normals,[1] between older and younger persons,[2, 3] between fatigued and rested truck drivers,[4] etc. In all such cases, the number of light-dark cycles per second at which a physically intermittent light was just perceived as a steady light was found to be lower for the more fatigued cases or those with lower metabolic rates than for normals or rested persons.

If it is shown that this variable clearly differentiates between normals and any clinically diagnosed psychoneurotic group, then flicker fusion frequency may be useful for measuring, more or less roughly yet objectively, the degree of disturbance possessed by various individuals, not only at the time of the original diagnosis but also at various stages of therapy as a check on the progress of therapy.

This question was formulated in response to a military assignment involving the study of a neurotic-like syndrome exhibited by many of the Army Air Forces combat veterans after their return to the United States. This syndrome was officially designated as "operational fatigue" and is described elsewhere very ably by Grinker and Spiegel.[5] Insofar as this syndrome was, on the surface, characterized chiefly by indications of severe hypertension, we shall refer to it simply as anxiety reaction. It should be noted that this reaction may be understood as normal in response to the combat situation. It is described as a neurotic-like syndrome only with reference to those for whom the reaction persisted, and in some cases became intensified, in post-combat life.

It was this group of aircrew returnees who served as the experimental group for our study of flicker fusion frequency. All testing was conducted at Army Air Forces Redistribution Station No. 2, Miami Beach, Florida.

Original Publication: Psychosomatic Medicine, vol. 9, no.4 (July-August 1947)

PROCEDURE

Fifty normal aircrew returnees and 50 anxiety reaction cases were selected, from 1 June until 23 June 1945, to report for a flicker fusion test.

1. From those returnees who were referred for psychiatric examination (approximately one-half the total processed at Station No. 2) during the course of routine medical processing, the psychiatrists selected 50 experimental cases showing fairly severe anxiety reactions.
2. From those returnees who were not referred for psychiatric examination, the medical officer at the final check station on the medical processing line selected 50 control cases.
3. Two testing conditions (A and B) were used, and the composition of the several groups of subjects was as follows:

	Condition A		Condition B	
	Officers	E. M.	Officers	E. M.
Control cases	16	9	19	6
Anxiety reaction cases	8	17	12	13

The apparatus used in this study was a General Radio Company "Strobotac," Model 631-B, which is capable of producing a variable oscillating light with a range of 600 to 14,500 cycles per minute. Because of certain extraneous light fluctuations which it was desirable to minimize, the apparatus was modified in the following manner:

1. The 5" diameter of the light source and reflector was cut down to 1¾" by placing an opaque cardboard shield in front of the apparatus. A circle of 1¾" diameter was cut out of the shield.
2. A single sheet of white bond paper was fixed to the back of the cardboard shield and acted as a translucent screen between it and the apparatus.
3. A fixation point on the shield was provided by drawing a cross with axes 5/8" long which intersected at a point 2" below the center of the stimulus light.

The physical characteristics of the test room situation were as follows:

1. The test room was 9' high by 9' wide and 11' long. Blackout curtains cut off all light from windows.
2. The apparatus was placed against a wall 9' wide, and equidistant from either side. A 7' wide portable movie projector screen was placed against the wall and behind the apparatus, in order that the background of reflected light would appear standard when the subject faced the apparatus.
3. Each subject was seated in such a manner that his eyes were level with the center of the stimulus light, and 24 inches distant. This distance insured a 5 degree angle of vision when the subject fix-

ated on the cross 2 inches below the center of the stimulus light. Vision was binocular.

4. The room was lighted by a 50-watt, 120-volt, G.E. Mazda lamp located in the center of the ceiling.
5. A General Electric fan effectively screened out sounds produced by the Strobotac motor and in this way completely eliminated possible auditory cues.

Upon entering the test room, the subject was seated, facing the apparatus. At this point a three-minute period, timed with a stopwatch, was given for the purpose of light-adapting the subject to the illumination level of the test room. During this three-minute period, the following data were recorded:

1. Time of day.
2. Age of subject.
3. Estimated visual acuity (by subject).
4. A short description of any strenuous exercise indulged in on the day of testing *(e.g.,* physical training).
5. Estimated hours of sleep on previous night.
6. A short description of any drinking (alcoholic) which might have taken place on the night prior to testing.

Standardized directions were read to the subject and ten measures of flicker fusion frequency were taken. These were separated by fifteen-second rest periods, during which time scores were recorded. The stimulus light was turned off as soon as the subject made a response, and turned on again five seconds before the start of the next trial.

1. For the first 50 subjects (25 control and 25 experimental), scores were obtained by beginning with a frequency of 3,700 per minute and gradually diminishing the frequency until the presence of flicker was reported. For the second group of subjects, a frequency of 2,000 per minute was used at first, and gradually increased until the absence of flicker (flicker fusion) was reported. Although the second method is the traditional one it was felt worthwhile to try both. These two methods are referred to as Conditions A and B.
2. The frequency of the stimulus light was controlled by a hand-operated dial. The rate at which this dial was turned was subject only to the very rough kind of standardization afforded by kinaesthetic control on the part of the examiner. The examiner looked away from the dial, the frequency scale and the subject during the progress of each test trial in order that kinaesthetic control should not be influenced by what could be seen.

RESULTS

In Table 12.1 a statistical summary of the results is presented for each of the two testing conditions.

TABLE 12.1

BASIC STATISTICS FOR TWO METHODS OF
MEASURING FLICKER FUSION FREQUENCY

	Condition A		Condition B	
	Fusion to flicker		Flicker to fusion	
	Control	Experimental	Control	Experimental
	(N = 25)	(N = 25)	(N = 25)	(N = 25)
	(Cycles per minute)		*(Cycles per minute)*	
Mean	3416	3248	2736	2613
S. D.	125	167	160	158

Fishers "t"= 3.93* Fisher's "t" = 2.69

r_{bis} = .62** r_{bis} = .45**

S.E. r_{bis} = .13 S.E. r_{bis} = .15

r^c_{11} = .98*** r^c_{11} = .96***

*   Difference between the means significant at the 1% level or better.
**   Correlation between flicker fusion frequency and psychiatric diagnosis (presence or absence of operational fatigue).
***   Corrected for twice the length by use of the Spearman-Brown formula.

It is apparent that the mean scores made by normals are significantly higher than those made by anxiety reaction cases, though there is considerable overlapping of the distributions. It is also evident that results for testing Condition A (fusion to flicker) seem to be somewhat more related to anxiety reaction diagnosis than the traditional testing condition, Condition B (flicker to fusion).

In order to evaluate the extent of the relationships between anxiety reaction and fusion frequency, it was considered desirable to determine the relationships between fusion frequency and some of the other variables in the test situation that might conceivably have affected the test scores. The intercorrelations of these variables and those of fusion frequency and psychiatric diagnosis are presented in Tables 12.2 and 12.3. Visual acuity and physical exercise are omitted

TABLE 12.2

VARIABLES FOR WHICH
INTERCORRELATIONS WERE COMPUTED

1. Flicker fusion frequency
2. Psychiatric diagnosis
3. Hours of sleep
4. Time of day tested (hours since 0001)
5. Age
6. "Alcoholism"*

*   For this variable the sample was split into those who drank more, and those who drank less, than one bottle of beer on the previous night.

because no distribution was obtainable (all subjects reported 20/20 vision and no exercise on the day of testing).

TABLE 12.3

INTERCORRELATIONS: CONDITION A (N = 50)

	1	2	3	4	5	6
1	—	.62*	−.06	−.41**	.01	.22
2	bis	—	.33*	−.44**	−.05	.60*
3	pm	bis	—	.10	−.14	−.09
4	pm	bis	pm	—	−.11	−.08
5	pm	bis	pm	pm	—	−.06
6	bis	tet	bis	bis	bis	—

*   The variables are so defined that these positive correlations indicate that normals slept more, drank more and got higher scores than the operational fatigue cases

** Fatigue cases tended to report later in the day.

INTERCORRELATIONS: CONDITION B (N = 50)

	1	2	3	4	5	6
1	—	.45*	−.04	−.09	−.05	−.14
2	bis	—	−.19	−.09	.50*	−.20
3	pm	bis	—	.11	−.19	−.24
4	pm	bis	pm	—	−.24	.13
5	pm	bis	pm	pm	—	−.07
6	bis	tet	bis	bis	bis	—

*   The variables are so defined that these positive correlations indicate that normals were older and got higher scores.

The intercorrelation tables suggest that flicker fusion frequency is not significantly related to any of the variables studied except that of psychiatric diagnosis. A clearer picture of this situation may be afforded in the table (Table 12.4) of partial coefficients of correlation where whatever slight degree of relationship between these other variables and fusion frequency is shown to have slightly obscured rather than exaggerated the degree of correlation between fusion frequency and psychiatric diagnosis.

TABLE 12.4

CORRELATION BETWEEN FLICKER FUSION FREQUENCY AND PSYCHIATRIC DIAGNOSIS WITH COMBINATIONS OF CERTAIN VARIABLES HELD CONSTANT

Coeffs	Cond'n A	Cond'n B
$r_{12 \cdot 3}$	.68	.45
$r_{12 \cdot 4}$	.54	.45
$r_{14 \cdot 5}$	.62	.55
$r_{14 \cdot 6}$	.62	.43
$r_{12 \cdot 34}$	.60	.45
$r_{12 \cdot 35}$	.68	.55
$r_{12 \cdot 36}$	.73	.43

Coeffs	Cond'n A	Cond'n B
$r_{12 \cdot 45}$	.54	.56
$r_{12 \cdot 46}$	.54	.44
$r_{12 \cdot 56}$	.62	.54
$r_{12 \cdot 345}$	.60	.56
$r_{12 \cdot 346}$	.68	.43
$r_{12 \cdot 356}$	.73	.53
$r_{12 \cdot 456}$	.54	.55
$r_{12 \cdot 3456}$	.68	.55

CONCLUSIONS

Flicker fusion frequency is a rather easily measured, almost physiologic function, and its relationship with other types of abnormal-metabolic rate states is fairly well known. Should the results of this admittedly preliminary study be confirmed by further studies, the measure of flicker fusion frequency may provide a means of assisting in the better evolution of therapeutic results with patients exhibiting anxiety reaction.

Although overlap in the distributions of normal and anxiety reaction ("operational fatigue") cases prevents fusion frequency from being used for purposes of initial diagnosis or screening, the results obtained in this study suggest the possible usefulness of this index as an objective check on the progress of therapy. Because this study has demonstrated what appears to be a fairly close relationship between flicker score and psychiatric diagnosis of anxiety reaction, it may be expected that flicker fusion frequency would rise during the progress of successful treatment regardless of what an individual's flicker fusion frequency might have been when first referred.

The results of this preliminary study are sufficiently promising to indicate that a larger number of cases should be obtained. Experience in the preliminary study indicates that it might be well to take certain additional precautions in future studies. These are as follows:

1. Attempt to improve the flicker source. It was observed that the Strobo-tac light source, which is a neon tube, emitted certain slight irregular extraneous light fluctuations which confused some of those subjects who showed high thresholds for flicker fusion.

2. Standardize the rate at which the frequency of the source light oscillations are increased or decreased during fusion testing by substituting mechanical for human control of the frequency dial.

3. Attempt better to match the anxiety reaction cases and the control cases with respect to time of day tested.

SUMMARY

Flicker fusion frequency has previously been found to differentiate between normals and cases exhibiting various types of abnormal metabolic-rate states. This experiment attempted, in an exploratory way, to study the relationship between FFF and an anxiety reaction state found rather frequently among Army personnel shortly after their return from Air Forces combat assignments overseas.

Fifty such cases (termed "operational fatigue" in the AAF) and 50 normal aircrew returnees were selected for testing under standardized conditions. Statistically significant differences were found between the mean FFF scores of the two groups although the distribution of scores overlapped considerably.

Because of the relationship between FFF and anxiety reaction ("operational fatigue") demonstrated in this study, it would be expected that the FFF scores of such patients would rise during the progress of successful therapy. Further research would seem to be indicated.

---

[1] ENZER, N., SIMONSON, E., and BLANKSTEIN, S. S.: The State of Sensory and Motor Centers in Patients with Hypothyroidism. *Ann. Int. Med.*, 15:659, 1941.

[2] BROZEK, J., and KEYS, A.: Changes in Flicker Fusion Frequency with Age. *J. Consult. Psychol.*, 9:87, 1945.

[3] ENZER, N., SIMONSON, E., and BLANKSTEIN, S.S.: The Influence of Age on the Fusion Frequency of Flicker. *J. Exper. Psychol.*, 29:252, 1941.

[4] LEE, R. H.: Fatigue and Hours of Service of Interstate Truck Drivers. IV: Critical Fusion Frequency of Flicker. *Publ. Health Bull.*, 265:195, 1941.

[5] GRINKER, R.R., and SPIEGEL, J.P.: *Men Under Stress*, Philadelphia, Blakiston, 1945.

CHAPTER 13

PASSIVE LEARNING FROM TELEVISION
(with Eugene L. Hartley)

W hen we speak about the processes of learning we usually talk about motivation, practice, achievement, new skills or insights attained — we usually talk, that is, about learning as active and purposive behavior. We think of it as the province of school and classroom. We know that there are other, more passive kinds of learning, but we focus less on these, in part because they are presumed to be less effective, in part because they have been less noticeable — at least until the rise of the mass media, especially the electronic media.

Much of what is taught by the mass media does involve passive learning, and especially so among young television viewers. This type of learning presents a difficult evaluation problem since the passively learned material is almost by definition unrelated to immediate needs or situations. If it were, the learning would be more than passive.

Critics of television recognize that later events or situations may trigger what has been passively learned and lain dormant. They have therefore been concerned about the content, especially the violent content of television that may be shown to children. However, few have asked how the child learns such content at the time of exposure, or how this may be different in process or consequence from the more active classroom types of learning. It is almost as if the more passive types of learning are presumed to be invisible, and therefore incapable of study. Yet most learning at most ages is outside the classroom, and much of it is passive.

The purpose of this paper is to identify some of the differences between passive and active learning, and to suggest some implications for education and for television.

A major distinction between passive and active learning is physical and concerns constitutional, inborn characteristics of the human being. In the visible history of research on communication influence such characteristics have been ignored in a one-sided emphasis on verbal data and the measurement of comprehension, recall, attitudes, and the like. The favorite research tool has been the

Original Publication: *Public Opinion Quarterly*, Vol. 34, No. 2 (Summer 1966). Delivered at World Association for Public Opinion Research, Amsterdam, September 1966.

interview. In the midst of the easily gathered verbal data many have lost sight of man's animal, mechanical, and physical properties, which define the limits, constraints, and conditions within which those verbal data function.

Research on those physical properties related to communication influence has been less visible until recently for several reasons. (1) Most of the pioneers (*e.g.*, Wundt, Helmholtz, James) died before the development of radio and television. (2) Most of the medical people who are interested in man's physical properties are not interested in the question of passive vs. active learning (to a great extent the same is true of experimental psychology). Furthermore, the branch of medicine most relevant to the question is among the more recent. This involves certain aspects of the study of the brain, specifically electroencephalography, which began its modern history in 1933 with Berger's classical work on electrical emanations from the brain. (3) The relevant work done within the field of physiology achieved little cohesiveness in U. S. academic circles until translation and publication in the early sixties of the major Russian accomplishments (*e.g.*, Sokolov[1]).

This research has relevance to the mass media in direct proportion to its age. That is, the older nineteenth-century research has the most relevance because it contains scientific observations that have been repeatedly rediscovered, repeatedly reconfirmed, and prior to its current relevance, repeatedly forgotten.[2]

Many of these observations concern some physical qualities of the phenomenon of attention. These acquire special relevance when attention is treated as the core aspect of human experience. For example, William James has said: "My experience is what I agree to attend to."[3]

James defined two types of attention, voluntary and involuntary, and noted that voluntary attention cannot be continuous; *i.e.*, voluntary attention is a continual returning of attention to its object when it wanders away. He said, *"Voluntary attention is always derived;* we never make an *effort* to attend to an object except for the sake of some remote interest which the effort will serve. . . . *There is no such thing as voluntary attention sustained for more than a few seconds at a time.* What is called sustained voluntary attention is a repetition of successive efforts which bring back the topic to the mind. *No one can possibly attend continuously to an object that does not change."*[4]

James's distinction between voluntary and involuntary attention means that much of thinking, learning, and reading represents a sequence of successive efforts to attend, while much of the viewing of life around us, films, TV, and other *changing stimuli* are far less likely to require effort. In other words, the change, the switching or the rhythmic process goes on inside man when he is working at the job of attention, *or* it goes on outside man and inside (*e.g.*) the moving film as it relieves man of that work. The alternation process, furthermore, has an upper ceiling. Posner's review of the evidence suggests that "the rate at which a man can perform repetitive tasks is limited. Such diverse movements as tapping the finger, moving the eyes, or saying short words can be made no more often than about *ten times per second.* Moreover, the limitation appears to be of the central nervous system rather than of the muscles themselves."[5] Without this ten-per-second limitation, we would not experience the illusion of movement when we looked at a motion picture film.

A single TV commercial had much to do with one of the authors' present interest in attention and rates of stimulation. This was the Clairol Nice 'N' Easy commercial, which used a slow-motion technique borrowed from the film "The Pawnbroker," starring Rod Steiger. That film introduced tricks of flash scenes as well as slow motion, but the Nice 'N' Easy commercial used only the slow motion. The commercial had exceptionally high recall scores but aroused absolutely no pupil response. This seemed quite unusual. Was the commercial learned without any excitement whatsoever, or was there another element present, an unmeasured response? Is the opposite of excitement just nothing? Is calm a flat emptiness?

The opposite of excitement is apparently relaxation, and relaxation is much more than a mere absence of excitement. That is, relaxation has physical properties which are just as real as, though different from, those of excitement. Some may be taken aback by the idea of a commercial which relaxes. However, once television gets out of the kitchen plumbing and into nurseries, romance, and springtime freshness, there are quite a few varieties of commercial to soothe the viewer. This dimension has simply not been measured.

With such measures of arousal as pupil, skin, heart, or respiration, an absence of excitement brings the measure back to a minimal baseline. No further information is produced. With brain waves, however, a decline in arousal would be evidenced by a slowing of so-called Beta waves, rhythmic frequencies emitted in the 30-40 cycles per second range. As relaxation appeared there would also appear the relatively slow Alpha waves of about 10 per second. These or their harmonics would largely replace or dominate the Beta waves. Alpha waves are not simply slow Beta waves; they are a new parameter and offer the promise of measuring physical tones of peacefulness and well being which might otherwise be looked upon only as verbal artifacts. In general, brain waves cover the full range of human response activity from peak arousal to deepest sleep.

Some special qualities of Alpha rhythms which need mention here are the following. (1) Internal Alpha responses can be stimulated by appropriate external rhythms or frequencies. The appropriate frequencies may vary slightly from person to person as a function of the variation in their spontaneous Alpha rates. (2) Some individuals produce Alpha responses quite easily, while some don't seem to have them at all, or only under the most restricted set of conditions. Some of these individuals may be individuals who cannot really relax. (3) The amenability of individuals to the external stimulation of Alpha is common enough so that the term "Alpha drive" has become established in the EEG literature. It means that one can literally drive down the brain frequencies to the slow levels of Alpha. (4) Another common term in EEG literature is Alpha "block-ing," which refers to the disappearance of Alpha in resting individuals when they open their eyes and look upon some scene or stimulus which elicits atten-tion or when they engage in "mental work." For some time, it was assumed that Alpha blocking occurred in response to all visual stimulation, but work by Morrell and by Walter indicates that there are many exceptions.[6] Again, it seems that some people block or unblock more easily than others. (5) Alpha, once driven, can be maintained even in the face of conditions that ordinarily block it.[7]

These qualities of Alpha rhythm suggest that there are innate constitutional differences in individual susceptibility to different types of communication in-fluence, in the efficiency of different types of study habits based on different degrees of required attention, even in response to drugs. Dr. Barbara Brown, for example, studied the EEG patterns and reported perceptions of 64 volunteers who were given doses of LSD.[8] It became clear that some respondents were constitutionally predisposed to experience more exaggerated perceptual distor-tions in their "trips" than others, while some respondents had predictably modest reactions. The excitement/ relaxation characteristics of particular individuals may prove to be chiefly constitutional characteristics, predominant over social and environmental influences.

The most special quality of passive learning is, by definition, an absence of aroused resistance to what is learned; resistance is exciting and a corollary, therefore, of active learning. This means that passively learned material has an important "advantage" which some have also associated with so-called sublimi-nal perception, extrasensory perception, or hypnotism. This advantage, how-ever, is not a property of the stimulus, but of the respondent; *i.e.*, he can learn passively so long as the material is acceptable to him, without conflict.

It is possible that the relaxed and successful character of passive learning can be enhanced by the artificial induction of Alpha rhythm, this with the aid of a flickering light. For example, if a person wants to give up smoking and wel-comes suggestion on this problem, then he may respond more successfully if the suggestion is made during an Alpha-induced condition. E.L. Hartley and Dr. Mali Thaineua, of the Ministry of Health of Thailand, have conducted a number of such experiments while both were at the East-West Center in Hawaii. The time may come when the mass media may create special programs to help peo-ple modify certain attitudes or behavior. We are all familiar with physical exer-cise programs on TV. Some day we may have TV exercises to cut down on (*e.g.*) smoking.

The distinction between passive and active learning involves a distinction between relaxation and excitement, two different aspects of what is usually called "interest." Too much of what we know about experience has been defined in terms of what excites, and little is known about what relaxes. This imbalance has been a function of the fact, now in need of redress, that excitement is (too) easily measured. In making this redress some particular opportunities may be listed:

1. For medicine there may be an opportunity to go beyond the routine procedures for EEG diagnosis of patients — *i.e.*, with the patient supine, resting and eyes closed. The patient may also be measured while performing some standard tasks with eyes open. Many psychologists and neurologists are curious about "normal" EEG reports of patients who are otherwise clearly known to be not normal. Perhaps such patients are EEG "normal" while near sleep, but not while trying to cope actively with tasks.

2. For early education there may be an opportunity to accept the fact that many children fidget in class, and that this interference with their attention is not to be blamed on parents, teachers, or the child. Mild drugging of these children, or training in relaxation through Alpha driving, may be dramatically helpful to their educational achievement.

3. For adult education television there may be an opportunity to design programs to help people stop smoking, to lose weight, to control drinking habits, etc.

4. For public television there may be an opportunity to accept without shame the fact that it has taught violence to an entire generation. The clear story of television violence is not that a new generation is more violent but that the new generation knows more violence. The political consequences of this may yet be what some would call "good" (*e.g.*, pacifist).

5. For students of attitude change and of the influence of the mass media, there is an opportunity to accept the fact that knowledge and information are more important than attitudes. The mass media have taught our society what it needs to know in order to have attitudes on a thousand serious matters which before television would elicit only "don't knows." This attention to serious matters is made possible in part because, as McLuhan has noted, television is a cool medium, one which people can attend calmly. The thesis of this paper is that for many people the attention to and learning about serious matters on television could only have been successful if done calmly, without excitement and without effort.

The next step in research on these matters is to record the brain waves of individual respondents performing simple everyday tasks, including the viewing of various television programs. By comparing immediate physiological response with later measures of what has been learned, we may begin to answer questions about just how much attention (arousal, interest) is required to learn what.

---

[1] E.N. Sokolov, *Perception and the Conditioned Reflex,* Moscow, Moscow U. Press, 1958. Translation by Pergamon Press, New York, 1962

[2] For example, in his final chapter Donald Broadbent (*Perception and Communication,* New York, Pergamon Press, 1958) reveals his debt to William James (referring to ch. 11,

Vol. 1 of James's *Principles of Psychology,* New York, Dover Publications, 1890). Turning to the work cited, we find James acknowledging his debt to Helmholtz and others. All report and confirm many of the same observations.

[3] Quoted in P.L. Wachtel "Conceptions of Broad and Narrow Attention," *Psychological Bulletin,* vol. 68 (1967), p. 427.

[4] W. James, *Principles of Psychology,* vol. 1 (New York: Dover Publications, 1890), ch. 11, pp. 416, 421

[5] M.I. Posner "Components of Skilled Performance," *Science,* vol. 152 (June 24, 1966), p. 1713. Italics supplied.

[6] L.K. Morrell, "Some Characteristics of Stimulus-Provoked Alpha Activity," *Electroencephalography and Clinical Neurophysiology,* vol. 21 (1966), pp. 552-561, and G. Walter, "Patterns in Your Head," *Discovery,* (February 1952), pp. 56-62.

[7] To some extent Alpha states may also be self-induced. Dr. Sato, editor of the *Japanese Journal of Psychology* at Kyoto University, reports in a personal communication that the Alpha rhythms of meditating Buddhist monks are restored after interruptions, but that the restoration takes much longer among novices than among experienced monks.

[8] B.B. Brown, "Subjective and EEG Response to LSD in Visualizer and Nonvisualizer Subjects," *Electroencephalography and Clinical Neurophysiology,* vol., 25 (1968), pp. 372-379.

CHAPTER 14

MASS MEDIA AND MENTAL MATURITY

W hen we speak about the processes of learning we usually talk about motivation, practice, achievement, new skills or insights attained, *i.e.*, we usually talk about learning as active and purposive behavior. We usually think of it as the province of school and classroom. We know that there are other, more passive kinds of learning but we focus less on these, in part because they are presumed to be less effective, in part because they have been less noticeable — at least until the rise of the mass media, especially the electronic media.

Much of what is taught by the mass media does involve passive learning, and especially so among the young television viewer. This type of learning presents a difficult evaluation problem since the passively learned material is almost by definition unrelated to immediate needs or situations. If it were, the learning would be more than passive.

Critics of television recognize that later events or situations may 'trigger what has been passively learned and lain dormant. They have therefore been concerned about the content, especially the violent content of television that may be shown to children. However, few have asked *how* the viewer learns such content at the time of exposure, or how this may be different in process or consequence from the more active classroom types of learning. It is almost as if the more passive types of learning are presumed to be invisible, and therefore incapable of study. Yet most learning at most ages is outside the classroom, and much of it passive. What seemed to be needed was a direct experimental approach to the nature of the response to media: What is happening during the moments of exposure?

LABORATORY STUDIES

The author's first attempt, in 1965 (Chapter 6 above), to study experiences during exposure suggested that television was a medium of "low involvement" as compared with print. Involvement was defined in terms of the number of personal connections between the stimulus and the viewer, *i.e.*, the number of *thoughts which came spontaneously to mind* during exposure and which linked

Undated Manuscript, ca. August 1970.

something in the content of the stimulus to something in the content of the viewer's own life. In 1967 Time Magazine sponsored and *Public Opinion Quarterly* published a small study in which the author reported that the same kinds of advertising in TV and print evoked in the TV form many fewer personal connections between the ad content and something in the life content of the viewer (Chapter 7 above). More recently, in a very much larger study, the Bureau of Advertising of the American Newspaper Publishers Association confirmed that TV versions of similar print ads evoked fewer personal connections.[1]

Television is popular, interesting and time consuming, and it is not meant as criticism to say that few thoughts occur during exposure. It is, however, very different from print. To learn more about these differences, an interest developed in conducting laboratory experiments on the processes of looking and of thinking, and also on the processes of attention and of relaxation.

In the laboratory, looking was defined in terms of the capabilities and limitations of the Mackworth stand mounted eye movement recorder in which the respondent's head is rendered immobile with the aid of a biteplate and a 6 x 8 inch picture is viewed at a distance of 18 inches.[2] Eye movements are recorded to produce a developed motion picture film of the viewed scene and a superimposed white spot or marker indicates the path of eye movements. Ten-second exposures are recorded, and from the developed film a plot is made of location of eye fixations, duration or dwell time, and shifts to new fixations. The type of equipment is described and photographed in the August 1968 cover story of *Scientific American* Magazine.

In and of itself, looking was of little concern in the particular research described since it started with the premise that the respondents were looking at the experimental ads. The concern was with how they were looking when communication or learning *was* taking place as compared with how they were looking when communication was *not* taking place, *i.e.*, what were the response qualities of looking-with-learning?

Of parallel concern were the stimuli themselves. How were easily learned ads looked at as compared with ads which were difficult to learn, *i.e.*, what were the stimulus qualities of looking-with-learning?

The respondents in such studies were brought to a laboratory, exposed to different ads for ten seconds each via the Mackworth Optiscan, and then interviewed for recall of the ads. Recall, therefore, was the criterion of learning. Additional respondents were brought back once a week for three weeks, without verbal interviewing, just to note the effects of repeated exposures on looking.

Of various scoring methods, the one of most interest concerned looking in only one place vs. looking all over, or "bunched up" vs. "spread out" looking. This was finally called focusing and scanning and was scored by dividing the total area of each advertisement into 1" x 1" cells and counting the number of different cells which were "looked into."

Initial findings presented an interesting paradox. On a respondent basis, scanning represents looking-with-learning, *i.e.*, the respondents who scanned more recalled more. However, on a stimulus basis, focusing represents looking-with-learning, *i.e.*, the ads which were scanned less were better recalled.

The resolution of the paradox is apparently this: ads which are easily learned require very little of the respondent; they communicate with little work on his part. But ads which do not learn easily do require the respondent to be more active, to look around, to scan.

So we have here a situation where at one extreme the work of communication must be done by the communicator via creation of an easily learnable ad or communiqué, or on the other hand where the work of communication may be done by the respondent or communicant via an ability to learn difficult communiqués.

At this point we had to ask, "How is it done?" For example, we began to suspect that scanning, as an active learning process, had something to do with the possibility of personal connections taking place between the stimulus and the viewer, but how? It also appeared that focusing permitted much learning without any effort at all, and again we had to say, "How?"

The work of William James suggested an answer. This turn-of-the-century Harvard psychologist had been the primary American exponent of the study of conscious experience, and as a student of the process of attention is still acknowledged as master by contemporary scholars of that subject.

James defined two types of attention, voluntary and involuntary, and noted that voluntary attention cannot be continuous, *i.e.*, voluntary attention is a continual returning of the attention to its object when it wanders away. He said, *"Voluntary attention is always derived*; we never make an effort to attend to an object except for the sake of some *remote* interest which the effort will serve. (p. 416) and *"There is no such thing as voluntary attention sustained for more than a few seconds at a time.* What is called sustained voluntary attention is a repetition of successive efforts which bring back the topic to the mind. No one can possibly attend continuously to an object that does not change."[3]

James' distinction between voluntary and involuntary attention means that much of thinking, learning, and reading represents a sequence of successive efforts to attend, while much of the viewing of life around us, films, TV and other *changing stimuli* are far less likely to require effort. In other words, the change, the switching or the rhythmic process goes on inside man when he is working at the job of attention, *or* it goes on outside man and inside (*e.g.*) the moving film as it relieves man of that work.

Now in these terms we may re-appreciate scanning as an interrupted series of discrete events. They permit the intrusion of a stimulus inside the head of the viewer in the form of a thought, and particularly in this case in the form of a thought connected to the stimulus. Thus, thinking, when taking place vis-à-vis a media stimulus requires that the respondent attend both to internal and external stimuli. It sometimes means that some of the external stimuli may be missed. It sometimes means that pressure to keep up will be felt, that is, to do two jobs of attention — one to the stimulus on the page or screen and one to the reaction inside the head. It is susceptible to motivation and effort, and may fairly at times be called mental *work*. One literally must "stop to think."[4] One must also *blind* oneself, to a degree, from external distraction.[5]

This matter of dual attention seemed to answer the "how" of scanning in such away that one could understand its relation to involvement or to thinking, but what about focusing where attention was easy, and uninterrupted, and some-how still seemed to communicate? What is there about the changing stimulus in film or TV that can relieve man of the work of learning? Is learning the right word to use, even qualified as passive learning?

We thought that the entertaining quality of film and TV might have some-thing to do with relaxation. Was relaxation not the opposite of work, and is it not associated with suggestibility? But how to measure relaxation?

With such measures of physiological arousal as changes in pupil size, skin temperature, heart or respiration rates, an absence of excitement brings the measure back to a minimal baseline. No further information is provided. With brain waves, however, a decline in arousal would be evidenced by a lessening of so-called Beta waves, rhythmic frequencies emitted in the 20–40 cycles per sec-ond range. As relaxation appeared there would also appear the relatively slow Alpha waves of about 8–12 per second, and as drowsiness appeared there would also appear the slower Delta waves of 4–7 per second. In general, brain waves cover the full range of human response activity from peak arousal to deepest sleep. So we decided to measure brain waves produced in response to television commercials.

The Neuropsychological Laboratory of New York Medical College serves the Flower and Fifth Avenue hospitals and also, when time is available, outside research clients. The paid subject in our experiment was a 22-year-old secretary who worked in the building. A high school graduate with a black-and-white television set at home, she had not served as a subject before. It is perhaps un-usual to report on one subject. However, our purpose was initially only to an-swer the question of whether there can be a clearly identifiable mode or pattern for the viewing of television. There was, and its clarity was rather impressive.

About half an hour after her lunch the subject was seated in a test room or cubicle, actually a light and sound controlled environment which could be viewed remotely via a television monitoring system. The cubicle had drapes, a comfortable couch, magazines on a cocktail table, and a simulated TV set in the corner at a viewing distance of seven feet from the subject. When the subject entered the cubicle, a single tiny electrode was fixed to the occipital region in the back of the head with the aid of a tiny quantity of jelly. It was referenced to both ears. A very fine wire lead ran from this to the wall where it apparently disappeared. It had no discernible weight and was not visible to the seated subject. The lead then went outside to a Grass Model 7 Polygraph, connected in turn to a Honeywell 7600 computer and a CAT 400B.

The subject was told: "We have fixed up this room a little bit like a living room at home. This is supposed to be a TV set. Just relax for a while. Look at one of the magazines here or read for a few minutes until some commercials come on the screen. Then watch the commercials. Don't be surprised if the commercials are repeated a few times. There will be three commercials shown. The commercials will be shown several times. The same ones will be repeated. When the commercials go off the screen, go back to the magazine and read or look a little longer."

The simulated TV set was a Fairchild 400 rear projector with an 8 x 11 inch screen. A tape cartridge held three different color commercials to be run in sequence three times for a total of nine viewings. We expected quite different initial reactions and a change in each with repetition.

In this situation analysis of the EEG data was first made on the total reaction to each of the nine viewings, or specifically to 56 seconds of each to eliminate transition responses. The type of analysis summed up the "spectrum" as it is called of all identifiable brain wave frequencies emitted during the 56-second "epoch" as *it* is called. In simple terms, one obtains a measure of how many seconds worth of each wave frequency appears during the 56 seconds.

Our computer program reported eleven "bands" or frequency-class intervals from 1.5 cycles per second up to 32 cps. The first four bands, up to 7.5 cps, are usually called Delta waves and are associated with drowsiness and sleep. We combined the four and called them slow waves. The next four bands from 7.6 to 12.33 cps are usually called Alpha waves and are associated with relaxation. We combined them and called them Alpha. The last two bands, from 12.3 to 31.8 cps, are usually called Beta waves and are associated with alertness, activity and arousal. We combined them and called them fast waves. We had more bands or categories programmed at the lower end of the scale because we were dealing with a seated, quiet subject.

The subject arrived, was seated and received her instructions. For about fifteen minutes she browsed through magazines while her EEG responses plus impressions from the TV monitor indicated a comfortable and relaxed adjustment to the surroundings. Just before the commercials came on, a full record was made of the EEG spectrum for the last 56 seconds of magazine reading. This involved a Max Factor advertisement which discussed different techniques for applying makeup. The subject reported later that she was very interested in this advertisement, and was a bit annoyed when the TV commercials came on. She also reported that she liked one commercial, disliked another, and was bored with all by the third exposure.

The print ad produced 5 seconds of slow waves, 16 of Alpha and 28 of fast waves all adding up to a picture of relaxed attention, interest and mental activity. As the first commercial came on, the subject looked up and an entirely new pattern or mix appeared, adding up to 21 seconds of slow, 18 of Alpha and 15 of fast. We say "pattern" because closer inspection and analysis showed that the wave patterns throughout were at any one moment mixtures of the overlapping wave actions. It was not some seconds of one frequency followed by some seconds of another but an overall state, mode or style of reception with elements of different wave types. Thus, the 21 slow, 18 Alpha and 15 fast in response to the first commercial roughly represented constant proportions of waves active in any one period within the 56 seconds. The 21-18-15 for the first commercial may be described as a relaxed condition with elements of both drowsiness and alertness.

We were surprised that the Alpha or relaxed element did not change significantly from print to TV but we took it as a sign of general relaxation in the situation. We had expected that the TV might be more relaxing, but not that it would instantly produce elements of drowsiness and a characteristic mode of response. Rather we expected that drowsiness or boredom might develop over time with the three repetitions.

The initial spectrum for the first commercial did not change significantly for the next two commercials. Apparently it was a characteristic mode of response. The 21-18-15 became 24-15-14 for the second commercial and 24-16-13 for the third.

The question arises as to how immediate was this characteristic mode of response. Did it appear in the first seconds of the first commercial or what? To answer this we analyzed spectra for three ten-second periods within the first exposure to the first commercial. Within seconds 2 to 12 we had two seconds of slow, four of Alpha and four of fast waves. Within seconds 25 to 35 we had four seconds of slow, three of Alpha and three of fast waves, and within seconds 46 to 56 we had five seconds of slow, three of Alpha and three of fast waves. In other words it was about half way through the first exposure to the first commercial before the slow waves predominated over the fast waves. We can say then that the characteristic mode of response took about thirty seconds to fully develop. Looking at just the first ten-second period, however, we can also say that slow waves were already half as common as the fast waves — as compared to the prior print viewing where the slow waves were only one-fifth to one-sixth of the fast waves. Thus the adaptation, quite reasonably, began immediately upon viewing the television stimulus.

What about repetition? Apparently it played a minor role. The second round of viewings went 22-20-13, 24-16-14 and 28-15-12. The third round went 24-16-13, 25-16-12 and 26-16-12. The slow waves gradually increased generally from 23 to 25 while the fast waves decreased from 14 to 12. More elements of drowsiness, less of mental activity — a fair indication of boredom. More noteworthy was the similarity of response to all three commercials, increasingly so with repetition. A most striking chart to see is the plot of all eleven bands of frequencies to each of the three commercials on third exposure. They comprise almost a single line rather than three lines. The differences between response to the three commercials on third exposure is less than the difference between any one commercial on the first exposure and that same commercial on second exposure. In short, the commercials evoked very little difference on first trial and none by the third.

The question arises as to the remaining sensitivity to the third exposure of the third commercial, by this time quite boring. Was there any increase in response during its viewing or was boredom constant throughout? To answer this we also analyzed spectra for three ten-second periods within the third exposure to the third commercial. Within seconds 2 to 12 we had six seconds of slow, two of Alpha and two of fast waves. Within seconds 25 to 35 we had four seconds of slow, three of Alpha and two of fast waves, and within seconds 46 to 56 we had four seconds of slow, three of Alpha, and two of fast waves. In other words, even on this last dull viewing the subject's initial preponderance of slow waves diminished a little as the commercial proceeded to the halfway point. Thus, it appears that there may be a little life left even in what appears to be a satiated condition. However, this is a very little life indeed.

It appears in this case then that the mode of response to television is more or less constant, and very different from the response to print. That is, the basic electrical response of the brain is clearly to the media and not to content differences within the TV commercials, or to what we in our pre-McLuhan days would ordinarily have called the commercial message.

It seems also clear, as suggested by the earlier studies of involvement or of eye movement, that the response to print may be fairly described as active, and composed primarily of fast brain waves while the response to television might be fairly described as passive and composed primarily of slow brain waves.[6]

MEDIA AND EVERYDAY THINKING

Laboratory research combined with ordinary observation seems to suggest two quite different types of everyday experience vis-à-vis the television and print media. Television seems to require only enough interest to maintain attention, and little effort is required to do so. Distraction, therefore, is no great problem, as the viewer can shift back and forth to other stimuli without concern. The media content arouses few thoughts and is easily forgotten, though easily recognized on second exposure. Response is not greatly affected by what came before or what will come next. The viewer is unaware of any particular impact of the material and cannot provide informed evaluations of that impact. Repetition of exposure to the material breeds familiarity up to the point where the stimulus becomes an accepted detail of life itself. No other effects occur . . . until a later and related action, choice, or decision situation triggers the accumulated learnings inherent in the exposure.

In contrast to television, print can quickly arouse a great deal of personally related thought. Attention is tense, distraction is not easily tolerable, and a variety of thoughts and feelings may be evoked. The viewer is conscious of the nature of his or her related conflicts resistances, evaluation, approval or disapproval, etc., and can report on some of these. The viewer may form new judgments, opinions and resolutions to take various actions. Some of this may take place after exposure, or in between exposures. However, a complete spectrum of information stimulus to action response may be represented in a single exposure. When this is so or when an action resolution does take place, another exposure to the same stimulus has little meaning since cloture has been achieved. To "do" more to the viewer, or to bring about further effects would require a change in the stimulus material.

It will be apparent that the nature of the learnings inherent in response to print is recognizable and familiar to us all. There is really no great problem then in evaluating their quite visible effects. They permit the mass media a modest power to offer new information to the viewer, but equally they permit the viewer a modest power to consciously evaluate, judge, resist or reject what is offered. The power to persuade or to change is thus limited, as it requires the intellectual participation of the viewer.

Now, let us return to the television viewing, where the more difficult problem lies and where the nature of effects has been less clear. Indeed, a measured absence of effects has sometimes been reported, but based, quite without relevance, on before-and-after measures of the effects of single exposures. The nature of the learnings inherent in intellectually uninvolving but frequently repeated stimulus material may be described in terms of processes far more elemental than "opinion" or "attitudes." These processes concern what is seen or perceived, *i.e.*, the information input itself more so than the value or interpretation placed upon it.

Repetition of the low involvement stimulus gradually builds a *potential* to see the object in a new way. This goes on without awareness and while the old ways are still entirely in force. One day the viewer may confront the object in a behavioral or action situation requiring an overt behavioral response. This requirement can eventually *trigger* the replacement of the old way of viewing the object with the new way. It is only at this point that the consequence of the many stimulus exposures is visible. Because this point may be far removed in space and time from the media exposure itself, the relationship may not be easily appreciated.

The differences between old and new ways may not be differences in basic content but only of emphasis or salience. For example, an object or person seen primarily as "reliable" may come to be seen primarily as "modern." The object is still seen as reliable and perhaps no *less* reliable than before, but this quality no longer provides the primary perceptual emphasis. Similarly, the object was previously seen as modern, and perhaps no *more* modern now — yet exposure to repeated messages may give modernity the primary role in the organization of what is seen.

Can such slight shifts in emphasis be important on important matters? When Hartley first introduced the concept of psychological salience, he illustrated it with a suggestion that Hitler did not so much increase anti-Semitic attitudes in Germany as bring already existing anti-Semitic attitudes into more prominent use for defining or reacting to particular daily events and situations.[7]

Shifts in emphasis may not bring new attitudes into place, but along with an action trigger they can suddenly reassemble the already existing and available perceptions and related attitudes. Then a real change takes place in behavioral response. Sometimes these behavior changes are quite surprising, both to the self and to the observer. They literally didn't know that he "had it in him."

To be surprised by a new response or act, in ourselves or close associates, is not unusual. What is unusual is an insistence by some students that all behavior changes must be preceded by attitude changes. Implicit in this error is an assumption that there is an attitude toward the topic or object at hand, and that *it* is the one that must change.

We may doubt that any individual has *an* attitude toward any single object or person, but instead a network of variously related attitudes and perceptions. Thus, toward a strange child one notes that it may be male, of a certain age, income class, race, deportment, etc., and each of these attributes can evoke a specific attitude or set of attitudes, *i.e.*, towards children, towards boys, towards the poor, the polite, etc. What will one finally do? How will one treat the strange child? Which of the many perceptions and related attitudes will be predominant?

It is likely that new behaviors or ways of response within a society may precede what opinion polls may be able to detect. Individuals may have to surprise themselves several times over before they have learned *that* they are behaving differently. Once this is realized the pressures of consistency may then bring about a parallel change in conscious verbal expressions.

It is suggested that it is these quiet gradual kinds of learning and change that are most characteristic of the underrated impact of mass media. These are changes that take time to produce, time to build potential, time for opportunities to trigger that potential, time for repeated acts to bring conscious awareness and a new verbal generalization.

So the media, and especially television, may bring more variety and differentiation into society but in some ways that are not strictly speaking intellectual, and which even challenge our use of the term "communication." Indeed, the field of *communication theory* is wedded to a view of someone preparing a message, the message carried across a distance (hopefully fast), and a receiver reading or decoding the message at the other end. It is a transportation type of theory with a communicator, a communiqué, and a communicant.

Mass communication theory has much to say about communicators, and influences on them and their media. It is also much concerned with patterns of diffusion of ideas, and it is very concerned with the selectivity and depth of audience responses. Somehow McLuhan seems to say that this has all been made irrelevant by the technological fact of television.

Television is not mass communication in our sense, says McLuhan. Nobody out there is trying to decode or receive any messages. Instead their eyes and ears have been "extended" into the situation portrayed on the screen. They are participating in an experience — even if it is passive participation. And unlike films, a significant portion of television is "live" or as they say in the computer field "in real time."

In terms of conventional mass communication theory one would ordinarily say that television is better or richer than radio because an extra dimension, that of video, was *added*, or richer than newspapers because the audio was added. This is a right conclusion from a wrong premise. Radio and newspapers as communication are deficient in that they must omit much information. Similarly television as experience is deficient in that reality is presented minus the feelings. This is McLuhan's "cool" medium, in consequence said to be breeding a generation yearning for feelings and meanings behind the superficial happenings and encounters in life around them.

Our EEG data confirms McLuhan in the sense that television is not communication as it has been known. Our subject was trying to learn something from a print ad, but was passive about television. If something happened to communicate, that's fine; if it didn't, it went by and was gone and no process of scanning or dual attention would worry over its shortcomings. The subject was no more trying to learn something from television than she would be trying to learn something from a park landscape while resting on a park bench. Yet television *is* communication. What *shall* we say of it, a communication medium that effortlessly transmits huge quantities of information *not thought about at the time of exposure*, but much of it capable of being stored for later activation?

The TV viewer is well equipped to *recognize* many things in life seen beforehand on television. So equipped he startles into an "Ah ha, I've seen you or this before." This startle is the beginning of an active response, but since this has not been thought out in advance of the time of exposure it comes out relatively unformed and shapeless. This is the awkward spontaneity of the younger generation, the tendency to act or react in a variety of new but faintly recognized situations where purpose or intent has not yet crystallized. It may look immature or enthusiastic to many observers, but it emanates from the ability to recognize as familiar a wide variety of things in life.

The print viewer, meanwhile, has paused and thought about what he has seen in print, has formed an opinion or mentally rehearsed a plan. When he recognizes something similar in real life he is ready with a relatively formed or "mature" response. However, print has allowed him to store relatively less information and so there is much that he does not recognize and to which he reacts not at all. So print man seems very selective, and reacts well or not at all. It looks very mature.

In short, television man, the passive media audience, is an active but clumsy participant in life, while print man, the active media audience, is a selective, less active and more mature participant in life. What, however, is the specific future for print media, and in general for the intellectual maturity of society?

A DIVISION OF LABOR FOR THE MEDIA

Compared with television, magazines have received little serious attention in the years gone by. There have been, for example, many weighty research reports on "The Social Impact of Television" and, prior to that, a still larger number on the role of broadcast radio in a changing world. Motion pictures have been the subject of innumerable investigations. But there is almost nothing on the significance of magazines and their special place in our society. Perhaps it is because they never appeared to be the dominant media, or merely because the printed word in any form — newspapers, books, or magazines — was old and familiar. It is almost as though we expect magic or some kind of super-impact from such 20th Century technical wonders as radio, TV and films but nothing other than comfortable security and loyalty from the old standbys of the printed word.

Some of the hue and cry about what mass media are doing to popular taste reflects this split. That is, radio, motion pictures, and television are attacked as villains, while newspapers and magazines come off more lightly. This is partly an accident of history since the printed word flourished long before the worst evils of the industrial revolution and, in fact, has had thousands of years to build — with the help of the Bible, at least — a long history of trust and respect.

Certainly the mass media differ greatly from each other in what they primarily offer to their audiences. At one extreme we have motion pictures and the world of sheer fantasy and escape. Of course, there are documentaries, news films, and educational films, but the primary content is sheer, escapist fantasy — and very pleasant it is. At the other extreme we have newspapers reporting the harsh reality of day-to-day life. Newspapers too may present fantasy and escape in the form of comics and special columns (even Sunday supplements and magazines) but the primary content is the anxious reality of the world's existence.

In between those two poles of timeless escape and immediate reality, we have two other primary contents. One involves entertainment, not so extreme as to induce complete lack of self -awareness but a more participative kind involving dancing, sports, comedy, and so forth. This is the province of radio and television. Finally then, we come to magazines, and here it seems that the primary content is what could be called *thoughtful guidance.*

This guidance is not escapist but appeals directly to the real situation and identity of the audience — there are magazines for men, for women, for teenagers, for mothers, for hobbyists, etc. Neither is this guidance a matter of harsh day-to-day reality. Magazines are withdrawn and detached from the daily deadline and crisis. They have the time to abstract and synthesize ideas — to take the time to present them with utmost care. Most magazines are of interest even if a year or two old. They are read and re-read, passed around among friends, and traded. They carry with them an intimate sense of ownership. There is "my copy" and "your copy," etc.

The guidance offered by magazines is of many types and as they are listed below you will no doubt think of radio, film, and television programs that have performed a similar function. However, such guidance from those media comes in passing, without much thought in the case of television, and as a secondary benefit of other major qualities. For magazines, these *are* the major qualities.

1. Magazines offer helpful guidance in that they re-affirm the sex roles, *i.e.*, some magazines are very obviously for women, some very obviously for men. These, in effect, create private audiences where intimate and personal problems may be raised and (especially in the more serious women's magazines) frankly discussed. If the problems are common to the sexes they have the added virtue of being discussed in a completely and unashamedly *partisan* manner, *e.g.*, with women reading the woman's viewpoint, on say fidelity in marriage, and men reading the man's viewpoint. While it may be said that the TV and films portray many of the battles between the sexes, it is the magazines that act as managers and seconds in between the rounds.

2. Magazines offer helpful guidance in that they assist us in coming to terms with the world. That is, people have only begun to think about world-wide events on a daily basis in recent years . . . as a result of World War II, the end of isolation, the atom bomb, fall out, Summit meetings, Vietnam, and because of television.

Now to walk around in the street with a "World View" is a serious matter. One can get so upset by the need to DO SOMETHING about this or that issue or one can get equally upset by impotent feelings of not being able to DO ANYTHING. And one cannot shut out the newspapers and news programs.

What the magazines give us, on a comfortable once-a-week basis, carefully analyzed, interpreted and digested, is an understanding of the world given in such a way that we come to feel the duty, even the virtue, of being *well-informed*. This feeling of being well-informed is a substitute, and a poor one admittedly, for positive action . . . but in consolation, and by way of contrast, let it also be noted that it is also a substitute for fear and panic.

3. Magazines provide helpful guidance in that they provide the reader with controlled shopping wherever and whenever he or she wants it. Compare the interest in, or at worst neutrality shown toward, magazine ads with the "issue" of commercials on radio and TV. The latter audience is in the position of listening to a salesman, and at times when the salesman is not always welcome. With magazines, however, the reader is in a position similar to that of browsing

through a self-service department store at the pace and in the direction he or she chooses — and this is "fun."

The really important thing about controlled shopping via the magazine is that it permits the reader to leisurely distinguish between his or her unrealistic desires for products and those that really and rationally belong in his or her home and budget. It is the antithesis of impulsive buying. It represents an opportunity for rational consideration and planning.

It represents the home study rehearsal and pre-planning that permits the reader to go out to Main Street and steer a steadier course than otherwise past the glittering displays, the eager salesmen, the special sales and other gimmicks to what he or she has carefully decided is really needed. It gives the reader a shopping strategy, so to speak, while shopping tactics are left up to the day-to-day opportunities and influences.

4. Finally, magazines offer helpful guidance on life goals, on what we think we should be getting out of life on this earth. This may sound rather strange, for would not all of us admit that what we want is happiness? Yet happiness has not always been the universally accepted goal of mankind that it is today — and if you look back over the popular heroes of the past 1000 years, you will see what is meant. For example, in the Middle Ages it was the spiritual man who was most looked up to as a model for everyday living. During the Renaissance it was the intellectual man. Toward the end of the 19th Century through the 1920's it was the successful businessman — the captain of industry who pursued a life of hard work and thrift in pursuit of economic success. For the totalitarian countries in the 30's and 40's it was the heroic or masterful man. Who are the new heroes and what are the qualities we should admire?

The popular heroes are figures from the sports and entertainment world — people who are disgustingly healthy and handsome, who appear to be having a lot of fun, or who are in ecstasy over their spectacular success. Their personal lives, their families, their hobbies, their *wholesomeness*, their essential normality (despite the talent which is a secondary matter) is splashed across page after page.

This normality seems to be the key to what we are after when we talk about happiness. It seems that for this period in our history, and thanks to the work primarily of Sigmund Freud — the man we most look up to as a model is the *psychiatrically healthy man.* Most people probably wouldn't accept the idea when put in those terms, but if in terms of happiness, etc., yes — that's what they want. Even the hippies, not quite so wholesome in our eyes, also seek happiness. They express it in the one word "Love." It's also true, however, that the hippies are challenging the concept that normal *equals* happiness. They say creative *equals* happiness.

It is up to the magazines to define when teenage high spirits are within the limits of safety and when they go beyond the limits (delinquency, drinking, drugs, etc.). It is up to the magazines to show what is fun, what is silly, what is dangerous, or what is square, half square, hip and way out. Now on the other side of our popular heroes, let it be noted that some magazines shout that many of the popular heroes are anything but wholesome and normal. And again, it is their abnormality — completely divorced from any interest in their talent that is the focus of attention and interest. In this sense, the hippies also provide an anti-hero. The focus for all magazines, though, is not primarily on the talent but on the normality or abnormality of the hero.

Interestingly, it was one section of the American magazine industry that was virtually wiped out by its failure to declare itself on the question of normality and wholesomeness. This was the comic book industry, which has been diminished two-thirds since a censorship was forced on it by a group of psychiatrically oriented citizens, these citizens pressing vigorously forward the views of a number of professional psychiatrists. In short, by word and picture, by illustration and analogy, by model and outright advice, the magazine is in the position of trying to hold up an image of what is the good life. And reception of all of this personal guidance requires attention and *thought*. By way of contrast, a recent international conference on television news coverage concluded, "One function of research might be to better understand the television viewers' lack of comprehension of the news. Numerous studies have indicated that even among viewers who watch diligently the comprehension level is very low."[8]

Television has acquainted the general public with the world at large. It has taught our society what it needs to know in order to have *some* kinds of attitudes on a thousand serious matters which before television would elicit only "don't knows". This attention to serious matters is made possible in part because as McLuhan has noted, television is a cool medium, one which people can attend calmly or as we would say on the basis of EEG results "passively". A thesis of this paper is that for many people the attention to and, at least, superficial learning about serious matters on television could *only* have been successful if done calmly, without excitement and without effort. That is, without the kind of thinking that can properly be called mental work. Television may be society's kindergarten or elementary school, while magazines represent its high school, and books perhaps, still, its university. In fact, television viewing is highest in the pre-school years and declines thereafter, while regular newspaper and magazine reading begins only in adolescence but grows and then continues as a life long habit.[9] The younger generation in America, though raised on television, largely rejects it as they enter the college years.

It is no criticism to describe television as society's kindergarten or elementary school. It is a prerequisite for admission to a higher education, *i.e.*, to the realm of hard thinking. Thus, television opens certain maturing influences to all, and print then, as always, finishes the job.

---

[1] Bureau of Advertising, American Newspaper Publishers Association, "What Can One Newspaper Ad Do?" August 1969.

[2] Norman H. Mackworth, "A Stand Camera for Line-of-Sight Recording," *Perception and Psychophysics*, March 1967.

[3] W. James, *Principles of Psychology*, vol. 1, (Dover: New York, 1890) ch. 11, p. 421.

[4] For example, Carter reports an experiment in which students did twice as much thinking in response to programmed learning with blank spaces in between some frames, as compared with the same program without blanks. See Richard F. Carter, "Research on Stopping Behavior", paper delivered at the *Pacific Chapter Meeting of American Association for Public Opinion Research*, San Diego, California, January 31, 1970.

[5] Kahnemann's work on pupil dilation during signal detection suggested that subjects engaged in concurrent mental activity were "to some degree functionally blind when they were engaged in thought." See Kahnernann, D; Beatty, J; and Pollack, I; "Perceptual deficit during a mental task," *Science*, vol. 157 (1967), pp 218-219.

[6] In addition to computer produced wave frequency rates, it is possible to visually examine the actual wave tracing produced. It is a physical record of the wave. Such examination shows the amplitude of the print waves to be consistently about five times that of the TV waves. It is tempting to attribute the short TV waves to monotony but probably more accurate to attribute the taller print waves to the fact that the print reader uses effort to converge his eyes onto the closer stimulus, and also endures a tension in the mastoid muscles of the neck as the head is bent slightly forward. It is possible that reading cannot be maintained without some such tension, and that in a *completely* comfortable chair with perfect head and neck support, the reader would fall asleep.

[7] Psychological salience was first discussed in this manner by E.L. Hartley, *Problems in Prejudice* (New York: Kings Crown Press, 1946), pp 107-115.

[8] "Criticism, Control and Objectivity," *Second Conference on Aspects of Television News Coverage*, Villa Fiorio, Grottaferrata, Italy (March 15-18, 1970), p.13, sponsored by International Broadcast Institute, 525 Via del Corso, Rome 00186.

[9] For example, one study shows that 59% of the 12-14 age group but 75% of the 15-20 age group read a newspaper "yesterday." Moreover, among the 59% of those aged 12-14, newspaper readership was 76% for those who aspired to a college education, but only 53% for those who did not. Television viewing in the 12-14 group was 38%. See "When People Want to Know, Where Do They Go to Find Out?" *Bureau of Advertising, American Newspaper Publishing Association*, 485 Lexington Avenue, New York, New York 10017.

CHAPTER 15

"TEMPORARY" EFFECTS OF COMMUNICATION

B efore-and-after impact measures of advertising and other communications typically ignore the direct data of the respondent's own experiences — that is, what happens between measures and during exposure to the stimulus. This leaves open the possibility that attitudes or perceptions may temporarily acquire qualities which are gone by the time of the "after" measure.

If otherwise stable attitudes or perceptions sometimes change during exposure to communication, then no matter how brief the effects, the consequences of repetition should be studied. With enough trials or exposures, the temporary or momentary effect may tip over into a fixed effect. It then would appear in the "after" measure without prior warning to those who confine themselves to before-and-after measures.

This view of a relatively ignored process would hold that many apparently gradual changes are gradual only in terms of the time to detect fixed or final effects, and that immediate and full-blown effects occur at least briefly at each exposure to the stimulus. In this sense, much advertising and communication may be considered to be at least momentarily successful, even with one exposure.

This view also would hold that many apparent changes are sudden only in terms of the unannounced appearance of final effects. These final effects may involve new attitudes and perceptions learned while the old ones still were completely in force, and new attitudes might displace the old with a suddenness and ease that would startle outside observers.

Thus, an old attitude might be *exchanged* for a new one without itself undergoing *change*. In this sense, much advertising and communication may be attributed excessive powers by those who see only the sudden effects of the most recent exposure and who are ignorant of the perceptual learning which took place during previous exposures, or those who are ignorant that previous exposures occurred.

In general, this view suggests that communication has great power to produce temporary effects, which have been overlooked, at least methodologically, for what they tell about the nature of change.

Original Publication: *Journal of Advertising Research*, Vol. 10, No. 1 (February 1970).

To illustrate this view, the present study attempts to (1) select some attitudes of conventionally proven stability, and (2) demonstrate their temporary flexibility in response to modestly varied versions of the same visual stimulus. A method for eliciting this variability also is discussed.

Earlier reports on the measurement of involvement with communication materials defined "involvement" as the number of connections — conscious bridging experiences or personal references — that the subject makes between the content of the persuasive stimulus and the content of his own life (Chapter 6 above). This definition necessitates a report of immediate experience or conscious reactions to the stimulus.

For this study, interview procedures were standardized, and a manual was made available for for coding of responses. The basic question asked of respondents was, "What thoughts came to mind *while* you were looking at . . .?" The procedure then was applied in studies comparing the impact of different media (see Chapter 7).

This procedure for reporting thought content during exposure then was supplemented and interrelated with measures of eye-movement and of pupil-size during exposure (see Chapter 9). A special virtue of these measures is that they permit repetition of the stimulus without the need always to repeat the verbal question. Instead, the two perceptual measures were used to signal at which repetition the processes of attention and arousal return to a pre-exposure baseline — for example, to signal when the active communication process is complete. At such time, the "after" part of a before-and-after procedure might take place with some confidence that the cumulative impact of stimulus exposures had had every opportunity to produce the intended effects.

In contrast to traditional before-and-after methods, the three measures of thinking, looking, and arousal concern what is happening during exposure. However, they concern responses *to* the stimulus and not directly about the intended effects of the stimulus.

An evaluation of the effectiveness of the stimulus also could provide valuable information about how the stimulus works, why it works (or doesn't), and even when to conduct an "after" measure. It might be suspected, however, that even with a single exposure, a direct test of effectiveness could be made. This, then, would complete a methodological circle in which the problem was to find a way to ask about the intended effects or purposes of a stimulus at the first exposure without asking *about* the stimulus itself.

The present procedure called for the respondent to make judgments about five well-known national companies. The companies are competitive in product quality, personnel recruitment, the value of shares to investors, etc. As part of a continuing program of corporate-image research, repeated national samples of respondents have been asked which one of the five companies they thought:

- has the highest quality products.
- is the best investment.

- does the most important research and development.
- they would most like to work for.
- does the most for its customers.

Other questions were asked in the same format, but only the five will be discussed. When asked questions over the telephone, the respondent first was told the names of the companies, then asked to write the familiar abbreviation of the companies' names (for example, "GE"). Thus, the symbols and questions constituted the stimuli. The questions also reflected corporate public opinion objectives.

COMMUNICATION AS STIMULUS

The present study began at the point when it was decided to ask these same questions, but using different ways of identifying the five companies. That is, an interviewer could say, "Which one of these and show an advertisement, a message, or another symbol signed by the company in question. Thus, the communication became part of the stimulus without any verbal attention directed to it and without any questions about it.

The objective of this study, then, is to establish that attitudes to the five questions are stable by conventional standards, then to investigate stability when the form of the visual stimulus is varied. This, of course, entails a shift from telephone to personal interviewing.

The visual forms to be investigated were six different versions of companies' signatures and/or monograms, one version ("GE") using the telephone interview procedure. In each comparison, the symbols to designate the competing companies were matched in form. Respondents were given 5 by 8-inch cards with the six symbols arranged vertically, then asked the five questions. Each version was shown to one-sixth of the total sample so no respondent would react to more than one version. The very few respondents who could not recognize the corporate identity of one or more of the symbols were not included in the analysis.

To preserve the proprietary nature of the data and yet be able to make a relevant report, the six versions of the stimulus are identified as I–VI, except III which is the personal interview equivalent of the telephone "GE." In addition, the five questions or attitudes listed above are identified as A–E, but in a different order.

In five quarterly telephone surveys conducted by Trendex between Fall 1967 and Fall 1968, the five attitudes, A–E, each varied from 2 to 4 percent with average overall readings of 19 percent, 19 percent, 13 percent, 8 percent, and 23 percent (Table 15.1). The range represents an instability factor *within* each set of attitude data (R/A) of .211, .311, .308, .250, and .130. It is not clear whether this degree of instability is a function of unreliability of measurement or changes in attitude, but the important observation is that the data appear as *largely stable*. When the same five attitude questions were asked personally by the Gallup Or-

TABLE 15.1

VARIATION IN ATTITUDE MEASURES ACROSS FIVE SURVEYS

Percent Who Choose "GE"

	'67 IV (1052) %	'68-I (1065) %	'68-II (1037) %	'68-III (1048) %	'68-IV (1039) %	Range	Average	RIA
A	17	18	21	18	19	4	19	.211
B	17	19	20	21	20	4	19	.311
C	12	12	16	14	12	4	13	.308
D	9	9	7	7	9	2	8	.250
E	24	22	25	22	24	3	23	.130

ganization in January 1969, but with six different visual stimuli as aids in identifying the companies being compared (Table 15.2), the instability (R/A) across forms was about *two to three times* that shown in Table 15.1 (.722 to .211, .500 to .311, .600 to .308, .500 to .250, and .536 to .130). The supposedly stable attitudes no longer appeared to be stable. In addition, certain of the forms are revealed as more desirable for certain purposes than are other forms.

CONCLUSION

It has been shown that verbal questions which elicit apparently stable responses produce quite different responses when the associated visual stimulus is varied.

TABLE 15.2

PERCENT WHO CHOOSE GENERAL ELECTRIC IN
RESPONSE TO SIX VERSIONS OF THE SAME STIMULI

Atti- tude	I (504) %	II (518) %	III (466) %	IV (488) %	V (516) %	VI (528) %	Range %	Average %	RIA
A	16	22	18	23	10	22	13	18	.722
B	20	22	20	31	20	22	11	22	.500
C	13	18	9	17	14	16	9	15	.600
D	10	13	8	13	7	14	7	14	.500
E	24	37	24	31	22	33	15	28	.536

Version III in Table 15.2 was intended to duplicate as nearly as possible the telephone version of the stimuli. The cards handed to respondents, therefore, contained the typed short-form abbreviation of each company, *i.e.*, "GE." The Gallup personal interview responses of 18 percent, 20 percent, 9 percent, 8 percent and 24 percent in January 1969 are almost identical to the Trendex telephone interview responses of 19 percent, 20 percent, 12 percent, 9 percent, and 24 percent of November 1968. Differences in response may not, therefore, be attributed to differences between the personal and telephone interview methods per se.

In the particular context of this study, attributions of product quality and other corporate virtues are shown to be highly susceptible to the influence of the communication at the time of exposure and interview. It is not suggested that the influenced response persists for any appreciable length of time, but that the momentarily influenced response may soon give way to the more stable response.

The question of how long the influenced response persists and how the frequency of stimulation affects its persistence or stabilization is open for further research. However, the question may be particularly fruitful for a better understanding of the role of the immediate perceptual experience in what is usually called "attitude change."

Meanwhile, a methodology has been developed to permit national pretesting of communication or advertising materials in such a way that the projection of corporate purposes or objectives — that is, public attributions of quality, value, etc — by such materials can be measured on single exposure and without any direct questions about the materials themselves.

CHAPTER 16

BRAIN WAVE MEASURES OF MEDIA INVOLVEMENT

E lsewhere I have suggested that television is a medium of low involvement as compared with print (Chapter 6 above). Involvement was defined in terms of the number of personal connections between the stimulus and the viewer: the number of thoughts which came spontaneously to mind during exposure and which linked something in the content of the stimulus to something in the content of the viewer's own life.

In 1967 *Time* sponsored a small study in which I reported that the same kinds of advertising in TV and print evoked in the TV form many fewer personal connections between the ad content and something in the life content of the viewer (Chapter 7 above). More recently, in a very much larger study, the Bureau of Advertising of the ANPA confirmed that TV versions of similar print ads evoked fewer personal connections[1].

Television is popular, interesting, and time consuming, and it is not meant as criticism to say that it is a low involvement medium. It is, however, very different from print, and perhaps even more so than is generally granted.

To learn more about these differences, I became more interested in laboratory experiments on the processes of looking and of thinking, on the process of attention and of relaxation. In so doing, I sensed that sooner or later I might develop a special viewpoint about the work of Marshall McLuhan. This is a report on that developing viewpoint.

Let us begin with looking. "Looking" was defined in terms of the capabilities and limitations of the Mackworth stand-mounted eye movement recorder in which the respondent's head is rendered immobile with the aid of a bite plate and a 6- by 8-inch picture is viewed at a distance of 18 inches.[2]

Eye movements are recorded to produce a developed motion picture film of the viewed scene and a superimposed white spot or marker indicates the path of eye movements. Ten-second exposures are recorded, and from the developed film a plot is made of location of eye fixations, duration or dwell time, and shifts to new fixations. The type of equipment is described and photographed in the August 1968 cover story of *Scientific American*.

In and of itself, looking was of little concern in the particular research described since it started with the premise that the respondents were looking at the

Original Publication: *Journal of Advertising Research*, Vol. 11, No. 1 (February 1971).

experimental ads. The concern was with how they were looking when communication or learning was taking place as compared with how they were looking when communication was not taking place — *i.e.* what were the response qualities of looking-with-learning?

Of parallel concern were the stimuli themselves. How were easily learned ads looked at as compared with ads which were difficult to learn — *i.e.*, what were the stimulus qualities of looking-with-learning?

The respondents in such studies were brought to a laboratory, exposed to different ads for ten seconds each via the Mackworth Optiscan, and then interviewed for recall of the ads. Recall, therefore, was the criterion of learning. Additional respondents were brought back once a week for three weeks, without verbal interviewing, just to note the effects of repeated exposures on looking.

Of various scoring methods, the one of most interest concerned looking in only one place vs. looking all over, or "bunched up" vs. "spread-out" looking. This was called focusing and scanning and was scored by dividing the total area of each advertisement into 1-inch by 1-inch cells and counting the number of different cells which were "looked into."

Initial findings presented an interesting paradox. On a respondent basis, scanning represents looking-with-learning — *i.e.*, the respondents who scanned more recalled more. However, on a stimulus basis, focusing represents looking-with-learning — *i.e.*, the ads which were scanned less were better recalled.

The resolution of the paradox is apparently this: Ads which are easily learned require very little of the respondent and they communicate with little work on his part. But ads which do not learn easily do require the respondent to be more active, to look around, and to scan.

So a situation occurs where, at one extreme, the work of communication must be done by the communicator via creation of an easily learnable ad or communiqué, or, on the other hand, where the work of communication may be done by the respondent or communicant via an ability to learn difficult communiqués.

At this point we asked, "How is it done?" For example, we began to suspect that scanning, as an active learning process, had something to do with the possibility of personal connections taking place between the stimulus and the viewer, but how? It also appeared that focusing permitted much learning without any effort at all, and, again, we asked. "How?"

ENTER WILLIAM JAMES

It was William James who came to the rescue. This turn-of-the-century Harvard psychologist had been the primary American exponent of the study of conscious experience. As a student of the process, of attention, he is still acknowledged as master by contemporary scholars.

James defined two types of attention: voluntary and involuntary, and he noted that voluntary attention cannot be continuous; it is a continual returning of the attention to its object when it wanders away. He said, "'*Voluntary attention is always derived;* we never make all effort to attend to all object except for the sake of some *remote* interest which the effort will serve' and '*There is no such thing as voluntary attention sustained for more than a few seconds at a time.* What is called "sustained voluntary attention" is a repetition of successive efforts which bring back the topic to the mind. No one can possibly attend continuously to an object that does not change'".[3]

James' distinction between voluntary and involuntary attention means that much of thinking, learning, and reading represents a sequence of successive efforts to attend, while much of the viewing of life around us — films, TV, and other changing stimuli — are far less likely to require effort. In other words, the change, the switching, or the rhythmic process goes on inside man when he is working at the job of attention, or it goes on outside man and inside (*e.g.*) the moving film as it relieves man of that work.

Now in these terms, we may re-appreciate scanning as an interrupted series of discrete events. They permit the intrusion of a stimulus inside the head of the viewer in tile form of a thought, and particularly in this case in the form of a thought connected to the stimulus.

Thus, involvement or thinking, when taking plate *vis-à-vis* a media stimulus requires that the respondent attend both to internal and external stimuli. It sometimes means that some of the external stimuli may be missed; it sometimes means that pressure to keep up will be felt — that is, to do two jobs of attention, one to the stimulus on the page or screen and one to the reaction inside the head. It is susceptible to motivation and effort, and it fairly may at times be called mental work.

This matter of dual attention seemed to answer the "how" of scanning in a way that one could understand its relation to involvement or to thinking. But what about focusing where attention was easy, and uninterrupted, and somehow still seemed to communicate? What is there about the changing stimulus in film or TV that can relieve man of the work of learning? Is learning the right word to use, even qualified as passive learning?

We thought that the entertaining quality of film and TV might have something to do with relaxation. Is relaxation not the opposite of work, and is it not associated with suggestibility? Furthermore, a particular TV commercial continued to pique our curiosity.

The particular TV commercial was the Clairol Nice 'N' Easy commercial which used a slow-motion technique borrowed from the movie film "The Pawnbroker." That film introduced tricks of flash scenes as well as slow motion, but the Nice 'N' Easy commercial used only the slow motion.

The commercial had exceptionally high recall scores but aroused no pupil dilation response. This seemed quite unusual. Was the commercial learned without any excitement whatsoever, or was there another element present, an unmeasured response? Is the opposite of excitement just nothing? Is calm a flat emptiness?

With such measures of arousal based upon changes in pupil dilation, skin, heart, or respiration, an absence of excitement brings the measure back to a minimal baseline. No further information is provided. With brain waves, however, a decline in arousal would be evidenced by a lessening of so-called Beta waves, or rhythmic frequencies emitted in the 13–40 cycle per second range. As relaxation appeared there would also appear the Alpha waves in the 8–12 cycle per second range, the slower Theta waves of 4–7 per second, and finally the Delta waves at 1–3 per second. In general, brain waves cover the full range of human response activity from peak arousal to deepest sleep. So we decided to measure brain waves produced in response to television commercials.

BRAIN WAVE EXPERIMENT

The Neuropsychological Laboratory of New York Medical College is engaged in basic and applied research, and frequently in practical applications. The paid subject in our experiment was a 22-year-old secretary. She was a high school graduate with a black and white television set at home, and she had not served as a subject before. Testing took place in November 1969.

About a half-hour after lunch, the subject was seated in a test room, actually a light- and sound-controlled environment which could be viewed remotely via a television monitoring system. The cubicle had drapes, a comfortable couch, magazines on a cocktail table, and a simulated TV set in the corner at a viewing distance of seven feet.

When the subject entered the cubicle, a single tiny electrode was fixed to the occipital region (the back of the head) with the aid of a tiny quantity of jelly. It was referenced to both ears. A very fine wire lead ran from the electrode to the wall where it apparently disappeared. It had no discernible weight and was not visible to the seated subject. The lead then went outside to a Grass Model 7 Polygraph, connected in turn to a Honeywell 7600 tape system and a CAT 400B computer.

The subject was told: "We have fixed up this room a little bit like a living room at home. This is supposed to be a TV set. Just relax for a while. Look at one of the magazines here or read for a few minutes until some commercials come on the screen. Then watch the commercials. Don't be surprised if the commercials are repeated a few times. There will be three commercials shown. The commercials will be shown several times. When the commercials go off the screen, go back to the magazine and read or look a little longer."

The simulated TV set was a Fairchild 400 rear projector with an 8 by 11-inch screen. (In a later retest with the same subject, an actual TV set and on-the-air stimuli were used, but with almost identical results.) A tape cartridge held three different color commercials to be run in sequence three times for a total of nine viewings.

Each of the commercials had some outdoor activity involving play, romance, or sports so that responses to the commercials might also reflect somewhat the responses that might be made to entertainment content as well as commercials.

The commercials were (1) a story about a boy who could run and play because his defective heart was artificially paced with a medical device developed by GE; it was a quiet, gentle commercial with pleasant outdoor scenes; (2) the classic and very gentle Nice 'N' Easy commercial; (3) a very explosive GE commercial showing star baseball pitcher Bob Gibson throwing fastballs at what looks like an unbreakable sheet of glass, actually a new product called Lexan.

Procedure

Analysis of the brain wave (EEG) data was first made on the total reaction to each of the nine viewings, or specifically to 56 seconds of each to eliminate transition responses. The type of analysis summed up the "spectrum," as it is called, of all identifiable brain wave frequencies emitted during the 56-second "epoch," as it is called. In simple terms, one obtains a measure of how many seconds worth of each wave frequency appears during the 56 seconds.

The computer program reported eleven "bands" or frequency class-intervals from 1.5 cycles per second up to 32 cps. The first 5 bands were combined and called "slow waves." The next four bands, from 7.6 to 12.33 cps, are usually called Alpha waves and are associated with relaxation. They were combined and called "Alpha." The last two bands, from 12.3 to 31.8 cps, are usually called Beta waves and are associated with alertness, activity, and arousal. They were combined and called "fast waves."

The subject arrived, was seated, and received her instructions. For about 15 minutes she browsed through magazines while her EEG responses plus impressions from the TV monitor indicated a comfortable and relaxed adjustment to the surroundings. Just before the commercials came on, a full record was made of the EEG spectrum for the last 56 seconds of magazine reading. This involved a Max Factor advertisement which discussed different techniques for applying make-up. The subject reported later that she was very interested in this advertisement, and was a bit annoyed when the TV commercials came on. She also reported that she liked the Nice 'N' Easy commercial, disliked the Bob Gibson commercial, and was bored with all by the third exposure.

Results

First, the print ad with five seconds of slow waves, 16 of Alpha, and 28 of fast waves all added tip to a picture of relaxed attention, interest, and mental activity, as shown in Figure 1.

As the first commercial came on, the subject looked up and an entirely new pattern or mix appeared, adding up to 21 seconds of slow, 18 of Alpha, and 15 of fast. We say "pattern" because closer inspection and analysis showed that the wave patterns throughout were at any one moment mixtures of the overlapping

wave actions. It was not some seconds of one frequency followed by some seconds of another but an overall state, mode, or style of reception with elements of
different wave types. Thus, the 21 slow, 18 Alpha, and 15 fast in response to the
first commercial roughly represented constant proportions of waves active in
any one period within the 56 seconds.

We were surprised that the Alpha or relaxed element did not change significantly from print to TV, but we took it as a sign of general relaxation in the
test situation. We had expected that the TV might be more relaxing, but not that
it would instantly produce a preponderance of slow waves and a characteristic
mode of response. Rather, we expected that it might develop over time with the
three repetitions.

The initial spectrum for the first commercial did not change significantly
for the next two commercials. Apparently it was a characteristic mode of response. The 21-18-15 became 24-15-14 for the second commercial, and 24-16-
13 for the third. Results are shown in Figure 2. There were, however, differences in the proportion of Delta and Theta which together comprise the "slow"
waves. These deserve closer attention in future studies.

The question arises as to how immediate was, this characteristic mode of
response. Did it appear in the first seconds of the first commercial or what? To
answer this, we analyzed spectra for three 10-second periods within the first
exposure to the first commercial. Within Seconds 2 to 12, there were two sec-

Figure 1

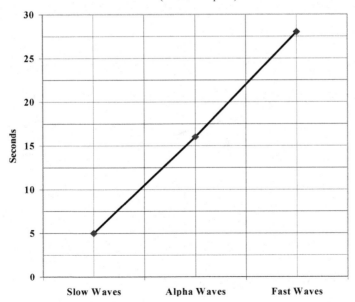

**EEG Response to One Exposure
of a Max Factor Print Advertisement**
(56 second epoch)

onds of slow, four of Alpha, and four of fast waves. Within Seconds 25 to 35, there were four seconds of slow, three of Alpha, and three of fast waves; and within Seconds 46 to 56, there were five seconds of slow, three of Alpha, and three of fast waves.

In other words, it was about half way through the first exposure to the first commercial before the slow waves predominated over the fast waves. We can say, then, that the characteristic mode of response took about 30 seconds to develop fully.

Looking at just the first 10-second period, however, we can also say that slow waves were already half as common as the fast waves, as compared to the prior print viewing where the slow waves were only one-fifth to one-sixth of the fast waves. Thus, the adaptation, quite reasonably, began immediately upon viewing the television stimulus.

What about repetition? The second round of viewings went 22-20-13, 24-16-14, and 28-15-12. The third round went 24-16-13, 25-16-12, and 26-16-12. The slow waves gradually increased generally from 23 to 25 while the fast waves decreased from 14 to 12.

More noteworthy was the similarity of response to all three commercials, increasingly so with repetition. The differences between responses to the three commercials on third exposure are less than the difference between any one

Figure 2

EEG Response to Each of Three
TV Commercials on First Exposure
(56 Second Epoch)

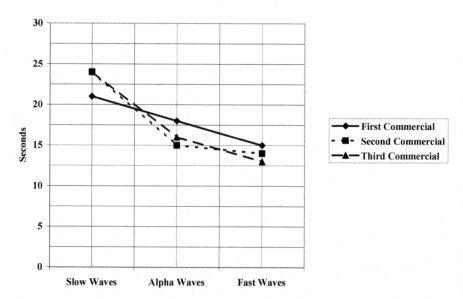

Figure 3

**EEG Response to Each of Three
TV Commercials on Third Exposure
(56 Second Epoch)**

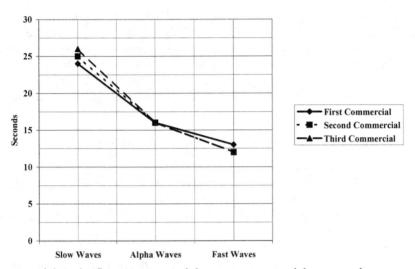

commercial on the first exposure and that same commercial on second exposure. In short, the commercials evoked little difference on first trial and almost none by the third as shown in Figure 3.

The question arises as to the remaining sensitivity to the third exposure of the third commercial, by this time probably boring and well-learned. Again, we analyzed spectra for three 10-second periods within the third exposure to the third commercial. Within Seconds 2 to 12, there were six seconds of slow, two of Alpha, and two of fast waves. Within Seconds 25 to 35, there were four seconds of slow, three of Alpha, and two of fast waves; and within Seconds 46 to 56, there were four seconds of slow, three of Alpha, and two of fast waves. In other words, even on this last dull viewing the subject's initial preponderance of slow waves diminished a little as the commercial proceeded to the halfway point. Thus, it appears that there may be a little life left even in what appears to be a satiated condition.

Interpretation

It appears that this subject's mode of response to television is very different from her response to print. That is, the basic electrical response of the brain is more to the media than to content differences within the TV commercials or to what, in pre-McLuhan days, would ordinarily have been called the commercial message.

It also appears, as suggested initially by the earlier studies of involvement or of eye-movement, that the response to print generally may come to be understood as active, and composed primarily of fast brain waves while the response to television might come to be understood as passive and composed primarily of slow brain waves. Further testing is indicated.

In addition to computer analysis of brain wave frequency rates, it is possible to examine visually the actual wave tracing produced. It is a physical record of the wave. Such examination shows the amplitude of the print waves to be consistently about five times that of the TV waves. We may attribute the taller print waves to the fact that the print reader uses effort to converge his eyes onto the closer stimulus, and also endures a tension in the muscles of (he neck as the head is bent slightly forward and turned. It is possible that reading cannot be maintained without some such tension, and that in a completely comfortable chair with perfect head and neck support, the reader would fall asleep.

OLD THEORY: LEARNING FROM MESSAGES

McLuhan might characterize our field of communication theory as horse-and-buggy, or at best a "Pony Express" type of theory. That is, we are wedded to a view of someone preparing a message, the message carried across a distance (hopefully fast), and a receiver reading or decoding the message at the other end. Ours is a transportation type of theory with a communicator, a communiqué, and a communicant.

Our mass communication theory has much to say about communicators, and influences on them and their media. It is also much concerned with patterns of diffusion of ideas, and it is very concerned with the selectivity and depth of audience responses. Somehow McLuhan seems to say that this has all been made irrelevant by the technological fact of television.

Television is not mass communication in our sense, says McLuhan. Nobody out there is trying to decode or receive any messages. Instead, their eyes and cars have been "extended" into the situation portrayed on the screen. They are participating in an experience — even if it is passive participation. And unlike films, a significant portion of television is "live" or, as they say in the computer field, "in real time."

In terms of our old mass communication theory, we would ordinarily say that television is better or richer than radio because an extra dimension, that of video, is added; or richer than newspapers because the audio was added.

This is a right conclusion from a wrong premise. Radio and newspapers as communication are deficient in that they must omit much information. Similarly, television as experience is deficient in that reality is presented minus the feelings. This is McLuhan's "cool" medium, in consequence said to be breeding a generation yearning for feelings and meanings behind the superficial happenings and encounters in life around them.

Our initial EEG data supports McLuhan in the sense that television does not appear to be communication as we have known it. Our subject was working to learn something from a print ad, but was passive about television. If something happened to communicate, that's fine; if it didn't, it went by and was gone and no process of scanning or dual attention would worry over its shortcomings. The subject was no more trying to learn something from television than she would be trying to learn something from a park landscape while resting on a park bench. Yet television is communication.

What *shall* we say of it, a communication medium that may effortlessly transmit into storage huge quantities of information not thought about at the time of exposure, but much of it capable of later activation?

NEW THEORY: LEARNING FROM EXPERIENCES

The TV viewer is well equipped to recognize many things in life seen beforehand on television. So equipped, he startles into an, "Ah ha, I've seen you or this before." This startle is the beginning of an active response, but since this has not been thought out in advance of the time of exposure, it comes out unformed and shapeless.

This suggests the awkward spontaneity of the younger generation, the tendency to act or react in a variety of new but faintly recognized situations where purpose or intent has not yet crystallized. It may look immature or enthusiastic to many observers, but it emanates from the ability to recognize as familiar a wide variety of things in life.

The print viewer, meanwhile, has paused and thought about what he has seen in print, has formed an opinion or mentally rehearsed a plan. When he recognizes something similar in real life he is ready with a formed or "mature" response.

However, print has allowed him to store relatively less information, and so there is much that he does not recognize and to which he reacts not at all. So print man seems very selective, and reacts well or not at all. It looks very mature.

In short, it is suggested that television man, the passive media audience, is a more active but "clumsy," experience-oriented participant in life, while print man, the active media audience, is a more selective, less active and more "mature" information or message-oriented participant in life. Never mind now which is better. McLuhan was aware of some such difference while none of our mass communication theory was relevant.

As to the question "Which is better?" we are handicapped by our greater familiarity with active and involved types of learning. Our understanding of how passive learning takes place is still deficient, and we are not yet sure how to measure its effectiveness in a fair manner.

While further work with brain waves seems indicated, it should be stressed that there is no evidence or speculative inference in this interim report to suggest that either print or television is "better" than the other, or that fast or slow brain waves are better than the other. Instead, we have a very great need to better understand the differences, and perhaps especially to better understand the significance of slow brain waves.

To do so we must hold in abeyance those historically built-in predispositions in favor of certain behaviors which currently seem more "mature."

Finally, we have previously pointed out in the analysis of eye movement patterns involving focusing and scanning that advertising which is easily learned requires very little work on the part of the respondent, but that advertising which communicates less easily does require the respondent to be more active. This observation based on eye movement data seems confirmed or paralleled by the present brain wave data. So the response to television is more passive simply because it is an easier form of communication. The task now is to determine just how easy or hard different communication or even educational materials should be made for optimal learning by various audiences.

---

[1] Bogart, L., Tolley, S.B., and Orenstein, F., "What One Little Ad Can Do," *Journal of Advertising Research,* vol. 10, no. 4 (August 1970), pp. 3-15.

[2] Mackworth, N.H., "A Stand Camera for Line-of-Sight Recording," *Perception and Psychophysics,* March 1967

[3] James, W., *Principles of Psychology* (New York: Dover Publications, 1890).

CHAPTER 17

WHY THREE EXPOSURES MAY BE ENOUGH

O ften a paper about advertising begins with the assertion that the American public is "bombarded" each day by a large number of advertising messages. (Dr. Britt's foregoing article quotes several of these numbers, ranging from 117 to 484.) Other papers emphasize not the bombardment, but the "filter" which blocks out, say, 90 percent of the total. It makes a great difference where you put your emphasis when you are trying to convey something about the power of advertising.

The joint ANA/AAAA industry presentation to the FTC in October 1971 produced surprise that so little was really known about the effects of advertising. This surprise was common to all parties, commissioners and industry representatives alike.

Ironically, the initiative taken by the industry to inventory its current expertise was what led to such unexpected and challenging consequences.

Some blamed the industry for having been overconfident, for not having done its homework, for having been remiss in its research, deficient in its concern for accountability, and (essentially) for being not at all as wise about advertising as some might have expected.

But how you handle the "bombardment" and "filter" views of advertising is central to a clear exposition of its power. As a matter of policy, appropriate statements should be made available by the industry.

I suggest that the root questions about the degree of impact, or persuasibility, or influence of television advertising have to do as much with the nature of man as with advertising. There are unsolved or unresolved questions, even at the level of understanding the nature of man.

HOW DO WE LEARN?

At one time, especially prior to 1900 and in the U.S., it was generally believed that an infant is born into a world of "blooming, buzzing confusion," and that as he matured he had to make order out of all this stimulation. Since that time, and more in Europe than in America, there has developed a different view: that the infant child is as if isolated on a remote island, and only occasionally does a lone message get across to him from the mainland.

Original Publication: *Journal of Advertising Research*, Vol. 12, No. 6 (December 1972)

When the first view prevailed it was considered very important to train young children into good *habits,* so that even if they did not understand the world they could cope with it in some routine behavior.

More recently the emphasis is on stimulating the child in an encouraging manner so that he will spontaneously make creative attempts, including those of insight and understanding.

The two views could hardly be more different. Indeed, the educational world has debated them for 75 years with sometimes one side in ascendance and then, after re-evaluation, the other.

This difference involves not only a different view of the child's (or man's) bio-physiological or reactive capacities but also of how children learn. Even though the psychologists of the day performed much of their research on learning on quite neutral laboratory rats, the proponents of each view seemed to find evidence to support their own views.

For example, American researchers noticed that rats confronted with a problem dashed energetically around the cage, trying one thing and another until by chance they accidentally performed the correct response and were rewarded, usually with food. They learned, as it was said, by trial and error — with much premium placed on energy and activity. If repeated often enough, they got the habit of the correct response.

Meanwhile, German researchers noticed that *their* rats confronted with a problem retired to a corner of the cage, remained quiet for a time — as if thinking the problem over — and finally went over and performed the correct response on one try. The rats learned by some process of abstraction rather than of energy.

Lord Bertrand Russell remarked one day that obviously there is a marked breed difference between American and German rats.

So here there is one view that sees the child adapting to an overstimulating world via useful habits, learned on the basis of frequent trials or (horrid school phenomenon) "practice." Opposed to it is a view that sees the child keeping the world at bay until reached or awakened, and capable, if encouraged, of insightful, one-trial acts of learning without repetition.

The problem is complicated by the fact that both views are correct to a degree. When my two children were young we called my son the German rat and my daughter the American rat. When he tried something new and failed, such as tying his shoelaces, he'd walk away from the problem and wouldn't try again for several days. On the second try and thereafter, he would always have it right.

When she failed to solve some new problem she would persist, get angry, and upset the whole house until she solved the problem or was helped to do so. This would happen repeatedly until she had the task well learned.

We spend a lot of money on repetition of advertising. Some explain this by noting that recall of the advertising will drop unless continually reinforced; others note that members of the audience are not always in the market for the advertised product, but that when they are, the advertising must *be* there. There's no choice but to advertise frequently. So we can have advertising campaigns of equal magnitude, but based on quite different assumptions about the nature of the effect.

Of course these two views are apparently quite opposite. One says that the ad must be learned in the same way that habits are learned — by practice. The other says that at the right moment (when one is "in the market") it just takes minimal exposure to achieve appropriate effects.

If you say this to the FTC, however (and it's been said), you seem, to them, to be saying two different things. If your ad has to be repeated endlessly to be learned, it probably isn't very powerful. If your ad has to be repeated just to be there at that critical moment when your viewer is "in the market" then it's got real one-shot power indeed.

This is like saying, if you're using the recall explanation, that schoolwork is hard, that the child must practice or else forget what he's learned. If you're using the "in the market" explanation, it's like saying that if the school curriculum and methods are truly stimulating, the child's mind will be open, creative, insightful, or "turned on." Those who believe in such stimulation say that practice is required only when you're forcing children to learn things they're not interested in, things that don't "turn them on." Well, you know the rest of that fight — but the same fight is not as easily recognized within advertising and mass communications.

People are confused about whether or not advertising is potent — and they are not getting any unified point of view from the advertising industry itself.

I would like to argue against single exposure potency and also against any large number of repeated exposures. It is important to understand how communication works and how people learn, and to do that some attention has to be given to the difference between one, two, and three — *i.e.,* the difference between the first, second, and third exposures. One to make ready, two for the show, three for the money, and four to go, or just what? Campaign effects based on 20 or 30 exposures I believe are only multiples or combinations of what happens in the first few exposures.

RECENT RESEARCH

First, I would like to note that the special importance of just two or three exposures, as compared to a much larger number, is attested to by a variety of converging research findings based on different research methods. In the April 1968 issue of the *American Psychologist,* for example, I reported ("Procedures underlying response to advertising") that an optimal number of exposures seemed to be about two to three. This was based on eye movement data conducted in a laboratory situation and in response to print advertising.

In September 1969 Grass published a similar finding (three to four exposures) in this *Journal* based on CONPAAD responses to television commercials. Both studies were primarily laboratory.

In September 1970, Colin MacDonald of the British Market Research Bureau gave an award-winning paper at the Annual Conference of the European Society of Market Research (ESOMAR), which reported purchase diary data interrelated with media data such that MacDonald identified two exposures as optimal. There are others as well but the point I am making should be clear, that a wide variety of research procedures agree on the special significance of just a few exposures as optimal.

AN EXPLANATION

Let me try to explain the special qualities of one, two, and three exposures. I stop at three because as you shall see there is no such thing as a fourth exposure psychologically; rather, fours, fives, etc., are repeats of the third exposure effect.

Exposure No. I is by definition unique. Like the first exposure of anything, the reaction is dominated by a "What is it?" type of cognate response — *i.e.*, the first response is to understand the nature of the stimulus. Anything new or novel, however uninteresting on second exposure, has to elicit some response the first time if only for the mental classification required to discard the object as of no further interest. Thus, the new stimulus, good or bad, has an initial attention-getting requirement even if it is quickly blocked out thereafter.

The second exposure to a stimulus has several implicit qualities. One is that the cognitive "What *is* it?" response can be replaced by a more evaluative and personal "What *of* it?" response. That is, having now fully appreciated just what is the nature of the new information, the viewer can now shift to a question of whether or not it has personal relevance. Some of this might occur during first exposure if the respondent is absorbing the commercial with great interest, but more likely, especially on television where you cannot rewind or reverse the film, there's enough missed the first time around so that elements of the cognate reaction are still present on second exposure.

Another element of second exposure, and unique to second exposure, is the startled recognition response, "Ah ha, I've seen this before!" The virtue of such recognition is that it permits the viewer to pick up where he left off — without the necessity of doing the cognate thing ("What is it?") all over again. So the second exposure is the one where personal responses and evaluations — the "sale" so to speak — occurs. This "What of it?" response completes the basic reaction to the commercial.

By the third exposure the viewer knows he has been through his "What *is* it's?" and "What *of* it's?," and the third becomes, then, the true reminder — that is, *if* there is some consequence of the earlier evaluations yet to be fulfilled. But it is *also* the beginning of disengagement, of withdrawal of attention from a completed task.

I suggest that this pattern holds true for all larger number of exposures. That is, most people filter or screen out TV commercials at any one time by stopping at the "What is it?" response without further personal involvement. The same person months later, and suddenly in the market for the product in question, might see and experience the 23rd exposure to the commercial *as if it were the second.* That is, now the viewer is able to go further into the nature of his or her reaction to the commercial — and then the 24th and probably the 25th might finish off that sequence with no further reaction to subsequent exposures.

The importance of this view of things is that it positions advertising as powerful only when the viewer, the consumer, or shopper is interested and that is largely outside the control of television or advertising.

Secondly, it positions the viewer as doing his business, reacting to the commercial — very quickly and thoroughly when the proper time comes around.

Many people have looked at the enormous TV budgets and repeat Scatter plans and assumed that the viewer had to be reacting slowly and gradually. It made TV look monolithic and successful on the basis of sheer mass and grinding momentum. It made large budgets seem especially advantageous or "unfair," and thoroughly distorted two of the common words in the English language: these words are "remembering" and "forgetting."

There is a myth in the advertising world that viewers will forget your message if you don't repeat your advertising often enough. It is this myth that supports many large advertising expenditures and raises embarrassing and, to some extent, needless questions about unfair market dominance.

The myth about the forgetting of advertising is based primarily on the erosion of recall scores. Yet the inability to recall something does not mean it is forgotten or that it has been erased from memory. The acid test of complete forgetting is if you can no *longer recognize* the object. Few TV commercials that *have been seen the* night before can be remembered the next day — *i.e.*, via recall. According to Gallup's TPT system only 12 percent can recall the average commercial. But at GE, we have shown photoscripts of TV commercials weeks after exposure and gotten 50 percent recognition.

Rather than continue the budget supporting myths renewed every day via the recall research technique, I would rather say that the public comes closer to forgetting *nothing* they have seen on TV. They just "put it out of their minds" until and unless it has some use, and then one day, "Ah ha!" — it springs to life again and the response to the commercial continues.

I am not critical of large TV budgets that provide many exposures. I am critical, and the industry will be criticized, if the power of those large budgets is misunderstood or mis-stated. The large budget is powerful because, like a product sitting on a shelf, you never know when the customer is going to be looking for you — so you must rent the shelf space all the time. But the nature of the customer's reaction is independent, rapid, decisive. He or she makes up his or her mind perhaps more than once during a campaign — but most frequently at some point in the second, or shall we say psychologically second, exposure to the commercial.

Within this perspective television advertising plays a modest, important, and thoroughly reasonable role in the marketing of goods and services.

CHAPTER 18

WHAT MAKES ADVERTISING EFFECTIVE?

A ny discussion of the effects of advertising must begin with the environment — a controlling factor that both defines and limits the possible effects. The environment of advertising consists of an intricate web of social, economic, and technological circumstances that direct an ad toward a particular audience through a particular medium. Obviously, the advertiser's primary concern in this environment is the consumer himself. How much attention does he pay to the advertising that surrounds him?

An answer to this question began in 1922 when a pioneer psychologist, Daniel Starch, devised a method for measuring readers' recognition of print advertising. In 1932 he established a readership research program that, through more than 240,000 interviews, annually surveys the readers of more than 1,000 issues of consumer and farm magazines, business publications, and newspapers.

To provide a reasonably precise answer to the question of how many people notice and read an ad, I chose the most common type of print advertising — the one-page, four-color ad — and totaled the Starch results for all such ads (20,347) in all issues of 47 major magazines in 1970. I found that 440 of readers claim to have noticed a particular ad and 35% read enough to identify the brand, but only 9% say they read most of a particular ad. In other words, almost half of all ads are noticed — a third to the point of brand identification — but less than a tenth are of enough interest to be read. Naturally, the responses vary depending on ad size, content, and position, on the receptivity of the reader (sex, age, and income), and on whether the reader is in the market for the product advertised. At any rate, only a small portion of advertising is fully perceived at any time.

The situation in television is similar. In the 1960s George Gallup, another psychologist who pioneered in media research as well as in public opinion research, instituted a survey in which, for example, a cross section of Philadelphia was telephoned the day after an evening of television and asked to recall the commercials on the prime-time shows. On the average, only 12% of those who had seen a particular program could recall its commercials.

It has been demonstrated in many ways that people filter out much of the huge quantity of advertising to which they are exposed. For example, in a study

Original Publication: *Harvard Business Review,* Vol. 53, No.2 (March-April 1975)

conducted in 1968 by the American Association of Advertising Agencies and Harvard University, 1,536 participants, representing a national sample, were equipped with counters and asked to register every advertisement they saw. Each person enlisted for half a day. The number of exposures per person fell more often into the 11-20 category than into any other, which indicates that the respondents' perceptual screens were very effective indeed.[1]

I mention these findings not to suggest that advertising is ineffective or impotent, but to point out the terrific competition for the consumer's attention. The reader is, so to speak, shopping for information, and he is aware of much product publicity that he hears and sees. But he fully absorbs or perceives only the portion that interests him. These research findings on attention help define the nature of advertising's very special and *restricted* ability to persuade.

In view of this limitation, it may be useful to discuss what can be expected of advertising — that is, what processes produce what effects. It may also help to spell out the differences in impact among one, two, and multiple exposures to an ad. Finally, it may be helpful to show how to use industry figures to avoid use of too little or too much advertising.

WHAT MAKES A SUCCESSFUL AD?

There seem to be three ingredients of successful advertising: information, rational stimulus, and emphasis. Few ads boast all three, but a good ad possesses at least one skillfully treated characteristic.

1. Information is the simplest ingredient. If your message contains news-such as the discovery of gold in California or a cure for cancer in spinach — the advertising skills brought to bear on it are not critical to the ad's success. The agency that first reported the American Dental Association's endorsement of Crest toothpaste had a rather easy job in producing an effective ad because the nature of the information almost guaranteed success. This is not a common phenomenon, but manufacturers of new products hope that their brainchildren will be accorded similar receptions.

2 Rational stimulus is the ingredient that provokes the consumer to evaluate, judge, and reach a decision. This response obviously is most common when the consumer happens to need or want the product or service in question. Involvement with the message is a prelude to, a substitute for, or a supplement to contacts with salesmen and stores. This rational process usually characterizes the reaction to ads for more expensive products and services; in such cases, an unwise purchase will haunt the shopper longer than if he had made a mistake buying a can of peas.

3 With the third ingredient, emphasis, the matter becomes more complex. Emphasis is particularly important in connection with less expensive products, products of relatively little importance to the consumer, and products with few differences among the brands represented. Consequently, the consumer is less interested in the advertising and is more likely to screen it out. The advertiser in

such cases is more likely to emphasize a single theme or one aspect of the product. Also, he repeats frequently to gain attention and make his message familiar to the public. This, the most difficult type of advertising, seems to be the most appropriate for television and its so-called captive audience. In addition it contributes the most irritating and the most entertaining commercials of all.

It also, however, receives the most criticism from citizens concerned with taste. The amount of advertising and media effort in comparison with the seemingly modest increments in brand preference seems disproportionate to many observers, who charge that the effort is wasteful. Or, at the other extreme, they claim that the endless repetition of simple themes produces in consumers a witless compulsion to go out and snatch up the product — whether they need it or not.

The fact is, however, that inexpensive and, what seem to some, trivial products also have to be purchased. For many people such products do not merit enough concern to require involved comparison shopping; rather, consumers put them with little reflection into their shopping carts. The advertiser, who cannot hold a long discourse with the shopper when his ad is seen or heard, can only hope that a residual effect will still be operating at the time of purchase. In short, advertising by emphasis aims for small, delayed effects, points that stick in the mind long enough to tip the scales in favor of Brand A over Brand B.

The exaggerated power that some critics attribute to repetitive advertising is based on an assumption that the consumer is being manipulated against his will by the message and "programmed" to buy the product immediately. It is not generally recognized that the advertising is designed primarily to produce an effect that persists after perceptual screening and forgetfulness have taken their toll. Most advertising has the modest goal of capturing attention and maintaining awareness; outright persuasion is a secondary consideration.

HOW MUCH ADVERTISING IS ENOUGH?

We spend a lot of money on repetitive advertising. Some experts explain this by noting that recall of an ad drops without constant reinforcement. Others note that members of the audience are not always in the market for the advertised product, but when they are, the advertising must *be there.* There's no choice but to advertise frequently.

I want to argue against single-exposure potency and also against much-repeated exposures. It is important to understand how communication works and how people learn, and before we can gain understanding, we have to examine the differences among the first, second, and third exposures. I stop at three because, as you shall see, psychologically there is no such thing as a fourth exposure; rather, fours, fives, and so on are repeats of the third exposure effect.

The importance of just two or three exposures, compared to a much larger number, is attested to by a variety of converging research findings based on different research methods (see Chapter 16 above).

The first exposure is by definition unique. As with the initial exposure to anything, a "What is it?" type of cognitive response dominates the reaction — that is, the audience tries to understand the nature of the stimulus. Anything novel, however unattractive it may be on second exposure, elicits some response the first time, even if it is only the mental classification required to discard the object as of no further interest.

The second exposure to a stimulus, if it is not blocked out, produces several effects. One may be the cognitive reaction that characterized the first exposure, if the audience missed much of the message the first time around. (This is most likely if the medium is radio or television, where the tape or film cannot be rewound or reversed.) More often, an evaluative "What of it?" response replaces the "What is it?" response; appreciating the nature of the new information, the consumer wonders whether it has relevance to him. If he absorbs the ad during the first exposure and finds it interesting, some of the "What of it?" response may take place then.

Another element of the second exposure, and unique to it, is the recognition response. "Aha, I've seen this before!" Such recognition permits the viewer or listener to pick up where he left off, without the necessity of repeating the cognitive step ("What is it?"). So the second exposure prompts an evaluation and, consequently the "sale" occurs. This "What of it?" response completes the basic reaction to the ad or commercial.

By this time the consumer is familiar with the message, and the third exposure constitutes a reminder, if a decision to buy based on the evaluations has not been acted on. The third exposure is also the beginning of disengagement and withdrawal of attention from a completed episode.

This pattern holds true, I suggest, for any multiple exposure. Most people filter or screen out TV commercials, for example, by stopping at the "What is it?" response. But these same people, suddenly in the market months later for the product in question, may see and experience the twenty-third exposure to the commercial as if it were the second — that is, the twenty-third exposure will be only the second time it really commands their attention.

Then the viewer is ready to absorb the message pared to a much larger number, is attested to by and evaluate it in terms of his or her needs. The twenty-fifth exposure, if not the twenty-fourth, will finish the sequence; subsequent exposures will arouse no further reaction. The viewer may still react to the commercial as entertainment or as an irritant, and while such a reaction may affect attitudes toward the advertiser, the industry, and the medium, these attitudes are probably irrelevant insofar as the response to the commercial message is concerned.

INDUSTRY MYTHS ABOUT MEMORY

Many people in and out of the advertising business, in looking at the enormous TV budgets and repeat scatter plans, assume that the agencies have evidence that consumers react slowly and gradually to commercials. That conclusion has made TV appear monolithic and successful on the basis of sheer mass and grinding momentum. To critics, it has made huge budgets seem especially advantageous and "unfair." Advertisers and their agencies, in using the television medium, have misused two common words in the English language, "remembering" and "forgetting."

There is a myth in the advertising world to the effect that viewers will forget your message if you don't repeat your pitch often. That myth supports large advertising expenditures and raises embarrassing and, to some extent, needless questions about unfair market dominance.

The myth is based primarily on the erosion of recall scores. Yet the inability to recall an ad or its message does not mean that the reader, viewer, or listener has forgotten it or erased it from memory. The acid test of forgetting is whether you no longer recognize the object. Few TV commercials seen at night can be remembered the next day. According to Gallup's prime-time survey, only 12% ran recall the average commercial.

But at General Electric we have shown photoscripts of TV commercials weeks after exposure and obtained a 50% recognition response. In my opinion, the public comes closer to forgetting *nothing* it has seen on TV. People just "put it out of their minds" until and unless it has some use. And then one day, "Aha!" — the image of the product springs to life again and the response to the commercial continues.

I am not critical of large TV budgets that provide many exposures. I am critical when the advertising industry misconstrues the power of those large budgets. The large budget is often a worthwhile expense because it gives an advertiser the power to be constantly heard — and this is necessary since he never knows when the customer will be looking for his product. But the customer's reaction is independent, rapid, and decisive. Furthermore, while the customer may make up his or her mind more than once during a campaign, it occurs most frequently at some point in the second — or let's say psychologically second — exposure to the commercial.

HOW TO DETERMINE THE BEST EXPOSURE LEVEL

When evaluating proposed advertising budgets and media schedules, an advertiser can try to ascertain the optimal exposure level for a product, brand, and target audience. At the least, one should be able to recognize in each schedule what portion of the frequency distribution is inadequate and what portion is probably excessive — that is, wasteful and possibly irritating.

The relevant data are well illustrated in Telmar reports or in similar reports from Interactive Market Systems, Inc. Access to such information in a timesharing computer service is included in an agency's or advertiser's contract with Simmons or TGI. Reports such as those shown here cost from $12 to $15 each. The type of report I shall discuss is based on the Beta Function Program; this

Exhibit 1

Sample report showing frequency distribution of exposures

Target audience
Media schedule
U.S. population base (000)
Gross Impressions (000)

NET Insertion level	% REACH Reach %	People	AVERAGE FREQUENCY Cume %	People
0				
1				
2				

program and the Metheringham formula are the two most widely used tools for estimating reach and frequency. For any given media schedule and target audience, the program provides a distribution of frequency of exposures as well as total impressions and reach.

Exhibit 1 is a skeletonized version of what is included in the program. First we have the target audience. This might be, for example, heads of households with incomes of $15,000 or more. Then there is the media schedule, the specific vehicles used and the number of insertions. For example, this schedule might include two insertions in *Reader's Digest,* two in TV *Guide,* three in *Harper's-Atlantic,* four in *McCall's,* five in *Argosy*, and six in *Seventeen.* Next, there is the population base, in thousands. Gross impressions are also stated in thousands. The reach is estimated to be 73%, or 9,483 divided by the target base in the U.S. population (13,023). Thus 73% of the target audience is considered to have been exposed to the advertisement at least once. The average frequency of exposure in this case is high, 2.80.

The most important information is in the three columns at the bottom,

Exhibit 2

Adults HH 115+
              1 TVG   1 17

Base: 30422

	Impressions		CPMG	
Gross	9707		0.00	

	%	Reach	CPMN	Avg. Freq.
Net	30.99	9429	0.00	1.03

Insertion Level	Reach %	People	Cume %	People
0	69.01	20993	100.00	30422
1	30.08	9150	30.99	9429
2	0.92	279	0.92	279

Exhibit 3					
Women					
	2 M C	2 17			
Base:		68386			
		Impressions		CPMG	
Gross		35274		0.00	
		%	Reach	CPMN	Avg. Freq.
Net		31.93	21385	0.00	1.62
Insertion		Reach		Cume	
Level		%	People	%	People
0		68.07	46551	100.00	68386
1		14.57	9966	31.93	21385
2		15.56	10641	17.36	11869
3		1.29	885	1.80	1228
4		0.50	343	0.50	343

which show (a) the number of exposures; (b) the frequency distribution, or the number of people reached *exactly* N times; and (c) the cumulative frequency distribution, or the people reached *at least* N times.

Now let's look at some actual cases, two small media schedules and then two larger ones. In *Exhibit 2* we have a target of adult heads of households with incomes of $15,000 plus. The schedule consists of only one insertion in TV Guide and one in Seventeen magazine. About 31% of the target audience is exposed at least once, while almost nobody is exposed twice (1% of the target group). This small schedule is popular because it achieves 30% reach — almost one third of the target audience. I question, however, the value of one exposure; schedules as small as this are possibly a waste of money.

The next schedule (Exhibit 3), aimed at women, calls for two insertions in *McCall's* and two in *Seventeen*. This schedule is clearly more effective than the first. While the reach is the same, the average frequency is significantly higher, and 16% of the audience is exposed twice.

The next schedule (Exhibit 4) is targeted for adult heads of households with incomes of at least $15,000. It lists two insertions in *Reader's Digest,* two in *TV Guide*, three in *Harper's-Atlantic,* four in *McCall's,* five in *Argosy,* and six in *Seventeen.* The reach is 75% and the average frequency, 3.4. More people are exposed twice (21%) than are exposed once (12%); 13% are exposed three times and 12% four times. It's a very solid schedule, but now, perhaps, we're beginning to overdo it a little. A few consumers have been exposed to the same message seven, eight, nine, ten, and more times.

In the last schedule (Exhibit 5), even more people are exposed ten or more times — and, mind you, I've been showing only schedules of print ads. I could show you many combined print and TV schedules where this frequency distribution gets very long indeed. In such cases the reach may be 90%. This is very gratifying; it means that nearly everyone in the target audience sees your ad at least once. But there is a price that you, we, or the advertising industry pays: every tenth U.S. citizen sees the ad more than ten times.

Adults							
	2 RD	2 TVG	3 HA	4 MC	5 ARG	6 17	
Base:		30422					
		Impressions			CPMG		
Gross		77290			0.00		
		%	Reach		CPMN	Avg. Freq.	
Net		74.73	22733		0.00	3.40	

Insertion Level	Reach %	Reach People	Cume %	Cume People
0	25.27	7689	100.00	30422
1	12.22	3717	74.73	22733
2	21.33	6488	62.51	19016
3	12.59	3830	41.18	12528
4	11.81	3592	28.59	8698
5	6.16	1875	16.78	5106
6	3.84	1169	10.62	3231
7	2.17	660	6.78	2062
8	1.34	409	4.61	1402
9	1.25	380	3.26	993
10	0.56	171	2.01	613
11	0.72	218	1.45	442
12	0.41	126	0.74	224
13	0.13	40	0.32	98
14	0.03	8	0.19	58
15	0.13	39	0.16	50
16	0.00	0	0.04	11
17	0.04	11	0.04	11

Exhibit 4

PROBLEMS OF SMALL AND LARGE ADVERTISERS

In the situations just examined, the small advertiser's problem is that he has to reach so hard for his single exposures — his "ones" — that he obtains few "twos" and "threes." He's getting less effectiveness than he thinks. On the other hand, the large advertiser is tempted to try to get everybody — that is, 100% reach. This is almost possible and is tempting when you already have 91% or 92%. If the advertiser gives in to this temptation, he inevitably subjects some of the audience to excessive exposure. So the advertiser also obtains excessive effects; he gets not just attention for his product and his advertising, but attention to the fact that the advertising is excessive. The consumer's reaction is "What do they think I am, a moron?"

The problem becomes complicated when the small advertiser, observing the large one, decides that he too wants a high reach. But with a high-reach, low-frequency schedule, he loses impact. If he stepped up his one-exposure reach and made two exposures his practice, he might double his returns. At any rate, he should find out what he is buying and obtain a report on each proposed schedule.

What the large advertiser loses with a high-reach emphasis is more difficult to say. By irritating consumers, he may be substituting a public relations problem for a sales problem. He may even give the advertising industry, his own industry, and the media a bad name. But apart from that possibility, he may be

Total Adults						
	4 R D	4 T V G	4 H A	4 M C	4 A R G	4 17
Base:		130326				
		Impressions			CPMG	
Gross		425938			0.00	
		%	Reach		CPMN	Avg. Freq.
Net		74.73	22733		0.00	3.40

Exhibit 5

Insertion Level	Reach %	People	Cume %	People
0	25.31	32987	100.00	130326
1	10.95	14266	74.69	97339
2	9.76	12721	63.74	83073
3	9.00	11727	53.98	70352
4	15.30	19939	44.98	58625
5	7.90	10301	29.68	38686
6	6.18	8060	21.78	28385
7	5.62	7323	15.60	20325
8	4.72	6146	9.98	13002
9	2.04	2655	5.26	6856
10	1.20	1558	3.22	4201
11	0.90	1177	2.03	2643
12	0.72	944	1.12	1466
13	0.22	282	0.40	522
14	0.08	106	0.18	240
15	0.06	78	0.10	134
16	0.02	31	0.04	56
17	0.01	13	0.02	25
18	0.00	0	0.01	12
19	0.00	0	0.01	12
20	0.01	12	0.01	12

indulging in a different kind of sin by paying for more than he needs. Does he really need a schedule in which half the exposures are reasonable — say, 50% of the target group is exposed up to five times — while the other half is exposed up to 20 times?

WHAT IS THE EFFECTIVE BANDWIDTH?

There is a well-known story about the man who knew that half his advertising was good and half was bad, but he didn't know which was which. I suggest that the bad half is a combination of too little and too much, and the effective middle range involves a bandwidth that is determinable through research. The lower limit of the bandwidth is dearly two exposures. The upper limit must be determined by tracking the target audience during a typical campaign to see when the upward slope of message recognition levels off.

You can start with a bandwidth objective on a judgment basis — one to be modified by research. Once, for example, I suggested to the advertising managers in a GE component that they start with the objective of exposing two thirds of their target group to at least two and no more than four exposures per month. While such an objective probably cannot be reached, it can be approached; and setting it can sharply differentiate some proposed schedules from others. The process clearly calls for a closer look at schedules, instead of leaving everything up to the agency.

NOT TOO MUCH, NOT TOO LITTLE

The effects of advertising on an individual are modest, but they are powerful in the mass and over time. Like erosion caused by shifting tides, little change occurs at any one moment, even though clear-cut effects appear eventually.

Good advertising gets attention, and its message lasts long enough through a few exposures to make one or two points. Optimally, these exposures should reach the target audience with an effective balance of a few exposures to most persons in the audience, rather than one exposure to many and many exposures to a few. Spillover exposures to nontarget audiences should be minimal. Ideally, the target audience should be exposed when it is in the market or during known shopping periods.

Advertising management needs precise information about audience attention and about patterns of reading, viewing, and shopping. But it is not enough to have great ads and fine media vehicles in which to place them; a good plan based on research is essential. Moreover, as in other areas of management, the numbers must be scrutinized with care.

---

[1] Raymond A. Bauer and Stephen A. Greyser, *Advertising in America: The Consumer View* (Boston: Division of Research, Harvard Business School, 1968), p. 178.

CHAPTER 19

MEMORY WITHOUT RECALL,
EXPOSURE WITHOUT PERCEPTION

I n each of two recent talks, to the AMA Attitude Research Conference in Las Vegas and to the ANA Media Workshop in New York, I pointed out the limitations of recall as an indicator of memory and tried to reposition the concept of perception. In Las Vegas I reviewed the implications of the new brain research on the theory of low involvement, in New York I reinterpreted some earlier data which suggested that three advertising exposures represented an optimal frequency. That two so different talks converged on a common focus suggests that there may be some value in looking at them together.

HIGH AND LOW INVOLVEMENT:
THE TWO BRAINS

In 1965 I had rejected what I thought was an overemphasis on the importance of attitude when I suggested that television advertising typically produced changes in behavior prior to changes in attitude, and that in-store purchasing triggered an accumulated potential for a shift in the salience of perceived attributes of an advertised object (Chapter 6 above). By contrast, it was typically in response to the print medium that one could expect to find in operation the more familiar model of AIETA (awareness–interest–evaluation–trial–adoption) or other hierarchy models — i.e., the classic "think before you act" rational approach to decision making revered in the schoolroom.

Low-involvement theory seemed to challenge the rule of reason and to confirm the idiocy of the so-called "boob tube" and perhaps even of advertising. Such fears were unreasonable, but the unknown is threatening. How can people learn without reasoning? When do insights occur apart from what we call thought or thinking? How much of behavior therapy, the encounter movement, Zen, ESP, and the new religions does make significant sense? What does this apparent downgrading of reason mean?

To me a psychologist is first a biologist. I have always looked to the physiological side of attention and learning for clues as to what was really hap-

Original Publication: *Journal of Advertising Research,* Vol. 17, No. 4 (August 1977), pp. 7-12

pening. For many years I maintained contact with Dr. Norman Mackworth of the Stanford Medical Institute, used his Optiscan device, and developed some views about the moving or actively scanning eye, the "working eye" (or brain) characteristic of reading, and the relatively motionless, focused, or passive eye characteristic of TV viewing (see Chapter 9 above). Now recently, Dr. Roger Sperry of the California Institute of Technology has begun to startle the world with his findings concerning the independence and separately specialized function of the right and left hemispheres of the brain.[1] Dr. Sperry arrived at this conclusion after examining 56 cases in which the *corpus callosum* connecting the two hemispheres had been surgically severed, most typically in an attempt to reduce the frequency and severity of seizures of epileptic patients. Sperry found that there was no readily apparent abnormality in behavior of these 56 individuals with separated hemispheres. How could that be, except if the hemispheres were largely independent in the first place?

With further research it became clear that reading and speaking are left-brain functions, while the perception of images is a right-brain function. Therefore, the medium of print is a left-brain function and TV largely or relatively a right-brain function. I would add that high involvement is more a left-brain activity and low involvement a right-brain activity; that gross eye movements activate left-brain activity, and that a motionless, focused eye tends to bring in right-brain activity. It is with these physiological views that I go on to matters of individual psychology and, specifically, to some questions about television and children.

It is no news that TV is a good and early baby sitter. It more likely replaces parenting behavior in large families than in small, in low-income families than in high. I refer here, for example, to the work of Clarke[2] and Zajonc.[3] Television teaches the young child to "learn to learn" in a very special manner to some extent before he can talk and, in many low socioeconomic status (SES) families or semiliterate societies, before he has ever looked at a book. So the child learns to learn by quick looks. Later, if the child is in a society where reading is required, he confronts the new "learn to learn" medium with the habit he has picked up earlier from TV. He tries to comprehend print via quick looks. It doesn't work. Learning to read is difficult, hard — and this comes as a surprise, an intolerable one in many cases. Years later, remedial reading may make up some of the lost ground. Meanwhile, there is a possibility that along with the lessened stimulation of reading behavior may go lessened stimulation of the left brain's capacities for abstract thought. In the smaller upper SES families where the book and reading are valued, the child may more likely be introduced to the book coincidentally with television and the latter may be rationed or even censored.

I suspect that the classes are moving apart psychologically and culturally. Even if incomes were mandated to be equal, the left-brain people and the right-brain people have different communication patterns. We may, therefore, split into two cultures, two increasingly separate societies. The Media Imperatives Study by the Simmons Company suggests that this is already happening. Going beyond the simple generalization that "everybody watches TV," they classified survey respondents into those whose print exposure was relatively high versus television, and those whose TV exposure was relatively high versus print. The SES differences were enormous. The advertising media implication is that to efficiently reach the High SES purchasers you should use print. Of course, once you reach them, you may still have a problem of what to do with them, and many advertisers are experimenting with new print formats, trying somehow to capture the kind of impact usually associated with television.

In considering communication behavior these days, it's all right to talk about differences in SES or in media habits, while it's not all right to talk about differences in intelligence. Aptitude tests are out of fashion and the concept of the IQ is under political attack. Nevertheless, the inventors of the IQ or of the standard intelligence tests, the Binet for children and the Wechsler for adults, took pains to include among the subtests that comprised their procedure the so-called verbal and performance tests. In the Wechsler, the overall IQ is an average of the verbal and performance subscores, giving them equal weight. There is in our society, however, a bias in favor of the verbal, in favor of the left brain, in favor of "thinking before you leap," even in favor of the idea that, except in the case of true (and mysterious) "genius," great scientific insights come as a conclusion to step-by-step research or reasoning. Our model of AIETA and other hierarchy-of-attitude models is this left-brain, verbal, "look before you leap," reasonable, or "rational" model. With a biological base, and acknowledging individual differences, it is not reasonable to ask if this model is valid. It is reasonable to ask for whom it is valid or perhaps when. Meanwhile, the newer behavior-before-attitude models redress an imbalance, an old bias, and are perhaps more appropriate for individuals of the newer generations, including the preliterate societies of the developing countries where TV will surely arrive long before the emergence of a mass print medium.

There is, then, no question of attitude-before-behavior theories versus behavior-before-attitude theories, just as there is no question of verbal versus performance skills on the Wechsler, or a left versus a right brain. There are two of everything, and an individual may avail himself of each. The challenge remains, however, that we "left-brain types" don't understand the right brain too well — the nonverbal skills, art, creativity (or at least the right-brain aspects of it). The future of low-involvement theory is in this nonverbal area.

The theory of low involvement asserts that repetition of exposure has an effect which is not readily apparent until a behavioral trigger comes along. Even then, the immediate effect is only a subtle restructuring of what was there all along — *i.e.*, a shift in salience. Now let us go back to the "not readily apparent effect" produced at the time of exposure. Just what is this effect? Is it what some people call "sheer exposure," and if so, what is that? What seems to happen is that we store a picture memory, an image memory, without words. There is no recall because recall is the word form of the picture. There is no recall because we have had only right-brain involvement. There is no left-brain involvement because no connections, associations, or thoughts occurred at the time of exposure. There is only a capacity — or an increased capacity, if repetition occurred — for recognition memory. An example of this process is the study by Roger Shepard, who had his subjects view 612 different pictures at their own pace, averaging six seconds per picture. Shortly thereafter they were shown 68 pairs of pictures, each pair consisting of one from the original series and one new picture. The pictures from the original series were identified with 98.5 percent accuracy. In another test with a one-week delay, accuracy was 90 percent.[4]

Advertising researchers have argued about the relative merits of using recognition or recall as measures of advertising effect. Because the criterion of recognition is much more easily achieved than that of recall, it has been criticized as being less sensitive. Underlying this "technical" controversy, however, is the fact that the use of recognition justifies modest advertising expenditures, while the use of recall justifies far larger expenditures. I would reposition the recognition versus recall problem with this proposed addition to the theory of involvement — *i.e.*, the nature of effective impact of communication or advertising on low-involvement topics, objects, or products consists of the building or strengthening of picture-image memory potential. Such potential is properly measured by recognition, not by recall. The use of recall obscures or hides already existing impact. The use of recall may be justified by advertisers who don't mind paying for a strategy that may include some "overkill." However, the use of recall obscures noncommercial cultural effects of the medium, especially television.

In contrast to the above, the proper measure of high-involvement impact is indeed recall along with clear verbalizing and correct perception of the stimulus. In this connection it is interesting that our tradition of research in public opinion has been heavily invested in reporting public reaction to the news, initially newspaper news. The news is very factual stuff, left-brain stuff. The continuous and very prominent reporting of public reaction to news probably over-represents the extent of that reaction, while the cultural impact of "right-brain" television, though presumed to be enormous, is difficult to demonstrate.

After World War I social scientists, led particularly by Harold Lasswell, had to work very hard to debunk the idea that propaganda via the mass media could enslave the public mind.[5] In a somewhat similar vein, the residual effects of Paul Lazarsfeld's work on personal influence[6] and Joe Klapper's review of the effects of mass media,[7] reassured us that the power of mass media had been overrated. But Klapper's review cited a bibliography of 272 studies, half of which had been published in 1950 or earlier, when television ownership in the United States was nil. The first TV-raised generation of Americans didn't face their TV sets until the end of the fifties. Ought we to have been so reassured? Have we not missed the massive cultural impact of television for simply having lacked the intellectual and methodological tools?

To develop those tools, to further our study of learning without involvement or of behavioral change without prior attitude change, we may have to study memory without recall. This is the right-brain form of learning. This is the area of the overlooked cultural impact of the mass media. This is the place where public opinion research techniques will have to be supplemented by a new generation of research methodology.

EXPOSURE OR PERCEPTION?

In an issue of this *Journal* I proposed a theory of advertising effectiveness oriented to the finding, from a variety of studies, that about three exposures were optimal (see Chapter 16 above). 1 characterized the first exposure as dominated by a cognitive "what is it?" type of response, the second exposure dominated by a more personally evaluative "what of it?" type of response, and the third exposure as both a reminder and also the beginning of disengagement.

Since that time, the application of the theory to media scheduling has run into the question of what is an exposure and, sometimes, what I meant as an exposure. Jack Hill of Ogilvy & Mather, in a February 1975 address to an ANA Television Workshop, decided that I meant that the respondent must at least perceive the commercial to have been considered "exposed." He then raised the question of what frequency of advertising is required to produce the desired frequency of perceptions. In January 1976 Walter Staab of SFM Media Service Corporation in an article in *Advertising Age* raised the same question, decided that I meant only sheer exposure when I said exposure, and cautioned that actual perception of the ad would be the more appropriate objective of scheduling and that this would require higher frequency of scheduled advertising.

Although Jack Hill decided that I meant perception and Walter Staab decided that I really meant exposure — or what the British call "opportunities to see" — the research on which the three-exposure theory was built does not favor one or the other. I had cited eye-movement data from my own research, and this involved forced exposure and, if you will, forced perception. In addition I cited CONPAAD data from Bob Grass of DuPont, also involving forced exposures. However, the most comprehensive body of data came from Colin MacDonald of the British Market Research Bureau. His were field survey data, using a panel design and based on opportunities to see, and no forced anything. The MacDonald research could suggest that sheer exposure (*i.e.*, without proven perception) is just as adequate an object of the three-exposure theory as is actual perception. Nevertheless, Hill and Staab and others assume "reasonably" that some perception is required, and they periodically ask how much frequency of sheer exposure is required to create perception.

To really get at this problem we need a better understanding of the terms *exposure* and *perception.* It might be helpful to first look at two related concepts to *look* and to *see.* These two variables permit a fourfold classification — *i.e.,* one can look *and* see, look but *not* see, neither look *nor* see, and, perhaps surprisingly, see *without* looking. The key is in the definition of *looking,* which sensory psychologists like Norman Mackworth call "direction of gaze." To the layman the equivalent concept is that *looking* means "looking at," that the head and open eyes are aimed at the object in question. But "looking at" does not guarantee seeing because the mind may be elsewhere — *i.e.,* one may not pay attention to what one is looking at. But what about seeing without looking? This involves the two phenomena of (a) peripheral vision and (b) conscious vision.

In the service, I used to think of peripheral vision as something that involved only the extreme right and left sensitivities of the eye. I was aware of the special training in night vision given to lookouts and sentries, based on the differential dark adaptation patterns of the extreme left and right sectors of the retina. It came as a shock to realize later that "looking at" an object or "fixating" on a particular stimulus can only be accomplished within a three-degree arc. Everything else is peripheral. Most of your vision is peripheral. As you walk down a street or drive down a road your direction of gaze and your focus of attention may be on a few items of special interest, but your total orientation to the scene is accomplished primarily by peripheral vision. This peripheral vision permits you to see without paying particular attention to what is seen. You're not especially conscious of that which is peripherally seen. You don't know that you have seen. Later you may even deny having seen. Much of what people call subliminal perception is merely peripheral seeing — *i.e.,* seeing without "looking at" and without being aware that seeing has occurred. It's just part of the selective process — *i.e.,* of all that there is available to see you decide what you should look at and what merits your attention. This kind of seeing can occur very quickly, under one tenth of a second, whereas to see, and to know that you have seen (a two-step operation), is usually a much slower phenomenon, occurring not faster than one-tenth of a second.

At this point, recall for a moment that the national averages for all full-page four-color Starched ads studied each year and year after year tell us that 50 percent of such ads are noticed, but only 10 percent are read. Many tend to assume "reasonably" that the 50 percent not noticed are not seen. That's a very leaky assumption. At the same time it's exceedingly difficult to say what percent of ads are seen since some of the seeing occurs quickly and without awareness. Consequently, conclusions about amount of exposure based on perception will always underestimate exposure.

The fact that Colin MacDonald's data on opportunities to see produce similar findings to the laboratory work of Bob Grass and to my own work seems to mean two things:

(1) first, generally, that most advertising is familiar and somewhat in the expected pattern or style for commercial products and brands. Here, the inference is that it only takes a very quick look, in most cases, to effectively get the message.

(2) second, and more specifically, that recall and attitude effects are not necessary for advertising to do its job of aiding in-store purchasing. I had proposed a theory of low involvement with advertising which suggested that faint impressions could build up into an in-store-triggered purchase — with very little trace of the advertising effect prior to that purchase. And this may include very little evidence of advertising perception prior to the purchase.

I conclude that quick and/or faint perceptions of product advertising, even unremembered, do their job in most cases and that the "actual" exposures are closer to the media-scheduled exposures than we give the media credit for. What does this say about the nature of advertising? Again, let's take the Starch ad norms as an example. Year after year Starch reports that the average noting for ads surveyed that year is about 50 percent, but that the average read most is about 10 percent. Remember that noting is simply a verified "yes, I looked at that ad." Now where do you want to position advertising? Do you want to say half of all ads are looked at, or do you want to say that 9 out of 10 are not read? What do you think the advertising process is all about? I suggest that ads are meant to be looked at, to communicate as quick as a wink, that 50-percent "noting" probably translates into something over 75-percent actual exposure. If an ad has to be "read most," or read slowly, then it's not really what we're talking about. The real ad is what's to look at. The example of television is even more striking. You don't even have to know how to read these, and commercials can get shorter and shorter and still do a job for the advertisers. As a practical matter and for immediate purposes, one need not perhaps be too concerned about whether or not exposure can be proven to have taken place. More and more, as an advertiser, I'm willing to assume it.

As a researcher, however, I do have a long-range interest in better measurement of exposure and have to take a different tack. I have to amplify still further my earlier statement that amount of advertising exposure based on perception will always underestimate exposure, to say more specifically that conclusions about amount of exposure based on recall data will greatly underestimate exposure, that conclusions about amount of exposure based on recognition data will somewhat underestimate exposure, and that sensitive tests of exposure are currently not in much use. A true test to pick up brief but valuable and often the most frequent type of exposure would force the recognition process to the extreme. Such tests may be laborious or difficult to administer, but the principle behind the suggestion is that advertising tests must "test the limits" or the "full range of effects." The easy-to-collect evidence of blatant exposure to advertising must be paralleled by the hard-to-collect evidence of brief exposure, otherwise the advertiser is not getting the full picture and is being shortchanged — especially if the bulk of his advertising does most of its effective work on the basis of brief exposures. So the practical assumption for the advertiser may be to assume exposure until that day when research can describe for him the full range of exposure.

I recently received a long-awaited copy of a paper by the eminent Donald Broadbent of the Department of Experimental Psychology at Oxford University.[8] In his paper Broadbent cites research to support the view that the perceptual system operates in a hierarchical fashion — *i.e.*, the eye (or mind) in selecting from the environment what it will attend to must reject a great deal in order to select what it will accept. This process of rejection is an active rather than a passive process, says Broadbent. Thus, to some small but measurable degree, one must note, perceive, or identify what one will not attend to in order to reject it. I suggest that this "pre-attentive process" leaves some trace of the rejected material, certainly not enough to be recalled, but perhaps enough, with repetition of the process and repeated rejections, to be recognized later on.

I'd like to amplify my previous comment about research to "describe the full range of exposure" with these conclusions. The main unresolved tasks for advertising research in this area are threefold:

(1) to explore more fully the unknown territory between what we now call perception and nonperception. The "make-believe" hard line between these two is contrary to nature. Perception is not an all-or-none matter.

(2) to explore the unknown territory between what we now call attention and nonattention. The selective process of attention involves more levels of attention than we like to admit.

(3) to get smarter about what lies between what we now call exposed and nonexposed. We may have to learn how to think more in terms of giving credit for partial exposure, for a half-exposure, for a quarter-exposure, and so on. These values also build up with repetition, just as do full exposures.

In general, let's not shortchange the remarkably sensitive capacities of the human eye and brain, and let's not shortchange the advertiser.

OVERVIEW

In my first paper it was the unexplored domain of the right-brain picture or image-sensitive function that compelled a focus on recognition measures as a test of nonverbal, nonrecallable memories. In my second paper it was the peripheral processes of selective attention, including Broadbent's active "pre-attentive processes," that compelled a focus on recognition types of measures. It is tempting to conclude that it is the right brain's picture-taking ability that permits the rapid screening of the environment — to select what it is that the left brain should focus attention on.

[1] Sperry, R.W., "Lateral Specialization of Cerebral Function in the Surgically Separated Hemispheres," in F.J. McGuigan and R.A. Schoonover (eds.), *The Psychophysiology of Thinking* (New York: Academic Press, 1973), pp. 209-229.

[2] Clarke, P., "Parental Socialization Values and Children's Newspaper Reading," *Journalism Quarterly,* vol. 42 (1965), pp. 539-546.

[3] Zajonc, R.B., "Birth Order and Intellectual Development," *Economic Outlook U.S.A.,* vol. 3, no. 4 (1976), pp. 62-63.

[4] Shepard, R.N., "Recognition Memory for Words, Sentences, and Pictures," *J. Verb. Learn. Verb. Behav.,* vol. 6 (1967), pp. 156-163.

[5] Lasswell, H., Smith, B. and Casey, R., *Propaganda, Communication and Public Opinion: A Comprehensive Reference Guide* (Princeton: Princeton University Press, 1946).

[6] Katz E., and Lazarsfeld, P., *Personal Influence* (Glencoe, Ill.: The Free Press, 1955).

[7] Klapper, J.T., *The Effects of Mass Communications* (Glencoe, Ill.: The Free Press, 1960).

[8] Broadbent, D., "The Hidden Pre-Attentive Processes," *American Psychologist,* vol. 32, no. 2 (1977), pp. 109-118.

CHAPTER 20

TOWARD AN IDEAL TV PRE-TEST

Although my primary "official" involvement has been with public opinion research, I have been dabbling with physiological measures for many years — searching for something that might be better than simple verbal interviewing.

Over the years my concept of "better than" underwent a number of changes. I even got used to the idea that it would keep changing. Consequently, I couldn't settle down happily with any one physiological system.

Then I got more interested in what "better than" meant or could mean, and I feel that this is more important than looking at the available physiological measures themselves.

Put another way, when I am sure *in what particular way* I want a physiological system to be better than verbal interviews, then I will simply draw up the purchase specifications and order the equipment.

Of course, that's easier said than done, for in this area of measurement equipment can be very costly, and very fancy, and very intriguing. So I don't very much want to look at it — for fear that I might adapt my needs to the equipment rather than adapting or ordering the equipment to satisfy my needs.

Well, I wouldn't be telling you all this if I wasn't beginning to feel that I did know what particular virtues I now wanted in a physiological system. But I think it's important to indicate also how I got to this point.

Essentially I had to come to terms with the nature of advertising itself, and its very special communication characteristics. These include rapid communication, based on brief or partial exposure, with low interest, little next-day recall, but nevertheless good recognition potential for what had been seen. That is, the visual images were usually retained even when there was no other (*e.g.* verbal) response to the advertising.

An important additional element to this passive portrayal is the very occasional presence of *thought*. Thoughts may involve irritation or annoyance, or more favorable and desirable forms of message involvement.

Since this is my picture of the nature of the advertising exposure, I would want to know:

Originally presented at AMA Annual Advertising Research Conference, Hotel Biltmore, New York City, May 16, 1978

- Is nothing happening? Is anything happening?
- Are the images registering but nothing else is happening?
- Are the images registering but irritating thoughts are occurring?
- Are the images registering and positive relevant thoughts are oc-curring?
- When does each of the above conditions prevail?

To answer these questions I want one or two electrodes attached to each side of the head, one or two on the left to pick up abstract activity like thinking and one or two on the right to pick up image response or imaging.

For each electrode I want a transducer to convert the full spectrum of brain wave frequencies present to a summary report on activity above and below a frequency of 12 per sec. That is, a rough differentiation between high and low activity or between Beta and Alpha.

Please note that I do not consider low activity, or a passive response bad. It's amazing how much can be communicated to passive audiences who can make use of the material even if they can't recall it unaided.

Please note too that I do not consider that the evaluation of commercials as "good" or "bad" is the primary objective of pre-testing. The primary objective of pre-testing is to find out *intimately* what happens when people are exposed to the commercial. The secondary objective is to evaluate *this* as good or bad.

Getting back now to my poor respondent sitting there with an electrode stuck on each side of his or her head. Actually the electrode is the size of a green pea and the connecting wire is as fine as silk thread. You don't even have to have a connecting wire because you can use an electrode which is also a radio transmitter and the signals can be picked up by an FM receiver thirty feet away. This has been used to study children's play activity, as well as adult football players (in the midst of a game). I want a computer read-out every few seconds of four figures, *i.e.*, the over/under 12 for the left brain and the over/under 12 for the right. It would be nice to have a live graph on a cathode tube.

Such a system will tell me about the extent of mental processing of the logical and pictorial content of the commercial as we move through it — and if there is a sharp increase in the left side Beta I will know that a thought has oc-curred, I will know when it occurred, and I will mark that content of the com-mercial down for later questioning. Like, "*What were you* thinking of when . . .?" On the other hand, if there is a sharp increase on the right side I would ask, "Tell me more about the part where . . .?" Here I will try for more detail on what the respondent saw.

So you see I still need interviewing to find out what within the commercial was most salient or critical, positive or negative, and why. But I wouldn't have asked if I didn't know *when* it happened. I *shouldn't* have asked if nothing hap-pened. And if I asked and the respondent had already forgotten, ten seconds later, I know in *what section* of the commercial something did happen and can *play it back* for reminder and comment.

Now let me comment on why I prefer to use brain data rather than such perceptual data as tachistoscopic, eye movement or pupil data on the one hand or such data on interest or arousal as PGR, heart rate, capillary dilation, voice tension, etc.

First I want to note that the memory of advertising is exceedingly poor as measured by unaided recall (*e.g.*, Gallup TPT norms of 12%) but exceedingly good as measured by recognition (*e.g.*, Starch, Krugman, Bruzzone). Put another way, respondents cannot tell you verbally what they have seen but they can acknowledge that they have or haven't seen it if you show them the ad in question. Put another way again, it is characteristic of advertising that verbal memory is poor and pictorial memory excellent. Neurophysiologists would say that the right hemisphere of the brain is more responsive to the characteristically low interest level of advertising than is the left hemisphere of the brain.

It is only recently that psychologists have begun to appreciate the enormous capacity of the brain for pictorial memory via recognition. And there is no explanation for it. This is new territory.

I quote to you from the *1978 Annual Review of Psychology*, Chapter II on "Visual Perception," by Ralph Norman Haber (p. 45):

> Four recent studies each demonstrated at least 90% recognition memory for pictures using 300, 600, 2500 and 10,000 pictures, respectively. Should we be surprised or reassured by the demonstration that one can recognize incredibly large numbers of candid photographs seen briefly once? No theory that I know of would have predicted these results, nor is any theory contradicted by them.

To me this is partially a testament to the fact that people can easily take in enormous amounts of even single advertising exposures without reacting to them in any other way except to retain them in the form of recognition memory. So in many cases, in the real world, the advertising has gotten inside the respondent but *nothing else happens*. I'd like to know more about the nothing else. Just as I'm interested in what parts of a commercial people are reacting to, I'm equally interested in what parts they're not reacting to. I particularly want to distinguish between verbal and pictorial reactions, between left- and right-brain activity — or recall potential vs. recognition potential.

Secondly, I'd like to note that this enormous capacity for intake of images means, among other things, that the relatively limited capacities of the optical perceptual system are bypassed in favor of the brain's more potent abilities. That is, the brain sees and selects faster than the eye can respond.

Psychologists used to talk about "selective perception," but in the past few years Donald Broadbent and Ann Triesman, the directors of the experimental psychology laboratories of Oxford and Cambridge respectively, have brought about a startling change in emphasis — which is now on "selective *response*." Thus, in the old days the eye was considered gatekeeper to the brain, and only admitted a small portion of what was "seen." Now we more likely think that everything is "seen" but the brain selects (very quickly) only a small portion to react to, *i.e.*, I say the right brain sees it all and selects only a little for left brain evaluation.

Ultimately, this is why I have to look to brain measures. It is here where the great capacities lie. It is here where the selection mechanisms operate. This is where the action is, and can be measured — during deepest sleep during drowsy or hypnotic states all the way up to wild excitement and even epileptic fits (the original brain "storm").

Again, getting back to my respondent stuck with two electrodes. How would I use the data? Even without later interviewing?

I have two electrodes, one for the left hemisphere, which is relatively more word, copy, slogan and theme oriented, and one for the right hemisphere, which is relatively more picture, rhythm and music oriented.

Each electrode reports the percentage of all wave frequencies over and under 12 per second, *i.e.*, Beta vs. Alpha, and this is numerically summarized for me every few seconds.

In the left hemisphere we could have high Alpha and low Beta (they tend to be inversely correlated), which to me suggests a very relaxed verbal or mnemonic activity such as memorizing, or we could have low Alpha and high Beta, which suggests thoughtful activity. Or we could have low Alpha and low Beta, which means perhaps that nothing is happening.

Simultaneously in the right hemisphere we could have high Alpha and low Beta, which suggests a very relaxed passive dwelling on the picture possibly deserving the term enjoyment. Or we could have low Alpha and high Beta, suggesting close scrutiny and examination of the picture. Or we could have low Alpha and low Beta, which again means perhaps that nothing is happening.

The two active conditions which are possible for each hemisphere provide a total of four qualitative types of response. Any one of these may be in evidence, or more, in some mix up to four.

The types of response are as follows:
1. If there is a thoughtful condition in the left brain and scrutiny in the right brain we presumably have an intellectual response with close evaluation of the stimulus.
2. If there is a thoughtful condition in the left brain and enjoyment in the right we presumably have evaluative enthusiasms such as "That's a good idea!"
3. If there is a mnemonic condition in the left brain and scrutiny in the right we presumably have a respondent taking it all in closely (and for later reaction).
4. If there is a mnemonic condition in the left brain and enjoyment in the right we presumably have a respondent singing the jingles of a commercial or responding to some other rhythmic is element.

To be sure all of this can be checked upon by later interviewing, but I did want to indicate that we are gradually learning about brain function to the point where we are no longer starting from scratch but can in fact formulate fairly specific hypotheses about qualitative response.

Once again, however, I'd like to stress the importance of when responses occur. Thus, all four of the responses above could occur at different times in the same commercial. Or nothing could occur.

I keep stressing this "nothing" because some of the most potent human responses can occur when the brain is peculiarly and/or apparently inactive. Thus, under hypnosis the brain is typically in an Alpha state though I'm not sure what the hemispheric differences are. Ditto for the almost asleep hypnogogic condition that various experimenters have used for studies of so-called "sleep learning." And what about the drowsy TV viewer propped up in bed after a long, hard day? I don't know — yet.

One point may be coming though in this ideal approach to measuring TV response, and that is that there is an awful lot of data which can be produced. What is the proposed strategy for handling *that* problem?

My particular personal bias is to concentrate on the single case, the single respondent, the sample of one. With Dr. Sidney Weinstein's help and the excellent facilities of his laboratory, this is what I've been doing in recent years. My attitude now is that when the researcher thoroughly and intimately understands the full response of one respondent to a TV commercial, if ever, then he might be daring enough to move on and try a second respondent.

Thus, the essential tactic is linked to the single case, the neglected tactic in advertising research. For fifty years and more the conventional wisdom in our research has been to learn a little about a lot of people. I suggest to you that to fully understand media qualities and the nature of advertising response it is time we learned "how to learn" about a single human unit or organism. After all, the tactic has proven quite successful, almost ideal, in medicine and in the physical sciences. So why not give it a try in advertising research?

CHAPTER 21

THE TWO BRAINS:
NEW EVIDENCE ON TV IMPACT

It is only recently that psychologists have begun to appreciate the enormous capacity of the human brain for the retention of pictures and images. Whereas relatively few images can be freely recalled, in comparison — and this is a very important point — a vast number can be correctly recognized.

Images are not especially amenable to conventional interviewing techniques because they are in the right hemisphere of the brain, which is, so to speak, silent. Words and speech, those things that are easier to obtain in interviews, are stored in the left hemisphere of the brain.

To ascertain the respondent's reactions, tiny electrodes are placed on three locations on the back of the head. Fine wires lead from the electrodes to the recording apparatus. The wires are so fine the subject is not aware of them while the test is under way.

Much response to advertising is right-brain, and I'd like to discuss what kinds of advertising evoke right-brain response. As an illustration I'll use some preliminary findings of research into brain hemisphere response to General Electric's "Thomas Edison" television commercials.

- All of the Edison commercials open with print superimposed — the name Thomas Edison and the calendar year. In our data, this addition of print supers always splits the audience. That is, among our cases, each individual reacts to the print with one brain hemisphere, or to the character Edison with the other brain hemisphere. I won't say this is good or bad, but I will say that different consumers react to different aspects of a commercial. In this way, the same commercial is seen by some people, read by others, heard by some as words, heard by others as auditory images.
- Some of the Edison commercials end with video alone, but we have one that adds voice-over. In our data, the voice-over diminishes the intensity of response. I won't say that this either is good or bad, but I doubt that the addition of voice-over was intended to diminish response.
- Response to so-called "print" was something of a surprise. The superimposed print on video, and the final logo itself without the voice-over, get a

Original Publication: Broadcasting Magazine "Monday Memo," January 29, 1979 right-brain response. But the words are not read; they are looked at. It is a word picture that is involved. The spoken names of unknown people are also pictured, for examination, by a right-brain response. While the spoken names of unknown people get a right-brain response, familiar names, with attendant associations, would more likely get a left-brain response.

- The right brain looks at things, dwells on them, inspects them and it all registers in a rather leisurely pattern until an idea creates a thought — which, relatively, is lighting fast. For example, there was a left-brain startled reaction to Edison's mention of his deafness, which could set off much respondent speculation. It is the idea of deafness and not a picture that is responsible for the left-brain response.

- In some of the commercials Edison told stories that created right-brain response only. Notice the vivid pictures which the story teller evokes:

  "The big test came at Niagara Falls in 1894. GE built a transformer and strung a line to Buffalo 26 miles away. The switch was thrown in Niagara. The lights came on in Buffalo' "

  "Alexanderson developed the equipment that made it possible to send a voice signal . . . a signal that would leap the ocean all the way to Europe."

  In stories like those the imagined scene is dominant.

- Other stories that evoked both left-brain and right-brain response dealt in ideas.

  "Because I had no hope of selling the light bulb if there was no electricity. And I had no hope of selling electricity unless there was a light bulb"

  "Steinmetz started working with alternating current. The type of electricity we all use today. I thought it was a fool idea. I favored direct current. Of course, that couldn't be transmitted more than two miles. But I didn't see that this was any real problem. That was the biggest blunder of my life."

Those last two examples are representative of insight, of learning, of teaching. And teaching, or being taught, appears to be the domain of the left brain while self-learning, or learning by experience, seems to be the domain of the right brain. Put another way, intentional learning takes place in the left brain and incidental learning in the right brain.

In about two-thirds of all our responses, the mental activity in the right brain was greater than in the left brain. This suggests that although TV is not exclusively a right-brain medium, it is relatively a right-brain medium. It would perhaps be more right-brain if there were less talk, if there were less verbal audio present.

On the other hand, what we call "print," or print advertising, is probably not really a left-brain phenomenon, since Starch norms of 50% "noting" and

10% "read most" for two-page, four-color ads strongly suggest that what advertising people call "print" is primarily a picture, or right-brain, medium too.

Those who wish to do research on comparison of qualitative differences among media might be reminded that within TV itself one can compare response to still and moving pictures, print and print-over, and voice and voice-over.

On the larger scale, the ability of respondents to show high right-brain response to even familiar logos, their right-brain response to stories even before the idea content has been added to them, the predominantly right-brain response to TV and perhaps even to what we call print advertising — all suggest that in contrast to teaching, the unique power of the electronic media is to shape the content of people's imagery and in that particular way determine their behavior and their views.

A virtue of the present research lies in its demonstrated ability to identify which media content creates thinking and which creates imagery without thought.

In the past the latter, which is, so to speak, "silent," has not been available for study by the techniques of verbal questioning or interviewing as we have known them. Now something new has been added. Students of media behavior may yet confront the embarrassing fact that television audiences give close attention for long periods of time to stimuli that create no thought and little recall. Why do they do it? What's happening? Perhaps a way has been opened to find out.

CHAPTER 22

MEDIA IMAGERY:
PERCEPTION AFTER EXPOSURE

In a January 29, 1979 issue of *Broadcasting* magazine I raised the following question about television viewing: "Students of media behavior may yet confront the embarrassing fact that television audiences give close attention for long periods of time to stimuli that create no thought and little recall. Why do they do it? What's happening?" (p. 14)

I propose to answer the question with the aid of a hypothesis first advanced in the August 1977 issue of the *Journal of Advertising Research* in which I suggested:

"It is tempting to conclude that it is the right brain's picture-taking ability that permits the rapid screening of the environment — to select what it is that the left brain should focus attention on." (p. 11)

In this view the right brain maintains a vigil, keeps watch on, or surveillance of the environment, and nudges the left brain into alertness when and as needed.

Since then, in reviewing the literature on vigilance, I found confirmation in the form of studies by the Drs. Stuart Dimond and Graham Beaumont of the Department of Psychology at University College in Cardiff, England which showed that left brain attention, though much more accurate than right brain attention in various tests of error detection, quickly tires — while right brain attention, though somewhat less accurate, shows almost no fatigue.[1] Thus, the so-called concentrated, selective, and conscious attention of the left brain is and should be used sparingly, as a rare and valuable resource. Meanwhile, right brain attention or vigilance, since it involves little fatigue, should no longer surprise us with its continuous activity and remarkable tolerance for sustained attention. We should accept the ability of children or adults to watch TV for zillions of hours per week, and find nothing remarkable about that *physiologically*. It is no more remarkable than the ability of a truck driver to drive his vehicle for many hours and to keep adequate watch on the road ahead.

Of course, both children and truck drivers, after a time, may have to fight to stay awake because of the hypnotic monotony of the situation. This is not because their brains are working hard, but because they are working very little.

Originally presented at AMA 11th Attitude Research Conference, Carlsbad, California, March 4, 1980.

Confirmation of the unique ability of the right brain to maintain sustained attention with relatively little fatigue is also provided in the form of a study conducted by Appel, Weinstein and Weinstein and reported in the August 1979 *Journal of Advertising Research.*[2]

In this study thirty women were tested in groups of five and exposed to twenty pairs of television commercials three times for a total of sixty exposures. The findings reported in the journal focused on differences between reportedly high and low recall commercials but did not comment on brain hemisphere differences in response over time; *i.e.*, over the sixty exposures.

In a subsequent discussion with the Drs. Sidney and Curt Weinstein, I asked what the left and right brain decrement had been over time. They then looked up the group means for the total thirty women tested for response to the first viewing of the twenty commercials, the second viewing, and the third viewing. Using their measure of "left-dominance index" (described on p.12 of their published report) they were startled and surprised to tell me that the means were 18, 10 and 5 respectively. That is, left-dominance declined exponentially over time leaving the right brain in predominance.

In the published report Table 12 on page 13 does report mean left-dominance scores for first, second and third trials but only for three pairs of commercials. The discussion focuses on the lack of significant differences between the commercials and ignores the left-dominance means for the low recall commercials as a group, which decline from 10.8 to 4.2 to 3.3 for the three trials, and it also ignores the left-dominance means for the high recall commercials as a group, which decline from 7.4 to 5.5 to 2.1.

Put another way, despite all of the micro-statistical analysis of the study, a gross total record of brain activity over time showed that the left hemisphere tires and gives way to the right. In some other laboratory testing situations this would be called "adjusting to the situation," "the overcoming of the novelty effect," or simply "habituation." It has always been suspected as a problem in single exposure pre-tests of commercials in theater situations *(e.g.*, Schwerin, ASI) where the initial response to the environment is atypical of natural viewing. What the group means of 18, 10 and 5 for first, second and third exposure signify here is that if you show the respondents enough commercials even in a semi-group situation, they will eventually tire to the point of achieving "natural" viewing — with the left hemisphere relatively "turned off" and the right hemisphere remaining alert.

Although at the micro-level of analysis the authors had prematurely concluded, and I quote, ". . .the study produced no evidence to support the belief that TV viewing is a right hemisphere activity" (p.12), nevertheless at the unreported macro-level of analysis the study represents the most compelling evidence to date that *natural* TV viewing is indeed a relatively right brain response.

Now, armed with the view that it is a right brain characteristic that sustains long periods of viewing TV, let us look at some of its implications.

At the 1979 AAPOR meeting at Buck Hill Falls, John Robinson of Cleveland State University presented some correlational data from studies of how people spend their time. He focused on time spent watching TV, and a long string of negative correlations between time with TV vs. time spent working, time spent shopping, time doing housework, etc. The one positive correlation (though low) was between time spent watching TV and time spent sleeping, especially among men. Similarly, though at a lower level, the array of coefficients for newspaper reading also showed only one positive correlation, and it too with sleeping, but only among men.

There are many questions and/or interpretations that could be put upon these data, but for me — I have this image of the typical American male sitting in front of his TV set with a newspaper unfolded across his lap, and he — sound asleep. The point I want to make is that each of the two media could contribute to sleep, but in a different way, the newspaper because it was fatiguing, and the television because it was relaxing.

The newspaper is described as potentially fatiguing because its physical format involves gross eye movements and highly selective choices of attention focus; *i.e.*, left brain attention. However, as one turns the pages, skips around from topic to topic, or seeks the "continued story" in later pages, attention is rested and refreshed. That is, natural *interruptions* to newspaper or magazine reading are more refreshing than frustrating.

The case with TV or movies is quite different. An interruption of a movie film is highly frustrating, and a major public complaint about TV is clutter and/or commercial interruptions. The frustration involved appears to be that the left brain has been "turned on" again thereby interrupting right brain relaxation. It's as if someone turned the lights on in the middle of a film in a movie theater.

In either case, without refreshing interruption of newspaper reading or annoying interruption of TV watching, the audience may eventually fall asleep — with the sleep of fatigue, or the sleep of relaxation.

Another set of implications of the view that the right brain sustains long periods of TV viewing is that we should take a closer look at the perception of images, both in TV and print, with special emphasis on those types of *sustained perception* called "after-images." But we might also describe these types of phenomena under the heading of *sustained exposure*.

In my 1977 talk to the ANA Media Workshop in New York (Chapter 18), I tried to reposition the concept of perception in light of the then-new brain research and suggested that advertising research try to cope with the "full range of effects," and especially to "describe the full range of exposure." The main unresolved tasks for advertising research in this area were described as three fold:

"(1)   to explore more fully the unknown territory between what we now call perception and nonperception. The "make-believe" hard line between these two is contrary to nature. Perception is not an all-or-none matter.

"(2)   to explore the unknown territory between what we now call attention and nonattention. The selective process of attention and nonattention involves more levels of attention than we like to admit.

"(3)   to get smarter about what lies between what we now call exposed and nonexposed. We may have to learn bow to think more in terms of giving credit for partial exposure, for a half-exposure, for a quarter-exposure, and so on. These values also build up with repetition just as do full exposures." (p. 11)

The emphasis in this call for a study of the full range of exposure was, on brief exposure because most advertising is meant to communicate "as quick as a wink," and we could profit from knowing more about brief and even "partial" exposure. At the other extreme, however, we also need to push back the limits of our concern by incorporating into the "full range of exposure" the description of those neglected concepts of longer exposure that also have been highlighted by new brain research.

Thus, it is within the context of the perception of images, that I wish now to discuss those outer limits of the definition of exposure suggested by the after-image.

In 1930 E.R. Jaensch published his classic work on eidetic imagery.[3] The full title was *Eidetic Imagery and Typological Methods of Investigation* but the subtitle was *Their importance for the psychology of childhood.* Indeed he made it quite clear that eidetic imagery was fairly confined to children. He did predict, however, that it would also be more common among primitive than among civilized people (p. 23).

Because of some criticism of methodology and not a little skepticism nothing much happened for thirty years, but in 1964 Haber and Haber carefully tested the whole enrollment of a New Haven elementary school of 151 children and found that 8% or 12 children were clear Eidetikers.[4] Their after-images lasted at least 40 seconds, and all 12 actively scanned their images whereas none of the non-eidetic children did so in response to any briefer after-images.

In Jaensch's time it was not known that the right hemisphere matured earlier in children than the left, and many parents bemoaned (and still do) the loss of their child's early artistic talents thinking it due to some fault in the educational environment. Perhaps it was, but not completely.

Partially perhaps. In the same year of the New Haven study Leonard Doob used the Haber method to study eidetic imagery among adults of the Ibo tribe in Nigeria.[5] Among rural adults eidetic imagery was quite common. However, among *urban* adults of the same tribe living in the provincial capital of Enugu (population 15,000) there was very little eidetic imagery reported, its absence presumably due to the process of acculturation.

On the whole, though, eidetic imagery in our society is a phenomenon of childhood and probably associated with periods of relative right brain dominance.

There is, however, another after-image process in our society, one which is not as dramatic as eidetic imagery in children but which is common to us all, and this has been best discussed by Ulrich Neisser in his 1966 classic *Cognitive Psychology*.[6] The focus here is on what he calls iconic memory.

It was first discovered and studied using brief tachistoscopic exposures of stimuli. It was clearly demonstrated that respondents can continue to "read" information in visual form even after the tachistoscopic exposure is over; *i.e.*, the visual sensation can outlast the stimulus, for up to a second if the post-exposure environment is relatively bright but up to five seconds if it is dark. Please don't minimize the importance of an extra second. You can make three eye fixations in a second and thereby absorb enough information to engage left-brain associative responses. That is, even in the brief exposure the response need not be passive.

To relate eidetic imagery and especially iconic memory to our previous concern with the concepts of perception and the limits of exposure, we would agree that "perception is an event over time." And so we must begin again to integrate new understandings.

Neisser says we must begin by abandoning a set of assumptions. He says, "Even psychologists who ought to know better have acted as if they believed (1) that the subjects visual experience directly mirrors the stimulus pattern; (2) that his visual experience begins when the pattern is first exposed and terminates when it is turned off; (3) that his experience, itself a passive — if fractional — copy of the stimulus, is in turn mirrored by his verbal report. All three of these assumptions are wrong." (p. 16)

Well enough! What are we to make of all this as it applies to advertising, to media, or to learning from media.

First, noting that all the available data on after-imagery apply to inanimate stimuli, I would suggest that print and outdoor advertising can perhaps be given more credit for some exposures, which though relatively brief physically are at the same time relatively long psychologically, and active in response. I don't think those media would object.

At the same time to achieve equivalent qualities in television advertising the viewer would have to STOP and dwell on what he or she has just seen. A compromise might be a slow motion technique such as used in the famous Nice 'N' Easy Clairol commercial of 1970. Its high recall but low pupil dilation scores intrigued me at the time, and still do. However, rather than slow motion a prepared full STOP might be optimal for the advertiser, but also anxious for media executives concerned about the set being turned off or the channel switched.

Even more so, for educational television the potential for greater effective-ness lies in knowing when to slow down the action, when to program carefully prepared stopping places.

This last is of course a researchable area, perhaps a new one. We might even consider the after-imagery of children to TV when programs are interrupted, either by accident or by design.

In the beginning of this paper I suggested that the right brain maintains a vigil, keeps watch on, or surveillance of the environment, and nudges the left brain into alertness when and as needed.

For educational television I would now conclude with the suggestion that they find out *how* and *when to* nudge, and this means, to some extent, "stopping the action."

In retrospect we were probably given a good hint of this at the 1977 APA Convention when Dr. Jerome Singer of Yale reported that while pre-schoolers were more attentive to the rapid-paced structure of *Sesame Street* the children learned more from the slow-paced *Mister Rogers.*[7]

---

[1] S.J. Dimond and J.G. Beaumont, "Differences in the Vigilance Performance of the Right and Left Hemispheres," *Cortex*, vol.9 (1973) pp. 259-265.

[2] V. Appel, S. Weinstein, and C. Weinstein, "Brain Activity and Recall of TV Advertising," *Journal of Advertising Research*, vol. 19, no. 4 (1979), pp. 7-15.

[3] Jaensch, E.R., *Eidetic Imagery and Typological Methods of Investigation*, Harcourt, Brace and Company (New York) 1930.

[4] Haber, R.N. & Haber, R.B. (1964) "Eidetic imagery: I. Frequency." *Percept. Mot. Skills*, 19, 131-138.

[5] Doob, L.W. "Eidetic images among the Ibo." *Ethnology* (1964 no. 3), pp. 357-363.

[6] Neisser, U., *Cognitive Psychology* (New York: Appleton-Century-Crofts, 1966).

[7] J.L. Singer *et al.*, "Preschooler's Comprehension and Play Behavior Following Viewing of 'Mr. Rogers' and 'Sesame Street'". Paper presented at the American Psychological Association, San Francisco, August 1977.

CHAPTER 23

A QUESTION OF SPEED OF COMMUNICATIONS

To me, to talk about advertising in an era of telecommunications touches a very special nerve.

I have never been able to shake off a view of the world largely influenced by a little familiarity with what is called "human factors research" or sometimes "human engineering."

Several events in the past two years have impressed me with the fact that the presence or absence of good human engineering is a highly variable matter in today's society — too variable!

Let me give you four examples . . . from Three Mile Island, from air to air combat in the F-15, from Prestel (the British version of Viewdata) and finally from some GE television commercials. All of these examples concern the interaction between numbers and letters on video screens, dials or instrument panels on the one hand and human operators or audiences on the other.

The official report of the *President's Commission on the Accident at Three Mile Island* was quite critical of the control room, but the chairman, John G. Kemeny, was even more frank in a subsequent article in the July 1980 issue of MIT's *Technology Review*. I quote him as follows:

> Now I'm afraid I got myself into serious trouble afterward because I remarked, within hearing distance of the media, that I did not think this particular control room represented the greatest glory of modern technology. In fact, I said it was at least twenty years out of date. I was greatly criticized for that. And rightly so, because my statement turned out to be false — we later discovered, in the documents of the NRC, a report written ten years earlier in which an expert had said that the control rooms were then twenty years out of date.
>
> We started out work with the prior conviction that the big problem was equipment. But our overwhelming conclusion was that the basic equipment was amazingly good; it was the control room that was terribly designed from the point of view of the people who had to use it. The commission's attention slowly but steadily shifted, almost completely, from equipment to people.

Originally presented at Conference on Newspaper Marketing in the New Era of Telecommunications, Waldorf-Astoria Hotel, New York, September 24, 1980.

This example of excess faith in technical equipment at the expense of attention to operators also appears in the financial side of the new electronic media (*i.e.*, of acquisitions in particular). I have sat in on some meetings where there seemed to be an atmosphere of gold rush fever in the air — with big money available for backing untried and untested systems; *i.e.*, untested on live people. I've been thoroughly startled by this apparent ignorance, or financially enthusiastic avoidance, of proper human factors research and evaluation.

At the other extreme from TMI is the most sophisticated human factors work on air combat where the human operator is recognized as a key element in the weapons system. An operations research team from the University of California conducted an analysis of mental requirements for successful air-to-air combat performance in the F-15. In the introduction of their report, in order to clarify what they intended to discuss, they introduced a quotation from Tim Gallwey's 1974 book *The Inner Game of Tennis* as follows:

> I ask students to stand at net in the volley position, and then set the machine to shoot balls at three-quarter speed. . . . At first the balls seem too fast for them, but soon their responses quicken. Gradually I turn the machine to faster and faster speeds, and the volleyers become more concentrated. When they are responding quickly enough to hit the top-speed balls and believe they are at the peak of their concentration, I move the machine to midcourt, fifteen feet closer than before. At this point students will often lose some concentration as a degree of fear intrudes. "Relax your mind . . . Let it happen." Soon they are again able to meet the ball in front of them with the center of their rackets. There is no smile of self-satisfaction, merely total absorption in each moment. Afterward some players say that the ball seemed to slow down; others remark how weird it is to hit balls when you don't have time to think about it.

The operations research team goes on to comment about this with these words:

> While man's technology, it seems, may be overtaking his capacity to think, it may not yet have even approached a skilled performer's ability to act. Such action faster than thought is not only a necessity when dealing with high-technology systems like that of the F-15, but even when there is time for thought the ultimate level of master performance is reached only by quieting the analytical mind.

I mention this example because of all the characteristics of operators or audiences which are critical to the success of electronic communication systems — an effective relationship to human capacities for speed of response is most critical, also least understand, and often grievously ignored. A key aspect of the problem is that mankind can be very fast in certain kinds of responses, but very slow about others. One must know the what and when of each, for some systems are too fast and others are too slow.

A good example is Prestel, which has been evaluated by Rex Winsbury of the Financial Times of London, who reported his research in a little book entitled *The Electronic Bookstall*. Winsbury was among the first to note the unexpected limitations on the number of words per line that could be effectively used on the screens of such devices, the similar limitations on number of lines, the need to use familiar words, the superiority of lower case over capitalized letters, etc. Here apparently was a class of devices or media which, in contrast to my example from the F-15 case, had to be slowed down in order to succeed. Why?

The why is suggested by my fourth example, a presentation which I put on at the 1978 Annual Conference of the Advertising Research Foundation at this same hotel. It showed some TV commercials in which the brain wave responses of laboratory subjects had been separately tracked in the left and right brain hemispheres for every three-second period within the commercials.

When we looked at those periods that contained print superimposed upon the picture we were surprised to find not a primarily left hemisphere response — which is known to be associated with verbal stimuli — but a right brain response — which is known to be associated with visual images. What we have concluded is that the words of the "supers" as they are called were perceived, recognized, understood but not *read*. That is, the process of reading occurs only when more complex word groupings are involved. It is slow and it is tiring.

Applied to Prestel we would say that Winsbury's emphasis on fewer but more familiar words meant that Prestel had to be slowed down to the point where reading could be replaced by recognizing, by scanning, by whatever you want to call it, it is not what we ordinarily call *reading*.

Words are not always words. Sometimes they are pictures, as you alter the medium. Even some languages are pictorial; *e.g.*, oriental. As you alter these formats and media you change speed, memory and fatigue levels. You must find out, because if you don't you will miss the opportunities for effective advertising in the new media.

Neil Borden said long ago that advertising to succeed must communicate as quick as a wink. I say that in the new era of telecommunications to succeed in advertising means that you must find out when you *can* speed up, and when you *must* slow down. If you want to retain Neil Borden's wink you at least have to decide whether its a wink of $1/3$-second duration or of three seconds. There's a world of difference right there.

In conclusion, the newspaper advertising implications of all this include the following:

    1. The line between what we call print and video has to be re-evaluated for each new system.

    2. The reading of a word, or words, can be slowed down until suddenly it's a word-picture. If that format can be maintained it may then be speeded up.

3. It is tiring to read words on a screen but relaxing to look at pictures. Either fatigue or relaxation can put you to sleep.

4. Newspapers have enjoyed a captive audience for advertising in part because the reader needs frequent rest stops. Television has enjoyed a captive audience for advertisers because the viewer is usually in a relaxed "good mood" and forgives (or almost forgives) the commercial interruptions.

5. Advertising in the new media will face such questions as whether to be short or long, whether words are to be recognized or to be read, whether the media context or the audience situation is right for content that is restful, even entertaining on the one hand — or informative, even provocative on the other hand. It is then a matter not of just "creating" advertising but of designing advertising or communications to the physical requirements of the medium, and to the physical capacities of the audience.

CHAPTER 24

SUSTAINED VIEWING OF TELEVISION

I n a January 29, 1979, issue of *Broadcasting* magazine I raised the following question about television viewing: "Students of media behavior may yet confront the embarrassing fact that television audiences give close attention for long periods of time to stimuli that create no thought and little recall. Why do they do it? What's happening?"

I propose to answer these questions with the aid of a hypothesis first advanced in the August 1977 issue of the *Journal of Advertising Research, in* which I suggested:

It is tempting to conclude that it is the right brain's picture-taking ability that permits the rapid screening of the environment — to select what it is that the left brain should focus attention on.

In this view the right brain maintains a vigil, keeps watch on or surveillance of the environment, and nudges the left brain into alertness as needed. Since then, in reviewing the literature on vigilance, I found confirmation in the form of studies by Drs. Stuart Dimond and Graham Beaumont of the Department of Psychology at University College in Cardiff, England, which showed that left-brain attention, though much more accurate than right-brain attention in various tests of error detection, quickly tires, while right-brain attention, though somewhat less accurate, shows almost no fatigue.[1] Thus the so-called concentrated, selective, and conscious attention of the left brain is, and should be, used sparingly as a rare and valuable resource. Meanwhile, right-brain attention or vigilance, since it involves little fatigue, should no longer surprise us with its continuous activity and remarkable tolerance for sustained attention. We should accept the ability of children or adults to watch TV for zillions of hours per week and should find nothing remarkable about that physiologically. It is no more remarkable than the ability of a truck driver to drive his vehicle for many hours and to keep adequate watch on the road ahead.

Original Publication: "Point of View," in *Journal of Advertising Research,* Vol. 20, No. 3 (June 1980)

Editor's note: The beginning of this piece is substantially identical to that of Chapter 21 ("Media Imagery: Perception After Exposure"). The two pieces go in rather different directions, however, so they are included in this volume as separate articles.

Of course, both children and truck drivers, after a time, may have to fight to stay awake because of the hypnotic monotony of the situation. This is not because their brain is working hard, but because it is working very little.

Confirmation of the unique ability of the right brain to maintain sustained attention with relatively little fatigue is also provided in the form of a study conducted by Appel, Weinstein, and Weinstein and reported in the August 1979 *Journal of Advertising Research.*[2]

In this study 30 women were tested in groups of five and exposed to 20 pairs of television commercials three times for a total of 60 exposures. The findings reported in the journal focused on differences between reportedly high- and low-recall commercials but did not comment on brain-hemisphere differences in response over time — *i.e.*, over the 60 exposures.

In a subsequent discussion with Drs. Sidney and Curt Weinstein, I asked what the left- and right-brain decrement had been over time. They then looked up the group means for the 30 women tested for response to the first viewing of the 20 commercials, the second viewing, and the third viewing. Using their measure of "left-dominance index" (described on page 12 of their published report) they were startled and surprised to discover that the means were 18, 10, and 5 respectively. That is, left dominance declined exponentially over time.

In the published report Table 12 on page 13 does report mean left-dominance scores for first, second, and third trials, but separately for high- and low-recall commercials. The discussion focuses on the lack of significant differences between the commercials and ignores both the left-dominance means for the low-recall commercials as a group — which decline from 10.8 to 4.2 to 3.3 for the three trials — and the left-dominance means for the high-recall commercials as a group — which decline from 7.4 to 5.5 to 2. 1.

Put another way, despite all of the microstatistical analysis of the study, a gross total record of brain activity over time showed that the left hemisphere tires and gives way to the right. In some other laboratory-testing situations, this would be called "adjusting to the situation," "the overcoming of the novelty effect," or simply "habituation." It has always been suspected as a problem in single-exposure pretests of commercials in theater situations (*e.g.*, Schwerin, ASI) where the initial response to the environment is atypical of natural viewing. What the group means of 18, 10, and 5 for first, second, and third exposures signify here is that if you show the respondents enough commercials even in a semi-group situation, they will eventually tire to the point of achieving "natural" viewing — with the left hemisphere relatively "turned off " and the right hemisphere remaining alert.

Although at the microlevel of analysis the authors had prematurely concluded that "the study produced no evidence to support the belief that TV viewing is a right-hemisphere activity" (p. 12), nevertheless at the unreported macrolevel of analysis the study represents the most compelling evidence to date that natural TV viewing is indeed a relatively right-brain response.

Now, armed with the view that it is a right-brain characteristic that sustains long periods of viewing TV, let us look at some of its implications.

At the 1979 AAPOR meeting, John Robinson presented some correlational data from studies of how people spend their time. He focused on time spent watching TV, and a long string of negative correlations between time with TV versus time spent working, time spent shopping, time doing housework, etc. The one positive correlation (though low) was between time spent watching TV and time spent sleeping, especially among men. Similarly, though at a lower level, the array of coefficients for newspaper reading also showed only one positive correlation, and it too with sleeping, but only among men.

There are many questions about and/ or interpretations of these data. As for me, I have this image of the typical American male sitting in front of his TV set with a newspaper unfolded across his lap, and he is sound asleep. The point I want to make is that each of the two media could contribute to sleep, but in a different way — the newspaper because it was fatiguing, and the television because it was relaxing.

The newspaper is described as potentially fatiguing because its physical format involves gross eye movements and highly selective choices of attention focus — *i.e.*, left-brain attention. But as one turns the pages, skips around from topic to topic, or seeks the "continued" story in later pages, attention is rested and refreshed. That is, natural interruptions to newspaper or magazine reading are more refreshing than mistreating.

The case with TV or movies is quite different. An interruption of a movie film is highly frustrating, and a major public complaint about TV is clutter and/or commercial interruptions. The frustration involved appears to be that the left brain has been "turned on" again, thereby interrupting right-brain relaxation. It's as if someone turned the lights on in the middle of a film in a movie theater.

In either case, without refreshing interruption of newspaper reading or annoying interruption of TV watching, the audience may eventually fall asleep — with the sleep of fatigue or the sleep of relaxation.

To sleep, perhaps to dream! Along with the relatively untiring qualities of right-brain observation goes, I believe, a limitless memory for images and pictures only a little of which can be recalled from memory, especially if you insist on using words to ask respondents to tell you about those images. It's hard to get at right-brain memory with left-brain probes. This is, in essence, the problem and challenge, for example, in psychoanalysis, and especially involves Freud's concept of the unconscious. Many neurophysiologists, like Dr. David Galin of the Langly Porter Neuropsychiatric Institute at the University of California, now view Freud's basic concepts as having physical and logical bases in fact. For example, Dr. Galin views the stored-up life memories of Freud's 'unconscious' as right-brain material and the difficulties of retrieving or integrating some of that material into conscious awareness as a function of the *limitations of left brain capacities* for sustained concentrated attention.[3] That is why psychoanalysis is such a time-consuming process. But it is also why briefer types of therapy may not produce permanent benefits.

Now I'd like to come back to television, and with the aid of the two notions — that concentrated left-brain attention needs frequent rest, and that the right brain easily absorbs and retains a limitless amount of material — I'd like to suggest why television and the electronic media have not made, but still can make, remarkable contributions to teaching.

The best use of TV for the stimulation of thinking, I believe, has come from the use of skilled faces — news commentators, talk-show interviewers, an occasional presidential candidate in debate, Pat Hingle playing the role of Thomas Edison in last year's GE centennial advertising. (Incidentally, we exposed three subjects to a sequence of eight Thomas Edison commercials but were unable to create any decrement in left- or right-hemisphere response. As Dr. Weinstein says, "Edison commercials were just too interesting.")

Magazines have learned. Faces are by far the most common feature on magazine covers. Faces are enormously interesting, even to six-week-old infants who have already begun to respond differentially to the "faces" made at them. A certain amount of human "imprinting" goes on.

I realize that the media refer to their stars as "personalities," but I would suggest that unknown faces on a magazine cover or in an ad can be just as interesting as the face of a well-known personality.

One of the implications of these remarks concerns the opportunity to multiply a thousandfold the skill of a "great teacher." When cable and cassette fragment the television market, I expect to see dozens of electronic classes and schools established, each oriented around a great teaching face, a face that knows when to pause, when to let students "stop and think" (even on expensive air time), when to stop actions on the screen to let students look inward to have personal thoughts.

I don't have high hopes that expensive national television would today be tolerant of what might seem the very slow pace of effective teaching. It is start and stop, start and stop, with many rest periods along the way. It is, after all, asking the students to do hard work, and some of them may not be previously familiar with the hard work of thinking. Note that Yale's Dr. Jerome Singer found that while preschoolers were more attentive to the rapid-paced structure of "Sesame Street," they learned more from the slow-paced "Mister Rogers."[4]

There is also a matter of keeping the eyes moving. If a student stares at a politely poised but stiff newscaster, the student will have to look away and back, and again away and back. He will have to work to maintain attention on the nonmoving newscaster. But if a newscaster were meant to be attended to as closely as a teacher, then he would accommodate the restless nature of close attention with little gestures, the moving of hands, the getting up and walking about the room, and all of this while still speaking effectively. These motions ask the student to *think along* (as opposed to "sing along") with the teacher, to ponder and speculate, to imagine and problem-solve without turning away. The motions provide rests (*i.e.*, rests for the left-brain hemisphere) and give time for thinking — without removing attention from the teacher. Instead of looking away from a wooden lecturer, one would stay with the effective teacher and perhaps watch him light his pipe or cigarette. What will teachers do when they've all given up smoking? How could anyone do a one-man show on Broadway without the lighting of pipes or cigarettes? Well, I suppose one could pull on one's beard, ear, or nose, or flick imaginary lint off one's clothing. The so-called "bits of business" of the professional actor are not just for the purpose of building a "character." On the contrary, they enhance communication.

Nature abhors a vacuum. The great teacher or great actor must control every response of the audience, especially the "rest stops." Timing is everything on the stage, on the podium, and in the classroom.

I think most of us, when we look back to our own education, think of the good teachers we've had, those who took us beyond the mere acquisition of facts into the exciting realm of hard thinking. This type of teaching, which is so rare, can be duplicated and preserved via electronic media.

Meanwhile, American television is producing and exporting all over the world right-brain images of a U.S. culture that is quite different from the traditional cultures of those audiences. The right-brain reservoirs of memory easily absorb all of this material, but offer no guidance as to what to make of it. Without such guidance from the medium, it sets the stage for local guidance, for new interpretations, for new teachers, and for new political leaders.

In the United States the child's absorption of television material may be said to represent unsupervised experience. Both here and overseas the buildup of memory banks without left-brain guidance can lead to new, possibly bizarre and unpredictable, trends or fashions.

To supplement all the new learned material, to integrate it with thoughtfulness, with thinking responses, is no mean task. The best way in schools is the tutorial way in which the teacher coaches the student over the more difficult hurdles. In therapy the best way may still be psychoanalysis, wherein the analyst helps to interpret patient blind spots, repressions, or other peculiarities emanating from the long accumulated, but not easily accessed, memory banks.

For the electronic media, I sense an educational explosion in the wings. As we now have superstar athletes, superstar entertainers, and even superstar news personalities, we are getting closer to superstar teachers. Fragmentation of the present mass audience for TV will do the trick. Our electronic classes and schools will have arrived.

Konrad Lorenz, in his preface to the 1965 reprinting of Charles Darwin's classic *The Expression of Emotions in Man and Animals*, describes Darwin as "a man who knows much more than he thinks he knows" (p. xi). In a way, television has done this for hundreds of million of people all over the world. They know so much, but cannot integrate or use what they know. A next step in the miracle of electronic media is to help them do just that.

---

[1] Dimond, S.J., and J.G. Beaumont, "Differences in the Vigilance Performance of the Right and Left Hemispheres," *Cortex,* vol. 9 (1973), pp. 259-265.

[2] Appel, V., S. Weinstein, and C. Weinstein, "Brain Activity and Recall of TV Advertising," *Journal of Advertising Research,* vol. 19, no. 4 (1979), pp. 7-15.

[3] Galin, D., "Implications for Psychiatry of Left and Right Brain Cerebral Specialization," *Archives of General Psychiatry,* vol. 31 (October 1974), pp. 572-583.

[4] Singer, J.L., *et al.,* "Preschooler's Comprehension and Play Behavior Following Viewing of 'Mr. Rogers' and 'Sesame Street'" Paper presented at the American Psychological Association, San Francisco, August 1977.

CHAPTER 25

THE EFFECTIVE USE OF PHYSIOLOGICAL
MEASUREMENT IN ADVERTISING RESEARCH

T he prevailing methodology of advertising research is represented by a mix of focused group interviewing, theater type pre-testing, and a large variety of sample surveys, some of them on a very large scale.

Taken as a whole this methodology has been limited in what help it can give to creative personnel, or in providing intimate insights into how advertising works.

There is room, I believe, for the added contribution of a laboratory type of function, the most commonly proposed being the physiological laboratory.

Over the years, however, the popularity of physiological measurement has run in cycles, with periodic enthusiasm over new measures followed in most cases by significant disillusion. Physiological measurement appears to be an approach with much promise, but which is poorly understood, and which keeps knocking on our doors with confusing claims. I'd like to clarify the situation, if I can.

In the beginning, there is adrenaline, which is produced when the body is aroused. When adrenaline goes to work the heart beats faster and more strongly and even enlarges. Blood flows to the extremities and increases capillary dilation at the finger tips and even in the ear lobes. The temperature of the skin increases, hair follicles stand up, the pores of the skin emit perspiration and the electrical conductivity of the skin surface is affected. The pupils of the eye dilate, electrical waves in the brain increase in frequency, breathing is faster and deeper, and the chemical composition of expired air is altered.

You have here a choice of perhaps fifty different measures, which to a great extent are all measuring the same thing, arousal.

Meanwhile, consider the cyclical enthusiasm for physiological measurement as partially a function of the fact that a young researcher in Cupcake, Idaho might suddenly discover that the temperature of the ear lobe correlates with interest in advertising. He gets very enthusiastic, and may forget, or simply not know that there are forty-nine other ways in which bodily arousal correlates with advertising (and other stimuli).

Originally presented at American Marketing Association, Twelfth Annual Attitude Research Conference, The Homestead, Hot Springs, Virginia, April 6, 1981.

The question of which of many different measures of arousal to use is to some extent irrelevant; *i.e.*, since they are all measuring the same thing. But some are more convenient to use, depending on the kind of stimuli you have in mind to test, whether you can make do with a laboratory environment or must require unobtrusive measurement of natural response, whether good equipment is available for a perhaps less preferred measure but not for the measure of first choice, and finally the state of your budget since some variables can be measured inexpensively and some only at great expense.

By and large the heart, lung, blood system and skin oriented variables can be measured. relatively inexpensively, while variables associated with the central nervous system (*i.e.*, eye and brain) are relatively more expensive. As I will discuss later, however, the major budgeting item in an effective system is not the pick-up of the variable, but how it is transmitted, communicated and displayed to the onlooker.

While the image we have of physiological research is that it is laboratory research, with respondents hooked up to gadgets, and researchers or clients "looking on" with interest, it is only a myth that it *has* to be this very obtrusive kind of research.

While I prefer a laboratory setting, I could have a completely unobtrusive system by sampling the expired air of respondents, provided that only one person is in the room. I could use the General Electric condensation nuclei counter which quite literally counts the number of nitrogen ions in the air sample. It is very sensitive at great distances, and capable of processing great amounts of air very quickly. The presence of nitrogen ions is a function of the urea and/or ammonia in the expired air, the same chemicals involved in perspiration or urination. The condensation nuclei counter was not originally intended for physiological research, but I ran across it at GE's R&D laboratories at Schenectady in 1968 and found that it might do the job.

I prefer, however, to use openly obtrusive measures and to confront, and hopefully to solve, the problems of the obvious artificial setting. In a nutshell that requires the use of habituated respondents, respondents who are tested long enough to have gotten over the novelty of the laboratory situation. This may take an hour or more, and varies somewhat from respondent to respondent. However, if you are really doing physiological research, the measure that you use must, to begin with, tell you when each respondent has calmed down to the level of, for example, "normal TV viewing," so that you may begin the real testing.

It is indeed awkward and expensive to treat each respondent in this custom-tailored manner, but it is essential. Otherwise the respondents are just too excited by their strange environment to give you anything like *representative samples of the kind of behavior in which you are really interested.*

If you are selling physiological research, it is hard at first to offer a standardized fixed price, not knowing how much habituation is required in order to simulate the desired samples of behavior.

Which brings up the matter of validity; the most misunderstood topic in physiological research.

A physiologist who is new to the world of advertising research will quickly find that what the industry wants to *buy* is the prediction of success or failure of new ads. The buyer asks the physiologist (1) if he can do so, and (2) if he can do so better than those researchers who use only verbal data.

The physiologist, often an enthusiastic former academic, and sometimes of high status, says "Yes," and "Yes" to both questions. This answer, coming from high academics (with no prior experience in advertising research) then sets the standards for claims made by others, including non-academics, who also sell physiological research. It also sets the standards for what the buyer thinks he "wants," or "needs."

But the right answers are "No" and "No." Physiological research is not good at predicting success of advertising, and certainly not better than verbal data, although perhaps no worse.

Anytime I hear a sales talk involving prediction or validity, I know that physiological research is being mis-sold or mis-bought, especially as it applies to television advertising. Why is that?

Because the great virtue of physiological measurement of animate stimuli such as television, its "unique selling proposition," its one great advantage over verbal data is that it is co-incidental; *i.e.*, not after the fact, not an exit interview, not dependent on what was remembered later on, but a live "blood, sweat and tears" response moment by moment synchronous with the stimuli.

When that fact is appreciated we will stop talking about prediction and validity. Instead, we will ask "what happens to viewers at second 1, second 2, second 3, etc., of the commercial. What parts, what words, what presenters, what gestures, what camera shots, what displays, what assertions turn the viewer on and off, from moment to moment?

While I would like to see physiological measurement focus on this virtue and get off the prediction and validity kick, I don't think it's going to happen until two conditions are fulfilled. One is that the moment by moment results, the "findings," must be displayed moment to moment on a video monitor so that both the researcher and the client can see them superimposed on the commercial itself, *i.e.*, again a "co-incidental" report format. There's a little extra hardware involved there, but it does permit the data to "speak for itself." It permits the report to consist of a tape, which can then be viewed over and over at will by the client.

The second condition is that the so-called "client" should be the creative personnel who made the commercial. Those clients should be free to compare their intended effects on viewers with the revealed effects, and thereby learn something more, about improving the commercial.

What kind of taped report we are talking about, of individual respondents, or of aggregated data?

The recommended principle is to test respondents individually to see whether an aggregated type of report would have the same graphic pattern as the individual. If the aggregate is *only* a statistical set of moment-to-moment averages, it has no value, no meaning, no validity for use by creatives. It would not be physiological research, it would not be psychological research. It would only be statistical research, and that would be quite a comedown for a physiological laboratory.

When there is not a statistical aggregate that is also true for the individuals then individual records must be shown.

Obviously, for each commercial to be evaluated in this way, the product of that evaluation cannot be known in advance, or sold in advance at a packaged price. It is research, not evaluation. It is description, not prediction. It is not even for general use with all creatives, but only for those who can make use of such feedback. These may be the better ones or the poorer ones among the creatives, or it may not related to their ability at all, but only to individual differences in preferred work habits.

Who's going to pay for such a service? Who would sell such a service? It may not be a very attractive endeavor financially, when described this way.

In an effort to sweeten the pot, I will discuss some additional values and virtues of physiological measurement, including a very general problem in advertising research, specifically, the large and depressing gap between what we could call good scientific practice on the one hand, and conventional ad pretesting on the other.

Scientific or experimental practice would require that the stimulus—as experienced by the respondent—be identified. It rarely is, but instead is assumed to be the ad, the commercial, sometimes the entire ad or commercial (as if it were a single stimulus).

Scientific practice would also require that the response as evidenced by the respondent—be identified. It rarely is, but instead the researchers impose selected measurements of types of responses in which they, the researchers, happen to have an interest, or a belief.

Until this gap between stimulus and response is narrowed, there can be little progress in understanding how advertising works, either in the general or the particular.

A special role for physiological measurement in narrowing this gap, would be to help identify what is stimulus, and what is response.

Imagine that you are the researcher, sitting in front of a screen which shows simultaneously, and in synch, the commercial and the respondents moment to moment physiological reaction. You have no prepared questionnaire or interviewer guide.

You see that the respondent's arousal increases gradually throughout the course of the commercial, or that it decreases. Each would suggest a different question to be asked of the respondent; *e.g.*, "You seemed to become more interested?" or "You seemed to be interested at first, but then less so?"

Or you might see that the respondent's arousal peaked at one or two places, and you could ask about those places.

Or you might find a level high, or a level low, and say "You seemed to find the whole thing interesting?" Or to find nothing of interest? Etc.

These types of questions are simple encouragements to the respondent to talk, and in that talk you will confirm what about the commercial was the stimulus, the object of attention, and what response, if any (*i.e.*, "what of it"), can be identified. Admittedly the latter is more difficult, but it is worth distinguishing between declarative responses "I noticed that," or "That's what got my attention going," and reactive responses such as those that I call connections, or thoughtful associations to content not in the commercial, but to content in the personal lives of the respondent.

I note parenthetically that low involvement is more common than high involvement, and that one connection or real thought per commercial per respondent is toward the high end of the continuum. All the more reason to identify such an important event, and to locate where and when it occurred during the exposure.

Now, say one identifies peak points of interest in a commercial and then, at the end of the commercial, one asks about those recently experienced peak points. That is, of ten or twelve seconds ago.

Just as unaided twenty-four hour recall, even among proven TV viewers, often produces zilch, so even a twelve second delay in the laboratory may lose valuable comment, especially from a non-verbal type of person.

And let's face it, what I am talking about here is how to encourage people *to* verbalize responses, people who might be able to answer structured but irrelevant test questions but who shy away from relevancy, people who would prefer not to commit themselves, people who usually end up in the "don't knows," especially in response to visual stimuli.

Now, if twelve seconds is too long to wait there is an alternative, which is to stop the commercial whenever a high peak (or a sudden drop) occurs, and ask immediately about what's happening.

You can see that the kind of interviewer that's beginning to take shape here, even though the data are physiological, is an interviewer that we would call clinical; *i.e.*, a skilled observer of the individual case, who proceeds in terms of the particular case (*i.e.*, respondent) to find out what's happening.

There is no training experience like this to teach one more about how advertising works, how communications work. One might require such experience of every so-called advertising researcher, of every so-called creative person in an agency. Some wouldn't like that kind of work or be good at it, but they would forevermore know something about the nature of advertising effects that they couldn't learn any other way.

Is agency management listening? Are the schools listening? There is a role for clinical communications research with physiological tracking as the procedural core.

There are historical precedents, without the physiological core. I refer to the anthropologist Elliot Chapple and his type of personnel interview called the "Interaction Chronometer," or to the sociologist Henry Lennard's content analysis of psychotherapeutic hours described in his book "The Anatomy of Psychotherapy." In general there have been numerous attempts to collect and to play back to respondents detailed observations of how they interact with another person.

My proposal is simply to do the same for interaction with media. However, since the human partner in this pair appears to be passive, we must look beneath the skin for the modest flickers of interactive behavior, hence the physiological measures.

If the clinical role of the researcher in this proposal seems a bit difficult, too demanding, too clinical, keep in mind that some of the questioning of the respondent might be handed over to the data itself. That is, a playback of the physiological measurement superimposed on the commercial can be shown to the respondent, and as a high point of reaction is shown the tape can be stopped, the researcher can look at the respondent, raise his or her eyebrows, adopt a quizzical expression, and wait ... and if the respondent still can't talk, he or she may at least be able to point.

So there are many possibilities for research on interviewing, and for research on advertising response.

Why haven't we had something like this earlier in the history of advertising research? One answer is that the advertising industry finds words so easy, they don't know that other people find words hard. Let me tell a personal story.

When I first came to Ted Bates Advertising in 1960 I came from the industrial design firm of Raymond Loewy Associated where I had been the research director.

A lady at Ted Bates said to me one day "Well Herb, how did you like working with the dummies (at Raymond Loewy)?" I didn't know what she meant. Finally, it dawned on me. She meant that they (the designers) didn't speak. Which was relatively true.

When I reported a research project to a team of designers there was usually silence until one took up a pad and pencil, drew a sketch, and then asked "Herb, do you mean like this?" Ten minutes later I might have thirty sketches of new product ideas.

The same report to an advertising group could end with a babble of questions and comments.

If you look at the Wechsler intelligence test, the form for children and the form adults, you will find that each is comprised of two sets of sub-tests leading to separate "verbal" and so-called "performance" or non-verbal IQ scores, which are then averaged to determine the overall IQ score.

An advertising person and an industrial designer might have the same IQ but the former would likely be high on verbal and low on non-verbal intelligence, while the designer would show the opposite imbalance. If they ever met, one would talk and the other would sketch.

Now here's an industry problem, in terms of IQ patterns. A person high on both verbal and non-verbal wouldn't be in the advertising business to begin with. That business attracts these who are high on verbal and who lack something on the other side. He or she is therefore very *glib*, brilliantly glib perhaps, *and knows it*. A very creative, but essentially verbal environment.

Of course, I'm exaggerating a bit to make the point. The point is that because of the emphasis on words, there is some hesitation in recognizing research that doesn't depend on words, on respondents that find it difficult to express themselves, and on responses that are hard to put into words. This hesitation handicaps agency management in providing creatives with meaningful (to them) research. This hesitation may become even more of a handicap to advertising management as electronics moves our audiences more and more into visual media.

This handicap has been evident in the past in connection with the positioning of print advertising. Despite a half century of Starch readership data and a million personal interviews, and the unvarying norms which from year to year show, for example, that the typical four color spread is noted by 50% and read by 10%, the medium is still called "print." That's a bias. It should be called a picture medium, or perhaps to fudge a little, a picture and headline medium. Put another way, just as television was the big advertising story in the second half of the twentieth century so photography was the big story of the first half, though it takes a reminder.

And there was not much research on photographs and pictures in that first half century, though there was plenty of "copy research."

It's not too late for that, although I wouldn't suggest a physiological laboratory for inanimate stimuli. I'd suggest a perceptual laboratory.

A physiological laboratory measuring biochemically stimulated moment to moment changes in arousal is fine for a moving stimulus like television. There's no big perceptual problem of where the eye is looking, because the movement of the stimulus leads the eye. The problem of identifying the stimulus is then to identify when arousal occurs.

A perceptual laboratory measuring response to a still picture must begin with an eye movement record to determine what is the stimulus content of the picture. Eye movement cameras have been around for twenty-five years, and while it takes very precise love and care to use them properly, they are on the whole still waiting.

When the newer electronic media such as Teletext or Viewprint put inanimate print and picture material on a TV screen, then we will really have to wonder what research tools to use. To date that field has been characterized by a seemingly inverse relationship between how much money is being invested in new systems and how much research is being done to evaluate them, a sorry condemnation of the field of communications research. I attribute this lack of research and evaluation in part to the advertising industry's ancient and fudging lack of distinction between the roles of pictures and of copy.

Well, so much for the past. What about the future? Here I want to say a few words about the special significance of brain research.

Earlier in this report I talked about fifty different ways to measure physiological arousal, all of them somehow stimulated by the injection of adrenaline into the bloodstream.

The whole idea then of a physiological laboratory is predicated on the assumption that the stimuli to be studied are arousing, or interesting. And of course, if you bring naive, unhabituated respondents into a physiological laboratory they certainly will be aroused by the novelty and adventure of the experience, and the consequent "hyping" of the stimuli.

This raises the awful possibility that with *habituated* respondents there just may be no adrenaline, and no arousal and no laboratory.

So we better have a clear idea of what habituation *is* in the first place.

The respondent who is thinking about the laboratory, the researchers, and the tests is not habituated. The respondent who has gotten used to these things so that he is content to look at the stimuli without thinking of laboratory, researcher or tests *is* habituated.

What diminishes during the habituation period is the number and types of non-relevant thoughts occurring to the respondent and their associated arousal. Meanwhile, the willingness to *look at* experimental stimuli continues.

Because brain data, thanks to the lateral specialization of the two hemispheres, can distinguish between "thinking" and "just looking" we can tell more confidently when habituation has been achieved, and when quote normal unquote testing can begin. In the June, 1980 issue of the *Journal of Advertising Research* in an article on "Sustained viewing of television," I reported, in effect, a minimum one hour habituation period for viewing of television commercials in a study by Val Appel and Sid Weinstein.

It is this insight into habituation of left brain "thinking" response which separate brain data from simple measures of arousal. That is, if you used one of these other measures and found a decline to some baseline during the first hour, you wouldn't know if that decline meant a decline of thinking, or of vigilant viewing or of both. Brain data can tell you when the relatively untiring viewing behavior is proceeding without the extraneous and non-relevant mental associations to the laboratory environment. In short, if nothing else, brain data permit a cleaner experiment via *the measurable elimination of the "laboratory" artifact.*

Brain wave data do have limitations. In 1970 I published data based on thirty second samples of respondents behavior. Over the years we reduced this to ten, to five and finally to three second readouts. Thus, it is not "moment to moment" data as with the simpler measures of arousal. The brain *waves* per se have a form and time span of up to 1½ seconds, and even evoked potentials require the cumulation of reaction across several seconds. I would therefore prefer to use brain data *along with* one of the simpler measures of arousal.

Now, I'd like to leave you with a few one-liners about an ideal physiological laboratory to measure animate stimuli (the problem of a perceptual laboratory to measure inanimate stimuli is in some ways more complex, and I'll leave that for another time).

First, design on paper the laboratory you want.

Second, discover that the equipment manufacturers will not quite have what you want and will suggest something different. Hold fast to your specifications!

Third, be prepared for the fact that the desired equipment will not at first work properly, even when the manufacturer is demonstrating it.

Fourth, hire a full-time "electronic junkie" to provide your equipment with tender love and care.

Fifth, take pains to identify in every piece of equipment that intercedes between response and feedback what is the lag, if any, since a few microseconds here and there can add up to an unknown out-of-synch condition between the portrayed stimulus and the portrayed response shown on the screen or tape.

Sixth, prepare each interviewer to go to work on a particular commercial by having it played to him or her fifty times, or until the interviewer can almost act it out in his or her sleep. In general, this type of laboratory makes a whole second look like a huge piece of time and makes a complete commercial seem like thousands of verbal, pictorial, gestural and other complex stimuli, which of course, it is. That's the going-in problem. So you must be intimately familiar with the commercial before getting intimate with a live respondent.

Seventh, if you find that a single respondent produces far more data than you can almost cope with, be encouraged that you're on the right track.

Eighth, if because of the above you begin to spend a lot more time with individual cases; *i.e.*, with single respondents, perhaps only one respondent studied repeatedly, you can console yourself with any of the following three justifications:

(a)   To a degree, and in response to certain stimuli, all individuals are alike, that is, "eyeballs *is* eyeballs," or the laws of vision apply to all. In a sense, when dealing with dark and light, noise and silence, you are dealing with a relatively unvarying biological part of the response and this should be identified.

(b)   The natural emphasis on individual respondents is indeed a new, or at least revived approach, which is gaining momentum, and which has recently been represented by Michel Hersen and David H. Barlow's book *Single Case Experimental Designs: Strategies for Studying Behavior Change*, published by Pergamon Press (New York) in 1976 and/or Thomas R. Kratochivill's Single *Subject Research: Strategies for Evaluating Change*, published by the Academic Press (New York) in 1978. Notice that the subtitles of both refer to the evaluation of "change." You will find that they fit nicely into problems of changing attitudes as well as changing behavior.

(c)   The final justification for studying individual respondents is the excitement you will feel at being able to do what most advertising researchers only dream about, and that is the experience of actually *seeing the immediate effects of advertising take place before your very own eyes.*

CHAPTER 26

NEXT STEPS — A PRODUCTIVE APPROACH TO MEASURING EFFECTIVE FREQUENCY

The past history of research on frequency of advertising has often involved compromise. Either advertising exposure was defined in terms of opportunities-to-see rather than in terms of proven exposure, the question of who in the household was really exposed was left open, the personally maintained diaries of viewing habits and/or purchases represented a weary chore, or the whole effort retreated into the laboratory in a preference for more manageable kinds of artificiality.

The various compromises were not without utility, for despite their limitations we learned a great deal about effective frequency. But now we wish to move forward, hopefully to take a quantum leap into new insights not previously possible. Part of this we all feel can be aided by new technology. However, it will be very important to use the new technology without being so overawed by it that we compromise relevant analytic objectives in order to be able to financially afford the technology.

For television advertising the "next steps" to move forward all involve stricter definitions: stricter definitions of exposure, stricter definitions of who is being studied, and stricter definitions of what we have loosely called product "purchase." If we become stricter on one of these, we will no doubt benefit, but to make a quantum leap forward with one research design, hopefully the ARF model for the next ten years, it will be necessary to tighten up on all these aspects simultaneously.

Now let me discuss each of these: exposure, subject identification, and product purchase and suggest what might be the next forward step.

We have long become accustomed to the great technological advance represented in the Nielsen audimeter. It's been around so long we take it for granted. But now that we're all excited by advances at the other end of our communication chain; i.e., the purchase scanning devices, we can't very well end up a research design with modern scanners and start up the same design with old fashioned personal viewing diaries, or even split cables with opportunities to see in one half the sample and no opportunities to see in the other. It's

---

Original presented at Advertising Research Foundation Key Issues Workshop, New York Hilton, June 4, 1982.

not only impractical to process output data in a modern way when the input data are old fashioned and crude, but it's unaesthetic.

So to begin you need something like the Nielsen audimeter to tell you, without bothering the individuals who are being studied, when the TV set is on and to what it's tuned. It doesn't have to be the audimeter, of course, since the *BehaviorScan* people themselves are developing an electronic feedback of the TV set status for 2,000 households. You will hear more about that from Gerry Eskin this afternoon.

So step number 1 is to start electronic as well as to end electronic. The TV set status in the household must be known. Even for those of you who like split cable, the implication here is that "natural" experiments (to use a term coined by Paul Lazarsfeld) are preferable to designed experiments.

Step number 2 is closely related to number 1, and requires not a techno-logical breakthrough but a sampling breakthrough; *i.e.*, knowing the TV set status, the next problem is "Who is exposed?"

Consider all the "noise" in past research on the problem. A member of a family turns on one of the possibly two sets in the home, leaves the room and is possibly replaced by a different member of the family, who possibly converses with someone else during the commercial, who possibly is not the same person who makes out the weekly shopping list, who is possibly not the same person who does the shopping. All these possibilities combined *possibly* reduce by 50% the reliability of any data collected in a study of advertising frequency and its effects on purchasing. What I propose is to drastically reduce all these possi-bilities, all this statistical noise, with one recommendation. That is, to study single person households only — at least to begin.

Now the probabilities are one TV set, less conversation, and the planning and shopping more likely done by the advertising exposed individual.

When I first made this recommendation at the first of two meetings held by ARF's Early Advisory Group to the Effective Frequency Project — perhaps half of those present expressed enthusiasm for the idea, and one of those present, Colin McDonald, will expand on it this afternoon. However, among some of the others there was a little concern over the representativeness of data from so spe-cial a group as single person households. So I turned to my GE associate, Peter Case, and asked him to look into the matter. Here is a summary of what he found about those households:

(1) First, there are 18,000,000 such households, comprising 22% of all households and 11% of all adults.

(2) Second, comparing the distribution of adults in single and multi-person households by age we find (see Table 26.1):

Women in single person households are much more likely to be 65 or over, and in multi-person households under 35

TABLE 26.1

DISTRIBUTION OF ADULT POPULATION BY AGE*

	Total 18+ (000)	18-34 %	35-54 %	55-64 %	65+ %
WOMEN in					
one person households	11,000	18	13	18	51
2+ person households	73,000	43	32	13	12
MEN in					
one person households	7,000	43	25	12	20
2+ person households	69,000	43	32	13	12
Total:	160,000				

*Nielsen projections of persons in TV households as of 1/1/82

       Men in single and multi-person households are very similar to men in multi-person households except for a small tendency to be more numerous in the 65 and over age group

(3) Third, comparing the distribution of TV viewing by adults by age in single and multi-person households we find, somewhat to our pleasant surprise, much less of a difference (see Table 26.2).

       Women in single person households in the 35-54 age group are slightly less likely to view TV than such women in the multi-person households.

       Men in the single person households in the 55 and over age groups are slightly less likely to view TV than such men in the multi-person households.

       A general observation from this and the previous slide is that the single person households present little or no problem of representativeness with regard to TV viewing and advertising exposure, but could *(e.g.,* if young women were not over-sampled) represent a problem in product usage.

       As a general footnote to this note that the same table as above was prepared for each TV day part and no significant differences were found.

   A more practical obstacle to using samples comprised of single person households is that one would sharply reduce the number of households available to study in those wired and scanned communities that provide us with the new technological opportunities. Thus, only 22% or about a fifth of their households may be usable. Nevertheless, I would infinitely prefer smaller studies and less data, if they were relatively free of the kind of experimental "noise" mentioned beforehand.

TABLE 26.2

TOTAL HOURS OF TELEVISION VIEWED PER WEEK*

	Total 18+	18-34	35-54	55-64	65+
WOMEN in					
one person households	39	33	31	39	43
2+ person households	36	32	37	40	44
MEN in					
one person households	30	27	32	30	33
2+ person households	30	26	29	35	40

* During the 4-week period Jan. 25-Feb. 21, 1982
Nielsen "National Audience Demographics" report, Feb. 1982

Step number 3 is the stricter definition of purchase, and here we are dealing not with the technological breakthrough provided by product and price scanners, but a conceptual breakthrough which allows us to go beyond "purchase" (as though it meant nothing except that the buyer *acquired* the product,) to the nature of the exchange between buyer and seller; *i.e.*, purchase at a discrepant price. The opportunity here is to avoid the unrealistic advertising *versus* promotion problem that has plagued market planning and research design alike, and to eliminate the fear or the possibility, for example, that a market test could be upset by a promotion war or invasion of some kind.

The view that the impact of advertising is measured by buyer resistance to price promotion, or that brand loyalty is a function of at what price discrepancy a brand "loyal" customer will substitute another brand — is a view developed by Bill Moran, who has been analyzing the price elasticities associated with brand loyalty, and even defining brand loyalty in terms of those price elasticities.

Put another way, the payoff of advertising observed in any new study of effective frequency must not be sales or purchasing, because that always under estimates the impact of advertising and overestimates the impact of promotion. More important it gives the manufacturer the false idea that he has a choice of one or the other.

It makes more sense in the final analysis of data in an effective frequency study to focus on brand loyalty; *i.e.*, to what extent do loyal customers exposed to how much advertising stay with their brand as the price discrepancies begin to favor an alternative? Similarly, to what extent do non-brand loyal customers exposed to how much advertising become brand loyal as price discrepancies diminish?

If the study will collect purchase price data on the purchased and the competing brands, and if the advertising and the promotion environment is treated as one symbiotic economic system, then the opportunity is presented to do much more than a study of effective frequency of advertising, because sooner or later someone will ask "Effective for what?" and the answer should be "Effective for profitability."

Thus, the conceptual breakthrough represented by Bill Moran's work on brand loyalty and price elasticity permits the opportunity, I suggest, to replace the term "effective frequency" with the term "profitable frequency." Up to now the area of research on effective frequency has been of interest primarily to agency and media researchers and a few large advertisers. I suggest that technological, sampling, and conceptual breakthroughs available to us can position the subject of *profitable frequency* as of vital interest to *all* advertisers.

What I have said up to now concerns some conceptual elements of research design. The implied logistics also deserve some mention.

For example, Nielsen audimeters are not available to us and BEHAVIOR SCAN won't have 2,000 households wired for another year, and that possibly to be reduced to 400 single person households. In addition Stu Tolley has made a number of reports to ARF based on the analysis of Project Payout and other purchase scanning studies which indicate a very low level of purchase frequency per week per store for most brands studied. Finally, the emphasis on brand loyalty data defined by price differentials would be oriented not only to events of purchase, but to changes in purchase patterns over time. All of this suggests that small numbers, slowly collected, will be the rule in this type of study, albeit expensive numbers to obtain.

ARF does not have to shoot for a large landmark study. Landmarks are often created in a modest way. For example, the little Arrowhead Project #9 is probably the most widely quoted of all ARF studies. This experiment on the reliability of rating scales, which established the acceptance of the constant sum method in the United States, was done on thirty or forty subjects. That is, the total sample was 630 women but the data per scale per product was based on 35 interviews each.

So rather than a large initial study on effective frequency ARF can begin with a prototype study on one brand category, to firm up the design elements for such studies, and to then initiate an ongoing data bank in which ARF member companies are encouraged and helped to conduct studies of their own, in return for depositing brand-confidential findings in the data bank. In short, ARF can fulfill its function by leading the way rather than by "doing the big project." You'll hear more about the data bank from Jim Spaeth right after lunch.

To begin the ARF project right now, even before all the technology is in place, we can start on research design. The results of a prototype study could be "written up" in advance with blank but fully annotated tables.

This type of self-imposed discipline proves that you know what you want when going into a new research area. It tends to prevent the research from becoming only an interesting fishing expedition. It keeps you from being swamped by tons of unusable data. It facilitates a tight and more economical contract with suppliers. It gets everybody on board and going in the same direction right from the start.

This afternoon Gabe Samuels, Al Rohloff and Colin McDonald will address the subject of research design and analysis, and they will be followed by Bill McKenna and Gerry Eskin discussing data collection.

I trust that all of this, taken together, represents the opening day ceremonies for a formal ARF project on profitable frequency of advertising.

CHAPTER 27

THE TWO FUTURES OF ADVERTISING RESEARCH: IMAGES VS. MESSAGES

I have always felt that the status of advertising theory and *theorizing* has been held back by the joint existence of two different *processes*, each capable of providing a clear view of 'how advertising works," and each valid for certain types of products and services, but all adding up to great potentials for chaos and confusion when the two processes get confused or contaminated with each other, *i.e.*, when their *distinctiveness* is overlooked.

In 1965 I introduced the concepts of low and high *involvement* with advertising and in subsequent years it enjoyed some success in highlighting the existence of two different processes. I would like to take a further step by making the difference sharper, by relating them to some basic processes, and by indicating the kinds of new measures of advertising effectiveness which they may imply for the future.

To go beyond the concept of involvement with advertising means, for me, to first broaden the subject matter from advertising per se to communication in general, and secondly to sharpen the focus to the point where one asks "What are the two ways in which the human being acquires new information?'

The most useful answer to this question comes from the Russian neuropsychologist, the late Alexander Luria, who distinguished between *incidental* learning and *intentional* learning.

Most of us in advertising or public relations are interested in intentional learning. It has to do with what we hope will happen when we get people *to pay attention* to our messages. That's what the industry is proud to charge high fees for, *i.e.*, to show that it can attract audience attention, then create enough interest to hold the attention, communicate some comprehensible new facts or ideas, create some persuasion, even induce a desire to purchase, vote or act in accordance with the objectives of the campaign. And so, the obvious measures for pre or post testing such campaigns are measures of attention, recall, comprehension, persuasion, intent to buy, or vote etc. There's lots of concepts here, lots of measurement tools, lots to talk about with clients and colleagues.

Originally presented at American Association for Public Opinion Research, New York Chapter, February 8, 1983.

But most communication, and much of advertising, does not require any of this. Incidental learning, things you pick up in passing, things you note peripherally, out of the corner of your eye (speaking both literally and figuratively), is what constitutes most of learning. It is done without direct attention to what is learned. You drive down a road vaguely noting highway signs, you enter a new room and automatically note its contents, you watch a TV show and become aware of its background content without any close or motivated attention.

George Gerbner keeps reminding us that young people learn that smoking or drinking alcohol is natural because the characters on TV and films are seen smoking or drinking. No one intended that this be so, but because it is 'natural" for the script to call for such behavior, it is unconsciously absorbed into what the audience accepts as natural behavior. So, natural behavior begets natural behavior, and it all happens incidentally to some other process, such as entertainment.

Now, those people in advertising and public relations who do try to create incidental learning via posters, billboards, simple slogans, or attractive logos, are in a conceptual quandary. They cannot fall back on concepts or measures of recall, comprehension, believability, persuasiveness, etc., because for the most part these measures *do not aptly.* Many advertisers operating on this simpler level of communication fall back instead on massive test marketing and end sales results because they just do not trust, rightly so I would say, their understanding of what processes *do* intervene between their advertising efforts and the final sales results. At times, and again understandably so, they are tempted to oversimplify and say that the sales effects of advertising are totally a function of advertising weight — and that this involves a one-step process of creating and maintaining a familiar visual environment for the brand or products.

Intellectually, this at the opposite extreme from an advertising rationale based on brilliant, persuasive advertising copy guided by equally brilliant research, and involving a step by step process of leading the consumer up a ladder or chain of processes from awareness to comprehension, to believability, to interest, to whatever.

Thus, the advertiser who seeks only to familiarize the public with his product and give it some simply recognizable image will expect to buy this familiarization by the GRPs and cost per thousand advertising exposures, and will want to make sure that his retail shelf space, his packaging, and his pricing are all appropriate to one another. That is, he will teach people that his product has a name, a look, a function, a retail location, a price, a guarantee. He will not expect any great customer loyalty to withstand price cutting by rival brands, or an out-of-stock or availability problem. Andrew Ehrenberg and Bill Moran have each contributed greatly to our understanding of the fragile limits of this kind of brand loyalty. In all of this kind of advertising, which may be the larger portion of commercial advertising, most of our research concepts do not apply. The goals appear too simple. We pass them by. Why make a closer study of simple 'familiarity' when there are so many more elegant variables to study or add to.

The kind of advertising that students of communication prefer to study is the more heroic (and financially more rewarding) advertising that motivates people to desire such and such a brand, and to seek it out even when the manufacturer has a makeshift distribution system. It seems more important to study this type of advertising. It seems that if we can motivate them to actually desire certain brands, come hell or high water, price wars or not, then we night even transfer what we have learned to the teaching of more important, non-commercial topics such as politics, health habits, or public safety.

But alas, there stands George Gerbner of the Annenberg School of Communication saying that to teach people to use auto seat belts you don't have to create great TV commercials you just have to show them people in TV shows getting into cars and *buckling up*, and stop showing them people getting into cars and *not buckling up*. So, again we're back to familiarity versus persuasion, or familiarity learned without close attention versus persuasion created in the heat of very close attention and interest indeed. Neither process has any monopoly on important issues or topics.

To summarize, I would say that advertising campaigns based on incidental learning and oriented to such goals as familiarity are *under-studied by researchers* because of the apparent simplicity of the process, and because the advertisers have learned that advertising cannot be *the* primary force in their commercial success, but only *a* major force equal with other major marketing forces or elements. Meanwhile, advertising campaigns based on intentional learning with an attentive audience have a surplus of concepts and extremely logical and reasonable measures which are so very *attractive* that they not only compete with each other but often get applied where they do not belong.

Now I have two types of suggestions. One is intended to attract more interest in the study and Measurement of the public's incidental (*i.e.*, without conscious attention) and gradual familiarization *with images*. The other suggestion is intended to bring about some greater degree of order in the use of the more numerous measures related to persuasion, and the public's conscious response to *messages*.

The first suggestion is to consider the *intensity* of images, possibly through the study of what are called after-images, and I will elaborate on that in a moment. The second suggestion is that what we now consider to be the study of the effects of persuasive advertising is really the study of after-effects, *i.e.*, the before and after differences in measurement, or the later effects that can be detected subsequent to the actual exposure. Put another way, the suggestion is to study the immediate or co-incidental effects.

The study of after-images is not new. It attracted a great deal of attention in Europe in 1930 when E.R. Jaensch published his famous book *Eidetic Imagery*. He found that a certain percentage of children, about 7% to 11%, could retain certain types of visual images for about five seconds after the stimulus had been removed from view.

This is not a function of memory. The image was still seen and experienced as being present, and it could be described in detail. This is also not so-called photographic memory which involves an effort to call back from memory a black and white representation of the original stimulus. Eidetic imagery is in living color, enhanced by color, retained in color although with special responses to certain colors. Other studies confirmed that a percentage of children are what are called "eidetikers." It was considered for many years that only children could be eidetikers and that the characteristic disappeared with maturity. I might have commented at the time that the right hemisphere matures earlier than the left brain hemisphere. That's why so many children with early artistic skills seem to lose them as they get older — through *no* fault of any educational system. But then Professor Leonard Doob of Yale University, the same Leonard Doob who wrote the first textbook on public opinion research in 1940, began doing perceptual research in Africa, and reported in 1964 that among rural members of the Ibo tribe of Nigeria eidetic imagery was as common among adults as among children, but that among Ibos who migrated to large towns this was not so.

Between Jaensch and Doob, the study of after-images lay fallow because Dr. Jaensch got into political hot water. He had become a Nazi in the late thirties and expanded his theory of eidetic imagery into a theory of personality types, based oil imagery tests, which became racist and German "super-race" oriented. So eidetic imagery got a bad name. However, by 1974 Marks and McKeller asserted that "all adults are eidetic to some degree," and in 1977 Ahsen suggested that eidetic imagery is "a normal, universal phenomenon which appears at all ages." There is good, but not yet complete evidence in support of these assertions.

In the nineteen sixties in the United States there developed an awareness of a more widespread, though less dramatic type of "after-imagery' involving after images of only one half second and not especially restricted to color. Ulrich Neisser of Cornell University reported in his 1966 book on *Cognitive Psychology* a large number of since replicated studies which demonstrated what he called an image icon. The point is that even black and white perceptual stimuli do linger on after the stimulus is removed, and that whether it is for a quarter second, a half, or more *it is measurable*.

I'm reminded of Jim MacLachlan's measurements of response latency recently applied and then reported by Bob Grass of DuPont at an Advertising Research Foundation conference. If we now apparently accept in advertising research that we can measure how long it takes for a person to formulate a response to a stimulus, it should not be too difficult to also consider for how long the exposure to a stimulus is really *experienced*.

At first television or any animate stimulus seems to be a problem, because all of the work I refer to was with inanimate images where the experimenter controlled the appearance of the stimulus. But I'm sure you've all seen films where later on you *could not* get certain scenes out of your mind, even when you tried.

We don't have too much time so I'll end this suggestion with two stories about Lucky Strike cigarettes.

In the early fifties, I met Ben Gedalecia, research director of BBDO. He liked to ask people for how long they thought the "Lucky Strike Green has gone to war" campaign was on the air during World War II. The mean estimate was two years. I tried it on my classes at Columbia, and again the mean was two years. The campaign actually ran for only six weeks.

Those of you who remember the campaign may report that when you were listening to it on the radio you had vivid images of three destroyers racing across a *green* sea, and a subsequent and heightened awareness of the new *white* Lucky Strike package.

At the time, Ben's respondents and my students were trying to answer the question about the length of that campaign. I suggest to you that what was being measured was not a function of memory or recall, but a function of the intensity of the original images initially evoked, and by their related tendency to persist for some time immediately after the final moment of the physical exposure to the stimulus.

At the present time Lucky Strike has a campaign called "Lucky Strikes Again," apparently to restore familiarization with the brand. I have become very gradually aware of it from billboards. With all due respect to its creators I find that it created no imagery in me at first, then an awareness of the play on words, and currently the striking of a match, a wooden match. I shall observe my further reactions with great interest. I'll have more to say on all of this at an ANA Research Workshop next December 13th in a talk entitled "Beyond Memorability."

So much for after-images, which by the way are not after *effects* of exposure but part of the immediate response.

We "scientists" do love controlled experiments, and we "applied researchers" do love to demonstrate the end *results* of studies of advertising effectiveness. So what goes on in between "before' and "after" is typically lost. That's one of the reasons why the so-called "creatives" who make the advertising copy in ad agencies have so little professional (*i.e.*, their profession) interest in our research. Our research ignores their product as such.

What is lost to the researcher in ignoring immediate effects is the knowledge of *where* and *when within* an advertisement a problem or a particular strength may occur. Consider that many advertisers routinely pre-test commercials for interest, comprehension, believability, memorability, etc., etc., assuming that any or all variables may be important criteria of effectiveness, and so all new commercials must pass a *battery* of tests. But measurement of what goes on during exposure to a particular commercial can indicate that when a problem arises, say thirteen seconds into a TV commercial, the problem happens to be specifically a loss of interest, or a loss of comprehension, or a loss of believability or whatever. Thus, the immediate effects reveal what is salient to the effectiveness of the particular commercial, or where the chain of awareness, interest, comprehension, believability etc., may have broken down.

Many of you know that I have been active in physiological measurement of response to advertising, but this is not because my primary interest is in the physiological variables as such. My primary interest lies in the fact that the physiological measures are continuous throughout exposure to the commercial. Thus, when high or low points of response develop during exposure, the location of those high or low points are a guide to *what should be asked* of the respondent. Often the meaning of the high or low point is clear enough even without post-exposure interviewing. Thus, physiological measures when carefully taken just happen to be extremely convenient.

Physiological methods are not the only means of studying immediate response. You can interview sub-samples of respondents 5, 10, 15 seconds into a thirty-second commercial to determine so far what have been their reactions. Or you can set up distracting stimuli to note when they may take effect in diverting attention, etc.

But perhaps the easiest and simplest way to improve the study of immediate effects is to exert more discipline in the coding of play back, recall, and similar conventional measures. All too often I have seen codes supposedly reflecting response to a commercial which indiscriminately lump together what I would call the "What is it?" type of cognitive response or perception and the "What of it?" type of evaluative response. Thus, a particular object in the content of a commercial might be played back because it was simply noted, because it was liked, or because it was thought relevant, and yet all tallies are lumped together because the object permitted categorization for tallying as "recall."

In closing, I would stress the *importance* of immediate effects because I think that researchers today can handle this problem, if they will accept its importance, and then decide to do something about it. On the question of images and after-images, however, I think we need instead some truly basic research. I intend to move in that direction and will welcome the interest and participation of any of my colleagues.

CHAPTER 28

BEYOND RECALL

Here in the shadows of Harvard it is appropriate to turn once again to William James and to reconsider his strong signals as to how to go about a more fruitful line of psychological inquiry than that of classical learning and memory experiments — or by analogy today's somewhat sterile emphasis on tested recall. James' signal was to study experience, mental experience if you will, thinking, consciousness, the moment-to-moment reality of living. It was not common or popular for a turn of the century psychologist to make such suggestions, and it is still an unmet challenge in this country.

A certain photograph burned in my memory for twenty-five years. It showed the dozen or so founding members of the American Psychological Association assembled in beards and frock coats at Williams College in 1905. There was James at one side of the photograph, but there at the other side was "Guess Who?" Sigmund Freud! What was he doing there along with James?

I came to understand that these two had more in common than the others. Quite apart from psychoanalysis, so-called Freudian theory, sex or the unconscious, Freud the European shared with James the lonely emphasis on the study of what people were thinking, or attending to, moment to moment — the everyday dribs and drabs of conscious experience. The artists, the literary leaders, knew quite well what James and Freud were offering, and led by James Joyce they created a new artistic consciousness of human experience. But it was too revolutionary for academe.

Some called it an emphasis on the stream of consciousness. For today's purpose I would call it the rhythm or pace of attention, especially as it refers to response to advertising.

Academic psychology didn't want to bother with varying rhythms and paces of experience or attention. It was discordant. It often lacked a logical flow. Stimuli and responses intruded upon each other in a messy sequence. It was neater to simply ignore what was happening moment to moment and then just "test" the residual "effects." Thus, the testers, sometimes the "researchers," prevailed over those who would study the psyche directly.

Now I would like to cite a few studies that have something to say about the flow of human experience during exposure to advertising. These will focus

Originally presented at Marketing Science Institute, Cambridge, Mass., Nov. 21, 1983.

somewhat on the ebb and flow of attention, which James said was never *continuous* but always involved an effort to bring attention back again and again to the object of study. Perhaps he exaggerated in the use of the term "never," but he did make the point that attention tended to be staccato rather than even.

In the mid-nineteen sixties I published some articles in *Public Opinion Quarterly* on what was called a theory of involvement, especially low involvement with television advertising. Along with the theory went a measurement system that evaluated degree of involvement in terms of the number of thoughts that each respondent or viewer experienced during response, thoughts which linked something in the commercial stimulus with something in the personal mental life of the respondent. These so-called connections were studied and reported.

The amount of thinking during exposure to advertising is typically low. For low involvement television the theory requires it. Yet the general low incidence of connections or thoughts was not lower numerically than the numbers that the industry is used to getting on Starch readership scores or from a variety of unaided recall measurement systems. So while measurement of involvement never became popular, it only joined a host of unpopular low incidence measures. We are here today in part because recall is unpopular, or more precisely "not liked." In fact, no measures are liked because all evidence suggests that only a little bit of something happens during or after exposure to advertising. Thus, we must look at all those little bits and use them all. There are no big bits and never will be.

One the of the by-products of studying involvement with, or thinking during exposure to advertising was the discovery that attention to interesting editorial matter, in print on TV, carried over to heighten interest in the following or appended commercial message.

While the real and desirable interruption of attention to commercials by relevant personal thinking made for a staccato rhythm, the inertial effects of maintained interest suggested a smooth rhythm. Of course, both rhythms represent real processes and are in no way contradictory.

My 1960's data were all laboratory, but in 1967 1 joined the General Electric Company and for fifteen years had the opportunity to confirm my impressions with on-the-air exposure and tracking data. Thus, in 1982 in the *Journal of Advertising Research* I showed with 56 corporate television shows that GE commercials did best in shows that had continuity in format, *i.e.*, stories, dramas, but did less well in comedy/entertainment shows punctuated by "acts," or in talk shows punctuated by different interviews. Sometimes the same commercials shown in a popular dramatic show did two to three times as well on exposed–unexposed attitude control measures as the same commercials in a discontinuous format.

If I doubted the GE data, I was highly gratified the same year to be exposed to the Gallup & Robinson data banks which contain ten years of data on the effects of varying show environments on commercial scores. I wish you would all see their presentations. The people there are exceedingly modest. The data are a gold mine.

One example here may suffice. It's one I like particularly and concerns the relative environmental effectiveness of different sports. Which does the poorest? Of course, the American pastime, baseball. But why?

Just think of baseball. The batter approaches the plate, scuffs his shoes, kicks the bat end, rubs the bat, adjusts his cap, etc. The pitcher goes through a similar ballet of expressive gestures. It is all stop and go, a stately progression of sudden activity replete with interminable minor interruptions. The opportunities for attention to wander are endless. By comparison the time between football downs is modest, and the pace of basketball or ice hockey is comparatively furious.

All of these clues and hints concerning the inertial effects of, shall we say, preceding attention upon subsequent attention demand that we study it directly and immediately, and that the riches to be gained are long gone in twenty-four hours, or simply distorted in questions and interviews. Much as I dislike focused group sessions as empirically "messy" they often seem to capture the immediacy of the equally messy but direct response.

However, let's not give up, for last year I read a marvelous study entitled, "Watching children watch television" by a four-person team of Anderson, Alwitt, Lorch and Levin. This was from the Department of Psychology, U. Mass at Amherst, not far from here. They observed and counted the number of times children looked at the TV set, and at other available stimuli, such as toys, other children, etc. and so we now particularly introduce the term *distraction* and its implications. I don't have to tell you what controversy exists in the broadcasting industry about how often the set is on in empty rooms or in front of socializing audiences.

Well, the U. Mass team at one point analyzed three hours of TV watching of sixty 3-, 4- and 5-year-old children in three-second intervals of looking, for a total of 26,664 looks. They found that the probability of looking at the TV increased with further looking and decreased with decreased looking; *i.e.*, inertia was quite evident in both directions. Equally interesting, however, was that they noticed a lot of partially attentive monitoring, much of it audio, and some by occasional looks, so that the child could return to attentiveness when desirable. Every time the content of the TV changed, *i.e.*, as each new "bit" of information appeared some children left off attention and others resumed. In all, a rather active and busy process in the stream of consciousness for a phenomenon which is often described in terms of a passive audience.

And here we may perhaps part with James who emphasized that attention is never continuous to allow for those instances where a degree of attention is so intense that no distraction is possible. Think of a person studying or working or perhaps watching a movie or even "glued to the television set" so tightly that, as they say, "a bomb could go off and they wouldn't even notice it."

This intensity is also not passive. It can be observed, and it can be measured. It is timely I think that one of the current physiological research groups has recently developed a measure of resistance to distraction while viewing commercials. I refer to your friend Sidney Weinstein of NeuroCommunication Research Laboratories and his service of brain wave measurements.

The new measurement provides for thirty tiny flashes of light to be superimposed on a thirty second commercial, too small for conscious notice but quite adequate for a brain reaction to each flash. However, when the viewer becomes interested the brain ignores the flashes of light.

So here you have a built-in physiological distractor that probes and elicits a brain reaction while the screen is blank or the viewer's attention is minimal, but is overridden and wiped out by strong interest in the real stimulus.

While such a measure will be useful in application, it confirms again that the moment-to-moment ups and downs of human attention can equally resemble a turbulent stream or a placid lake. All that variety of experience and response is there for the study of it, in addition to today's timid emphasis on the mere results.

You have asked me to talk about "Beyond recall?" and I say that theory, laboratory research, tracking data, commercial data banks, and even physiological copy tests are all hinting that the advertising industry itself is not a very quick supporter of direct research on the advertising process, that *most of the human response* to advertising, that is, the direct response is rarely studied, that the techniques for doing so are still primitive (and might profit greatly from a little investment in the area).

I am also suggesting that to broaden advertising research and its company of "researchers" to research on advertising one will once again have to join with psychologists, anthropologists, students of mental imagery, psychoanalysts and artists who for almost eighty years since the founding of the American Psychological Association have been trying to say that the study of everyday mental experience, the study of thinking, of reverie, of the ebb and flow of consciousness and attention is the ultimate goal of any psychology, even as in this case a psychology of advertising. In short, we are in need of a research focus on what might be called "the advertising experience."

To the extent that this involves the nature of consciousness, and the content of thinking we must learn how to study images rather than just words, nonverbal memory rather than just recall, and always the unexpected "triggers" for what memories may be dormant. While Tom Ryan stressed the rise of sales promotion activities somewhat in opposition to advertising expenditures, those sales promotion activities may also be thought of as additional "triggers" or an extra boost needed for television advertising which has been made less effective overall by the switch to shorter and more frequent commercials.

Remember also that it was the Mike Ray MSI-sponsored study of "clutter" that showed the major problem to be not total commercial time per se, but the increased number of interruptions whether due to more commercials or more station promos.

To develop the implications and applications of this way of thinking, we will have to go beyond the measurement of attention, or "Are they looking or not," to the question of degree of attention, *i.e.*, "Are they *only* looking, or is something (anything) else happening?"

Television recall, I fear, has been teaching audiences *only* to look as commercials became shorter. I suggest that as researchers interested in what *is* happening to advertising audiences we should be able to show what is being lost (and possibly could be regained) when the viewer's attention becomes so casual. To do this requires not only a study of aftereffects, but a study of immediate experience.

CHAPTER 29

MEASURING MEMORY: AN INDUSTRY DILEMMA

Thirty years ago, in 1955, there took place what Darrell Lucas called "probably the finest example of experimental design ever reported on advertising research."[1] Sponsored, planned, and supervised by the Advertising Research Foundation; executed by the Alfred Politz organization; and usually referred to as the PARM study, it was officially entitled: "A Study of Printed Advertising Rating Methods."[2]

The major findings of this study concerned differences between recognition and recall measures of memory for advertising. Although some of the major findings were quite clear, what is not clear is how the industry has managed to repeatedly forget them in the ensuing years. I say repeatedly because the findings do get excitedly rediscovered from time to time and must then be once again accepted or ignored.

The thirty-year time gap is important, because, statistically, the industry is overdue for a once-and-for-all acceptance of the findings and their implications. I say "statistically overdue" on the basis of the work by Thomas Kuhn on *The Structure of Scientific Revolutions,* which is the title of his famous book in which he demonstrates that the great discoveries and insights of the preeminent scientists of history were not immediately accepted, but each, on the average, required about twenty years of professional debate, resistance, discussion, etc.[3] So, the PARM study of thirty years ago is, I say, overdue by some ten years for serious appreciation. We may even speculate as to why it has taken this long. Indeed, we hope it has only taken this long, and that we will not have to do it all over again in another ten years.

What the PARM study did, essentially, was to take a single issue of *LIFE* magazine and apply recognition and aided-recall measures to all the advertisements in that issue. Taking the methods used by the leading practitioners Starch and Gallup & Robinson, ARF trained Politz field staffs in their methods and used them with national samples of readers. Thus, any bias inherent, in the Starch or Gallup & Robinson staffs was removed, and their relatively small and controversial samples (in the hundreds) were upgraded to national samples for this one-time and historic test of precision in the measurement of memory. The scores achieved in this large study were then compared with the scores on the same ads measured in the usual way by the Starch and Gallup & Robinson staffs

Original Publication: *Journal of Advertising Research* Vol. 25, No. 4 (August 1985) (also appeared in Marketing Review, Feb. 1985, as a talk given at an AMA Breakfast Conference on February 7, 1985).

and on their own typically small samples. So what we have here is an evaluation of the modest commercial rating service as purchased by advertisers when those methods are treated to full scale sampling procedures and other objective refinements.

To the surprise of many, the recognition measure on Starch scores achieved very high reliability, and significantly higher than the recall scores. For example, there was 85 percent agreement between the PARM and regular Starch scores for women and 74 percent for men. By contrast, the aided-recall scores showed 68 percent agreement between PARM and Gallup & Robinson for women and 37 percent for men.

In those days the then-president of ARF, Sherwood Dodge, and such leading analysts of the day as Darrell Lucas, reacted to the study findings with elaborate language to describe and praise the stability of Starch scores and their typically small samples, pointing out that nothing would be gained by enlarging them. Yet, over the years, and still today, it seems always to be some kind of fashionable requirement for young and even some older advertising research types to grumble about the "small" and/or "sloppy" samples used by Starch. I have heard this grumbling through all my experience in advertising, and it is, in light of the facts, startling nonsense. But why? Why don't they know the relatively simple facts involved?

Secondly, the study suggested that recognition and recall measures were different in nature, and that one did not therefore have the simple choice of just which one was "better," or more reliable. That is, in some advertising situations you needed one or the other and in some you needed both. So, again, over the years the popular arguments of one method *versus* the other have been irrelevant. Unfortunately, in 1956, Sherwood Dodge muddied the waters somewhat by prematurely concluding that recognition and recall were measuring the same thing but that recognition was an "easier" test of memory (because of the higher norms). However, analysis of the data reveals that the Starch scores did not significantly erode over time (*i.e.*, in the weeks after exposure to the latest issue of *LIFE*), whereas the recall scores did erode significantly and quickly. Thus, the Starch scores seemed to measure a kind of memory that involved no forgetting, while the recall scores did. Darrell Lucas,[4] and later Bill Wells,[5] said that this meant that recognition was not a measure of memory at all but was a behavioral measure of whether or not the respondent had been exposed to the advertisement. But this cuts a fine hair then as to the memory of having been exposed. Yet, Lucas and Wells knew that the difference was somehow real. Wells speculated that the recognition measure could be a measure of attentiveness (*i.e.*, attention-getting quality) of the advertisement, and recall a measure of its meaningfulness. Now, all of this took place long before the awareness of brain hemisphere research and the current distinction between pictorial and verbal memory. We know now that right brain memory for pictures and images is extremely high with relatively little forgetting, and that memory for words is relatively low with much forgetting. Put another way, the next time someone says to you, "I can't remember your name, but I never forget a face," you must remind yourself that this is generally true of everyone, and a physical fact of nature. So, today, we would even more strongly indicate that recognition and recall scores, while both measures of memory, are measures of different kinds of memory. The refinements added to the earlier insights of Lucas and Wells do not change the implications very much. These are primarily that the measures are different, and one does not have a choice of which one is better. There is no "better."

Here again, the industry has not caught up with the facts. For example, when they do, they will demand recognition measures for television to use alongside of the recall measures for television and to parallel those of print. In the mid-sixties the Television Bureau of Advertising conducted a careful study of recognition of television commercials, but did not report it, and in 1970 the Starch organization tried unsuccessfully to market a recognition testing service for television. Perhaps they were premature. Both the Television Bureau of Advertising and Starch used a series of still photos to represent the commercial. There is now only one such measure available, Bruzzone. He too uses a still-photo technique, but through the mail!

The need for new recognition-type measures for television is underscored by the gradual extinction of the recall phenomenon from that kind of advertising, as shorter and shorter commercials increase the number of commercials that are aired. In this connection I cite the Bogart and Lehman JAR article of February 1983 in which they compare data on national samples of 1965, 1974, and 1981, where respondents were asked to identify the brand in the last commercial they saw just prior to the telephone interview.[6] This is no 24-hour recall. This is immediate recall. The results of their study were: In 1965 correct brand identification was 18 percent; in 1974 it went down to 12 percent; in 1981 it went down to 7 percent. Now correct brand identification is not the whole story. Perhaps, as it becomes extinct, some easier recall data will live on. But do not be alarmed; it is just a trend!

In summing up the situation identified by the PARM findings and elaborated upon in the light of subsequent related research, we have an advertising research situation in which the audience for advertising, at least for low-interest, low-involvement, repeat-purchase products, is best described as an audience that recognizes the pictures and images but cannot recall the words. We are all like the person who claims, "I don't remember your name, but I never forget a face."

The paradox, in terms of research, is that when we want to evaluate an advertisement or a campaign we typically in our research confine ourselves to words — *i.e.*, to the low-cost telephone with its word-for-word questions and its word-for-word answers. What we get back from the audience is a predictably weak response, suggesting little impact of advertising.

I suggest that the industry is comfortable with such a modest image of its powers, in part because it rationalizes the need for larger advertising budgets, and in part because it has kept the Federal Trade Commission and social critics at bay.

It may in the process keep researchers at bay too, that is, keeping their influence down. Recall measures "make sense" to agency management. They find the logic of it appealing. But any time researchers encourage such comforting use of a questionably reliable measure, they become vulnerable eventually to a variety of attacks and limitations.

The times are changing, however, for today the PARM findings are being taught to MBA students in the Harvard-MIT community. The advertising clients of tomorrow may be more empirically minded on this issue. For example, the most recent review and reappraisal of the PARM findings appears in the Spring 1983 issue of *Marketing Science* entitled: "Recall, Recognition, and the Measurement of Memory for Print Advertising" by Richard Bogozzi and Alvin Silk, both of the MIT faculty, in their Sloan School of Management. I would just like to quote a few lines from their concluding discussion:

> It has frequently been advocated that reliability and sensitivity be employed as criteria in selecting a testing procedure or service (Axelrod, 1971; Young, 1972) but this recommendation appears not to have been widely adopted due to the limited availability of relevant information about reliability. In a survey of leading advertisers and agencies, Ostlund, Clancy and Sapra (1980, p. 19) found that "very few of the advertiser and agency respondents claimed to employ any formal standards of reliability, sensitivity and validity in judging the worthiness of copytesting methods, whether applied to television or to print" and went on to observe that "it is strange that there has not been greater demands for full documentation on at least the reliability of alternative copy-testing methods in widespread use" (p.22, 23).[7]

What is most strange is that this situation has persisted for thirty years in the face of available facts.

---

[1] Lucas, Darrell B., "The ABC's of ARF's PARM," *Journal of Marketing* vol. 25, no. 1 (1960), pp. 9-20.

[2] Advertising Research Foundation. *A Study of Printed Advertising Rating Methods.* 5 vols. New York: Advertising Research Foundation, 1956.

[3] Kuhn, Thomas, *The Structure of Scientific Revolutions.* (Chicago: University of Chicago Press, 1970).

[4] Lucas, *op. cit.*

[5] Wells, William D., "Recognition, Recall and Rating Scales," *Journal of Advertising Research* vol. 4, no. 3 (1964), pp. 2-8.

[6] Bogart, Leo, and Charles Lehman. "The Case of the 30-Second Commercial,." *Journal of Advertising Research* vol. 23, no. 1 (1983), pp. 11-19.

[7] Bogozzi, Richard, and Alvin Silk, "Recall, Recognition and the Measurement of Memory for Print Advertising" *Marketing Science* (Spring 1983), p. 125.

CHAPTER 30

A PERSONAL RETROSPECTIVE ON THE USE OF PHYSIOLOGICAL MEASURES OF ADVERTISING RESPONSE

Having been exposed from earliest years to my father's stories of his 1917-18 World War I experiences at Le Bourget and Etampes airfields in France, I was determined to go to Randolph Field, Texas, then known as the "West Point of the Air." Since two years of college were required I enrolled at CCNY in 1939, but when the two years were up found myself majoring in a psychology department which was unique at the time, *i.e.*, (1) it had a high altitude (simulation) chamber, and (2) it offered courses in applied physiological psychology. On graduation in 1942 I went into the Army Air Corps, not as a pilot, but as an aviation psychologist.

In 1944 after two years of work on air crew selection and training problems I completed my first physiological project, which was to develop a physical (*i.e.*, non-verbal, non-interview) measure of reactions to prolonged stress among combat crews. The successful procedure, based on differential threshold responses to a flickering light correlated highly with independent psychiatric diagnosis, and when declassified in 1947 was published in *Psychosomatic Medicine*.[1]

Post-war, along with many other former military psychologists I entered the business world, first in the area of personnel research, but gradually moving over to marketing and communication. By the late nineteen fifties I was once again involved with physiological problems in my role as research director of the industrial design firm of Raymond Loewy Associates. As the firm produced an endless supply of new package designs, corporate logos, stores, restaurants, shopping centers, highway signs, aircraft interiors, automobiles, etc., I was able to introduce a variety of tachistoscopic, eye-tracking and other visual tests to determine under various conditions which designs were most visible, attention-getting, and appropriate to what the designer and client had in mind. It was in

---

Undated Manuscript, ca. 1986

Editor's note: This was written in 1986 and is an updating of a 1981 paper (Chapter 24) that was presented to an AMA Attitude Research Conference. The new personal elements themselves justify separate inclusion of the piece, and a number of the changes and additional substantive observations are of interest as well.

these years that I began a long collaboration with Dr. Norman H. Mackworth of Stamford University. "Mac," was inventor of the "Optiscan," prototype eye-tracking camera, descendants of which are now used by the two commercial eye tracking services in the United States.

In the early nineteen sixties I moved over from industrial design into advertising, and after my initial introduction to that field at Ted Bates Advertising was lured into the Interpublic Group by Russell Schneider and Dr. Herta Herzog. They wanted me at Marplan, in part, to head up a perception laboratory which Marion Harper had approved in order to apply the techniques of pupil dilation measurement developed by Dr. Eckhard Hess, then chairman of the department of psychology at the University of Chicago.

Over the years Hess and I had many running battles over whether the pupil response was "directional" *(i.e.,* expanding with liking and contracting with disliking). I never did see a contraction as he defined it. To me the pupil response measured arousal, good or bad, period. Despite Hess's battles with me, and others, on this point it did, as a measure of arousal, prove useful. On taking the job in the first place I immediately set out, with general approval, to do a small validation test. With the help of friends at Hallmark Cards and Georg Jensen, Inc., we arranged to conduct field tests of pupil responses to greeting cards and to sterling silver patterns. The rank order of pupil responses was later compared with the sales rank of the tested items for the previous period. Rank order correlations were +.4 for cards and +.6 for silver patterns. The number of cases (N=23) was too small to conclude statistical significance but the results on reliability and sensitivity were encouraging (see Chapter 4 above). Note, however, that the correlations between verbal ratings and sales were about the same as those between pupil and sales.

In the following years several hundred new television commercials were tested via pupil response. Those were the days when Marion Harper set up a large budget for the creative group to spend on research, entirely on their own. It came to be routine for some groups to use pupil tests on all their new commercials, whether the client saw or paid for them or not. But the most interesting research finding was that among one hundred and sixty commercials the peak pupil response between 4 and 10 seconds after the onset of the commercial correlated +.83 with the average response for the total of sixty seconds. That meant that very early on the respondents made some form of "decision" or subjective commitment as to whether the commercial was or was not something they would watch closely or with interest. This finding, evoking recollections of what sociologists called "definition of the situation" or what psychologists called a "frame of reference" also suggested that in the real world many commercials would be quickly tuned out and either not watched, not absorbed, or not remembered. It also reminded us that forced exposure in the laboratory, at least after the first few seconds, may in many cases be producing data of only academic interest. In this sense television is similar to print advertising, *i.e.,* if the picture and headline doesn't immediately arouse interest few readers will bother to read the body copy.

In the late sixties a combination of reduced research budgets, controversy over the "directionality" of the pupil, and changed personnel led to the gradual demise of pupil measurement at Marplan, although eye-tracking research lived on. My own view of this demise sees it more in terms of the trade secrecy which kept Dr. Hess's elaborate and precise stimulus preparation procedures from being made available to others. Thus, when other enthusiasts attempted pupil measurement without adequate technology their results were bound to be contradictory with one another. This did not help the reputation of pupil research. Considering the unique financial investment which Interpublic made in such research it was understandable, however, that they should have sought competitive advantages and exclusive use of it.

By 1967 1 had joined the General Electric Company as manager of corporate public opinion research, which included responsibility for evaluation of corporate advertising. An informal agreement at the time of joining GE was that I would pursue my "hobby," as I called it, of physiological research, or "fooling around in the laboratory" to the extent of one percent of my departmental budget. This was more than adequate for me since I preferred working in the laboratory with very small samples, and was not then attempting to build a new measurement service in that area, but only to learn more about the nature of response to advertising.

For the following fifteen years I did pursue small scale laboratory research and it was helpful in stimulating a variety of professional articles having to do with advertising theory (see, *e.g.*, Chapter 18 above). Much of the work involved research on brain wave response to advertising, which perhaps does hold the promise of a new and better-standardized measurement service for advertising. During the same period of time however I tried to systematize what were the requirements for an ideal physiological measurement system, and to understand better why previous attempts had not been as successful as could be desired. Clearly none of the systems have been completely understood. Often their unique qualities were appreciated, but without an appreciation of the general principles involved.

A general understanding would begin with the subject of adrenaline, which is produced when the body is aroused. When adrenaline goes to work the heart beats faster and more strongly and even enlarges. Blood flows to the extremities and increases capillary dilation at the fingertips and even in the earlobes. The temperature of the skin increases, hair follicles stand up, the pores of the skin emit perspiration and the electrical conductivity of the skin surface is affected. The pupils of the eye dilate, electrical waves in the brain increase in frequency, breathing is faster and deeper, and the chemical composition of expired air is altered. There is a choice therefore of perhaps fifty different measures, which to a great extent are all measuring the same thing, *i.e.*, arousal.

The question of which of many different measures of arousal to use is to some extent irrelevant; *i.e.*, since they are all measuring the same thing. But some are more convenient to use, depending on the kind of stimuli one has in mind to test, whether one can make do with a laboratory environment or must require unobtrusive measurement of natural response, whether good equipment is available for a perhaps less preferred measure but not for the measure of first choice, and finally the state of the budget since some variables can be measured inexpensively and some only at great expense.

By and large the heart, lung, blood system and skin oriented variables can be measured relatively inexpensively, while variables associated with the central nervous system (*i.e.*, eye and brain) are relatively more expensive. However, the major budgeting item in an effective system is not the pickup of the variable, but how it is transmitted, communicated and displayed to the onlooker.

While the image of physiological research is that of laboratory research, with respondents hooked up to gadgets, and researchers or clients "looking on" with interest, it is only a myth that it *has* to be this very obtrusive kind of research. While I preferred a laboratory setting, I could have had a completely unobtrusive system by sampling the expired air of respondents, provided that only one person is in the room. I could have used the General Electric "condensation nuclei counter" which quite literally counts the number of nitrogen ions in the air sample. It is very sensitive at great distances, and capable of processing great amounts of air very quickly. The presence of nitrogen ions is a function of the urea and/or ammonia in the expired air, the same chemicals involved in perspiration or urination. The condensation nuclei counter was not originally intended for physiological research, but I ran across it at GE's R&D laboratories at Schenectady in 1968 and found that it might do the job, if respondents could be tested one at a time in atmospherically controlled environments.

The question of unobtrusive measurement had been discussed back in Marplan days when respondents were peering into boxes to record pupil dilation or participating in eye-tracking tasks that required their heads to remain immobile throughout the test. At one time Dr. Hess proposed putting the respondents in a "box" (*i.e.*, a room) equipped with hidden cameras which could photograph their eyes at a distance. The U.S. Army Human Engineering Laboratory at the Aberdeen Proving Ground in Maryland does just that. As the world's most advanced eye-tracking laboratory, with fully computerized scoring, it goes even further. Thus, while their respondents do go into a special room with remote cameras at work, they sit in an easy chair while viewing the test stimuli, and are free to move naturally in the chair. This is possible because the remote camera is continuously being aimed at their face and eyes by a camera operator who is also remote and invisible.[2] It is the opinion of the staff (Dr. Richard A. Monty, et al) that eye tracking data from respondents whose head positions and movements are restrained produce research findings which are largely artifacts of the measurement procedure.

I preferred, however, to use openly obtrusive measures and to confront, and hopefully to solve, the problems of the obvious artificial setting. This requires the use of habituated respondents, respondents who are tested long enough to have gotten over the novelty of the laboratory situation. This may take an hour or more, and varies somewhat from respondent to respondent. The measure to be used must, to begin with, indicate when each respondent has calmed down to the level of "normal" television viewing, so that the real testing may begin. It is indeed awkward and expensive to treat each respondent in this custom-tailored manner, but it is essential. Otherwise the respondents are just too excited by their strange environment to provide anything like representative samples of the kind of behavior in which you are really interested.

The use of habituated respondents became a dramatic issue in 1969 when I began collaborating with Dr. Sidney Weinstein. At the time he was director of the Neuropsychological Laboratory of New York Medical College. Since then he has set up his laboratory in Danbury, Connecticut. But in 1969 I asked him to record the first brain wave data comparing response to magazines and television. The seated respondent, a secretary, was asked to read a magazine for some time. Then a television set was turned on and she shifted her attention to it. The change in brain wave patterns was instant and dramatic shifting from fast to slow frequencies and from large to small amplitude waves. The results (Chapter 15 above) were of much interest. I tell the story here because the later publicity surrounding publication of the article often referred to the tests I had made on "my secretary." I had to repeatedly emphasize it was Dr. Weinstein's secretary who was the subject, and that this made all the difference. She was quite accustomed to being used as a "guinea pig" by the laboratory staff and was not at all impressed by the gadgetry encountered in her daily work environment. She was a clearly habituated respondent.

A physiologist who is new to the world of advertising research will quickly find that what the industry wants to buy is the prediction of success or failure of new ads. The buyer may ask the physiologist (1) if he can do so, and (2) if he can do so better than those researchers who use only verbal data. The physiologist, often an enthusiastic former academic, and sometimes of high status, says "Yes," and "Yes" to both questions. This answer, coming from high academics (with no prior experience in advertising research) then sets the standards for claims made by others, including non-academics, who also sell physiological research. It also sets the standards for what the buyer thinks he "wants," or needs." But the right answers are "No" and "No." Physiological research is not good at predicting success of advertising, and certainly not better than verbal data, although perhaps no worse.

The great virtue of physiological measurement of animate stimuli such as television, its great advantage over verbal data, is that it is co-incidental; *i.e.*, not after the fact, not an exit interview, not dependent on what was remembered later on, but a live "blood, sweat and tears" response moment by moment synchronous with the stimuli. When that fact is appreciated we will stop talking about prediction and validity. Instead, we will ask "What happens to viewers at second 1, second 2, second 3, etc., of the commercial. What parts, what words, what presenters, what gestures, what camera shots, what displays, what assertions turn the viewer on and off, from moment to moment?

While I would like to see physiological measurement focus on this virtue and get off the prediction and validity kick, I don't think it's going to happen until two conditions are fulfilled. One is that the moment-by-moment results, the "findings," must be displayed moment to moment on a video monitor so that both the researcher and the client can see them super-imposed on the commercial itself; *i.e.*, again a "co-incidental" report format. There's a little extra hardware involved there, but it does permit the data to "speak for itself." It permits the report to consist of a tape, which can then be viewed over and over at will by the client.

What kind of taped report — of individual respondents or of aggregated data? The recommended principle is to test respondents individually to see whether an aggregated type of report would have the same graphic pattern as the individual. If the aggregate is only a statistical set of moment to moment averages, it has no value, meaning, or validity for use, especially by creatives. When there is not a statistical aggregate that is also true for the individuals, then individual records should be shown.

There are some very special virtues of such an approach, and some special applications, most especially to the most general problem in advertising research, which is the large and depressing gap between what we could call good scientific practice on the one hand, and conventional ad pre-testing on the other. Scientific or experimental practice would require that the stimulus — as experienced by the respondent — be identified. It rarely is, but instead is assumed to be *the* ad, *the* commercial, sometimes the entire ad or commercial, as if it were a single stimulus.

Scientific practice would also require that the response — as evidenced by the respondent — be identified. It rarely is, but instead the researchers impose selected measurements of types of responses in which they, the researchers, happen to have an interest, or a belief. Until this gap between stimulus and response is narrowed, there can be little progress in understanding how advertising works, either in the general or the particular. A special role for physiological measurement in narrowing this gap would be to help identify what is stimulus, and what is response.

Imagine a researcher, sitting in front of a screen which shows simultaneously, and in synch, the commercial and the respondent's moment to moment physiological reaction. There is no prepared questionnaire or interviewer guide. One can see that the respondent's arousal increases gradually throughout the course of the commercial, or that it decreases. Each would suggest a different question to be asked of the respondent; *e.g.*, "You seemed to become more interested?" or "You seemed to be interested at first, but then less so?" Or one might see that the respondent's arousal peaked at one or two places, and he or she could ask about those places. Or one might find a level high, or a level low, and say "You seemed to find the whole thing interesting?" Or to find nothing of interest? Etc.

These types of questions are simple encouragements to the respondent to talk, and in that talk one can confirm what about the commercial was the stimulus, the object of attention, and what response, if any, (*i.e.*, "what of it") can be identified. Admittedly the latter is more difficult, but it is worth distinguishing between declarative responses "I noticed that," or "That's what got my attention going," and reactive responses such as those that I call connections, or thoughtful associations to content not in the commercial, but to content in the personal lives of the respondent.

I note parenthetically that low involvement is more common than high involvement, and that one connection or real thought per commercial per respondent is toward the high end of the continuum. All the more reason to identify such an important event, and to locate where and when it occurred during the exposure.

Now, say one identifies peak points of interest in a commercial and then, at the end of the commercial, one asks about those recently experienced peak points. That is, of ten or twelve seconds ago. Just as unaided twenty-four-hour recall, even among proven TV viewers, often produces nothing, so even a twelve second delay in the laboratory may lose valuable comment, especially from a non-verbal type of person.

What I am suggesting here is how to encourage people *to* verbalize responses, people who might be able to answer structured but irrelevant test questions but who shy away from relevancy, people who would prefer not to commit themselves, people who usually end up in the "don't knows," especially in response to visual stimuli. Now, if twelve seconds is too long to wait there is an alternative, which is to stop the commercial whenever a high peak (or a sudden drop) occurs, and ask immediately about what's happening.

The kind of interviewer that's beginning to take shape here, even though the data are physiological, is an interviewer that we would call clinical; *i.e.*, a skilled observer of the individual case, who proceeds in terms of the particular case (*i.e.*, respondent) to find out what's happening. There is no training experience like this to teach one more about how advertising works, how communications work. One might require such experience of every so-called advertising researcher, of every so-called creative person in an agency. Some wouldn't like that kind of work or be good at it, but they would forevermore know something about the nature of advertising effects that they couldn't learn in any other way.

If the clinical role of the researcher in this proposal seems a bit difficult, too demanding, too clinical, keep in mind that some of the questioning of the respondent might be handed over to the data itself. That is, a playback of the physiological measurement superimposed on the commercial can be shown to the respondent, and as a high point of reaction is shown the tape can be stopped, the researcher can look at the respondent, raise his or her eyebrows, adopt a quizzical expression, and wait — and if the respondent still can't talk, he or she may at least be able to point.

Well, so much for general principles. What about the future? Here I want to say a few words about the special significance of brain research.

Earlier I mentioned the fifty different ways to measure physiological arousal, all of them somehow stimulated by the injection of adrenaline into the bloodstream. The whole idea then of a physiological measurement laboratory is predicated on the assumption that the stimuli to be studied are arousing, or interesting. And of course, if you bring naive, unhabituated respondents into a physiological laboratory they certainly will be aroused by the novelty and adventure of the experience, and the consequent "hyping" of the stimuli. This raises the awful possibility that with habituated respondents there just may be no adrenaline, and no arousal and no measurement worth taking.

So we better have a clear idea of what habituation *is* in the first place. The respondent who is thinking about the laboratory, the researchers, and the tests is not habituated. The respondent who has gotten used to these things so that he is content to look at the stimuli without thinking of laboratory, researcher or tests is habituated. What diminishes during the habituation period is the number and types of non-relevant thoughts occurring to the respondent and their associated arousal. Meanwhile, the willingness to *look at* experimental stimuli continues.

Because brain data, thanks to the lateral specialization of the two hemispheres, can distinguish between "thinking" and "just looking" we can tell more confidently when habituation has been achieved, and when "normal" testing can begin. I reported, in effect, a minimum one hour habituation period for viewing of television commercials in a study by Val Appel and Sid Weinstein (Chapter 23 above).

It is this insight into habituation of left-brain "thinking" response which separate brain data from simple measures of arousal. That is, if you used one of these other measures and found a decline to some baseline during the first hour, you wouldn't know if that decline meant a decline of thinking, or of vigilant viewing or of both. Brain data can tell you when the relatively untiring viewing behavior is proceeding without the extraneous and non-relevant mental associations to the laboratory environment. In short, if nothing else, brain data permit a cleaner experiment via the measurable elimination of the "laboratory" artifact.

Brain wave frequency data do have limitations. In 1970 I published frequency data based on thirty-second samples of respondents' behavior.[3] Over the years we reduced this to ten, and finally to five second readouts. Thus, it was not "moment to moment" data as with the simpler measures of arousal. The brain *waves* themselves have a form and time span of up to 1½ seconds. At the present time, retired from General Electric and in my own consulting business, I am working with Dr. Weinstein on a procedure that does permit (*e.g.*) sixty measures per minute. The compromise is that the measures are not at one second intervals, but involve a random pattern of probes and measures that average out to one second. But this adaptation of a procedure based on "cortical evoked potentials" is another story, and just emerging from the developmental stages. It is an attempt to measure resistance to distraction while viewing advertising. I mention it in part to bring this retrospective up to date (October 1983).

In closing I'd like to list a few one-liners of advice about setting up physiological laboratories to measure animate stimuli (the problem of a perceptual laboratory to measure inanimate stimuli is in some ways more complex, and I'll leave that for another time).

1. Design on paper the laboratory you want.
2. Discover that the equipment manufacturers will not quite have what you want and will suggest something different. Hold fast to your specifications!
3. Be prepared for the fact that the desired equipment will not at first work properly, even when the manufacturer is demonstrating it.
4. Hire a full time "electronic junkie" to provide your equipment with tender love and care.
5. Take pains to identify in every piece of equipment that intercedes between response and feedback what is the lag, if any, since a few microseconds here and there can add up to an unknown out-of-synch condition between the portrayed stimulus and the portrayed response shown on the screen or tape.
6. Prepare each interviewer to go to work on a particular commercial by having it played to him or her fifty times, or until the interviewer can almost act it out in his or her sleep. In general, this type of laboratory makes a whole second look like a huge piece of time and makes a complete commercial seem like thousands of verbal, pictorial, gestural and other complex stimuli, which of course, it is. That's the going-in problem. So one must be intimately familiar with the commercial before getting intimate with a live respondent.
7. If you find that a single respondent produces far more data than you can almost cope with, be encouraged that you're on the right track.
8. If because of the above you begin to spend a lot more time with individual cases; *i.e.*, with single respondents, perhaps only one respondent studied repeatedly, you can console yourself with any of the following three justifications:
   (a) To a degree, and in response to certain stimuli, all individuals are alike, that is, "eyeballs *is* eyeballs," or the laws of vision apply to all. In a sense, when dealing with dark and light, noise and silence, you are dealing with a relatively un-

varying biological part of the response and this should be identified.

(b) The natural emphasis on individual respondents is indeed a new, or at least revived approach, which is gaining momentum, and which has recently been represented by Michel Hersen and David H. Barlow's book *Single Case Experimental Designs: Strategies for Studying Behavior Change*, published by Pergamon Press (New York) in 1976 and/or Thomas R. Kratochivill's *Single Subject Research: Strategies for Evaluating Change*, published by the Academic Press (New York) in 1978. Notice that the subtitles of both refer to the evaluation of "change." You will find that they fit nicely into problems of changing attitudes as well as changing behavior.

(c) The final justification for studying individual respondents is the excitement you will feel at being able to do what most advertising researchers only dream about, and that is the experience of actually seeing the immediate effects of advertising take place before your very own eyes.

---

[1] Krugman, H.E., "Flicker Fusion Frequency as a Function of Anxiety Reaction," *Psychosomatic Medicine*, vol. 9, no. 4 (1947), p. 269.

[2] R.A. Monty, "An Advanced Eye-Movement Measuring and Recording System," *American Psychologist*, vol. 30, no. 3 (1975).

[3] "Mass Media and Mental Maturity," Chapter 13 above. The published version of this piece has not been located.

CHAPTER 31

ADAPTING EXISTING SURVEY DATA BANKS
TO SOCIAL INDICATOR PURPOSES

There is a fool in one of Molière's plays who was delighted to discover that he had been speaking prose all along without knowing it. I wonder where the line should be drawn when we look back at our own experiences in survey research. Have we been speaking "social indicators" all along, but didn't know it, *i.e.*, until the term became fashionable? Must we really start anew with a blank page?

Before answering this question, let's review some definitions. Kenneth C. Land in his recent (American Sociologist, Nov. 1971) article, "On the Definition of Social Indicators" notes that . . .

The term "social indicators" (or one of the related terms, "social accounts," "social bookkeeping," "social intelligence," "social reporting," or "monitoring social change") has become part of the vocabulary of professional social scientists, social commentators, legislators, and governmental administrators in recent years. Literature relevant to social indicators includes early programmatic statements (Bauer, 1966; Biderman, 1969; Gross, 1966; Moore and Sheldon, 1965; and National Commission on Technology, Automation, and Economic Progress, 1966), scholarly and legislative works (Ferriss, 1969; 1970; Gross, 1967a,b; Mondale, 1969; Sheldon and Moore, 1968; U.S. Department of Health, Education and Welfare, 1969), and several recent reflective and sometimes critical evaluations of the preceding and related items (Bell, 1969, Duncan, 1969; Land, 1971a; Olson, 1969; Sheldon and Freeman, 1970).

Three recurring claims for social indicators arising from the exigencies of public policy decisions are that social indicators can help (1) to evaluate specific programs, (2) to develop a balance sheet or system of social accounts, and (3) to set goals and priorities. These claims have recently been criticized by Sheldon and Freeman (1970) who, with regard to the setting of goals and priorities, remark (1970:99) that although it is foolish to argue against the use of indicators in planning

Undated Manuscript, ca. 1972

and development or to expect them to disappear as a means of influencing politicians and their electorates, it is naive to hold that social indicators in themselves permit decisions on which programs are to be implemented, and it is especially naive to hold that they allow the setting of priorities. Sheldon and Freeman's point is that priorities and goals are more dependent on national objectives and values than on assembled data. Furthermore, with respect to the evaluation of specific programs, Sheldon and Freeman (1970:100) argue that this use of indicators would require one to be able to demonstrate statistically that programs, rather than uncontrolled variables, determine the outcomes (measured by the indicators). According to them there is no possibility at the present time of meeting the requirements of controlling for contaminating variables with available indicators. Sheldon and Freeman (1970:102) argue also that the claim that social indicators can be used to develop a system of social accounts is not reasonable because there is no social theory capable of defining the variables of a social system and the interrelations between them, and such a theory is an essential prerequisite to the development of a system of social accounts. In brief, the Sheldon-Freeman paper constitutes the most caustic critique thus far of some of the claims that have been advanced for social indicators. The authors go on to argue that the social indicator movement can contribute to the more modest and realistic goals of (1) improved descriptive reporting, (2) analysis of social change, and (3) prediction of future social events and social life.

For our purposes the more modest view of social indicators held by Sheldon and Freeman is quite satisfactory. None of the definitions moreover limit the data to survey data and all including the Sheldon-Freeman view concern indicators of social *change*. If then we are mainly speaking social change, we can go back to Molière's France but in a more serious vein, to the France of August Comte, the father of sociology and one of the first to describe a science of society in terms which included the need for indicators of change. And there is already too much social change data behind us to ignore without galloping off for more data — even if that's an easier way to raise money. A number of long-established research centers in this country *can* study their own past data, if they dare. Very few people have made this a specialty. A notable exception is Hazel Gaudet Erskine who brilliantly edits the Polls section of the *Public Opinion Quarterly*.

To dare to look at past data is to look at what seems like "old" data. The opinion survey profession overvalues current and newsworthy data, rarely stops to look back or take stock. It identifies and competes more with journalism than with the social science, and looks forward to each new and latest survey with never slackening anticipation. As an industry, it contributes to a repository for old survey data at Williams College. Meanwhile, a few lonely scholars do a little long-term analysis.

It does not have to be so. Old data can be re-analyzed to see what indicators they may hide. Let me describe our still young efforts to put one of our regular opinion surveys on a "social indicator" basis. Of course, our opportunity to learn was limited in part by the nature of what we had to work with. However, if others try with their data, they will have the opportunity to learn other things. If several were willing to try, we might together learn a great deal in six months.

The data I will use as an example involves repeat national samples surveyed four times a year back through 1965. It is called the General Electric Quarterly Index of Company Relations (QICR). We are now working on survey number thirty-three. The survey is used to track the corporate reputation, issues in which the company has an interest, and a variety of topics which we judged (at the time of inclusion) to be of imminent, potential or growing interest to one or more divisions of the company. Some questions have been asked every time, some only annually, some at longer but regular intervals and some erratically. Since the company is so very much diversified, there are few topics of national concern which are not represented. The question is, "Do these past data hide trends which when detected and/or carried forward could provide more sensitive indicators of subtle social change?"

To look backward, however, past the trends which have already been discovered and reported, one has to do some things which are different. To begin, you may simply have to turn some tables upside down, *e.g.*, tables of response to open-ended questions. Instead of looking at the main responses to major trends already somewhat in evidence, you may want to look harder at the trends of the little numbers at what is usually the bottom of the table.

If you do that, however, you'll complain that the N's are small, and that the numbers may be unstable. But you won't know. You won't know enough about their stability because the survey field has held the science of statistics at arm's length. It does so by attaching to every survey report appendix a p.q. error estimate formula and a rule of thumb table of confidence limits. These are monotonously the same in all survey reports without regard to the survey content or the variance of the individual questions. Our typical appendices were born decades ago in the days of quota sampling. They are nonsense today. They are destructive today. They stand between the survey worker and the practice of statistics.

The nub of it all is that each and every question in a survey has its own limits of error — and beyond the matter of sample size. It is the variance which is hidden even in a simple "Yes-No" response, but which still can be uncovered and measured. The trick, as you guessed, is to use a replicated sample. But you may say that's okay for new surveys; the old ones have been done a different way. Not so. Thanks to Jerry Greene of Marketmath and my associate, Joan Black, the card decks of our "old" surveys have been sorted into five equal replicates based on a random treatment of the *last* digits (not the identifying first digits) of the interview identification number. The variances across the five then become the basis for a whole new approach to significance testing, and more importantly, to trend-fitting over time.

I've oversimplified the procedure but the point is that you *can* go back and clean up old samples and you can go back to small "unstable" numbers to fix precisely their degree of stability. With firmer numbers then you can afford to look more carefully at the growth of trends and of issues. We are so used to seeing new issues "burst" upon the stage of public consciousness, when in fact some that we have tracked, such as those involving the environment, had been measurably growing for years prior to the "burst."

So much for sampling. Unlike Molière's fool, we have not been speaking statistics, and not seriously studying emerging trends, but we could and should. Now another way of recapturing old survey data is to reconsider our questions and what they mean. Let us say that in looking backward we had wished that we had measured such supposed trends as anti-materialism and/or anti-technology, but that we had asked no questions on the subject per se. At one point, this was somewhat the case with us.

Well, we didn't have questions on materialism per se, but we did have re-peated questions on such things as (1) what one liked and disliked about one's present dwelling place and what one would like most in a new place, (2) what one would do with an extra amount of income, (3) how one felt about renting and leasing (*e.g.*, cars) as opposed to owning, (4) the number and type of electri-cal appliances in the home, and (5) still others. Each showed some trends, but taken together a few such items may say much more than the sum of the parts.

Let me speculate: Suppose we find that among private home owners with a given amount of land, there is a trend toward a preferred ratio of more house space to less yard and outside space, that there is a growing inclination to lease things that stay outside the home proper, such as automobiles, but no inclination to give up, say, shopping for food or cooking of food within the home.

If we found trends like that, we would probably say that it isn't anti-materialism or a rejection of more goods per se, but something in the area of privatization and intimacy, of living more in the home, family or pad — as against the outside. It would suggest less of anti-materialism perhaps but more of the growth of counter influences. Put that way, it needn't threaten marketers but only alert them to new styles of consumption.

I would like to show you one graph that helps greatly, I think, to better un-derstand one of the major and supposedly new trends in life style — that is, all those life styles which are tinged with such labels as "cop out," on the one hand or alienation on the other. I refer to all anti-establishment searches for a counter-culture. In hearing such words and phrases we tend to assume not only rejection of older values but also withdrawal from issues, a retreat, aided per-haps by drugs, into a smaller, more personalized and sensuous world. But rejection and search do not always involve withdrawal, and those who assume that the counter-culture means withdrawal of world involvement are greatly mistaken.

All of our thirty-three surveys have opened with the question, "What are you most interested in or concerned about lately?" The open-ended answers help us to rank the major issues of the day, *e.g.*, concern over the economy or of Vietnam. One of our analytic categories is an over-code for all personal concerns mentioned. International and domestic concerns together exceed the personal concerns. But the thirty-three measures of personal concern taken since 1965 do give us an indication of whether our society overall is drifting more towards "copping out" or more towards greater involvement with the world at large. The answer seems clear: mentions of personal concerns have drifted downward from about 50% to 30%. Our society is involved, despite all the experimentation with new life styles. It is a society that does care about the world outside the pad, and gives it increasing attention.

Having made suggestions on re-computing sampling error and on re-grouping of questions for analysis or re-phrasing the meaning of questions, the third suggestion should concern respondents. If we seek to study social change, we are confronted here by the fact that our national cross-sections do not include any extra numbers of respondents for such reputed pacesetters in social change as the young, the blacks, the bohemians and Californians. How are you going to give appropriate attention to the reputed carriers of the counterculture in a national cross-section?

We have found it useful to cumulate certain types of respondents from survey to survey and report on them as a separate category only every second, fourth, or eighth survey as their numbers reach say 400. This has been done both forwards and backwards in time. It helps us therefore to think sometimes of our thirty-three surveys of 2, 000 each as a bank of data containing 66, 000 plus records. One might only identify only say 400 young Californians per year out of such a bank, but at least there are seven years over which to compare responses.

Now to summarize: I have said that existing survey data banks can be adapted to social indicator purposes if they will sharpen their sensitivities to social change in several ways.

1. Treat survey data as social scientists rather than as journalists. Get over the attitude that "old" data have lost their value.

2. Don't disregard the smaller percentages and less common answers as statistically unstable. Do convert all samples, past and present, to a replicated basis and determine the individual stabilities of individual questionnaire items.

3. Look at the meaning of groups of questions which may have in common some large meaning not represented in any of the individual questions.

4. Look at the total pool of respondents across all samples to see how many pacesetter or style-setter respondents can be singled out for cumulative analysis, and if necessary supplement current cross-section samples with special sub-samples. The national cross-section is not the best device for studying social change. It is only a beginning.

In conclusion, may I say that the current interest in social indicators is a welcome challenge to present survey procedures. This challenge calls for a great deal more precision, precision which *can* be provided. The question is, *will* it be provided?

CHAPTER 32

INNOVATIONS IN PUBLIC OPINION RESEARCH

The kind of innovation that interests me concerns corporate information needs, or the needs of other large institutions interrelating with
our society as a whole.

At GE we do seem to be on some kind of methodological trend line covering the past ten years. It sort of goes from reliance on one shot surveys to periodic (*e.g.*, quarterly) surveys — to panels (*e.g.*, with three contacts per
respondent per year) — to continuous interviewing, say at the rate of at least ten
respondents (*i.e.*, one-time respondents) per day. The trend isn't quite that neat
in terms of events but conceptually that's the direction.

I think we're on this trend because of some seven questions we have raised
and some things learned, and I'd like to share these with you just that way. With
questions like these: –

*1.   What is public opinion?   (It's about time we answered **this** one.)*

Paul Lazarsfeld used to distinguish between liberated and spontaneous
opinion. Liberated opinion was inside the respondent's head before the pollster
came along. The pollster's question then released or liberated the opinion,
which had been there all along. Spontaneous opinion doesn't exist until the
pollster asks his questions — thereby stimulating an answer.

Consider now the opinion data which you use or read about. How much of
it is liberated, how much is spontaneous? Do you know? Does it matter?

Liberated opinion carries with it the implication that respondents may have
thought, talked, listened, seen and/or read or done something about the subject.
It is active. Spontaneous opinion carries with it an implication of potential, *i.e.*,
that respondent might react in this and this way if exposed to effective stimulation.

It's expensive to find out if opinions are liberated, as it usually requires
open-ended evidence initially, although one can ask structured questions about
the frequency with which respondents have thought, heard, read, seen, etc.

Liberated opinion is probably more like what the layman has in mind about
"what is public opinion?", but the pollsters with syndicated newspaper columns,

Originally presented at the Market Research Council, Yale Club, New York, March 19,
1976.

hard-pressed for interesting news, often report spontaneous opinion data on odd subjects, thereby giving an impression overall that there is much more opinion out there in the land than in fact there is. On any important issue, however, we should all know how much of such opinion is already active, and how much, at best, only potential.

Joan Black of our public opinion research department is in the near future going to publish a paper on active opinion.

2.   *What is a public issue?   When may opinion be said to have emerged?   Or again, but this time in a different way we ask, how much opinion is out there anyway?*

One Tuesday last year I got an excited call from a product department expressing alarm about a (false) report n page one of the *Wall Street Journal* concerning one of our high technology products. I was asked about the feasibility of doing a survey to assess the impact or damage of the report.

I asked if the caller anticipated that the story would make the front pages two days in a row. The answer, "No." I then pointed out that we had made a study of what we call "blips," disturbing events which we had tracked, some of which did and some of which didn't turn out to be problems or issues. Going back over many years and comparing awareness with news treatment we generalized that the issue threshold for us was a minimum of three days of page one news treatment and 1½% public awareness. On these grounds the product department skipped the survey and relaxed somewhat as the days passed.

The moral here is that it is useful to consider how much opinion there is on a subject — and also to have your survey procedures in place when the unexpected happens. We were not in place to catch all of these events but we would have been with continuous interviewing.

3.   *What is private opinion?   What are the distinctions between how a respondent generally views the world, perhaps reflecting mass media impressions, and how he views his own individual condition or immediate neighborhood?   When do the two intersect?*

Many of our economic forecasters are amazed that the public is less concerned about unemployment rates than about inflation, and that the public seems willing to live with an 8% rate for quite some time into the future. This is not what had been predicted. "Unrest" had been predicted.

It is hypothesized that in this context unemployment is something that is happening to "the other guy" — possibly a minority guy — or gal. In some areas, however, the visibility of middle class unemployment may evoke a different response. How visible must it be before the individual personally identifies with the public view of the problem?

We talked before about thresholds for emerging issues and mentioned 1½% awareness. In the present context, however, I'd talk about "tipping points." For example, Oscar Cohen of the ADL studied white flight from ten cities for an article in the old *Reporter* Magazine. He said that the tipping point was on the average 38%, *i.e.*, whites perceived the neighborhood as "going black" and hence fled but not before the percentage of black population reached about 38%.

It is equally instructive then for forecasters to look at local unemployment rates to assess at what point job security actually does outweigh inflation as a community concern, and where.

From a marketing point of view the same applies to the introduction of many new products especially with regard to the respondents' view of these new items on the one hand as only fads ("probably won't last") and fashions ("this is the new 'in' thing").

How much visibility does it take before one perceives that a fad has arrived? How much does one have to hear about it before deciding it has caught on as fashionable? How much is "everybody" when "everybody is doing it?"

Thus, does the private view or world intersect with the public view — a matter of rates, of thresholds and the need for close observation of the human experience.

4. *When is public opinion?*

Most supermarket shopping, and a lot of other shopping too, takes place Thursday evening, Friday and Saturday. Why advertise then, at least on TV (why poll then?) They're out shopping. Why not advertise only on Monday, Tuesday and Wednesday, when they're home and relaxed? When you can get their attention just before they begin the shopping part of the week. Thus, on Monday, Tuesday and Wednesday you can perhaps build attitude potentials to subsequently complete with sales, promotions and point of sale stimuli on the last three days. The end of the week is too hectic for initial attitude build-ups. The housewife has too much internal mental clutter to sort out the TV clutter.

This is a parody (although some advertisers are now scheduling this way), but just what is the sequence of events and effects on a day-to-day basis? Must pollsters arrive late onto the scene, letting the news events of the day, the established issues, dictate what questions should be asked? Must pollsters arrive too early on the scene, asking questions about nonexistent issues but the answers to which they hope will make headlines? Is there not public opinion research capable of staying on, with the public, and capturing the flow of experience?

At times the inability to stay with the public leads to a polling disaster. The last two weeks of Truman's 1948 campaign against Dewey showed that you had to keep on interviewing right up to election day, because things were still happening — events and effects — the political campaign was an important variable. So that's the way you hang on to a good record for accuracy in predicting presidential elections — of demonstrating validity — you keep on polling as long as you have to.

By the same token the dozens of presidential trial runs in between elections have no validity, *i.e.*, the validity of one is incompatible with the other. So — election polling is at its best when it is doing frequent interviews during the actual political campaign, when the pollster (expensively it is true) is staying with the public.

5.   *What's going to happen?*

In recent years Futurism, including the Delphi technique, has fallen out of fashion among serious social scientists. The boomlet in "social indicators" of 1972-73 evaporated almost as soon as it got started. Despite the truism that crystal balls always get popular at the end of each century, the confidence in the ability of the polls to predict anything complex or subtle is very low.

There is perhaps a solution from advertising research where the best copy research on how a respondent feels about an ad is based on a prior and clear understanding of what the ad means to him. That is, the response has to be closely related to the actual nature of the stimulus. And we must not get these two types of data mixed up.

An example from public opinion research. In 1970 Congress was preparing to vote for or against funding the SST, a supersonic transport plane that bothered the environmentalists. GE was involved because it had the contract to provide the engines for the new plane. What was Congress going to do? Vote "for" or "against"? I said "against.

For years we had been routinely tracking public attitudes toward the SST and a lot of other environmentally related issues, and noticed that the trend line had adopted a trajectory that would soon achieve a majority "against" the SST. Among the various reasons for being "against" the SST, three reasons (and only three) were rising steeply (a) the cost, (b) the fear of danger to the upper stratosphere and (c) the noise problem.

Against the objections to the SST the Nixon Administration had launched a public information campaign in the form of a sixty-minute, chart-packed presentation by William Magruder (not the Jeb Magruder of Watergate). We heard that the Congress had given Magruder a standing ovation for this tremendous presentation and that he was taking it "on the road." I caught the show at the Waldorf Astoria in New York City, where the Sales Executive Club had asked Magruder to perform.

It was quite a performance. There was indeed a standing ovation. Magruder was a star salesman — of Magruder. What he did was to take 24 objections to the SST and "demolish" them in sixty minutes flat. It was an astonishing display of talent.

But 24 objections in 60 minutes is less than three minutes per objection, and three salient objections had to compete for attention with 21 non-salient objections. From a communication effectiveness point of view it was a splendid disaster. I said that the SST was lost, that the administration was not answering the public's objections. The applause in Congress was for Magruder (at the time) and his sales image and not for the SST problem. Both the stimulus (Magruder's presentation) and the response (a standing ovation in Congress) were misperceived by the administration, and by the press and so they were in for a surprise. They had not spent some years listening to the public on this matter and thereby having the capability of evaluating the campaign as the public would.

6.   Is the public ignorant or shrewd?

In one month last year four different national polls featured in their news releases or in their reports the "fact" that the public over-estimated the average amount of corporate profits. Some referred to the fact that the over-estimate had been getting worse over the years. Of course this kind of information scares management and causes them to reach out for program of "economic education.

The findings are baloney. Not one of the polls bothered to find out what the respondents meant by "profit," especially those that "over-estimated" profit. The temptation to infer that the public was ignorant of economic life (on this issue, where it's supposedly safe to indulge such a temptation) was too much.

An intensive study of this question with open-ended probes to discuss its meaning reveals that, yes, the average percent profit is estimated at about 25%. However, this average describes practically nobody, since the distribution of estimates is bi-modal.

The low estimators, by profit, mean what business and the *Wall Street Journal* mean by profit, and their estimates are on target. The high estimators in this bi-modal distribution mean, by profit, what the man in the street means — "mark-up" — and they too are on target. They are the ones who are responsible for the rising estimate of profits as inflation and prices rise.

When you ask the "profit" and the "mark-up" respondents about the use of the funds obtained, the high-estimating "mark-up" respondents are twice as likely to say that profits are used for such nice things as R&D, pensions, etc. So, "profits" are not clearly bad. What is bad is high prices, and given any semantic opportunity to complain about high prices, the public will do so. Very shrewd! Fools the omnibus pollster every time — especially if that pollster is looking for a headline!

Seriously, we have learned to beware of allegations about the public's lack of information. If you listen closely you often find that their semantics may be different, but their information base and understanding is just fine.

7.   Finally, a very practical question designed to bring some of this down to earth. How should we evaluate our corporate advertising?

As you may know DuPont gave up on magazine advertising and moved all its corporate budget into television. The magazines they used were invited to visit with them and view the research which led to the corporate decision. Experience within corporate GE has been somewhat similar in that it's been easy to document the favorable impact of TV on attitudes toward the company but very difficult to make the equivalent demonstration for magazines.

But there is hope for magazines because of our trend data, which not only routinely tracks attitudes towards GE, and viewing of GE TV shows, but magazine readership as well. Here are a few generalizations covering the past five years.

- In every quarter viewers of a GE Theater TV show had significantly higher attitude scores than non-viewers — viewers of two shows significantly higher scores than viewers of one show — viewers of three shows (in the fewer quarters where we had three) no higher scores than two shows. Two per quarter seems optimum.

- Looking at all gaps in our magazine advertising for each major magazine used in the five years, there were no drops in attitudes score associated with going out of the book and no increases associated with going back into the book for periods up to six months. My hunch is that a year "out" or (for a new book) "in" would show a difference. We may get a chance to look at this.

- Experience with one major magazine sharply affected our attitudes toward the whole category of magazines. We had not been advertising in it. The average attitudes of its readers towards GE consistently tracked below the national average year after year. We started advertising in the book and stayed in. The readers' scores rose through the national average, leveled off significantly above the national average and have stayed there ever since.

- We're trying to replicate the above demonstration with a small magazine, somewhat new. We agreed to advertise in it, in exchange, in part, for the names of a sample of subscribers. We then separated the sample into four equal parts and will do four waves of our standard tracking interviews. We shall see if the introduction of our advertising achieves our attitude objectives.

With some of the larger, and established magazines in which we have been advertising, the only way in which we can demonstrate their effectiveness is unfortunately to stop advertising for a year or so. It's all in a good cause though.

CONCLUSION

In summary —
- We should distinguish between active and potential public opinion. We should know how much of it is taken personally and affects behavior.
- We should be able to "stay with the public," to see what happens, to understand their reactions to real or proposed campaigns. We should get a very good look at the information and understanding that they bring to an issue
- We should know how much effect different amounts of advertising has

on them and over what periods of time.

Well, there are some of the interests that spark innovations in public opinion research at General Electric. Taken together they underlie our slow but steady drift towards continuous interviewing. With continuous interviewing you listen to the public even while not too much is going on, but you increase the volume when things start to happen. You review the data and accumulate it in a variety of "before" and "after" time periods to take advantage of opportunities for "natural experiments."

This approach is Aristotelian in its emphasis on observation. It is what social psychologists would call "phenomenological" in its attempt to hook up external stimuli with individual response. It's frugal in its emphasis on running at low speed when nothing is going on. And it's good to be able to turn up the volume (*i.e.*, increase the interviewing rate) when people really do have something on their minds. In that way we may even eliminate the "Don't know" response, or at least the "problems" of the "Don't know" response.

CHAPTER 33

PUBLIC ATTITUDES TOWARD PRIVATE ENTERPRISE AND BUSINESS

B usiness leaders have been repeatedly urged to do more about defending the system against public attack. The most common proposal is that they should sponsor economic education programs to improve public understanding.

This suggestion creates uneasiness within management because it is controversial — especially within management. While management knows that business is under attack, it knows too that government, that the "establishment," that all major institutions have been under attack. Is there something special and different about attacks on business that need so special a remedy as economic education? Is economic education the relevant variable, or is it something else? What in fact is the real problem? Most of the discussion about economic education focuses on it as a proposed *solution*. A solution to specifically what?

Research on public opinion has escalated in recent years and much new and relevant data are available for review and analysis. That is a prime purpose of this report. But some of the older public opinion data have been frequently cited as evidence for the alarm that management should feel toward public attacks. Some of those key older studies especially need to be re-evaluated in the light of newer and more extensive data.

The plan of this report is organized around the following six sections:

I. A re-evaluation of the *most publicized data, i.e.,* the data on "declining confidence in our institutions" (Harris Poll)

II. A re-evaluation of the *most disturbing data, i.e.,* the data on "the public's distorted ideas about how much profit companies make" (ORC Index, "The 1976 Study of American Opinion" by U. S. News and World Report)

III. Trends in the desire to regulate large companies from General Electric's *Quarterly Index of Company Relations (QICR)*

IV. Career plans of young people (General Electric QICR)

V. The most recent and comprehensive study of the subject ("National Survey on the American Economic System," Ad Council, Inc. for Department of Commerce, 1976)

VI. Summary

Unpublished Manuscript, May 18, 1977.

I. The Most Publicized Data —
"Declining Confidence in Our Institutions"

One of two recent reviews of these data has been published by Harvard's Professor Seymour Martin Lipset (in an article entitled "The Wavering Polls," *The Public Interest*, No. 43, Spring 1976, pp. 70-89, and reprinted as a separate by the American Enterprise Institute). Let Professor Lipset speak for himself:

There are, of course, many other issues involved in interpreting opinion from surveys. The picture presented can appear very different, depending on how the answers to the same questions are presented. Thus, a number of polling organizations have inquired as to the confidence the public has in the people in charge of various institutions — medicine, Congress, major companies, the Supreme Court, etc. All the surveys agree that confidence, as expressed in responses to these questions, has been eroding since the mid-1960's, although it must be mentioned again that the percentages reported giving the same response to the same question for the same institution at about the same time have varied considerably.

One polling organization, the market research division of Procter and Gamble Company, noting the variation in responses to such questions, recently undertook an experiment to see how much expression of confidence in different institutions may be varied by using different terms to describe them. They divided their sample into three groups and asked them whether they "have a great deal of confidence, a moderate amount of confidence, or no confidence" in a number of institutions, giving each third a different term for the same institution. Some of the results are presented in Table 33.1.

It is clear from looking at these results that a sharply different picture of the level of confidence in different institutions emerges when different words are used to depict them. Fifty percent have a great deal of confidence in "established religion," but only 35 percent feel the same way about "organized religion." Almost two-thirds (63 per cent) are very positive about the "Army, Navy, and Air Force," but the high level of confidence declines to 48 per cent for the "Military," and drops way down to 21 per cent for 'Military Leaders." More than a third (35 per cent) express no confidence in "election polls," but only 18 per cent have the same negative view of "Public Opinion Pollsters." Twenty-one per cent have a great deal of confidence in "Organized Labor," but only seven per cent have the same view of "Big Labor." The responses reported in this table tell us a great deal about the public's sentiments, but just as important, they illustrate in detail the instability of such replies — the extent to which it is possible to vary the public's view by changing the way in which institutions are labeled.

It is also important to recognize that one gets a very different image of the confidence level of the country depending on whether a survey organization reports and discusses the proportion of respondents voicing "great confidence" while lumping together those indicating "some confidence" with "hardly any confidence at all," or makes the break between any confidence and none at all. The most widely circulated poll reports published in the press, those conducted by the Harris organization, usually give only the "great deal of confidence" figure — which in recent years has been under 50 per cent, often well under that figure, for the leaders of most institutions.

TABLE 33.1

*Level of Confidence in Different American Institutions,
Using Different Terms**

INSTITUTION	GREAT DEAL OF CONFIDENCE	MODERATE CONFIDENCE	NO CONFIDENCE
Army, Navy, and Air Force	63%	31%	6%
The Military	48	45	7
Military Leaders	21	59	20
Established Religion	50	41	9
Ministers and other Religious Leaders	35	56	9
Organized Religion	35	49	16
Television News	31	58	11
Network Television News	25	69	6
Television News Commentators	23	66	11
Colleges	2	52	46
Professors	9	62	29
Business	20	73	7
Business Leaders	18	68	14
Big Business	12	62	26
Organized Labor	21	53	26
Union Leaders	12	63	25
Big Labor	7	66	27
Public Opinion Pollsters	14	68	18
Public Opinion Polls	16	55	29
Election Polls	20	45	35
United States Presidency	30	53	17
Executive Branch of Federal Government	18	62	20
Federal Government	16	69	15
Government	20	64	16
Elected Government Officials	5	65	20
Congress	7	74	19
Politicians	2	53	45
Politics	4	65	31

* Source: Market Research Division of Procter and Gamble Company

But if we look at the per cent of those who say they have "hardly any confidence," a quite different picture emerges. According to a 1975 NORC survey, for all except the leaders in the political realm (the executive) and organized labor, the proportion indicating a lack of confidence runs only from a tenth to a fifth, while even for politics and labor the proportions are all under 30 per cent. Or to put the matter another way, from 71 per cent to 92 per cent of respondents indicate "some" or "a great deal of confidence" in various key institutions. Is the confidence glass more full or more empty? The implications of the results are debatable, but Harris, in reporting the low proportions voicing "a. great deal of confidence," concluded in October 1975: "In short, there is a leadership vacuum in this country across the board."

Apart from the rejection of Harris' conclusions the reader should especially note words or terms which elicit the more negative ratings of the various institutions. The most damaging terms were "Leaders" — as in "Military Leaders," "Organized" — as in "Organized Religion," and "Big" — as in "Big Business" or "Big Labor." It appears that it is not that the institutions themselves have declined so much in confidence, but that the public is increasingly skeptical about the uses of the power available to those institutions.

None of the other institutions show so marked a variation on the "No confidence" side of the ledger as does the institution of business. It goes 7% for "Business," 14% for "Business Leaders" and 26% for "Big Business." This is the first of several findings which suggest that the attack on business is primarily an attack on *big* business and not on the free enterprise system generally. That is, it is the powerful, or presumably too powerful aspects of business that are suspect.

The second recent review of the data on confidence in public institutions is provided by Professor Everett C. Ladd, Jr. in the 1976-77 Winter issue of *Public Opinion Quarterly* ("The Polls: The Question of Confidence," pp. 544-552). After examining data from Harris, Yankelovich and others, Ladd concludes as follows:

> All sorts of indicators attest to the fact that the public mood has darkened over the past 10 years. People are angry at the actions and inactions of various groups of leaders, feel the society has fallen far short of its promise in a number of areas, believe their individual viewpoints are inadequately attended to, and so on.

> I must conclude, however, that here the polls have too often only confirmed the obvious. Only a nation of idiots could look at the events of the last decade and say, "Gee, isn't it all so wonderful!" Of course people are upset. The mere fact of dissatisfaction is scarcely remarkable. How deep is the dissatisfaction? What consequences does it carry for national life? What sorts of actions are called for to improve citizenry assessments? Questions like these need more examination.

Available data surely do not sustain the argument that the U.S. has experienced any sort of a legitimacy crisis — or that the country is at the beginning of one. This is not to say that the argument cannot be made, only that the polls do not support it.

We cannot even assert confidently from poll data that the United States has undergone (or has not undergone) a loss of confidence in the constitutional air broadly defined — in the basic *constituent institutions and processes* of the society. Here the public has been giving contradictory clues, perhaps because it is itself unsure what it feels, perhaps only because the instruments employed in assessing its response are imperfect. My guess is that the public is saying that "the institutions are about as good as human beings are likely to get, but the mix of fools and knaves in the current leadership cohorts has been a bit too rich." But at this stage in the inquiry of the polls, that can only be a guess.

While the review by Lipset, leaning very heavily on the special study by Proctor & Gamble, suggests that the particular problem is public mistrust of power, the somewhat more broadly based review by Ladd cautions us that the whole inquiry into the question of public confidence is still in an early stage of development.

As a postscript to the above both Harris (Feb 17, 1977 *Chicago Tribune*) and Roper (May 3, 1977 *Wall Street Journal*) reported increased confidence in business compared to the year before.

II. The Most Disturbing Data —
"The Public's Exaggerated Ideas About
How Much Profit a Company Makes"

Since 1965 the Opinion Research Corporation has repeatedly publicized the "exaggerated ideas" of "The average person's estimate of after-tax profits on sales." They stress, for example, that the 29¢ per dollar estimate is about five times the actual amount. Similarly, a May 19, 1975 Gallup Poll release featured the sub-head "Hold Distorted Ideas of Profit Margins," and the then-current issue of *The Cambridge Report* also featured the same type of data on its first page. Those who hear or read of such findings easily make the inference that the public considers corporate profits as "swollen or excessive." However, the ORC surveys which show a 29¢ average profit estimate also show, but without relevant comment, that the same survey respondents consider about 25¢ as "reasonable." Over-estimated or not, therefore, the 29¢ figure itself does not carry the connotation of unreasonable or too high (ORC Public Opinion Index, January, 1977).

Similarly, the 1976 Study of American Opinion sponsored by *U.S. News & World Report*, and using a somewhat different survey procedure, comes up with a national median estimate of 14.4¢ for what a typical manufacturer actually keeps on profit out of a sales dollar, but 13.8¢ as to what a typical manufacturer *should* be able to keep (pp. 48-50). The American public is *not* against profits.

Before leaving the subject, we ought to look more closely at the questions asked by ORC and by *U.S. News & World Report*. The ORC question on "What percent profit on each dollar of sales do you think the average manufacturer makes, after taxes?" elicits an average estimate of 29¢ while the *U.S. News & World Report* question on "Out of every sales dollar about how much of that sales dollar do you think the manufacturer is able to keep as profit (after all costs and taxes are paid)"? elicits an average of 14. 4¢. In other words, if you merely remind the American public that costs and taxes are involved, the resulting estimate of profit drops (from the ORC estimate) by fully half.

Another perspective on the inflated 29¢ estimate from ORC comes from a 1973 study by GE's *Quarterly Index of Company Relations*. Concerned about the meaning of "profit" to those who answered the ORC question, GE repeated the ORC question within its own survey and did obtain a 25% (or 25¢) average estimate. However, most estimates were well above or well below the average suggesting the possibility of two different meanings. So this follow-up question was asked — "People figure profit in a number of ways. I'm going to read you some things manufacturers pay for and ask you if you think of them as being paid for out of the percent profit or not."

Some things were equally likely to be judged as paid out of profit by both those who estimate low and those who estimate high profits; *e.g.*, dividends to stockholders. But other things were much more likely to be judged as paid out of profit by the high estimators — 33% of low but 55% of high estimators thought that "construction of new buildings or plants" was paid for out of profits — 25% of low but 50% of high estimators "Research to produce technological breakthroughs" — 18% of low but 45% of high estimators "Retirement benefits" — *obviously high profits are not all bad*!

While none of the pollsters who had been belaboring the public's inaccurate estimate of profits over the years had said outright that this was BAD, the inference was always blatant. Our data suggest that public confusion about amount of profit is in large part a confusion of profit with retail mark-up (*i.e.*, with prices). Since profit is a difficult term at all levels (see R.M. Estes "Large Scale Investments and Competition" 3/6/75) perhaps it had best, as Estes suggests, be dropped.

An important research implication of the confusion between profits and mark-up is that one should look with a skeptical eye on any trend data about public attitudes towards profits. For example, the cover page of the January, 1977 ORC *Public Opinion Index* is headlined "The Public's Growing Criticism of Corporate Profits" — this on the basis of a chart on page 9 which shows the trend of answers over the years to a question — "In all industries where there is competition, do you think companies should be allowed to make all the profit they can, or should the government put a limit on the profits companies can make?"

The trend lines show a 2:1 predominance in favor of profit from the mid-1940's through the mid-60's and then in 1971-73 a reversal! Does this really mean a change in attitudes towards actual profit or, since it appeared at the end of Vietnam and the emergence of inflation as the public's priority concern, is this just another manifestation of concern over prices; *i.e.*, profit as retail mark-up? The ORC report is silent on such matters.

In general, we may conclude that the public is liberal about what they consider to be a reasonable profit, but is inclined to confuse profit with retail mark-up, and gets very personally concerned therefore when higher profits are seen as being a consequence of higher consumer prices. Such concern is, of course, one of the characteristics of periods of inflation.

"People figure profit in a number of different ways. I'm going to read you some things manufacturers pay for and ask you if you think of them as being paid for out of the percent profit or not."

	TOTAL (1072) %	AFTER-TAX PROFIT ESTIMATE Less than 10% (269) %	10%- 30% (356) %	Over 30% (274) %	Difference between +30% and −10%
Dividends to stock-holders	58	65	55	56	− 9
Bonuses for top level executives	46	40	45	52	+12
Construction of new buildings or plants	42	33	41	55	+22
Rainy-day funds to see a company through recessions	39	36	38	43	+ 7
Research to produce technological breakthroughs	35	25	34	50	+25
Creating new jobs	32	32	26	41	+ 9
Retirement benefits	29	18	23	45	+27
Pollution controls	26	20	22	37	+17
Shorter working hours	21	19	17	30	+11

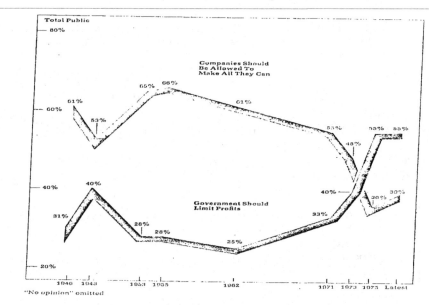

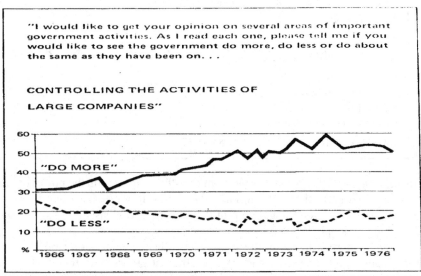

III. Trends in the Desire to Regulate Large Companies
(FROM GENERAL ELECTRIC, *QICR* 1976-IV)

Desire for government control of large companies had increased from about a third "more control" in 1966 to a high point of sixty percent in the first quarter of 1975. It has since declined to fifty percent. Meanwhile, the nature of

"You said you would like the government to do more about controlling the activities of large companies. Please tell me more about that."

SAY "DO MORE":	'73 IV. (570)	'75 I. (1041)	'76 IV. (1046)
POWER	%	%	%
Big companies too powerful	21	14	14
Stop interference in elective/ legislative process	13	11	10
Get away with too much	8	9	6
STRUCTURE			
Enforce anti-trust monopoly laws.	12	5	4
Break up large companies	7	11	10
Acquisitions, mergers, conglomerates	8	6	
MARKETING			
Control prices	13	25	15
Product quality, safety, service	7	6	4
FINANCIAL			
Raise taxes, plug loopholes	11	11	16
Control profits	7	19	8
OTHER			
Protect small business	17	8	8
Pollution	2		
Employment policies	12	14	11

(Other specifics less than 5% each)

concern has shifted away somewhat from the 1973 emphasis on the power of big business, and protection of small business, and away somewhat from the 1975 emphasis on price control and on profits to a current emphasis on raising taxes and plugging loopholes.

The important lesson of the above data is that the attacks on large companies change over time, and may involve different groups over time. There is then perhaps no one answer to attack, but only current answers to current attacks. It is also interesting to note that some of the attacks on large companies or big business (as in 1973) are on behalf of small business. In general, the 7 major attacks concern the power or size of companies on the one hand, the inflation related concern over prices, or the newer interest in inequities of the tax structure.

IV. Career Plans of Young People

An underlying consideration in the evaluation of attitudes towards business is the change in values among young people — especially changes in their choices of jobs and careers. Since 1968 national samples of college students have been asked about their choices 35 times within the quarterly QICR surveys conducted by General Electric.

The chart on the next page shows a major change since 1969 in that the number of college students who have wanted to work in education has declined by about half. Those wanting to work in industry or business declined from 1968 through 1972, but increased in number since, almost regaining the 1968 level. Self-employment increased steadily from 1968 through 1974, and has since leveled off at about twice the 1968 level.

The evidence here suggests increased or at least continued strength for the entrepreneurial spirit and for support of the business system. While it does not mean that attacks on the system will necessarily decrease, it does mean that the ranks of those who choose to enter and participate in the system will remain numerically strong.

V. The Most Comprehensive Study

On October 23, 1974 the Secretary of Commerce asked the Board of Directors of the Advertising Council, Inc., to take action on the need to strengthen public understanding of the economic system. The Board enlisted the services of Compton Advertising, whose research department conducted "The National

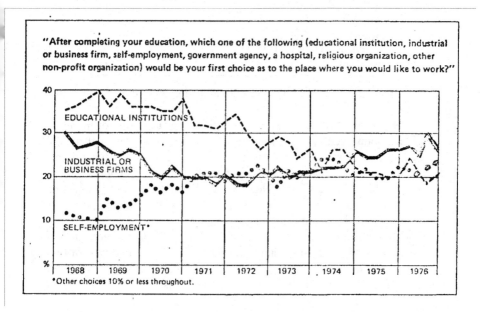

"After completing your education, which one of the following (educational institution, industrial or business firm, self-employment, government agency, a hospital, religious organization, other non-profit organization) would be your first choice as to the place where you would like to work?"

EDUCATIONAL INSTITUTIONS

INDUSTRIAL OR BUSINESS FIRMS

SELF-EMPLOYMENT*

1968 1969 1970 1971 1972 1973 1974 1975 1976

*Other choices 10% or less throughout.

Survey on the American Economic System," an intensive study based on a national sample of 3, 000 interviews. A preliminary report was compiled in March 1975 and a final report distributed in 1976. The findings below are taken from the Highlights section (pp. 13-17) of that report.

When describing the U.S. economic system, many Americans talk in personal terms rather than the language of economics. Four out of ten base their description on the personal freedoms and opportunities for economic mobility inherent in the system for everyone — for the worker as well as the entrepreneur: Anyone is free to choose or change his job, free to start a business, free to improve his condition by his own initiative.

As the following summary of principal comments shows (Table 33.2), interpretations of the system in terms of broad economic concepts are far less frequent than personal interpretations.

TABLE 33.2
Descriptions of the U.S. Economic System

		%
Personal freedoms, opportunities		36
Economic/job mobility	*18*	
Anyone can start a business	*10*	
Personal/political freedoms	*10*	
Opportunity for initiative/creativity	*10*	
Free enterprise, free economy, private enterprise		19
Supply and demand system		13
Profit system		6
Government involvement: regulation, anti-trust laws, etc.		8
Don't know		11

The freedom described above is individual freedom, entrepreneurial freedom.

This view of the economic system from the standpoint of the individual looms even larger in attitudes toward the system. More than half of the public at large express their favorable attitudes toward the American system in terms of these personal freedoms and opportunities for mobility (Table 33.3). Note below that these considerations are much more important than the system's physical benefits of goods and services as determinants of attitudes.

The above suggests that the public values its political and economic freedom per se more highly than its famed consumer life style. This type of finding or comment has not previously received much attention. It suggests that public appreciation for the material benefits of our system is not the key or the suffi-

TABLE 33.3
What Is Good About the System

	%
Personal freedoms, opportunities	54
Economic/job mobility	*25*
Personal/political freedoms	*22*
Anyone can start a business	*14*
Encourages initiative/creativity	*10*
Free enterprise, free economy, private enterprise	9
High standard of living, wide variety of goods and services	12
Nothing	10
Don't know	7

cient justification of that system. Apparently, the freedom is. An earlier indication of this came from a May 1975 Yankelovich survey which found that "94% of Americans insisted that 'we must be ready to make sacrifices if necessary' to preserve the 'free enterprise system'" (see previously cited review by E. C. Ladd, Jr., p. 551).

At the same time, the great majority of Americans express negative attitudes, but these are mainly complaints and frustrations about the state of the economy at the time of the fieldwork plus other contemporary economic, political and social issues. The most frequent of these responses are shown in the table following (Table 33.4).

Concern over inflation is the number one criticism of the system. Profits as such are not mentioned. Criticism of business is criticism of "big" business.

TABLE 33.4
What Is Not Good About the System

	%
Inflation	27
Unemployment, recession	8
Big business creates shortages/has political/tax advantages/tends to be monopolistic	18
The wealthy have power/tax advantages	7
There is uneven distribution of wealth	5
Too much foreign aid causes shortages; imports mean fewer jobs	7
Dishonest politicians	7
Too much government regulation	6
Too little government regulation	2
Everyone is out for himself	5
Nothing	6
Don't know	5

TABLE 33.5
What Americans Mean by Changes

	%
Stop inflation	21
Eliminate unemployment	6
Tax reforms	20
Reforms in big business — enforce anti-trust laws, control profits	19
Cut overseas aid and imports	13
Reform welfare programs	10
Improve health/social security benefits	10

When the respondents are asked about necessary changes in the system (Table 33.5) or about the amount of regulation of business (Table 33.6) their criticism is, again, that "big" business needs reform, and while some say there is too much regulation of "business," more say there is not enough regulation of "big business."

VI. Summary

1. The public is more confident in our institutions than trusting in the leaders of those institutions.

TABLE 33.6
**Opinions on Current Amount
of Government Regulation**

	%
Too much at present	35*
Principally:	
Of business	11
Of prices	4
It is inefficient . . . wastes money	3
Of wages	2
Of foreign trade	2
Not enough at present	56*
Principally:	
Of business, especially big business	20
Of prices	20
Of wages	6
Of inflation	4
Of foreign trade	2
Right amount at present	19

*13% gave a qualified response, i.e., "too much" in some respects and "not enough" in others.

2. The public values its freedoms and mistrusts the power available to the leaders of large institutions.

3. The public values free enterprise, and the entrepreneurial spirit, and mistrusts "big" business. Some of the attacks on big business are even made in the name of free enterprise, or for the protection of entrepreneurs.

4. Levels of confidence and of trust have risen somewhat in the past two years.

5. The public is permissive in its attitude concerning corporate profits, even high profits, but tending to confuse profit with retail mark-up takes a dim view of high profits (*i.e.*, prices) during periods of inflationary concern.

6. Attacks on big business vary in nature over time. The issues and battlegrounds can change significantly from year to year.

7. The ranks of those who choose to enter and participate in the economic system will continue to be numerically strong; *i.e.*, large numbers of young people continue to choose self-employment and/or careers in business. The trend is upward.

In sum, attacks on the economic system are not the problem, nor are attacks on business or attacks on free enterprise. The problem is the attacks on *big* business. The problem is, can you trust the powerful leaders of big business to have the citizen's interests at heart? The problem is how to reassure, and how to achieve trust. This is probably not a matter of economics or of economic understanding.

The problem is complicated by the fact that when under attack representatives of large companies often react instinctively *as if* the attack is on the free enterprise system. In defending that they feel virtuous, even patriotic — a sense of "righteousness" is in the air. It appears to the critic, however, that the defense is evasive, irrelevant and often pompous. How can we avoid this common scenario? Must we educate big business? After all, it has been somewhat misinformed by some of the pollsters (*e.g.*, by Harris re public confidence in business, by ORC re public attitudes towards profits).

The problem is also complicated by the fact that certain large companies or industries have *always* been mistrusted. For example, Huey Long maintained a very successful career by periodically attacking the Standard Oil Company (N.J.). It is not clear that industry can handle the problem of trust in a united way. Some companies or industries may have to lead the way, perhaps in opposition to others.

The intellectually fashionable issues of public members of Boards, of social audits, and of public accountability are probably valid symptoms of the problem of needed trust. While these particular forms of reassurance may or may not be welcome, other perhaps more acceptable forms of reassurance might be investigated rather than leave all innovation (and credit) in this area to the critics of big business.

CHAPTER 34

HOW TO MISINTERPRET PUBLIC OPINION RESEARCH AND UNDERESTIMATE THE POTENTIAL OF CORPORATE ADVERTISING

A few months ago the president of a major company spoke before a friendly business audience about a certain environmental problem. The excellent talk was well received and he was encouraged to have it printed on the "Op Ed" page of the New York *Times*. It attracted favorable comment there and his agency was then ordered to prepare a related campaign of national advertising. The advertising materials, ads and scripts, were subsequently made ready.

I received a worried telephone call from the company's advertising manager. He wanted to know, since we had some experience with a similar environmental problem, did we have any research to advise him about the public's likely acceptance or rejection of their imminent advertising campaign?

The upshot of the discussion was that I advised him to stop treating the ad program as an extension of his president's speech and start treating it like an advertising program — by pre-testing it intensively.

The program was eventually cancelled, not because the president's point of view was rejected by the public but because the reasoning was too complex to be efficiently comprehended and communicated — *in an advertising format.*

So to begin I'd like to define corporate advertising as only one avenue of the many which are available to businessmen that want to speak up.

A speech is speaking up and has certain values. I'm in favor of more speeches. A speech reprinted in the Op Ed pages is just that and has certain values. I'm in favor of more speeches being reprinted in the Op Ed pages. A long paid editorial is fine too, and I greatly admire the Mobil campaign in Op Ed. In my view, however, that's not advertising.

Advertising has to communicate quick as a wink. It is characterized by Starch magazine scores averaging a high 50% "Noting" but a low 10% "Read Most." Gallup TPT norms for next day recall of exposed television commercials are only 12%.

Originally presented at Association of National Advertisers Corporate Advertising Workshop, Hotel Plaza, New York, October 26, 1978.

Therefore, advertising is rapid communication, based on partial or brief exposure, with little next day recall but nevertheless good recognition potential for what has been seen.

Mass advertising is a difficult, challenging, professional activity. It is *quite* different from speech-making or editorial writing. So let's talk about corporate advertising, and why its potentials are largely unexplored.

I've already implied the major internal reason. Ad agencies are afraid that when the client for whom they do product advertising also asks them to do corporate advertising — they will be dealing not with the client's advertising manager, who understands what they do and can do, but with top management who may arrive on the scene with a pre-determined idea of what is to be done. Sometimes this means turning good speeches into bad ads. Who needs that kind of business? Who needs failure?

I'm sure many of you are familiar with this reason, and I won't dwell on it. I'll shift instead to the major external reason as to why the potentials of corporate advertising are largely unexplored . . . and here I want to talk about some bad public opinion research, or bad interpretation of opinion research. I want to talk about alleged research findings on *credibility* of corporate advertising.

The problem of credibility is typical of the confusion between corporate spokesmanship (*i.e.*, speeches and editorials) and corporate advertising. A pertinent example of that confusion is represented in the talk given to this very workshop on November 29, 1977 by Eric Weiss of the Sun Company, and since reprinted in the March 1978 issue of AMA's *Management Review*.

It was an excellent speech, and I wrote to Mr. Weiss complimenting him on it. But I also took exception to his remarks on credibility. These remarks:

> In short, I would conclude that the credibility of *advertising on issues* and the credibility of, at least, oil company spokesmen and speeches is so low that efforts in that area are counterproductive. If your audience is convinced that you are incredible, you are well advised to say as little as possible; you should also be certain that whatever you do say agrees with the facts as your audience will perceive them.
>
> Thus I reject the suggestion that there is a solution to the question of mistrust through economic education, explaining business to the public, or really making them see things our way. But I am also convinced that business will pursue the advertising path and, in pursuing it, will simply reinforce the public in its mistrust.

Granted that Mr. Weiss tried to limit his observations to the oil industry, and granted that he wisely rejected the panacea of economic education, his remarks have since been quoted by others as evidence of the ineffectiveness of corporate advertising on issues in particular and to some extent generally. This is a drag on the entire field of corporate advertising.

What I am most concerned about is that Mr. Weiss presented *no* direct evidence on credibility of any advertising. What he did was to show the results of some questions by Yankelovich and by Cambridge Research, which asked respondents which of a variety of information sources they would find most and least believable. That is, he reported people's opinions about believability. He showed no evidence on reactions to any advertising. He referred to no case histories on the effectiveness of particular corporate advertising programs.

The need for actual case histories rather than opinion research is underscored by the fact that people don't like to admit that they are influenced by advertising — any advertising.

Furthermore, it is well known in the research community that "testimonial evidence" (*i.e.*, what people think *of* an ad) is rejected — by advertisers and agencies alike — as evidence of advertising effectiveness in favor of actual reactions (*i.e.*, how people react *to* an ad).

Even in corporate campaigns the first concerns in preparing good advertising are to find out if the advertising will attract attention and be understood. The criterion of credibility is way down on the list and may not be involved at all — depending on the message.

I attribute Mr. Weiss's over-interpretation of public opinion data to an attempt to make a generalization that would hold for both corporate spokesmanship *and* for corporate advertising. It doesn't work, because they are different. Credibility is often a problem in spokesmanship, but significantly less so in advertising.

Another perspective on opinion research and credibility is represented by the alleged decline in public confidence in business. A great deal of media attention has been given to this in recent years ever since Lou Harris first began publicizing his opinion research on this matter.

It doesn't inspire advertising personnel to believe that they are working on behalf of a "loser" or that they are working against the tide.

However, in the past year or two a number of very thorough evaluations have been made of the alleged decline in public confidence in business.

I refer here to the Winter 1977 issue of *Public Opinion Quarterly* and a report by Professor Everett Ladd of Yale University on the topic "The Question of Confidence."

I refer here to the August 1978 issue of *Public Opinion* Magazine and the report by Professor Seymour Martin Lipset of Stanford University entitled "How's Business?"

The net conclusion of such evaluations is that the polls show not *a* decline in public confidence in business but public *declines* in aspects of all large organizations, business, government, and labor equally.

Second, they show not a decline in the institutions themselves but in the leadership of such institutions.

Thirdly, they show that the leaders are specifically mistrusted as having too much power and for being too self-interested.

In all, it is concluded that neither the American economic system nor its institutions are under significant attack. It is the leadership which is mistrusted. Of course, I mean leadership generically, not as individuals.

Well, if this is so, corporate spokesmanship is indeed in big trouble. But corporate advertising, which represents the institution, the organization, the company, may not (perhaps oil companies excepted). I refer here to the absence of evidence on lack of credibility of specific corporate advertising campaigns.

Well, I don't mean to gloat on behalf of corporate advertising, but if corporate advertising can be encouraged and inspired to succeed what is then its relation to the difficult problems of the credibility of spokesmanship?

Consider this: spokesmanship is verbal. It's made up of words. It is the area of argument and counter argument.

Advertising is pictorial and graphic. To communicate "quick as a wink," good ads depend on picture, headline and logo. Body copy is read by only 10%. Words are of minor importance. Many fine ads use no words at all.

Using pictures alone you can communicate that the X company
- does interesting things
- does important scientific work
- is a good place to work
- makes high quality products
- is a good investment
- provides good customer service
- helps its local community
- cares about people
- helps solve problems of the environment

All of that is corporate advertising. It succeeds when the images portrayed by the ad cumulatively contribute to favorable impressions about the company.

Why do corporate advertising? Certainly not for its own sake, and not for the favorable impressions themselves. Those favorable impressions or attitudes are supposed to affect behavior.

We used to say they affect these types of behavior. We used to say that we want people
- to buy our products
- to invest in our stock
- to take jobs with us
- to vote to accept our plants into their communities

I think now that we should add another kind of desired behavior — to distinguish further between corporate spokesmanship and corporate advertising.

We should desire favorable impressions about our companies so that in addition to buying our products, investing in our stocks, etc., etc., we would like people to be willing to listen to what our spokesmen have to say; *i.e.*, to "lend them an ear" without prior skepticism or cynicism.

So, on the question of corporate spokesmanship it is corporate advertising which must build the receptive, or at least tolerant, audiences

Put another way, in building corporate reputation through advertising we should expect, as one of its by-products, greater public interest in corporate spokesmanship.

I think it's rare for advertising agencies to fail when they have clear and reasonable objectives. I think it's exceptional for them not to fail when the objectives are unclear.

Corporate advertising with a dose of corporate spokesmanship thrown in is not an assignment that agencies or agency personnel are delighted to get, and that's a terrible drag on creativity.

But if you can keep the spokesmanship out of it — and let the advertiser cope with that — I think you will see that corporate advertising can provide a great new assist to that spokesmanship.

That assist is going to be much more urgently needed in the years ahead, because the face of American politics is undergoing significant change.

As a function of distrust in leadership, and now I'm talking about the leadership of the Democratic and Republican parties, the 25-35 age group (the baby boom of WW II) in particular is cynical, is registering as political independents, and prefers to support special issue-oriented groups where they can trust the official representatives to in fact "vote" their way.

Thus, Washington is alive with lobbies and lobbyists and the regular parties decline in influence. Lobbying will become more visible, more controversial for a while, but in the long run another accepted form of democratic process.

Business and companies must be part of this process and increasingly so. It is one of many kinds of special interest groups and must protect its interests.

It will be encouraged to increase its spokesmanship, if it isn't scared off by fears of lack of credibility.

Meanwhile, credibility is not the problem of corporate advertising — it is one of the *targets* of corporate advertising — *i.e.,* to build credibility for corporate spokesmanship.

The two can only succeed *hand in hand*, and by recognizing the *differences* between them. Those differences are clear.

Advertising is pictures; spokesmanship is words — and pictures must lead the way.

CHAPTER 35

UNDERSTANDING PUBLIC RESPONSE TO MASSIVE NEW TECHNOLOGIES

Many of the future challenges to managers of the General Electric Company will be external. Economic trends, governmental regulations, worldwide competition, inflation, materials shortages and social changes are just a few examples.

Another external challenge and the focus of my message this morning is public opinion — the thoughts, interests and reactions of various segments of the general public — which can be important catalytic agents operating for or against the success of any major business effort.

I would like to share with you this morning how public opinion reacted to three major technologies, all of interest to the General Electric Company — the proposed U.S. supersonic transport plane, the Apollo Space Program and the current nuclear power situation. I would like to explore this morning why each enjoyed, or enjoy less public support than their sponsors expected.

I hope this prelude to your work at the Conference will be helpful to you in your discussions and as *examples* you may use, as you present subsequent sessions of the course.

My purpose, then, is to evaluate changing public attitudes toward technology as illustrated by three specific case histories. In search of useful generalizations I will rely upon public opinion tracking data — specifically on GE's Quarterly Index of Company Relations (QICR) which since 1964 has been interviewing national samples of adults and of college students every three months.

To begin I'd like to remind the audience that the technologies in question all came about through presidential initiatives, all were war or defense related in origin, all were challenges to industry and technology, and all proved technically feasible — even if the SST finally came about in the form of an Anglo-French product, and the nuclear industry is still struggling with various problems.

The modern process of presidential initiatives in technology was begun in World War I with President Wilson promising the aid of America's industrial

Originally presented at General Electric Co. Professional Employee Management Seminar, Marriott Hotel, Stamford, November 5, 1979. The slides are not available, but the text discussion of the slides is reasonably descriptive.

might to the Allies, and the most dramatic technical example of this aid in the form of the "Liberty" aircraft engine.

A product of Detroit, the Liberty engine concentrated more horsepower in less weight than was thought possible at the time. It was an unsurpassed engineering marvel for more than a decade, and made feasible the post-war establishment of a U.S. Air Mail service.

Unfortunately for the Allies, the Liberty engines shipped to France in 1917-18 were "diplomatically" married to a British designed de Havilland airplane body manufactured in Canada. The marriage was unsuccessful, *i.e.*, the plane tended to nose over on takeoffs and landings. So the American pilots in France continued to fly in French airplanes. After the war the Liberty was more happily married to an American airplane, the Curtiss "Jenny," and became the backbone of the U.S. Air Mail.

Early in World War II President Roosevelt demanded from industry 50,000 warplanes, thought impossible of production at the time. He got them. He asked for an atom bomb and got that too. And Truman used it. Eisenhower initiated Atoms for Peace, as if it were a continuation of the Marshall Plan, and somehow about that time industry was also offered, and accepted, a nuclear energy business. Kennedy asked us to go to the moon and so we did. Nixon asked for an American SST and was *refused*. Let's start with that.

I

The American aircraft industry had a history of doing costly development work on new airplanes in the form of bombers contracted by the Air Force. When the military plane proved successful a passenger version was then adapted. This was no longer possible in the supersonic jet era where the military and civilian requirements differed too widely. To afford a next step in passenger plane development the industry asked government for financing.

Unfortunately for the SST, a growing environmental movement targeted the plane as controversial. As the Congressional vote on the SST approached in the Fall of 1970 public opposition reached the halfway mark and majority opposition looked imminent.

- Slide I indicates a two year drop in support from 55% to 50% as the crucial vote in Congress approached in the Fall of 1970.

The rising public concerns were noise, cost, and pollution — this last in the form of danger to the ozone layer.

- Slide II shows that among SST opponents the concern over noise rose from 5% to 20% and concern over cost from less than 1% to 7%.
- Slide III shows that among SST proponents there were slight declines in such specific benefits as faster travel, and increases in the more vague virtues of progress and efficiency.

- Slide IV shows a different form of the question documenting an approaching majority disapproval of SST prior to the Congressional vote.
- Slide V shows the results of the probes among these SST opponents in which air pollution (*i.e.*, concern over danger to the upper atmosphere) rose from 1% to 14%.

The possibility that the American aircraft industry would lose leadership to other countries did not budge this opposition.

- Slide VI shows still another form of the question leading to a specific probe about foreign SST's.
- Slide VII indicates that 72% of opponents say they would not change their minds.

From a business point of view, the product was somewhat premature because the era of quiet jet engines was still two to three years away, and the public had yet to experience that relative quiet.

From a business point of view, the large American SST was planned to be economical and profitable. The very small Anglo-French Concorde with only eighty passengers is a highly uneconomical airplane, and in retrospect makes public concerns about cost appear (erroneously) to have been valid. Meanwhile, the concern about danger to the ozone layer has disappeared.

So why did Mr. Nixon fail to win Congressional approval for the SST?

Mr. Nixon appointed a very talented William Magruder (not Jeb Magruder of Watergate) to take the case for the SST to Congress and to the public. Magruder was a former test pilot and airline official, a brilliant and articulate man. He gave a sixty-minute presentation to Congress and received a standing ovation. He repeated the presentation to other groups around the country and also got standing ovations. I saw the performance in the Waldorf Astoria ballroom, hosted by the Sales Executive Club of New York.

Magruder was great. In sixty blazing minutes, articulating what seemed like hundreds of statistics, he demolished twenty-four objections to the SST. He was impressive! All the sales executives present wished he was on their team. But there were only three salient rising objections to the SST — noise, cost, and pollution — and in Magruder's presentation these three had to compete for attention, comprehension and memory with twenty-one others — at less than three minutes each. Magruder was able to sell the SST to its proponents but did not sell the product to its opponents.

From a business point of view, the SST offered insufficient product benefits to a public that was still enjoying the superior speed of conventional jets over the then recently displaced prop planes. National aviation "leadership," which the President stressed, was not a highly motivating concept at the time, although it apparently did mean something to the British and the French. Americans who are not familiar with the biennial Paris Air Show at Le Bourget have no idea of the intensity of international competitiveness involved. It is the super "Olympics" of aviation, as well as its biggest retail store.

The failure of the American SST may be attributed then to a questionable product benefit of greater speed, a defensive communication program that lacked focus, and a too early, by three years or so, commitment to unnecessarily high noise levels.

It should be noted that the defeat of the SST was hailed as a great victory for the environmentalists, even though environmental factors turned out not to have been significantly involved. It was also the high point of environmental sentiment, which has been trending down since — though still at very high levels.

- Slide VIII shows two questions asked repeatedly over the years about a variety of government activities.
- Slide IX, for example, shows the trend of declining, though still majority desire for the government to "do more" about water pollution. The trend is paralleled at a less than majority level in willingness to pay more for this action.
- As you note the similarity of the shape of the trend lines for other examples such as air pollution (Slide X), public transportation (Slide XI), parks and wilderness (Slide XII), and controlling noise (Slide XIII) you will note that the high point of these concerns was about 1971-72 after the defeat of the SST. That defeat, often hailed as the most significant specific victory of the environmentalists, was ironically followed by some decline in such sentiments. The years 1973-75 were particularly marked by oil embargo, recession and inflationary concerns, and appeared in these data to have created the first general "trade-off" adjustment of Americans to the economic aspects of environmentalism.
- Now let me show you another slide about controlling noise (Slide XIV). This is the trend on controlling noise of jet aircraft. Because it shows the steepest decline during the 1973-75 period of oil embargo, recession and onset of inflation, a decline from majority to minority levels, I attribute to it not only the public's rising "trade-off" awareness of the economic costs of environmentalism, but also, in this case, to an actually declining decibel trend for jet aircraft.

II

The Apollo Space Program, the "space race" to beat the Russians to the moon, always had the very visible support of American presidents, the scientific community, the television networks — but not the support of the majority of the public. While anticipation of the first moon landing was momentarily pleasing, support diminished again thereafter since we had "won the race.

- I apologize for the difficult detail of Slide XV but some of you may be familiar with it from a *Journal* of *Communication* article published in the Fall of 1977 (Chapter   above). It indicates a 2-to-3:1 preponderance of public desire to "do less" rather than "do more" about space exploration and increasing opposition with each of the successful moon landings.

It is unfortunate that President Kennedy defined the program with a *terminal* objective — to reach the moon. In a sense public support for the Apollo Program had been designed to self-destruct on the initial achievement of the program's major objective. It is also unfortunate that no one told the Russians that they were in such a race. They showed then and show now little interest in the moon but are establishing one record after another for keeping space crews aloft for three and four month periods. Skylab may have fallen but there are Russians whizzing overhead most seasons of the year.

It is unfortunate that Apollo involved so many as six televised landings on the moon because each repetition increased opposition. NASA and the networks didn't believe it at the time, so heady was the sponsor excitement. While the public enjoyed the spectacle enough to watch TV, the message really communicated to them was that this was all very expensive, and where was the benefit?

- Slide XVI shows that the major reasons for saying that the government should do less on space was that they "should spend the money elsewhere," a level 58%, and it was a "waste of money," which went from 19% to 33% from 1969 to 1972, during the period of the successful landings.
- Slide XVII shows that among the declining supporters of Apollo the increasingly cited reasons were learning and progress. As in the SST case the opponents are specific about *lack of benefits* while the proponents cite broader values.

From a business point of view, we could say that the Apollo program floundered because of inadequately defined objectives and benefits, and an exaggerated faith in television reach and frequency. The sponsors were exceedingly proud of their product, certainly with good reason to them, but the public retained a financially skeptical attitude — even in the face of the most lavish and spectacular product promotion.

Since the days of the Apollo program NASA has responded to public concerns about the cost of space exploration and developed a re-usable shuttle plane, the Rockwell Industries-designed "Enterprise," which is launched piggyback off a Boeing 747 in flight. If that 747 were an SST, the costs of the shuttle might be even less than they are today.

III

The third and still current case history is nuclear energy.

It is, of course, an established industry and in that sense a success, and the public is still apparently majority pro-nuclear even after Three Mile Island.

- Slide XVIII shows two open-ended questions used to track each of the fuels used by public utilities. Slide XIX shows the results for nuclear before and after Three Mile Island. Only a minority mention nuclear at all, and I'll come back to that. Meanwhile, note that "spontaneous" proponents of nuclear declined from 21% to 19% to 17%, while opponents increased from 8% to 17% and then receded to 13%.

The nuclear business inherited from the military a difficult technical problem in the form of storage of radioactive wastes. Even today the major portion of these wastes are a by-product of military weapons production rather than of power plant operations. The nuclear business also inherited in the seventies a "No More Nukes" movement from "Ban the Bomb" movement of the fifties and sixties. President Eisenhower's "Atoms for Peace" theme has yet to take firm hold, here or overseas.

I'm sure you're all aware of many of the hopes and fears associated with nuclear power, but there is one element of the impact of Three Mile Island that you may not know of, and which is one of the keys to an understanding of public response. It is the question of how many of the public know that nuclear power plants provide electricity. Until Three Mile Island only a little over a third of the public mentioned nuclear when asked what fuels are used to make electricity.

- Slide XX shows increased awareness of nuclear *to make electricity* from 41% before to 56% after Three Mile Island but dropping back to 48% in the following quarter.
- Slide XXI shows a similar increase in awareness on the local level, but increasing growth in such awareness.

*   *   *

Now to summarize. What have we observed in common for these three cases?

First, that what we would call consumer benefits were simply not communicated, or not communicated adequately. In the SST and Apollo cases some argue that there were none, while in the case of nuclear the key benefit was not widely perceived. This is not to say that the benefits of national technical leadership were not recognized by the public in the case of the SST, or no longer recognized in the case of Apollo, but that as remote and impersonal benefits they were not sufficiently valued; *i.e.*, they were not perceived as benefiting the individual citizen. Presumably, a stronger case could have been made to the individual citizen, if that need had been perceived by the policy-makers of the day.

Secondly, we would note that neither presidential sponsorship, favorable media treatment, or successful product performance nor all of those taken together are sufficient to make up for the lack of communication of benefits to the individual citizen.

Thirdly, we would note that the proponents of at least SST's and space exploration tend to cite values *(e.g.,* progress, learning) rather than benefits.

We could make a modest recommendation, that U.S. presidents need advisors in technical communication. Something more than an after-the-facts public opinion analyst; *i.e.,* advisors who are sensitive to the needs of effective public communication planning at the earliest stages of technical product or program design. The issues at stake are to some extent technological, but at least to an equal extent they are issues of effective communication planning.

In closing, I'd like to make clear that the public's faith in the values of science and technology has not eroded, and has recently increased; *i.e.,* in 1977 and 1979.

- Slide XXII shows a question used to track changes in values over the years, and slide XXIII shows the track for science and technology. It declined somewhat during the oil embargo and recession years of 1972-73, but has regained strength, especially in 1977 and 1979. Why not 1978?

Faith in science and technology is more and more focused on expectations that science Will specifically come up with solutions to the energy challenge *(i.e., benefits),* and this has displaced medical advances as the major public contribution expected from science.

- Slide XXIV suggests that in 1978 the importance attributed to science declined apparently because the increased expectations of energy solutions in 1977 were not fulfilled. Now expectations are even higher than in 1977 for energy solutions, and science is even more clearly "on trial."

A final suggestion is that science and technology will increasingly need direction, interpretation, and communication to live convincingly in a world of "issues."

To guide that direction, interpretation, and communication you will increasingly need to keep track of the public response.

CHAPTER 36

MEASURING PROGRESS

I'm going to report to you today on how we track our corporate reputation and the forces that influence it. This is quite apart from any advertising testing that we do, or any media analysis that we do.

My files contain a "Report on Field Survey for General Electric Company" conducted by Barton, Durstine & Osborn with the cooperation of Lord & Thomas and Logan in 1926. That report compares findings with an earlier study conducted in 1924 but I don't have a copy of that one.

Between 1926 and 1964 there were many years that attitudes toward GE were surveyed by Dr. Henry Link of the Psychological Corporation. There were other years when Opinion Research Corporation did the job. But in 1964 we settled down with an in-house system that has been used, quarterly, ever since. It is called QICR or the General Electric *"Quarterly Index of Company Relations."*

Although QICR is an extensive and somewhat expensive procedure, its basic principles can be faithfully duplicated on a small and modest scale, or on a larger and even more extensive scale if desired.

QICR interviews three separate national samples of 1,000 respondents each. New samples are interviewed every three months. Interviews are conducted on the telephone using the facilities of the Trendex Corporation in Westport, Connecticut.

The three samples of 1,000 respondents each include two comprised of adults, and one of college students. Interviews cover a wide variety of topics of social and economic importance but about midway in each interview respondents are asked about their attitudes toward companies, including GE.

Prior to QICR in 1964,the usual way to ask about GE was to focus on GE and obtain some rating of favorability. But when average favorability as so measured hovered in the 90% range there was little sensitivity for measured improvement. That is, only about 10%, or the difference between 90% and 100% was practically available for measurement of changes over time.

The more sensitive instrument adopted in QICR was to force a comparison between GE and four other prestigious companies. That is, we forced the re-

---

Originally Presented at Association of National Advertisers Corporate Advertising Seminar, Hotel Plaza, New York, October 17, 1979

spondent to make a harder and more discriminating choice. With five companies represented, any one company by chance would be chosen 1 in 5 times for
an average of 20%. For most companies there was now lots of room for measured progress or improvement over time.

We used only a total of five companies because this seems to be the most
that the average telephone respondent can hold in his or her head when asked,
"Which one of these five companies does the best job of . . . ."

We ask respondents to write down the names or initials of the companies
before we ask the company comparison questions.

Which companies should be compared with GE? There are only a relatively small number that are as well known to the public at large. From among
those we picked four to use with one of our samples of 1,000 adult respondents,
and a different four for the second sample. The third sample of 1,000 college
students has still a different line-up of companies.

By making *comparisons* with other companies we get a more sensitive,
thoughtful response. By using different groups of companies with different
samples we get a check on whether GE itself is really improving, *i.e.*, regardless
of who it's compared with, or whether some measured change is only an aberra-
tion due to the decline of one or two of the other companies.

Sometimes one of our managers says, "Why do you use Company X? Why
don't you compare us with Company Y?" Although his logic may be reasonable
at the time, once we change a piece of the system, our data bank, and the validity of our trend lines is destroyed. So we must be consistent, as any other true
measurement system must be consistent.

In making the comparisons of GE with four other companies, we ask the
following ten questions, our "image profile" as we call it.

"Which one of these five companies . .

- does the most new and interesting things?
- is doing the most important research and development?
- does the most for its customers?
- would you most like to work for?
- would you consider the best investment?
- has the highest quality products?
- does the most for the communities in which it is located?
- cares most about people?
- does most to help solve problems of the cities?
- does most to help solve problems of the environment?

What do we do with the answers? Well, six weeks after the end of interviewing we distribute to 350 plant managers and up (including the Board of Directors) a top-line or "HIGHLIGHTS" report.

Here are the answers to the first question for the first group of companies.
Zooming in on the Consumer Group of Companies, you can see the comparison
— with the other company names blacked out. Moving to the right you see the

second group, Image-Growth. Moving again to the right is the third group. The current quarter's findings are compared with the previous four quarters.

Then we go on to report the second question, and the third, and so forth.

For each group the choices for each company are also averaged for the ten questions and reduced to a three-digit ratio which for convenience we call a "batting average." For each company the average batting average by chance alone would be .200 (*i.e.*, the equivalent of 20%). As you can see, some companies bat over .200 and some under. I have, of course, blacked out the other companies.

Six weeks after the QICR "Highlights" report (*i.e.*, twelve weeks after interviewing has ended) we issue a more detailed QICR "Analysis Report." Here the same data which was shown in the "Highlights" report and compared with the previous four quarters is, among other things, charted for the past fifteen years.

This then is a brief sketch of our basic data. We do ask other questions about the companies compared. For example, when the ten questions of the image profile are completed we ask, "Did any of these companies do anything recently that you did not like?" and for those who say, "Yes," we then ask, "What was that?"

At the very end of the survey we indicate that the survey was sponsored by General Electric and would they like to make any comment or suggestion to General Electric?

As Dave has mentioned, we also separately compute image profile and batting average figures for those respondents who have seen zero, one, two or more of our TV shows in the past quarter, for respondents who have read one or another magazine in which we have advertised, etc. We also compare such image responses among those who are vs. those who are not aware of some boo-boo we may have committed, or among those who side *with us* or *against* us on some controversial issue. The system is infinitely flexible and leads to a well used data bank.

If you wished to do the same, but on a smaller scale, you could
- survey 1,000 rather than 3,000 respondents
- conduct surveys once or twice a year rather than every three months
- buy a relatively few questions into an omnibus poll (Gallup, Roper or others) rather than sponsor an entire questionnaire or interview

You could spend 10% of what we do and still have a viable instrument. Note that our own questionnaires carry a lot more freight than just attitudes towards GE; *i.e.*, we probe many topics and issues of other interest to the company.

However, to have a true measurement system you would have to stick with *a* system and see how you trended over time. If your company lives in a rapidly changing environment it would be preferable to survey frequently even if you would thereby afford fewer questions each time.

If a major objective is to track the influence of your corporate advertising on your image (by comparing attitudes among the exposed vs. non-exposed) then the frequency of surveying should be geared to the frequency of advertising. The more continuous the advertising the more frequent the survey, to catch the recent impact of advertising before it is lost.

In closing, I would stress that the QICR system is designed to track changes *over time*, to detect trend changes early in their lifecycle, and even to make short range predictions of what is likely to happen next. One can only perfect such a system by investing in it as a long run commitment, and sticking to it. Thus, in recommending the system to you we suggest you try to do it however modestly, but frequently and persistently.

It is especially gratifying to me to see how QICR has been used as a pivotal planning element in our corporate advertising, and here to tell you about our current advertising plans is Karl Koss.

CHAPTER 37

TRACKING THE EFFECTS OF CORPORATE ADVERTISING

This morning I would like to illustrate some uses of tracking and to indicate some of the things we feel we have learned thereby about corporate advertising. So I'll be talking about media allocation, frequency, flighting, effects of program context on commercials, and some differences between types of corporate campaigns.

The tracking itself is a simple procedure of three thousand telephone interviews every three months. The trick is to keep it going year in and year out through various changes in management. This requires some repeated education of management to keep them from suggestions for "improving" the measurement system with changes that cut short the existing trend lines.

The present tracking system is distinguished, therefore, primarily because it has been in place for seventeen years, and produced seventy consecutive quarterly reports. The interview itself consists of three types of content:

(1) Questions about current affairs and public issues of interest to the company.

(2) Questions about large companies — top-of-mind awareness, competitive ratings of some large companies (including GE), open-end queries on any recent dislikes caused by any of the large companies, rated knowledge of company products, etc.

(3) Questions on magazine readership, viewing of GE television shows, and identification of company slogans.

What can be learned from seventy data points like this collected over seventeen years?

CORPORATE AD EFFECTIVENESS
ABOUT AS EXPECTED IN MAGAZINES

First, you can do *historical* measurement of media effectiveness. For example, we took the ten magazines we advertised in over a five-year period and charted what quarters we were in each book and out of each book. In some magazines we were in for a few quarters, out for a year and back again. In some we were out two years and back in again. In some we started advertising half

Originally presented at Association of National Advertisers Advertising Research Workshop, Hotel Plaza, New York, December 9, 1981 way through the years under study, while in some we were in for the first half of the period and then out for the remaining half. Did it make any difference? That is, did the corporate reputation ratings of GE change among the readers of each of the magazines, during the periods when we were advertising and when we were not advertising? No, with one exception, they did not.

Mind you, we are not talking about evaluating an ad, an ad campaign, or a year's advertising effort. We are talking about years of advertising or not advertising.

Ten magazines were involved and with one exception it just made no difference. Now we are not the only corporate advertiser to make this discovery. The DuPont Company went out of corporate magazine advertising for several years specifically because its research showed no benefit from such advertising. However, they did go back in, and GE never went out.

I think many corporate advertising people have a faith in print magazines, and perhaps blame themselves as much as the medium if the advertising doesn't work (and mind you, nobody's Starch scores are very encouraging!). I think there is a faith that print can really do the job, if only one knew how. There is a creative challenge to advertisers which of course they share with their agencies, and as the goals of corporate advertising evolve and clarify perhaps print will become a more effective context for corporate messages.

AN EXCEPTION TO THE RULE

I did mention an exception to these otherwise uniformly negative results, and it is an important one, the kind of exception that almost "proves the rule," if you understand it correctly. This exception helped to keep our faith up.

There is a magazine, which shall be nameless, that we started advertising in halfway through the study period in question. In the years prior to GE advertising, the GE ratings of readers of that magazine were well below the national average of GE ratings. As we began advertising, those ratings began to climb. In a year they were up to well above the national ratings, and they stayed above throughout the rest of the years in which we advertised.

What was different about this phenomenon was that our Starch scores sometimes differed in pattern from the other magazines. The typical corporate ad in a national magazine enjoys the average 50% "noted," 10% "read most" scores you are familiar with. GE ads average a bit higher, say 55% noted and 12% read most. In the exceptional magazine, however, where attitudes toward the Company were favorably affected, the Starch rating" was only a little higher for GE ads, but the "read most" was sometimes significantly higher; i.e., more people read.

Although we call magazines a "print" medium, the Starch scores generally have been telling us for years that it is really a picture medium, since it is usually a picture and perhaps a headline that gains attention. When we say, however, that our ads were being read, which is so unusual, we realized that we were fulfilling the classic if not the actual role of magazine advertising, *i.e.*, to get people to read, and perhaps even to think.

Such a finding, or such a view, becomes more important if or when or as our advertising objectives change, and might-place more emphasis on thought-provoking messages. Then we would have to consider the formats and the contexts which promoted, not the brief attention, which has been characteristic of advertising, but more sustained involvement.

THE EXPERIENCE IN TELEVISION

Now television was-an entirely different story. Here, we could not miss detecting attitude effects of corporate advertising no matter what. People who were exposed to one of our corporate shows per quarter typically produced higher GE ratings than those who were not exposed, and those who were exposed to **two** shows produced higher scores than those exposed to one show.

Of course, some shows had much bigger audiences than others, and program choice is also an area of research. Since 1971 we had 56 corporate TV shows, including 11 documentaries, 23 GE Theaters, 14 Barbara Walters, and 8 variety shows. But if you trichotomize the attitude impact scores of these shows, trichotomize the Nielsen % of household viewing scores, and then cross-tabbed the two variables in a 3x3 table, it turned out that only the GE Theaters tended to enjoy both high attitude impact and large audience size, so we are back-1-n-GE Theater and plan to -be there in 1982.

Again. context is important, in this case, program context. But even after you decide on a show type — say GE Theater there are differences in the impact of one theater presentation and another on the commercials used. For example, the attitude impact of our January 1980 GE Theater "Once Upon a Family" was three times greater than another GE Theater *using the same commercials.* That's something we'll not soon forget. It is another one of those exceptional findings that keeps us fascinated by the potentials of advertising.

HOW TRACKING CAN FACILITATE EXPERIMENTS IN ALLOCATING MEDIA DOLLARS

Let's take a look at the allocation of media dollars around the year. A historical view of the past indicates that company-wide there have been marked variations by quarter, with the first and third quarters receiving less and the second and especially the fourth quarter receiving the larger share of the dollars.

This condition, if viewed historically, sets up the possibility of conducting what Paul Lazarsfeld used to call natural experiments," in this case, in flighting or media weight. Rather than, for example, to purposely go out and design an experiment to test doubling or halving of advertising expenditures, why not take advantage of the "natural" doubling or halving that takes place during the year as a matter of course. Those are a matter of record. They represent the stimulus in the experiment. If you've been tracking response over the year and over the years, there's your experimental design.

Looking at the data this way permits several generalizations. For example, if you markedly increase expenditures in one quarter, and then go back to baseline for the following three or four quarters — you may find that the one quarter increase produced a significant increase in attitude impact for that quarter, about half of which was retained through the following two quarters.

This type of generalization is not based on GE data alone because our GE ratings are comparative; i.e., GE is pitted against other major companies. We consequently pick up the ratings for these other companies as well. Using LNA reports we have been made aware of any sudden increase in their corporate advertising expenditures and have, therefore, been able to see the generalization working in these cases as well.

Incidentally, the major reason for these relatively rare but sudden increases in advertising expenditures are corporate re-organizations, which involve a lot of advertising for one quarter, but then simmer down. Yet they are real, they are in nature or natural, and they represent opportunities to learn about the advertising potential of large amounts of money temporarily injected into the system.

THE VALUE OF THEMES AND SLOGANS

I should note, however, that while large money may be "temporarily" injected into the system, the advertising content injected into the culture may live on forever. For example, in tracking awareness and correct recognition of our company slogan, "Progress for People" (used in the late seventies), we achieved levels of 21% to 23%, which always fell far short of the 35% to 40% that continued to be enjoyed by "Progress is our most important product." This latter slogan, which we hadn't used in over ten years, just kept merrily on its way without any help from us. It had become part of the culture. Similarly, I think "The pause that refreshes" is probably still the slogan of Coca Cola in the popular culture.

In his book, *Reality in Advertising*, Rosser Reeves argued against unnecessary changes in themes, slogans, and even campaigns, on the grounds that the old campaign inadvertently became the main competition for the new campaign. Changing campaigns he said was like "stopping the money."

Certainly our experience with such slogans as "Men helping man" in the early seventies, and "Progress for people" in the late seventies, tends to support Reeves' view, but again there are exceptions. For example, our new theme, "We bring good things to life," had a steeply rising slope of increased awareness and recognition never seen before in our history. Its trajectory was almost vertical. That theme achieved parity with "Progress is our most important product" within twelve months, achieving over 50% levels, and thereby, I would say, entering the U.S. culture. This is qualitatively different from just entering marketplace awareness. Thus, when advertising content enters the culture it shows up in conversation, in New Yorker cartoons and in many non-marketplace con-texts. But it carries a corporate image message with it, wherever it goes.

Why is "Good Things" an exception? Perhaps because it is not a slogan, which implies just words, but also a melody, and also an accompanying set of pictures or visual images. It was perhaps more fully designed for the several communication capabilities of television.

TRACKING THE NEW MEDIA

We are of course, all of us, still learning about the potentials of television just as we are being forced to think about the newer electronic media.

One of our recent campaigns gave us the opportunity, again somewhat un-expectedly, to think a bit about what are called "infomercials." The campaign was the "Edison" campaign in which the actor Pat Hingle played t ' he part of Thomas Edison in a series of two- and three-minute commercials. Pre-test groups characteristically reported that they thought they were viewing a docu-mentary until the logo appeared at the end. The tracking data also made its spe-cial contributions. It showed an inverse correlation between age of respondent and impact on attitude; i.e., the younger viewers were affected the most. This may be because Thomas Edison was not as well known to them as he was to the older generation, and hence there were surprising things to learn about him. But it may also reflect, even in these times of supposed youthful cynicism, a special respect for aged wisdom. Perhaps such respect hasn't gone out of style after all -even though it may have required the considerable theatrical talents of Pat Hin-gle to bring it out. On the whole, however, it can be said that, especially for younger viewers, this series of commercials was thought-provoking. Surely, that is one of the skills that a corporate advertising component would like to have available for use, as needed, and in anticipation of new electronic media formats and contexts.

In closing, I would like to specify what may be the single most valuable aspect of tracking, and which underlies the several examples I have given of its use by the company. This is the making visible of exceptions to customary ex-pectations, or to conventional or normal trends in the data. You just cannot see an exception unless you have been measuring the normal trend. If you don't know that an exception has occurred, you don't get the chance to ask "Why it happened?" and "Is it good?" or "Is it bad?" The exceptional responses and re-actions represent our opportunities to learn new things about the effects of ad-vertising.

CHAPTER 38

CORPORATE ADVERTISING AS "THOUGHT PROVOKING" MESSAGES

Many years ago I visited Norman Mackworth at Stanford Medical Institute when he was working with Karl Pribrim. Pribrim would surgically remove very tiny slices of brain tissue from rhesus monkeys and Mac would try to determine what impairment in perceptual behavior, if any, could be noticed later on. Outside his office on the day of my visit there were stashed about a dozen monkey filled cages, and of course I had to see them.

Mac asked if I would like to know what kind of pictures the monkeys like to look at. He showed me into a laboratory with a large wooden box occupied by a monkey. On one side of the box there was a hole, a peephole, just large enough for a monkey to put his eye to it if he wanted to see what was going on outside. Meanwhile, inside the box there was food and toys, so the monkey really had a choice. The pictures outside the box were shown one at a time. Each time the monkey's eye appeared in the peephole it was timed. After a while it became clear which pictures the monkeys liked to look at. Of the great variety of types of pictures, the clear winner was the face of a very old, very distinguished looking monkey, the wisest (looking) I had ever seen, a veritable chief justice of the Supreme Court of rhesus monkeys. Thus, respect for age, and presumably aged wisdom is a strong element in rhesus monkey society.

This respect for age is less clear in human society. At least it seems less clear to the older person that such respect still exists. I am reminded of a set of GE commercials called the "Thomas Edison" series with the actor Pat Hingle playing the part of Tom Edison. He appeared in these commercials in his laboratory, telling stories about science. His manner was that of a one-man show, playing Edison as an elderly person with many pauses in the monologue. The role was that of a person who could make you stop and think.

Our research on these commercials found them very effective indeed. However, we also found an inverse relation between our measures of effectiveness and the age of viewers. Younger viewers showed more attitude shift on our

Originally presented at Corporate Communications Workshop, Marketing Science Institute Cambridge, Mass., May 1981 measures and older viewers showed less. This was an unexpected finding which refuted a notion that these commercials made GE look old-fashioned.

One of the frequent criticisms in our society is from elders who complain that young people don't respect age. Yet here *was* a case of young people respecting age and wisdom.

What is there about these commercials that makes them effective? What is there about older statesmen, human or monkey?

Maybe it's because they must, or have learned to, speak slowly — thereby giving the audience, even forcing the audience, to *stop* and think.

Now this then concerns the questions of when to stop and how often and how long to stop. All of these are important matters in the theater, but can you take the time in commercials. Can you identify good stopping places efficiently, so as to make the most of them in the relatively short time available?

I am reminded of Professor Richard Carter (of the University of Washington's School of Journalism) and what he calls his "stopping technique." He distributes a story or article to his students, asks them to read, and asks them to make slash marks after each word or phrase at which they took a moment to stop reading and to reflect about what they had been reading. Professor Carter would analyze these stopping places to determine what were the conceptual units of the article or message, as opposed to their mechanical or even literary units.

I myself insert slash marks in the texts of speeches I am to deliver. To me they are signals to pause. It would be nice if I could get an audience to apply Carter's stopping technique to their reception of my speech. Did they stop where I paused; *i.e.*, where I planned for them to take an extra moment to think about what I was saying, or did they stop at places I hadn't expected them to? Just how good was my speech plan, my proposed timing?

The opportunity to slow down or to stop is inherent in reader response to print media, but harder to arrange in television advertising where every second has a large price tag on it. The trend toward shorter commercials, and even the recent interest in Professor Jim MacLachlan's research on "time compression," is all testimony to the difficulty of advocating any contrary view involving the slowing of response. Yet, we are speaking here of corporate advertising which has different goals than that of consumer advertising, and so the point of view must be advocated, at least for its exploration and evaluation. Fast commercials may be fine for communication of a single fact or impression, but no so fine for the provocation of thoughtfulness.

Some consumer advertising has experimented with slow commercials. The Clairol "Nice 'N Easy" commercial was actually shown in slow motion and was aired successfully as a unique mood commercial of its day. Coca Cola created a sixty-second commercial showing just a large cold bottle of coke with beaded moisture glistening on the glass bottle. The background audio indicated, via a subdued babble of voices, that a party was going on. It was left to the viewer to "imagine" the scene, or any similar scene in his own life. It was a daring combination of still photo and animated unstructured audio. The absence of visual action provided an opportunity for the audience to think about the stimulus.

Why does one have to slow down to get people to think? Because they can't do the two things at once! They can't watch a moving stimulus, trying to understand it, and at the same time step back and think about it in personal terms at least they can't do that the first time around when the stimulus is new and they are trying to "take it in." To think "about" the stimulus, they have to look into their heads, perhaps even close their eyes. They have to scan their own memory banks, their own "internal grids" as some cognitive psychologists would say. They have to review their own situation to see where and if the stimulus has relevance. So, somehow, the stimulus must be slowed or stopped or the viewer will just skip part of it and do his own stopping — which the advertiser might unappreciatively bemoan as a temporary loss of attention.

A major reason for the required multiple exposure of typical commercials is so that people can *evaluate* the message content the second or third time around. All they can do the first time is simply to learn what the message is saying.

Some areas of television technology are catching up with the need to create multiple exposures in one viewing. I refer here to the developments in the instant replays of football plays. Nowadays each play is re-shown to the audience from three different camera angles. This creates perceptual insights that cannot be achieved from one angle, and somewhat puts the garrulous announcer out of business. The successful experiments of the past 1980-81 football season in broadcasting some football games without the ubiquitous "commentator" were made possible by this instant replay photography.

At the other extreme from "instant triple replays" are some of the new corporate documentaries seen on public broadcasting. I refer particularly to the Occidental Petroleum half hour film on shale oil. This film shows the company confronting the problem of how best to get some oil out of a particular hill or mountainside. First, it shows the proposed solution as discussed by the foreman and the boss, then it shows the same plan in diagram, and finally it shows the plan in action. It is so to speak a replay of the same plan in three formats, (1) head to head talk, (2) charts and diagrams, and (3) on the scene mining activities. When the first plan does not fully succeed, another one is developed, and again shown in triple format. I learned a great deal about shale oil, pleasantly and fast.

Now, is the "instant triple replay," at any speed, effective because it is triple, or because it is three *different* types of perspective on the same topic? We have this question in our corporate television shows wherein, over a one to two hour program we insert half a dozen corporate commercials. But those corporate commercials are all of a family with a similar purpose. Is this repetition? Should it count as multiple "frequency?" It's not the same commercial shown six times, but it's not six completely different commercials either.

We have some reason to believe, based on experience with rotating the order of these commercials, that we may be getting the best of both worlds, "both" meaning the benefits of sheer repetition (as with the identical commercial repeated) and the benefits of a variety of perspective on the same topic (as in the instant triple replays).

Underlying this view is an age-old argument in the field of psychology as to the effectiveness of practice on learning, with some advocating so-called "massed learning" involving few but long practice sessions and others advocating so-called "spaced learning" which emphasizes many short practice sessions. I'm sure that you have confronted this tactical issue when you had to memorize a lot of material in school, when you had to decide either to study all term long or "cram" for exams at the end of the term, or when perhaps in subsequent years you had to decide on buying a package of six one-hour tennis lessons or a different package of twelve half hour lessons.

This problem has been complicated in recent years, at least in the academic world, by a new point of view which asserts that it is the total time in practice, whether massed or spaced out that really matters. The "total time hypothesis," as it is called, has been verified in some cases but not in others.

Does it apply to corporate television commercials? My view is that it depends on the context. That is, if you control the environment of the messages with a corporate sponsored show, then the commercials can build upon one another just as if the several problems shown in the Occidental Petroleum documentary were all parts of a single story.

However, the show context must be hospitable. It too must be on a single theme, a football game, a dramatic story, *not* a "variety" show. Thus, corporate commercials are never put in what is called "spot" advertising; *i.e.*, scheduled at the discretion of the broadcaster. Corporate advertisers therefore talk about the need for a "show case" for the corporate commercials. This works to create a build from commercial to commercial within the show, by showing different perspectives on the same problem, by achieving (in effect) a long commercial of six minutes' total time.

This type of advertising is qualitatively different from consumer advertising, where the objective as once put by Neil Borden is "to communicate as quick as a wink." By comparison, the provocation of thought in some corporate messages is closer to the goals of classroom education — and may eventually have much to teach the classroom educators.

I do not say that corporate advertisers uniformly recognize this quality of their advertising, but as they gain more experience with a greater variety of information objectives via issue or advocacy advertising, or via the longer commercials that may be required for interactive communication on VCR's, two way cable, and direct merchandising to the home, etc. — they will have to recognize that the boundaries between selling and educating are breaking down.

Thus, the company that has the best films on how to properly apply house paint may sell the most product.

At the present time networks do not offer a large choice of suitable programs for corporate advertisers, "suitable" meaning a suitable showcase for corporate commercials plus a well-defined target audience. This however is one of the many promises of the new media technologies. In time, thought provoking corporate messages will be a major focus of the advertising industry.

Meanwhile, I would like to close these comments with three perhaps outrageous hypotheses.

(1) Despite media assertions to the contrary, I suggest that there is less genuine corporate advertising today than ten years ago — simply because serious, potent TV commercials can't readily fit into the noisy, light hearted, low involvement programs of today's television world.

(2) Where you do have corporate advertising in corporate programs and have independent measures of effectiveness of the program (as a program) and the commercials (as commercials) then I would suggest that

- a good show makes a good commercial better (but)
- a good show makes a poor commercial worse

In other words, you can't mix good and poor quality.

(3) There is a great need to look away from fast, allegedly "efficient" communication and to identify the particular profitability of slow teaching on mass media.

CHAPTER 39

REPETITION REVISITED:
APPLICATION OF THE THREE EXPOSURE
THEORY TO CORPORATE ADVERTISING

Ten years ago, in the December 1972 issue of the *Journal of Advertising Research*, I suggested, based on a variety of research, that three exposures was typically the optimal frequency for television advertising. The first exposure was described as producing a cognitive or "What *is* it?" type of response, the second exposure by a more evaluative "What *of* it?" type of response, and the third exposure by recognition of prior familiarity with the commercial and the beginning of withdrawal.

These ideas have been put to much use and drawn much comment over the years. One popular modification, by Al Achenbaum, was to add the term "effective" to "frequency" to create the term "effective frequency", and to raise the proposed optimal number of exposures from three to about six.

But that's not what I want to talk about today.

My earlier views on frequency, as well as the public comments about those views, concerned the broadcasting or airing of commercials whose frequency of media exposure could be counted as separate incidents. That is, a product commercial could appear X times per evening in separate spots and X times per week on separate nights, etc. Most airing of commercials is of this spot and separate, or separated in time nature. At the other extreme, you wouldn't repeat the same commercial back to back, although you might have two related commercials back to back.

When I left the advertising agency world of Madison Avenue to join the General Electric Company, I found that corporate advertising was different. It appeared only in company-sponsored shows, a so-called "showcase" for its commercials, and showed six commercials per hour, twelve in a two hour show. All the commercials differed in specific topics, but all were somewhat similar in format and objective, an objective usually described as reputation or image-building.

Confronted with this practice over the years, I couldn't help thinking about how the three-exposure theory did and didn't apply. What is the optimal num-

Originally presented at American Marketing Association, 13th Attitude Research Conference, Phoenix, Arizona, February 10, 1982.

ber of commercials within a company sponsored show? How differentiated are the commercials in their effects? Is a series of six related commercials in a sheltered environment equal to six exposures, or is it experienced to some extent as one long but interrupted, single commercial? How much generalization of effect is going on?

Obviously this is quite a different world of advertising from TV spot advertising of products and services. But perhaps there is an opportunity to learn something of general value about advertising. Clearly, some very general questions can be asked.

Almost as soon as the ink was dry on my 1972 article on the three-exposure theory, I began to feel the presence of a different kind of theory breathing down my neck. This theory goes under the title, in academic circles, of "The Total-Time Hypothesis" and appeared in the October 1967 issue of the *Psychological Bulletin* in an article by Elaine Cooper and Allen Pantle. I guess I always knew that I would have to come to grips with it, and that-someday I would want to.

"The Total-Time Hypothesis states that a fixed amount of time is necessary to learn a fixed amount of material regardless of the number of individual trials into which the time is divided." Unquote. That's the opening sentence of the article by Cooper and Pantle. Bang out of the box!

Those of you who are familiar with the educational or teaching controversy over so-called "massed" vs. "spaced" practice; *i.e.*, the question of whether it is better to hold few but very long practice sessions, or many but very short practice sessions, will realize that the total time hypothesis tends to knock much of that debate into a cocked hat, and to suggest that it is an irrelevant debate. It's as if someone said that all of your experience in the flighting or pulsing of ads and campaigns was unrealistic because it was only total exposures during the campaign that counted no matter how they were allocated over time.

I'm neither advocating nor taking issue with the total time hypothesis, because it isn't a case of it being valid or not valid. Like a lot of other hypotheses its history, in this case since 1967, has shown that it is true sometimes for some things. Most important, it raises fruitful questions.

For example, questions about the six to twelve different GE commercials within a company sponsored television show. The topics varied from jet engines, to computerized medical procedures, to auto safety, solar energy, etc., but the overall message, if they were seen together, was that GE was doing interesting things and important research. Nowhere was that said specifically, but it was there implicitly and it was consistently measurable in audiences responses.

Because we were dealing here with a generalized attitude response the specific factual content of the commercials had to be understood by the viewer. We had here not the teaching of a brand name to be measured by store shelf recognition, but the memory of stories and facts associated with an attitude of respect.

Obviously the technical stories told in the commercials had to have some high involvement connection to the viewer; *e.g.*, health and safety interests.

But because a generalized impact on specific attitudes was sought, the number of examples given (i.e., the number of independent or separate sixty second commercials), may be irrelevant. Usually they are back to back in pairs. I could call that one exposure. Even three in a row could be one.

In terms of the general objectives why not consider the twelve one minute commercials as one twelve-minute commercial interrupted by show content? Or as one commercial sausage cut for convenience into a dozen little weenies. Does it make any difference, and if so, what kind?

Assuming high involvement and close attention, isn't this saying that the effective message here is a one exposure commercial? Or, that the different examples of company technical activity must approach a critical mass in one sitting in order to achieve the one generalization? Or, that the purpose of a company sponsored show is primarily to hold the viewer throughout and insist that he or she see all the individual pieces of the same message?

There is some evidence to support such a view, a view that the various commercials, the dozen weenies, can be treated as one big sausage.

For example, GE corporate commercials do have measurably more impact in a dramatic show, the "GE Theater," than in a sponsored variety show. The former, the GE Theater, is itself one big sausage, a dramatic story interrupted or cut into pieces by the interruption of the commercials, while the variety show is a series of individual entertainment acts with less consistent content and less intrinsic rationale for maintaining or keeping the audience in its seats for the full two hours.

For example, some corporate commercials have been lengthened to two and three minutes, and some of these in turn have been combined to create a documentary film. Thus, the commercial advertising is transformed into programming and educational material.

I think it is important to note that advertising can reach a point where it changes over into education, and important to understand where that point occurs, and how the change is brought about. The time is approaching when low involvement product advertising may have to take on an information bearing or educational load as the electronic media fragment into cable, satellite and cassette. When the "infomercial" comes on stream we will be dealing with long and involving messages which will strive for comprehension and freely usable retention rather than mere brand name or package recognition.

Let me approach the subject backwards now, not from the sixty second weenies to the big sausage, but vice versa, starting with the sausage. I once saw a documentary film on PBS by the Occidental Petroleum Company. Its manifest purpose was to show how shale oil could be mined. Its latent purpose, presumably, was to position Occidental as a capable, conscientious and worthy company.

That twenty minute film could have been broken up into at least three segments, nine easily, and more if necessary. The individual segments could have been "commercials".

The film showed three different experimental approaches to producing shale oil from a particular mountain in the Western Rockies. Each of the three methods is shown in three different vignettes, one in which Armand Hammer, the company president, is discussing the procedure with his chief engineer, another in which the method is portrayed by vivid graphs and models, and yet another in which a mine foreman and workers actually put the procedure into action within the mountain.

When the film was over, I knew a lot more about shale oil than I ever expected to know. I had been exposed repeatedly to various methods of mining shale oil, but no two methods were visually the same. Either it was the same method shown in different ways or different methods. None of the material was specifically repeated, but all of the material was inter-connected via subject matter and the cast of characters. I understood some of it, remember most of it, and will always remember, unaided, the experience. My respect for Occidental is permanently enhanced.

If the material was broken up into nine or more segments and shown as commercials on repeated occasions, and if I happened to see them all, I might'(I'm not sure) end up just the same as if I saw them all together. So perhaps I do endorse the total time hypothesis and equate the one long exposure with several short ones, but only with an involved audience.

Thus, the outer limits of the three exposure theory is that with highly involving material the ideal commercial to aim for is one long thought provoking commercial which does well on comprehension and unaided recall, while with low involvement material the ideal commercial to aim for is a frequently repeated short commercial requiring no mental work, which does not require recall, but which achieves high recognition value for one or two vivid symbols.

With material in the medium range of involvement or where you have a creative choice between going high or going low——the problem is time. If your marketing or political goals are short term, you would have an advantage in going the high involvement way. If you have longer term goals, you can go with a lower involvement approach. Overall the virtue of the total time hypothesis as it applies to repetition and frequency is that it offers on many topics and issues, a choice of which way to go.

Most advertising agencies and media in the past fifty years have gone the low involvement way, and that's where the creative talent is today. With the protected formats provided by the newer electronic media, some of the campaigns can be shifted to higher involvement, and agencies may want to build new resources of creative and other talent to cope with that very different approach.

CHAPTER 40

TELEVISION PROGRAM INTEREST AND COMMERCIAL INTERRUPTION

One of the admonitions about television clutter addressed to advertisers is that commercial interruption of an engrossing show limits the effectiveness of the interrupting commercial. For example, this is claimed by G.A. Soldow and V. Principe,[1] who review viewer opinion data and report, "Further, it was found that commercials are particularly objectionable when they interrupt interesting programs. Thus, the more interesting the program, the less effective the commercial."

Without contesting viewer opinion that interrupting commercials are sometimes "objectionable," it is very questionable that this makes them less "effective." To demonstrate the falsity of this equation we will introduce data on attitude impact in types of TV programs where the commercials *do* interrupt a story versus types of programs where the commercial comes at a natural break, such as the break between separate interviews with different talk show guests, or between separate acts in a variety show.

The distinction between *viewer opinion* and *impact on viewers* is important for several reasons. For example, it keeps open for the advertiser the choice to opt for lower or higher quality, and as a separate matter for more or less interesting programs. It keeps open for the viewer the choice to complain about immediate frustrations, and as a separate matter to complain about national or other cultural effects. It keeps open for the networks, or even the advocate, the choice to air unpopular but effective public service messages. By contrast, it is only confusing and inhibiting to equate momentary with long-term effects, or to equate opinions with behavior.

The data concern all 56 corporate television programs sponsored by the General Electric Company during a ten year period: 1971-1980.

The data come from quarterly national surveys that General Electric has been conducting regularly since 1964. Two types of data are relevant to this article. One is the measurement of attitudes toward General Electric. This is done by asking ten questions about company image, and which of five companies, including GE, is best on each of those ten image dimensions. An average

Original Publication: *Journal of Advertising Research*, Vol. 23, No. 1 (Feb. 1983), pp. 21-23.

score for the ten is called, within GE, the company "batting average." The second set of relevant data consists of questions about recent exposure to briefly described television shows, including the recent corporate show, but with sponsorship not identified.

The two pieces of information above are put together to compare the GE "batting averages" among those respondents exposed versus not exposed to the show in question. The difference is treated as the attitude impact. (This impact will be considered to be the impact of the commercials as influenced by the show context, *i.e.*, while the four types of shows varied markedly, the technical "progress" type of corporate commercial involved as relatively constant until 1980, with the advent of the "We Bring Good Things to Life" campaign.)

The comparison of exposed versus unexposed does not, without before and after measures, constitute a controlled experiment. However, the possibility of selective exposure was unlikely in the absence of a TV "series" with weekly frequency, a continued story, and a "following" of loyal audience. That is, the TV shows involved here were "specials," and only the Barbara Walters show may be presumed to have had an audience "following." Even so, Nielsen demographics indicated fluctuations from show to show depending upon who was to be interviewed on the show, just as is indicated similar fluctuations in response to the announced story topic of the GE Theater.

The manner of measuring impact, as briefly described, is less relevant for the purpose of this piece than the fact that the resulting batting average differences for the 56 shows were trichotomized into three equal-sized groups representing relatively "high," "medium," and "low" impact. The question is simply which type of show was most frequently in the high group.

TABLE 40.1
Shows Ranked by Impact

Type*	Date	Show
Theater	1/80	"Once Upon a Family"
Special	3/73	"Conquista"
Variety	5/80	Cheryl Ladd Special
Special	4/72	"In Search of the Lost World"
Theater	2/78	"See How She Runs"
Theater	4/74	"Larry"
Theater	1/79	"Champions: A Love Story"
Variety	6/77	To the Queen
Walters	12/77	Ball, Parton, Winkler
Theater	12/76	"The Secret Life of John Chapman
Walters	8/78	Parton, Winkler, Osmond, Crosby (R)
Theater	12/77	"Tell Me My Name"
Theater	12/78	"Amahl and the Night Visitors"
Special	7/72	"In Search of the Lost World" (R)
Theater	1/75	"Miles to Go Before I Sleep"
Special	1/72	"Hollywood: The Dream Factory"
Theater	11/74	"Things in Their Season"

Type*	Date	Show
Special	1/73	"Bellevue"
Theater	2/74	"It's Good to Be Alive"
Special	1/73	"Big Horn"
Special	5/73	"Bellevue" (R)
Theater	12/74	"I Heard the Owl Call My Name" (R)
Theater	2/75	"In This House of Brede"
Walters	7/79	Reynolds, Shah-Iran, Wayne (R)
Theater	9/80	"See How She Runs" (R)
Theater	5/75	"Larry" (R)
Walters	12/76	Streisand, Carter
Special	3/72	"The Champions"
Walters	12/79	Somers, Stallone, Wonder
Theater	11/79	"The Streets of L.A."
Theater	8/77	"Just an Old Sweet Song" (R)
Walters	11/78	Alda, Ross, Martin, Hussein
Walters	5/79	Moore, Burns, Reiner, Pryor
Special	11/71	"The Eagle and the Hawk"
Variety	9/78	GE All Star Anniversary
Walters	4/77	Taylor, Shah-Iran, Jordan
Walters	7/77	Taylor, Shah-Iran, Jordan (R)
Walters	4/78	Osmond, Jackson, Matthau, Mondale
Special	12/72	"Getting There First"
Walters	5/77	Hope, Crosby, Foxx
Theater	12/75	"In This House of Brede"
Variety	4/79	John Denver's Rocky Mtn. Reunion
Variety	12/80	OMNIBUS
Theater	8/74	"Tell Me Where It Hurts" (R)
Walters	1/77	Ford
Theater	3/76	"Twenty Shades of Pink"
Theater	4/78	"The Secret Life of John Chapman" (R)
Theater	11/80	"Skyward"
Theater	3/74	"Tell Me Where It Hurts"
Variety	6/80	OMNIBUS
Variety	12/80	Happy New Year, America
Ballet	6/76	Bolshoi Ballet: "Romeo and Juliet"
Walters	6/77	Castro
Theater	9/76	"Just an Old Sweet Song"
Special	4/73	"Love and Hate"
Walters	5/78	Reynolds, Landon, Ali

* Key to Show Types
Special: Documentary Special (GE Monogram Series)
Theater: GE Theater
Walters: Barbara Walters Special (interviews)
Variety: Variety entertainment
(R): Repeat broadcast

The 56 shows are ranked in Table 40.1 in order of impact, and the types of shows are indicated as GE Theater, Documentary Specials, Barbara Walters

Specials, and Variety Entertainment. Table 40.2 summarizes how often each was in the high, middle, and low impact groups.

TABLE 40.2
Summary of Shows' Impact

	N	*High Third*	*Middle Third*	*Low Third*	*High Total*
Interrupted contexts					
GE Theater	(23)	10	6	7	44%
Documentaries	(11)	5	4	2	45%
	(34)	15	10	9	44%
Natural Breaks					
Barbara Walters	(14)	2	8	4	14%
Variety show	(8)	2	1	5	25%
	(22)	4	9	9	18%

That 44 percent of the shows with true commercial interruption are in the high third, as compared with only 18 percent of the shows with natural breaks, is more than adequate data to dispel the notion that interruptive commercials are less effective. Even a pair of equal percentages would be evidence against the notion. But what about the reverse? The 44 percent to 18 percent here suggest that commercials interrupting interesting shows are *more* effective. Can that be?

It is not a new idea, or a new finding. In 1967, I reported a series of small studies with the tentative conclusion that "involvement with advertising tends to be consistent with interest in the editorial environment, *i.e.*, greater interest 'carries over' to produce higher involvement" (Chapter 7 above).

Despite the above, it is not suggested that interest in shows "carries over" to interest in any or all interrupting commercials, and thereby makes them more effective. That remains to be investigated. It is suggested, however, that when an interesting show is interrupted by an interesting commercial the momentum of aroused interest does carry over.

In an admittedly biased way, I would suggest that General Electric corporate commercials are of greater interest than is typical of television commercials.

In a speculative way, I would suggest that someday we will come to know that interesting shows increase the effectiveness of interruptive but interesting commercials, and diminish the effectiveness of interruptive commercials of less interest. To complete the paradigm it must also be suggested that uninteresting shows diminish the effectiveness of interruptive but interesting commercials. In all, quality begets quality!

---

[1] Soldow, G.A. and V. Principe, "Response to Commercials As a Function of Program Context," *Journal of Advertising Research*, vol. 21, no. 2 (April 1981), pp. 59-65.

CHAPTER 41

THE "DRAW A SUPERMARKET" TECHNIQUE

T
he use of projective techniques of an essentially verbal character has now become well established in opinion research. For special types of problem, however, nonverbal methods may also be considered. In the case described here such a method was developed in response to a problem in store layout and design.

The general problem was to provide guidance to supermarket planners about those aspects and areas of present-day store layouts which create conflict and tension in the shopper. To some extent this guidance was already available in the form of traffic and conventional interviewing studies. What still seemed desirable, however, was a technique for enhancing the conventional interview process by recording the shoppers' stereotyped perception of supermarkets before the verbal questioning or "formal" interviewing began.

The technique selected was a drawing task and used as its materials a No. 2 lead pencil — without eraser — and a sheet of plain white bond paper 8½ x 11 inches. However, on each sheet of paper a simple rectangle 5½ x 7 inches was drawn in advance. This was meant to represent the outlines of the most common (110 x 140 foot) supermarket.

Fifty housewives in New York and adjacent suburban areas were then asked to "draw a supermarket." Some had to be reassured about "just making a quick sketch" or "not having to reproduce any particular supermarket" — although concern over drawing skill was the more common cause for resistance. As each drawing was completed and the parts labeled, interviewing began. Special emphasis in the interview was placed on the content of the drawings.

Three aspects of the drawings were of primary interest. These were (1) store departments omitted, (2) order in which departments were drawn, and (3) space allotted to each department. The range of these responses may be described as follows:

1. The meat department was omitted in about 1 out of 10 drawings, produce in 1 out of 5, dairy in 1 out of 5, dry groceries in 1 out of 4, etc.

2. The produce department was drawn first in about 2 out of 5 drawings, meats in 1 out of 5, dairy in 1 out of 6, dry groceries in 1 out of 6, etc.

Original Publication: *Public Opinion Quarterly*, Vol. 24, No. 1 (Spring 1960), pp. 148-149.

3. The meat department was, on the average, drawn about 50 percent larger than the dry groceries department. Actually, it is only about one-third as large as the dry groceries department in a store of the dimensions involved. Produce was drawn 80 percent as large as dry groceries, though it too occupies only about a third of the space actually allotted to dry groceries.

These data suggest that supermarkets do look quite different to different shoppers and, more important, different from actual dimensional layouts. In the present case they have provided a vivid representation for discussion of respondents' feelings and, when used as illustrations of interview findings, have proven useful in communicating the various shades and nuances of those findings to store planning and design personnel.

CHAPTER 42

THE ROLE OF MAGAZINES IN AMERICA:
TODAY AND TOMORROW

The panel has been asked to take up a topic that has received strangely little serious attention in the years gone by. There have been, for example, many weighty research reports on "The Social Impact of Television" and, prior to that, a still larger number on the role of broadcast radio in a changing world. Motion pictures have been the subject of innumerable investigations. But there is almost nothing on the significance of magazines and their special place in our society. Perhaps it is because they never appeared to be the dominant media, or merely because the printed word in any form — newspapers, books, or magazines — was old and familiar. It is almost as though we expect magic or some kind of super-impact from such 20th Century technical wonders as radio, TV and films but nothing other than comfortable security and loyalty from the old standbys of the printed word.

Some of the hue and cry about what mass media are doing to popular taste reflects this split. That is, radio, motion pictures, and television are attacked as villains, while newspapers and magazines come off more lightly.

This is partly an accident of history since the printed word flourished long before the worst evils of the industrial revolution and, in fact, has had thousands of years to build — with the help of the Bible, at least — a long history of trust and respect.

But the reformers, who see the new leisure of modern industrialism applied to frivolous rather than worthy and serious pursuits, seem to feel cheated out of the fruits of their crusade against illiteracy and poverty. They abhor the entertainment appeal of "TV and movies" and worry over the future of our youth.

Certainly the mass media differ greatly from each other in what they primarily offer to their audiences.

At one extreme we have motion pictures and the world of sheer fantasy and escape. Of course, there are documentaries, news films, and educational films, but the primary content is sheer, escapist fantasy — and very pleasant it is.

At the other extreme we have newspapers reporting the harsh reality of day-to-day life. Newspapers too may present fantasy and escape in the form of

Originally presented at Magazine Publishers Association, 39th Spring Conference, The Greenbrier, May 6, 1958.

comics and special columns (even Sunday supplements and magazines) but the primary content is the anxious reality of the world's existence.

In between these two poles of timeless escape and immediate reality, we have two other primary contents.

One involves entertainment, not so extreme as to induce complete lack of self-awareness but a more participative kind involving dancing, sports, comedy, and so forth. This is the province of radio and television.

Finally then, we come to magazines, and here it seems that the primary content is what I would call helpful guidance.

This guidance is not escapist but appeals directly to the real situation and identity of the audience — there are magazines for men, for women, for teenagers, for mothers, for hobbyists, etc.

Neither is this guidance a matter of harsh day-to-day reality. Magazines are withdrawn and detached from the daily deadline and crisis. They have the time to abstract and synthesize ideas — to take the time to present them with utmost care. Most magazines are of interest even if a year or two old. They are read and re-read, passed around among friends, and traded. They carry with them an intimate sense of ownership. There is "my copy" and "your copy," etc.

The guidance offered by magazines is of many types and as I mention them you will no doubt think of radio, film, and television programs that have performed a similar function. I can only note again that such guidance from those media comes in passing as a secondary benefit of other major qualities. For magazines, these *are* the major qualities.

1. Magazines offer helpful guidance in that they re-affirm the sex roles, *i.e.*, some magazines are very obviously for women, some very obviously for men. These, in effect, create private audiences where intimate and personal problems may be raised and (especially in the more serious women's magazines frankly discussed. If the problems are common to the sexes they have the added virtue of being discussed in a completely and unashamedly *partisan* manner, *e.g.*, with women reading the woman's viewpoint, on say fidelity in marriage, and men reading the man's viewpoint. While it may be said that the TV and films portray many of the battles between the sexes, it is the magazines that act as managers and seconds in between the rounds. In short, "vive le difference."

2. Magazines offer helpful guidance in that they assist us in coming to terms with the world. By this I mean that Americans have only begun to think about world-wide events on a daily basis in recent years . . . as a result of World War II, the end of isolation, the atom bomb, fall out, Summit meetings, etc.

Now to walk around in the street with a "World View" is a serious matter. One can get so upset by the need to DO SOMETHING about this or that issue or one can get equally upset by impotent feelings of not being able to DO ANYTHING. And one cannot shut out the newspapers and news programs.

What the magazines give us, on a comfortable once-a-week basis, carefully analyzed, interpreted and digested, is an understanding of the world given in such a way that we come to feel the duty, even the virtue, in being *well-informed.* This feeling of being well-informed is a substitute, and a poor one admittedly, for positive action . . . but in consolation, and by way of contrast, let it also be noted that it is also a substitute for fear and panic.

3. Magazines provide helpful guidance in that they provide the reader with controlled shopping wherever and whenever he or she wants it. Compare the interest in, or at worst neutrality shown toward, magazine ads — with the "issue" of commercials on radio and TV. The latter audience is in the position of listening to a salesman, and at times when the salesman is not always welcome. With magazines, however, the reader is in a position similar to that of browsing through a self-service department store at the pace and in the direction he or she chooses — and this is "fun."

The really important thing about controlled shopping via the magazine is that it permits the reader to leisurely distinguish between his or her unrealistic desires for products and those that really and rationally belong in his or her home and budget. It is the antithesis of impulsive buying. It represents an opportunity for rational consideration and planning.

It represents the home study rehearsal and pre-planning that permits the reader to go out to Main Street and steer a steadier course than otherwise past the glittering displays, the eager salesmen, the special sales and other gimmicks to what he or she has carefully decided is really needed. It gives the reader a shopping strategy, so to speak, while shopping tactics are left up to the day-to-day opportunities and influences.

4. Finally, magazines offer helpful guidance on life goals, on what we think we should be getting out of life on this earth.

This may sound rather strange for would not all of us admit that what we want is happiness?

Yet happiness has not always been the universally accepted goal of mankind that it is today — and if you look back over the popular heroes of the past 1000 years, you will see what I mean. For example, in the middle ages it was the spiritual man who was most looked up to as a model for everyday living. During the Renaissance it was the intellectual man. Toward the end of the 19th Century through the 1920's it was the successful businessman — the captain of industry who pursued a life of hard work and thrift in pursuit of economic success. For some European cultures (the totalitarian countries) in the 30's and 40's it was the heroic or masterful man.

In this country, however, when the thrifty and hard working captain of industry was replaced as a popular hero, there began a period which saw the "happiness" orientation achieve dominance for the first time.

Who then are the new heroes and what are the qualities we should admire?

The popular heroes are figures from the sports and entertainment world — people who are disgustingly healthy, handsome, who appear to be having a lot of fun, or who are in ecstasy over their spectacular success. Their personal lives, their families, their hobbies, their *wholesomeness*, their essential normality (despite the talent — which is a secondary matter) is splashed across page after page.

This normality seems to be the key to what we are after when we talk about happiness. It seems that for this period in our history — and thanks to the work primarily of Sigmund Freud — the man we most look up to as a model is the *psychiatrically healthy man*. Most people probably wouldn't accept the idea when put in those terms, but if in terms of happiness, peace of mind, etc., yes — that's what they want.

Well then, it becomes the role of the magazines to define what is the normal healthy life. It is Mickey Mantle romping with Mickey Jr.

It is up to the magazines to define when teen-age high spirits are within the limits of wholesomeness and safety (*LIFE* goes to a teenage pajama party) and when they go beyond the limits (delinquency, drinking, drugs, etc.)

It is up to the magazines to show what is fun, what is silly, what is dangerous.

Now on the other side of our popular heroes, let it be noted that magazines, especially those such as *CONFIDENTIAL*, shout that many of the popular heroes are anything but wholesome and normal. And again, it is their abnormality — completely divorced from any interest in their talent — that is the focus of attention and interest.

The focus for all magazines then is not on the talent but on the normality, the healthiness of the hero.

Interestingly, it was one section of the magazine industry that was virtually wiped out by its failure to declare itself on the question of wholesomeness. I refer to the comic book industry, which has been diminished two-thirds since a censorship was forced on it by a group of psychiatrically oriented citizens. These citizens pressing vigorously forward the views of a number of professional psychiatrists.

In short, by word and picture, by illustration and analogy, by model and outright advice, the magazine is in the position of holding up an image of what is the normal, healthy and, therefore, so-called "happy" life.

*   *   *

So much for the role of magazines in America today, a role of providing helpful guidance in re-affirming the sex roles, providing us with a comfortably informed world view, permitting controlled and rationally planned shopping, and orienting us toward the life goal of "happiness" or psychiatric normality.

What about the role of magazines tomorrow?

I do not see any change in the magazine's role of helpful guidance, though I do see changes in the particular content of that guidance. The world continues to change, and in the opinion of some, at an accelerating pace. Our new problems and needs for guidance rapidly replace older ones.

Thus, in the area of the sex roles, we will very soon be confronted with such technical innovations as the birth control pill, and not so soon but not so distant either, by the complex issue of prediction and/or control of the sex of the fetus.

On the social side of the sex role problem, we may be increasingly confronted by a situation wherein the so-called "modern" American woman appears more and more as a throw-back to the old-fashioned girl, her feminist revolution interrupted by the bland utopia of "togetherness." She may appear to be out of step with some of her sisters in other parts of the world, and not helping to meet the talent and professional manpower crises, especially in science, which are rapidly overtaking America.

Another aspect of sex role problems is the increasing average age of the U.S. population. This suggests the possibility of a widening of the romantic love complex to include love at older ages, and possibly producing more mature love themes than "moon," "June," and "croon."

So much for the area of sex roles, an area which will continue to be subject to all the stress and strains of the world's technical and social development.

In the other areas of guidance, we have new problems, developing which are at least of equal impact. As our population grows, and as the super-city, the so-called megalopolis, begins to dominate all else, including suburbia — the problems of maintaining an effectively workable representative democracy will increase. It seems to me that the continuing debate over editorializing in the mass media must finally be resolved in the direction of some, perhaps as yet unknown, form of editorializing. What this will do to the magazines' role of providing a comfortable world view, especially in an age of increasing literacy, is unknown. We may possibly find ourselves in a golden age of mass intellectual debate and exploration aided and abetted primarily by the descendants of what are now our news magazines. We may also see a split in these ranks similar to that between the tranquilizer and the lift drugs. We could have a sharper break — even on a highly intellectual level between "don't give a damn" and "give a damn" magazines. A crude prototype situation is perhaps represented in existentialism and affiliated movements in Paris.

In the area of controlled shopping we have to deal with such considerations as the fact of increasingly beautiful and vivid magazine advertisements, increasing brand faith, and the increasing dignity and prestige of the magazine itself. If consumers are so able to rehearse their shopping while browsing through their magazines, it seems reasonable that it would not be too difficult for other social changes (*e.g.*, population, housing, changing roles of women) to accidentally have an impact here which would tip over great masses of consumers into ordering directly from their magazine ads. In. this sense, we could change the name of Madison Avenue to Sears Roebuck Avenue.

Now finally in the area of life goals, what are the chances of retaining the goal of happiness, peace of mind, psychiatric normalcy? Not very much I think.

For one thing, the psychiatric world itself, or at least the world of the psychological sciences broadly defined, has gone beyond the issue of normalcy, mere "adjustment" and contentment to begin to deal with the requirements of effective utilization of aptitudes and abilities. It is even admitted that a little bit of anxiety may be a good thing. We discover once again the virtues of motivation and drive — just at a time in this world when talent, especially scientific talent, becomes spectacularly in demand. Thus we may be entering a period when not peace of mind happiness — but creativity, enthusiasm, talent, and ability better represent the cultural goals. A period when our citizens will not be divided in status by symbols of material wealth and comfort but by education, intellect, and constructive achievement.

This may sound "good." However, it will bring its share of problems, as has any other system of life goals, and there is no reason to believe that these problems will be less intense, less painful, or less difficult to solve. So, no matter where we look, the need for helpful guidance, on a carefully, thoughtfully, *routinely* comfortable basis will continue to exist — and with it the magazine no doubt forever.

CHAPTER 43

FAST LEARNING AND SLOW FORGETTING OF ADVERTISING CAMPAIGNS

One of the most provocative questions in the advertising industry is "How much advertising is enough?" The answers vary with the situation, of course, but if not *for* the question we would be less likely to learn the nature of those specific conditions where advertising may be typically insufficient or typically excessive. I would like to offer some perspectives on a few built-in limitations to the role of advertising. Hopefully, the specifications of the limitations will also sharpen the sense of the contributions of advertising.

Hindsight is a wonderful aid. From 1967 to 1983 1 regularly had the opportunity at General Electric to examine quarterly survey data on national telephone samples of adults and college students. One question always included was, "Please identify the company that uses the following slogan." This was followed by six slogans (per respondent) and the right and wrong answers recorded.

Now, you may recall that in the late sixties and early seventies many large companies gave up their traditional slogans in response, I would say, to the felt need for a more socially contributory image. So, General Electric gave up "Progress is our most important product" and tried first "Men helping man" and then "Progress for people" in the seventies. Westinghouse replaced "You can be sure if it's Westinghouse" with "We serve people." DuPont replaced "Better things for better living through chemistry" with "There's a world of things we're doing something about." Many other companies did the same. I will talk only about the G.E. case, but the results are similar.

Well now first. There I was at the start of the seventies with no more "Progress is our most important product" being advertised. Its recognition stood at about 50%. 1 awaited the decline, and it came. A drop to about 35% in the first year. But there it stayed, year after year. Meanwhile, "Men helping man" leveled off at about 5% and the later slogan "Progress for people" leveled off at about 20%. In each case it took about a year to reveal the general level of success to be achieved by the new slogans.

Originally presented at Fourth Annual Advertising Research Foundation Research Quality Workshop, New York Grand Hyatt Hotel, September 15-16, 1986.

It is tempting to add the reduced levels of the old slogans with the levels achieved by the new slogans. They of course would add about 50%, *i.e.*, where the old slogan would have been if maintained.

It is important to note that the old slogans persisted in adult samples, *i.e.*, there was a limit to *forgetting*, the 35% recognition may persist until all the sample respondents are dead. But in the college samples the level did decline inexorably, down to 15% by the late 70's. But this is not *forgetting*. This is a case where they were cut off from the opportunity to learn the slogans in the first place.

What makes the G.E. case especially interesting is that at the end of the seventies an entirely new kind of campaign was introduced, "We bring good things to life." Its success and industry fame were spectacular. In one year recognition among adults was up to 40% and for college students about 60%.

This was very heartening indeed, but lo and behold, the levels for the old slogan suddenly spurted up to almost 45% in the same year, after dawdling along at 35%, having been given up ten years previously. So, it seemed that with adults the learning for the new slogan reinforced memories of the older slogans as well. So you have two slogans, two images of General Electric. Which is the right one? Both. They are not in conflict. In other corporate situations this may not be so, but here no conflict.

The higher levels achieved by the college samples, involving a trajectory which was about vertical, may in part be explained by an intentional youthful appeal built into the new TV commercials, but also by the fact that no response to the commercial was drawn off for reinforcement of older commercials. In this respect the young people were "tabula rasas," or empty buckets waiting to be filled.

This naive quality of the young makes them favorite targets for political parties, as well as advertisers. New campaigns look best when aimed at the young, and if the market is really a young market then it is feasible to change campaigns frequently and successfully — as with the case of soft drink companies. How pleased the advertiser who can describe his campaign as "contemporary" — for all those tabula rasas may make the campaign look very good.

One last word about the G.E. data. If you add the levels for "We bring good things to life" to the same time levels for the old slogans, then the adult and college samples are about equal in their familiarity with G.E. I say "about equal" because there are some missing points in the college data and I have to project a bit here.

Well, what have we learned here? In his book, *Reality in Advertising*, Rosser Reeves says, "Changing the campaign is like stopping the money." That is not the case here. Most simply because the old campaign went right on doing a job, and the new campaign did not conflict with it.

It gives one pause, however, to consider just how many supposedly dead campaigns are still out there alive and well and doing their job — often aided and assisted by present "new" campaigns.

I suppose that research personnel are expected to drop measurements of old campaigns when they are officially replaced by new ones. Apparently this would be a mistake, and where possible, should be remedied. Old campaigns are not dead until proven dead, and we shall find many that just will not die.

It is tempting to bring forth new campaigns. It only takes about 9 months, but then you may have to live with the results for the rest of your life.

Let us turn now to a different kind of non-forgetting. Not non-forgetting of campaigns but of individual TV commercials.

This past winter I was engaged in an experiment with the Starch INRA Hooper organization — to establish a new TV recognition measure to match their longstanding print measures. The TV recognition question required interviewers to show to respondents a picture board with a number of photos representing the full commercial. The problem at the time was how many pictures to show — 4, 8 or 12? The pictures came from 35 mm shots of 3/4" video tapes of the commercials — the pictures then arranged on an 8½ x 11 page to show the story presented by the commercial. The 12 picture format contained three rows of 4 pictures each, the 8 picture format contained 8 of the original 12 in two rows, while the 4 picture format contained 4 of the previous eight in one row. Thus, all pictures were the same size and cumulatively identical in context.

Picture boards for ten different commercials were shown to respondents in personal interviews conducted by the Roper organization. To our surprise, the recognition of commercials was not affected by the number of pictures used to elicit that recognition. Thus the average recognition of the same commercials was 35% in the 4 picture format, 34% in the 8 picture format and 38% in the 12 picture format. We had expected that the greater number of pictures would aid recognition and produce higher levels, but this was clearly not the case. I wonder now if we could have tried 1 picture?

In short, aiding does not work with this type of recognition, and it comes as a surprise to those used to *recall* scores that go up as the amount of aiding increases.

In our view this is a possible explanation of the greater reliability of recognition over recall scores (as shown by ARF's PARM study). The reasoning is that aiding helps recall because recall involves an effort to remember and takes a little time, whereas recognition appears to be an instant "all or none" reaction.

I would suggest a test of this hypothesis by timing responses to recall and recognition questions, and would propose that responding to the recall questions involve a delay or response latency of 1–2 seconds or more, while recognition responses — made without the effort of "trying to think" — would average less than a second.

In fact, something like this has been found to be so in a study of compressed speech conducted by DuPont. They found that speeded up radio commercials for a household paint product were 25% more effective with those commercials that were devoted to brand image but not so with informative commercials that required the audience to stop and think, *i.e.*, speeding up the commercial did not help when the audience needed time to think.

In my previous discussion of the relative ease of learning and lack of forgetting of corporate slogans I didn't make the point then, but slogans are abbreviated symbols meant to bypass thinking. One *chants* slogans, for example. Put that way, the data on slogans and on commercials have much in common. But here are the specific hypotheses suggested:

1. Emotional and/or mood advertising (or slogans) communicate quickly, as compared to informative or rational advertising. It lends itself to short commercials, possibly very short commercials.

2. Much repetition of short, mood commercials (or slogans), while possibly not very efficient (since their recognition doesn't decline much anyhow) is nevertheless not too irritating. That is, if it doesn't insist that you "stop and think," it is not really "intrusive."

3. Researchers who use recall techniques with various degrees of aiding should add to their measures *response time* as an indicator of the amount of mental effort or thinking involved by the various types and degrees of recall aiding. It says much about the initial experience of the viewed commercial.

4. Researchers who study recognition should push that procedure to its limit to see how little it may require the respondent to correctly recognize even the briefest of commercials. Here is where we may finally confront Neil Borden's old principle that "Advertising must communicate as quick as a wink."

In general, it seems clearer than ever to me that recall and recognition are two very different processes in the overall response to advertising. To pursue those differences will provide, I think, the opportunity to learn how the effective stimulation of thoughtfulness differs from the stimulation of emotion and/or mood.

CHAPTER 44

LIMITS OF ATTENTION TO ADVERTISING

A cademic research suggests that human memory for pictures is almost limitless. At the same time repeated national surveys of recall of television commercials suggests a limit to how much advertising people can remember. The academic research is typified by that of Roger Shepard, who had his subjects view 612 different pictures at their own pace, averaging six seconds per picture. Shortly thereafter they were shown 68 pairs of pictures, each pair consisting of one from the original series and one new picture. The pictures from the original series were identified with 98.5 percent accuracy. In another test with a one-week delay, accuracy was 90 percent.[1] Since then, similar studies using 2,500 and 10,000 pictures showed similar results.

This suggests that there maybe only very modest physical limits to what humans can see and remember having seen when politely forced to attend (as in experiments and pretests).

The relevant advertising research is best represented by Bogart and Lehman, who demonstrated that the ability to remember the last commercial one had seen (when queried over the phone) declined from 18 percent in 1965 to 12 percent in 1974 to 7 percent in 1981, which was a period of years during which the number of commercials being aired increased greatly.[2] In a recent 1988 speech at the University of Illinois, Bogart commented more broadly:

> The volume of messages disseminated has been growing at a much more rapid rate than the number to which people are actually exposed. Just between 1967 and 1986, the number of TV, radio, magazine, and newspaper advertisements disseminated in the United States increased by 133%. The number of TV messages alone increased by 257%, with more channels and shorter commercials. The number of TV messages to which the average person is exposed grew 128% in that period, the total number of messages by 73%. But the human capacity to absorb and make sense of this swollen flow of attempted persuasion hasn't changed one iota in those twenty years.[3]

Original Publication: "Point of View," in *Journal of Advertising Research,* vol. 28, no. 5 (October-November 1988). Also presented at ARF Forum on Advertising Effects, Arrowwood Conference Center Rye Brook, New York November 1, 1988. The text here includes comments and suggestions for further research ("Additional Thoughts") from the presentation version that were omitted from the published version.

Taken together, the academic and the commercial perspectives indicate that people can attend but are somehow less able to recall at some point of excess. While Bogart suggests that the limit is one of retention, I suggest it is one of attention (*i.e.*, people can but will not attend) and will discuss the processes involved.

In April 1967, Horace Schwerin reported that it is easy to lose half the audience or more in the first 16 seconds. His research concluded that, "The opening sequence of any commercial is of key importance, since advertisers must capture and hold the attention of viewers to retard them from mentally or physically tuning out."[4]

The critical number of seconds may in part be a function of the particular measurement technique employed. In 1968, I reported that using a quite different (physiological) technique a different number of seconds was found to be critical. For example, among 160 commercials the peak pupil dilation response between 4 and 10 seconds after the onset of the commercial correlated +.83 with the average response for the total of 60 seconds (Chapter 9 above). This phenomenon is found in magazine reading as well. The whole technique employed by Paul Lyness to pretest magazine ads is based on it. That is, he lets the respondent see the test ad for a few seconds, takes it away, and then asks if they would like to view it again and more closely.[5]

The three references above suggest that viewers take a little time to come to some sort of "decision," or make some form of mental commitment to view or not to view, or to attend closely or not closely to the balance of the commercial. Whatever the exact time it takes to do this, it seems to be a regular phenomenon of advertising exposure. It suggests again that we should not speak only of captive audiences "watching" TV advertising but also of active audiences "monitoring" the advertising and distributing their attention selectively, with closer attention to involving commercials, with less to the others, and preserving a certain economy of effort overall, *i.e.*, by limiting their attention.

While the viewer is actively monitoring the TV and being selective about his or her degree of attention, he or she is still captive to the first few seconds required in order to be selective. An extreme example of this point would be to say that even if a viewer rejects a commercial "instantly" he would have to accept or know what it consisted of, in the first part of "instant," in order to reject it. Psychologists would say, "Perception precedes perceptual defense." In 1977, Donald Broadbent, director of the psychological laboratory at Cambridge University, called these processes "the hidden pre-attentive processes."[6]

I would emphasize the role of being "captive" and the need to economize in one's efforts. For example, as more and shorter commercials abound, the total number of demanded "decisions" increases and the total amount of potential "captive time" increases. In effect, the amount of work demanded has increased. This happens even with no increase in overall commercial air time.

Further, the captive period of a 10-second commercial may be a larger proportion of its total length than that of a longer commercial. Thus, if it takes 4 seconds for a viewer to realize that he or she is being exposed to a good taste/soft drink commercial, the 4 seconds are 40 percent of a 10-second message, 13 percent of a 30-second message, and 8 percent of a 60-second message. While it may take slightly longer to recognize the nature of a more leisurely commercial, it is not likely that the increase in recognition time would keep up with the proportion of total time.

So, in recent years there has been approximately a doubling of the decisions that might be made to attend or not, along with an increase in the demanding kind of intrusion represented by the captive audience state. In the absence of trend data on recognition (as opposed to the recall data from Bogart), or the television equivalent of Starch "Noting," one cannot know for sure that people are resisting the captive state and reducing their attention in the first part of a commercial. Data on exposure, therefore, may not necessarily show a decline. Yet, if recall is dropping one can say that people are "deciding" more often than before *not* to attend the rest of the commercial and to resist the active mental processing that make for such recall.

It is perhaps preferable for the industry that audiences have responded by altering their attention patterns rather than by public complaint. Still the alterations which permit avoidance of increased audience labor should be appreciated. In effect they permit the medium to continue its role as a source of entertainment and relaxation.

The first line of defense is to switch channels, zap, etc. It looks threatening to the advertising because it is so overtly rejecting, but it is not a very efficient defense for the audience because it takes too much attention or concentration. A far more efficient and comfortable defense for the audience is to create opportunities for distraction, to spend more time viewing television with others present, and unrelated (to the TV) conversational opportunities to talk. Also, one might expect more television viewing to be combined with cooking, eating, and general housework, or homework for children. One might want to find out if, as the "exposure opportunities" were increased by the medium, these "distraction opportunities" would be increased by the audience. Would total exposure remain the same, or would it become less as the audience becomes more practiced at inattention to advertising?

There are also covert distraction opportunities, with eyes-on-screen but thoughts elsewhere, and waiting for what comes next., It is perhaps the purest form of learned and/or practiced inattention. It is a third line of defense when other distractions are not available; but all types of distraction are rest stops which permit some degree of renewed attention to the medium.

It is hard to make a definitive evaluation of these mechanisms in the absence of industry studies on audience behavior. Take the number of people in the room, for example. The distractions provided reduce attention to advertising at any one time, but over time it provides rest stops that may permit longer exposure and perhaps some additional attention to advertising. What is the net gain or loss for advertisers as the room audience increases from one to two to three to four and the time in the room also increases? How many commercials are attended in various situations? When does fatigue appear? How are these things to be measured? Shouldn't we count the successful distractions as well as the successful exposures, and then relate the two? We like to say that communication is a "two-way process," but when will we seriously observe and measure the audience process at all, much less give it equal time?

An important academic beginning was made, and since followed up, by Dan Anderson and his colleagues at the University of Massachusetts. They counted "looks" or "looking behavior" as children distributed their time between playing with toys and occasionally looking at a TV set in the room. We need similar studies on listening, on talking, on the audience environment overall.[7]

In one area of the study of attention, commercial research has followed up the leads provided by academic research, and this is in the acceptance of human capacity for attention to the pictorial, visual, or image aspects of advertising. Thus, it is now better understood that passive learning and recognition of such pictures may hold up — even in the face of a decline in verbal recall. For example, Young and Robinson of Tatham, Laird and Kudner,[8] Singh and Churchill of the Universities of Kansas and Wisconsin, respectively,[9] and Lukeman of ASI Market Research, Inc.[10] have all reported new copy-test procedures involving the joint use of the recall and recognition (of pictures) methods, the latter as a measure of attention. Starch introduced a new service to track attention to new advertising campaigns with representative national samples and personal interviews (Roper) and storyboard recognition tests of commercials.[11] All of this indicates an end to the old recall *versus* recognition memory controversy and a vindication of the views expressed by Lucas[12] and later by Wells[13] in response to the PARM studies by the ARF.[14] They said that recognition was a measure of whether or not the respondent had been exposed to the advertisement. Wells speculated that recognition was a measure of attentiveness. Apparently, they were right.

In time to come, especially if advertising increases, audiences may absorb the pictorial aspects, but without the sense of the advertising. It is the processes which permit this to happen that the industry now needs to study.

Additional Thoughts

In light of the above, I offer two general challenges. First, I suggest that TV program audience figures are not an adequate guide to the size of advertising audiences, and that as the program viewing audience per set increases from 1 to 2 to 3 the increases in advertising audience increase significantly less so — because of the increase in distraction or *the viewing of one's fellow viewers*. Thus as program audiences go from 1 to 2 to 3 advertising audiences may go from 1 to 1.4 to 1.8. The numbers are hypothetical; the mathematical function is not yet known. It is not a difficult question to put on the research table, and it might make a good ARF project.

Second, I suggest that in the competition for attention among commercials, the ads are achieving successful attention, but — at their outset, and increasingly — *at the expense* of the advertising *messages* which are *not* being communicated.

Parenthetically, both these suggestions could be taken as rationale for increased advertising expenditures. One, to make up for inflation in the audience figures, and two, to make up for the advertising messages that are not being communicated. You may prefer more positive reasons for increased advertising, but in this forum we should consider all reasons, both the "good" and what may seem like the "bad."

I don't want to refer only to television. The situation is not too different in print advertising, where a respectable ad "noting" average is just below 50% nationally but is trailed by a "read most" average of about 9%. I compare the "read most" in print to the recall in TV. In both cases the ads are learned so much better than the ad messages.

The situation is not too different in supermarket merchandising. Shoppers pushing a cart down an aisle at the rate of one foot per second can sweep twelve feet of shelf space with their eyes. But only so many brands and package facings can fit into twelve feet, and the number of products and brands keep increasing, faster than increases in store size or shoppers' time can keep up with, even with an average of 1/12 second to register on the eye, and perhaps hopefully in the mind of the shopper. So what do the manufacturers do, but encourage purchase selection *before* the cluttered store shopping, via discount coupons.

At one time we used to say that advertising encouraged impulse buying, so that we would spontaneously pick up our familiar and respected brands, but coupons have intruded on the impulse and the pick-up. More and more advertising of packaged goods has the primary goal of protecting the product price. Bill Moran can tell you much more about this then I can, but I would like to note that it is a daily requirement, a daily function — a "good" reason for increased advertising.

I'm not too pleased with the trends we are looking at. Some of the supermarket windows are so cluttered with double discount and other stickers that they resemble graffiti.

In so many areas — in TV, in print, and in retailing — one may have some cause to fear mental gridlock with regard to the attention of consumers. And yet, the consumer's freedom to ignore all of this hullabaloo is his or her first line of defense against invasion of privacy, and in turn the industry's primary protection against regulation. A better understanding of how the viewer, reader, shopper defends him or herself will benefit all parties in this would-be communication. I think that such understanding can be attained via specifically targeted research. Of course, *my* answer would be "more research," but to quote Andrew Ehrenburg,

If in doubt, find out,
For if you don't, you won't.

[1] Shepard, R.N., "Recognition Memory for Words, Sentences, and Pictures," *Journal of Verbal Learning and Verbal Behavior*, vol. 6 (1967), pp. 156-163.

[2] Bogart, Leo and Charles Lehman, "The Case of the 30-Second Commercial," *Journal of Advertising Research* vol. 23, no. 1 (1983), pp. 11-20.

[3] Bogart, Leo, "Advertising: Art, Science, or Business?" The James Webb Young Fund Address. University of Illinois, April 7, 1988.

[4] Schwerin, Horace. Quoted in *Media/scope,* April 1967, pp. 56-57.

[5] Lyness, P. Speech given at the Association of Canadian Advertisers, Toronto, May 3, 1966.

[6] Broadbent, Donald, "The Hidden Pre-Attentive Processes," *American Psychologist* vol. 32, no. 2 (1977), pp. 109-118.

[7] Anderson, D.R.; L.F. Alwitt; E.P. Lorch; and S.R. Levin, "Watching Children Watch Television," in *Attention and Cognitive Development,* G.A. Hale and M. Lewis, eds. New York: Plenum Press, 1979.

[8] Young, C.E., and M. Robinson, "Guideline: Tracking the Commercial Viewer's Wandering Attention," *Journal of Advertising Research* vol. 27, no. 3 (1987), pp. 15-22.

[9] Singh, J.S., and G.A. Churchill, Jr., "Response-Bias Free Recognition Tests to Measure Advertising Effects," *Journal of Advertising Research* vol. 27, no. 3 (1987), pp. 23-36.

[10] Lukeman, Gerald, "How Recall Scores Come About: The Underlying Structure," in *Transcript Proceedings of the 34th Annual Advertising Research Foundation Conference,* New York: Advertising Research Foundation, 1988.

[11] Wilson, W.J., and Herbert E. Krugman, "Recognition of TV Commercials: A New Starch Measurement Service," in *Transcript Proceedings of the 32nd Annual Advertising Research Foundation Conference*, New York: Advertising Research Foundation, 1986.

[12] Lucas, D.B., "The ABC's of ARF's PARM." *Journal of Marketing*, vol. 25, no. 1 (1960), pp. 9-20.

[13] Wells, William D., "Recognition, Recall and Rating Scales," *Journal of Advertising Research,* vol. 4, no. 3 (1964), pp. 2-8.

[14] Advertising Research Foundation. A *Study of Printed Advertising Rating Methods,* 5 vols. New York: Advertising Research Foundation, 1956.

CHAPTER 45

HIGH RESOLUTION TELEVISION
AND VIDEO GAMES OF THE FUTURE:
SOME PSYCHOLOGICAL IMPLICATIONS

T
he television set, as we know it today, is an instrument basically unchanged in physical design for over a quarter of a century. Thus, "an entire generation brought up on TV," as they say, has been brought up on a particular type of TV set, a type which now technically obsolete can be replaced by something quite superior, but let us just say by something quite different. Suppose this does happen, and it may, what about the newer generations brought up on that different TV? Will it make a difference in personality and behavior, and if so, how and why?

Equally important, however, suppose because of the vast economic investment in present-day TV sets the change to a new system does not occur — but that because of the possibility of that change we did investigate the new system and found that personality and behavioral factors were involved. That knowledge would have to alter our understanding of the past and present day effects of television on society. We would have to reject certain generalizations about the universal, and inevitable social effects of television per se.

We would also have to recognize that somewhere a purely technical choice had been made about TV equipment in such a way that made cultural history. Not a bad history, necessarily, nor a good one, but a different one than would have been implicit in alternate choices. We might also conclude that among the many new types of electronic media emerging into our lives, including HDTV, one could and probably should pre-determine some of the human and social consequences in advance. The purpose of this essay is to suggest some of the likely impact of HDTV, and to do this by taking its widely agreed upon physical characteristics and confronting them with some of the things that we already know about human characteristics.

You may feel that the human characteristics I shall cite are narrowly psychological, based on what is called the application of a "human engineering" or "human factors" approach, but if they do link up to vast social implications then they must be accepted as useful tools, and somewhat overlooked tools as well.

Originally presented at American Marketing Association, Grand Hyatt Hotel, New York, January 24, 1984.

To begin, let me contrast our present low definition TV set as we know it in this country with what is being proposed for HDTV, primarily by the pioneers of better quality television, NHK, the Japanese Broadcasting Corporation. The main characteristics involved are a switch to pictures made up of 1,125 lines compared to the present 525 lines — an effective doubling of picture resolution, and a wider screen of width to height ratio of 5:3 as compared to the present 4:3, *i.e.*, more like a movie screen. There are other virtues of the new system, and various obstacles to its early adoption, but these two qualities above are enough to consider for the purposes of this essay.

It is generally claimed by proponents that the finer optical resolution and wider picture will be less fatiguing, permit closer attention, and greater involvement. I have no quarrel with those assertions. I agree with them. But they do leave much unsaid because these same assertions followed through to their ultimate consequences change, I would suggest, the function of TV viewing, after the social situation of viewing, and would be more highly valued in Japan than in the United States.

THE FUNCTION OF VIEWING: FROM RELAXATION TO EDUCATION

In most Western cultures the primary function of TV viewing is entertainment and relaxation. Heavy viewing is common. However, heavy viewing is made possible in part by the barriers to close attention, i.e., pictures of poor quality resolution invite casual attention, and also encourage subject matter of relatively low information content (*i.e.*, entertainment) also inviting casual attention. Ultimately the heavy viewer may fall asleep because long periods of casual and undemanding observation are very relaxing. Thus, the fatigue of present day television is a pleasant fatigue — called "relaxing with television."

In a system with finer optical resolution and a wider screen, close attention is greatly enhanced, and to a degree even required by the system. Because of the much greater information content that is programmable and the freedom to make left and right scanning movements of the eyes (without going off screen), the viewer will be able to give close attention to varied educational materials that don't work on today's screens. That type of demanded close attention is not visually fatiguing on an optical level. But the mental work of giving close attention — rather a high degree of attention — will be mentally fatiguing after awhile, and the viewer will have to shut off the set to rest, relax, or go to bed. The viewing itself will not be relaxing. Here when we speak of fatigue it is uncomfortable fatigue, i.e., and there are limits to how much the viewer can take.

So the entertainment and relaxation function of HDTV will shift somewhat toward the educational, in its narrow and broad senses, and the viewer may not be able to watch for as long. He may have to keep an old fashioned present day TV set around the house, just to relax from his chores on HDTV. This doesn't mean that HDTV won't provide newer and more exciting video games, but relaxing is not the right word for them. To the degree that they involve more rapid eye movements, however, they are a precursor of the close attention of HDTV.

THE SOCIAL SITUATION OF VIEWING:
FROM FAMILY TO PRIVACY

Because present day television does not demand close attention and because the squarish shaped screen permits easy peripheral distraction left and right, the viewer is able to attend to stimuli from on the screen and off, even to chatting comfortably with others about the on-screen stimulus. No tension is involved. It is the making of "family viewing." The high levels of ambient light in the room also help to make the TV set just one of many stimuli in the room. Thus, present day TV is social and family.

The wide screen, like the present wide screened and darkened movie theater, eventually requires silence, at least in most adult audiences when the movie is good. Social behavior in movie audiences during the performance is sometimes tolerated, but it is not the rule. The situation is solitary. The audience stares.

With present day TV young children often sit closer to the set than do adults in order to concentrate. More gross eye movements are thereby made possible without peripheral off-screen distraction. By comparison the normal 30 of focus at seven to -twelve feet distance from the set necessitates little eye movement.

Distance is important. A special room for TV encourages distance, encourages casual rather than close viewing, and keeps the scene relaxing. The lower resolution helps because the 525 lines are less visible at distance. Even a certain amount of the ever present flicker at 60 cycles per second is less noticeable at distance.

A fine resolution in and of itself in HDTV, however, permits closer viewing — again a deterrent to social viewing, pleasant distraction, or the piece of architecture known as the TV room. The newer generation will be able to study their TVs in small private places.

If HDTV permits close attention, in a private way, it may perform somewhat like today's book, and yet in some ways still not as efficient as that book. Even HDTV viewed like a book may not be as easy to view for long periods as books are easy to read for long periods. In book reading the reader controls the pace of the reading, and provides himself with innumerable rest stops, some of which are conscious and some of which are not. HDTV suggests a captive audience without those involuntary, unconscious rest stops, and while it might provide the viewer with a stop/start button to "take a breather," go to the bathroom, etc., it is the involuntary stops and rests (even turning the page) that make long book reading possible.

Let's ask still again: why couldn't HDTV present printed material of high resolution to be read like a book? Because the wide screen, so pictorially superior for closely viewed pictorial material, is too wide for close and comfortable reading. Someday the wide screen may be built that could be rotated 90 degrees to become a tall screen for print. Meanwhile, one could resist the temptation to make use of the entire width of the screen for print, and use instead only an appropriate part.

MORE HIGHLY VALUED IN
A MASS MERITOCRACY LIKE JAPAN

It may be accidental that HDTV is being pioneered in Japan, or it may just reflect their general electronic skills, but consider the large role played by television in Japanese life.

Nielsen provided data comparing the United States to available data on Tokyo, Osaka and Nagoya show equal TV ownership of 98% each in the two cultures, more multiple set ownership in the U.S. 55% to 53%, but more color TV ownership in Japan 96% to 83%. There seems to be more viewing in Japan, i.e., the percent of households using TV in the average minute, 8-11 PM any day in the Fall of 1981 was 70% in Japan to 63% in the U.S., and the average hours of TV usage per day per TV household between April 1980 and February 1981 was 7:58 for Japan and 6:35 for the U. S.

The Japanese don't have large rooms in their homes. They can't simulate advances in TV by going the big screen route of the Americans. If they stepped back to a comfortable viewing distance, they'd be in their neighbor's bedroom. The average American living room has been estimated at 15 x 15 feet.

The Japanese are more studious, have a greater desire to learn and to achieve educationally than do Americans. A high resolution, close-attention wide screen can have great impact in a meritocracy like Japan. Moreover, this meritocracy is a mass phenomenon rather than an elite phenomenon. For example, Leonard Silk in the 11/17/82 *Wall Street Journal* summarized studies to emphasize the high quality of Japanese primary and secondary education. He goes on, and I quote

International surveys show that, in both mathematics and science, the average scores of Japanese youngsters are higher than those of any other country — much higher than in the United States.

An American educator, Thomas P. Rohlen, finds that the great accomplishment of Japanese primary and secondary education lies not in its creation of a brilliant elite but in producing a high average level of capability in its graduates. "The profoundly impressive fact," he writes, "is that it is shaping a whole population, workers as well as managers, to a standard inconceivable in the United States." (page D2)

An up-to-date and devastating report about educational achievement of American youngsters compared with other countries, is represented by Barbara Lerner's article "American Education: how are we doing?" in the Fall 1982 issue of *The Public Interest*. In it she cites Professor Robert Thorndike's review of the studies sponsored by the International Education Association wherein the so-called "hard work variable" is identified as the only really important one. Thorndike described it as a measure of "grim effort." I quote further from the article

In fact, it proved to be the single most powerful school variable in the entire IEA survey, not only as a predictor of achievement in reading, but in virtually every other subject studied. In many cases, it was just about the only school variable that did correlate with achievement. Wolf described the American situation this way: "Outside of the homework variable, there was little consistency in the results. A variable that showed an independent relationship with achievement in one subject at one population level often failed to appear in the analysis at another population level in the same subject. The positive relationship between homework and achievement held fast, however, not only in America but in all other nations studied as well." (p. 72)

Now, try mixing American style homework with American style television, and homework comes out the loser. But imagine what Japanese children and Japanese homework could do with HDTV, a screen with resolution and dimensions suitable for thoughtful attention to complex and detailed stimuli!

Aside from these considerations, what does all this say about certain technical choices made in our society; technical choices made with little regard for "human factors" or "human engineering" considerations?

I'd like to make three points: one, that this lack is capable of producing disaster as in the infamous and badly designed operator control room at Three Mile Island; two, that its presence approaches high art in the aerospace achievements of the U.S., which the public rejected as wasteful and/or elitist; and three, closer to home now for this audience, that the human factor consideration is being treated today with relatively little concern by those planning the new electronic media.

Recent evidence of this low level of concern is contained in a Marketing Science Institute Working Paper, Report No. 82-110 (November 1982) entitled *Benefit Segmentation: An Industrial Application* by R.T. Moriarty of the Harvard Business School and D.J. Reibstein of the Wharton School. To test some hypotheses about benefit segmentation they happened to choose the information technology industry as their test case, and gathered data from 300 companies that had recently made major acquisitions of data terminals.

Those who had made the decision to purchase were interviewed, and also filled out various ranking and rating forms. The various product attributes influencing purchase were then treated to a variety of statistical reduction processes.

In the first unreduced ranking, the attribute "Visibility, size and color of screen" ranked 26 in importance out of 33 variables.

After both conceptual and statistical reduction, the re-labeled attribute "operator" ranked 10th out of 14 variables. The leading attributes were service, reliability, manufacturer stability, software, comparability, delivery, speed, price, etc.

This is no condemnation. The number one ranked variable of service or service time is indeed understandable. Where would we be without the TV repairman? Yet, to avoid the repair problem generally we somehow compromise on relatively inferior products, which help to produce relatively inferior workers and students.

As we approach the exciting era of new electronic media, I hope for a more favorable balance of technical choices. It may be hoping for too much, but I would like to suggest that what we call "intelligence" can be created by design. The telecommunications industry in the United States would happily interpret that to mean the design of more intelligent computers. Alas, I mean more intelligent humans.

Higher quality video games can also be created by design, if entrepreneurs would be willing to market games that had more operator control built into them. At the present time the games are exciting because of the modest illusion of control which the operator feels. Yet these levels are at the lower end of what is possible from an engineering point of view. At the upper levels are mock-ups of advanced fighter aircraft and simulated combat flying with reality levels of the highest order. Thus, the human factors or human engineering profession is capable of providing a sense of real control, in contrast to modest illusions, although it comes expensively. However, a little added expense provides proportionately a great deal of added control, or certainly illusions of control.

Television and video games thus share in common a level of marketing success based on a minimum provision (to the public) of higher quality technology. You should realize, however, that the technology to provide high quality is available and that the futures of television and of video games can be quite exciting, and also quite different from what they may seem today.

CHAPTER 46

SOME CONSEQUENCES OF HIGH DEFINITION TELEVISION

From July 9 to July 14, 1989 an international conference on science, technology and world affairs met in Santa Fe, New Mexico. The summary conclusion by the conference chairman S.P. Kapitza of the USSR (he is the son of the Nobel laureate in physics) began as follows:

In attempting to sum up some of the deliberations of this conference, and I expect that is what I am to do, it would be best first to say why we are all here. We are here because the world is passing through a transition. With good authority it has been said that the Cold War is over. Now that a war is over, you have the victors and the vanquished. You know who won — Japan and West Germany. I suppose you can guess who lost. That is why we are now disarming ourselves. Losing this strange war is just as strange as fighting it. The war was never fought outright.

Etc., etc. This was in July!

I will talk about the Japanese. Different speakers will view the Japanese with alarm but for different reasons. I will "view with alarm" the Japanese and high definition television, and in the following manner.

The television set, as we know it today, is an instrument basically unchanged in physical design for almost half a century. Thus, "an entire generation brought up on TV, as they say, has been brought up on a particular type of TV set, a type which now technically "obsolete" can be replaced by something quiet *superior*, but let us just say by something quite *different*. Suppose this does happen, and it may, what about the newer generations brought up on that different TV? Will it make a difference in personality or behavior, and if so, how and why?

The purpose of this discussion then is to suggest some of the likely impact of HDTV, and to do this by taking its widely agreed upon physical characteristics and confronting them with some of the things that we already know about human characteristics. You may feel that the human characteristics I shall cite are narrowly psychological, based on what is called the application of a "human

---

Originally presented at Market Research Council, The Yale Club, March 16, 1990.

Editor's note: This is an updated version of the previous chapter (Chapter 44), which appeared in 1984. The new material was significant enough to warrant separate inclusion.

engineering" or "human factors" approach, but if they do link up to vast social implications then they must be accepted as useful tools, and somewhat overlooked tools as well.

To begin, let me contrast our present low definition TV set as we know it in this country with what is being proposed for HDTV, primarily by the pioneers of better quality television, NHK, the Japanese Broadcasting Corporation. The main characteristics involved are a switch to pictures made up of 1,125 lines compared to the present 525 lines — an effective doubling of picture resolution — and a wider screen of width to height, the so-called "aspect ratio," of 5:2 as compared to the present 4:3, *i.e.*, more like a movie screen. There are other virtues of the new system, such as improved color rendition and better sound quality. I am interested primarily in the new aspect ratio, and its consequences.

It is generally claimed by proponents that the finer optical resolution and wider picture will be less fatiguing, permit closer attention, and greater involvement. I have no quarrel with those assertions. I agree with them. But they do leave much unsaid because these same assertions followed through to their ultimate consequences change, I would suggest, the function of TV viewing, alter the social situation of viewing, and would be more highly valued in Japan than in the United States.

In most Western cultures the primary function of TV viewing is entertainment and relaxation. Heavy viewing is common. However, heavy viewing is made possible in part by the barriers to close attention, *i.e.*, pictures of poor quality resolution invite casual attention, and also encourage subject matter of relatively low information content (*i.e.*, entertainment), also inviting casual attention. Ultimately the heavy viewer may fall asleep because long periods of casual and undemanding observation are very relaxing. Thus, the fatigue of present day television is a pleasant fatigue — called "relaxing with television."

In a system with finer optical resolution and a wider screen, close attention is greatly enhanced, and to a degree even required by the system. Because of the much greater information content that is programmable and the freedom to make left and right scanning movements of the eyes (without going off screen), the viewer will be able to give close attention to varied educational materials that don't work on today's screens. That type of demanded close attention is not visually fatiguing on an optical level. But the mental work of giving close attention — rather a high degree of attention — will be mentally fatiguing after awhile, and the viewer will have to shut off the set to rest, relax, or go to bed. The viewing itself will not be relaxing. Here when we speak of fatigue it is uncomfortable fatigue, *i.e.*, and there are limits to how much the viewer can take.

So the entertainment and relaxation function of HDTV will shift somewhat toward the educational, in its narrow and broad senses, and the viewer may not be able to watch for as long. He will have to keep an old-fashioned present day TV set around the house, just to relax from his chores on HDTV. This doesn't mean that HDTV can't, for example, also provide newer and more exciting video games, but relaxing is not the right word for them. To the degree that they involve more rapid eye movements, however, they are a precursor of the close attention of HDTV.

Because present day television does not demand close attention and because the squarish shaped screen permits easy peripheral distraction left and right, the viewer is able to attend to stimuli from on the screen and off, even to chatting comfortably with others about the on-screen stimulus. No tension is involved. It is the making of "family viewing." The high levels of ambient light in the room also help to make the TV set just one of many stimuli in the room. Thus, present day TV is social and family.

The wide screen, like the present wide screened and darkened movie theater, eventually requires silence, at least in most adult audiences when the movie is good. Social behavior in movie audiences during the performance is sometimes tolerated, but it is not the rule. The situation is solitary. The audience stares.

With present day TV young children often sit closer to the set than do adults in order to concentrate. More gross eye movements are thereby made possible without peripheral off-screen distraction. By comparison the normal 31 of focus at seven to twelve feet distance from the set necessitates little eye movement.

Distance is important. A special room for TV encourages distance, encourages casual rather than close viewing, and keeps the scene relaxing. The lower resolution helps because the 525 lines are less visible at distance. Even a certain amount of the ever-present flicker at 60 cycles per second is less noticeable at distance.

A fine resolution in and of itself in HDTV, however, permits closer viewing — again a deterrent to social viewing, pleasant distraction, or the piece of architecture known as the TV room. The newer generation will be able to study their TVs in small private places.

If HDTV permits close attention, in a private way, it may perform somewhat like today's book, and yet in some ways still not as efficient as that book. Even HDTV viewed like a book may not be as easy to view for long periods as books are easy to read for long periods. In book reading the reader controls the pace of the reading, and provides himself with innumerable rest stops, some of which are conscious and some of which are not. HDTV suggests a captive audience without those involuntary, unconscious rest stops, and while it might provide the viewer with a stop/start button to "take a breather," go to the bathroom, etc., it is the involuntary stops and rests (even turning the page) that make long book reading possible.

Let's ask still again: why couldn't HDTV present printed material of high resolution to be read like a book? Because the wide screen, so pictorially superior for closely viewed pictorial material, is too wide for close and comfortable reading. Someday the wide screen may be built that could be rotated 90 degrees to become a tall screen for print. Meanwhile, one could resist the temptation to make use of the entire width of the screen for print, and use instead only an appropriate part.

HDTV may become more highly valued in a mass meritocracy like Japan. Let us, for example, consider television and education in Japan.

Nielsen data comparing the United States to available data on Tokyo, Osaka and Nagoya show equal TV ownership of 98% each in the two cultures, more multiple set ownership in the U.S. 55% to 53%, but more color TV ownership in Japan 96% to 83%. There seems to be more viewing in Japan, *i.e.*, the percent of households using TV in the average minute, 8-11 PM any day in the Fall of 1981, was 70% in Japan to 63% in the U.S., and the average hours of TV usage per day per TV household between April 1980 and February 1981 was 7:58 for Japan and 6:35 for the U.S. These data have not been updated as of late 1989.

The Japanese don't have large rooms in their homes. They can't simulate advances in TV by going the big screen route of the Americans. If they stepped back to a comfortable viewing distance, they'd be in their neighbor's bedroom. The average American living room has been estimated at 15 x 15 feet.

The Japanese are more studious, have a greater desire to learn and to achieve educationally than do Americans. A high-resolution, close-attention, wide screen can have great impact in a meritocracy like Japan. Moreover, this meritocracy is a mass phenomenon rather than an elite phenomenon. For example, Leonard Silk in the November 17, 1982 *Wall Street Journal* summarized studies to emphasize the high quality of Japanese primary and secondary education. He goes on:

> International surveys show that, in both mathematics and science, the average scores of Japanese youngsters are higher than those of any other country — much higher than in the United States.

> An American educator, Thomas P. Rohlen, finds that the great accomplishment of Japanese primary and secondary education lies not in its creation of a brilliant elite but in producing a high average level of capability in its graduates. "The profoundly impressive fact," he writes, "is that it is *shaping a whole population* workers as well as managers, to a standard inconceivable in the United States."(page D2)

A devastating report about educational achievement of American youngsters compared with other countries, is represented by Barbara Lerner's article "American Education: How Are We Doing?" in the (Fall 1982 issue of) *The Public Interest*. In it she cites Professor Robert Thorndike's review of the studies sponsored by the International Education Association wherein the so-called "hard work variable" is identified as the only really important one. Thorndike described it as a measure of "grim effort." I quote further from the article.

> In fact, it proved to be the single most powerful school variable in the entire IEA survey, not only as a predictor of achievement in read-

ing, but in virtually every other subject studied. In many cases, it was just about the only school variable that did correlate with achievement. Wolf described the American situation this way: "Outside of the homework variable, there was little consistency in the results. A variable that showed an independent relationship with achievement in one subject at one population level often failed to appear in the analysis at another population level in the same subject." The positive relationship between homework and achievement held fast, however, not only in America but in all other nations studied as well. (p. 72)

Now, try mixing American style homework with American style television, and homework comes out the loser. But imagine what Japanese children and Japanese homework could do with HDTV, a screen with resolution and dimensions suitable for thoughtful attention to complex and detailed stimuli!

There, I have viewed with alarm.

Meanwhile, the actual availability of HDTV is a toss-up. On September 21st, a congresswoman asserted in a speech before the House that American industry no longer has the technical ability to produce HDTV. On September 29th the Secretary of Commerce announced that the department was abandoning plans to provide a "focused initiative" to support U.S. development. In November there were various rumors about U.S. – Japanese combinations to produce the product. In December there was speculation that American know-how in optic fiber and cable technology could leap frog the Japanese advantage in electronics, *i.e.*, "To make fiber optic the vehicle for HDTV signals would leap frog the present obstacle of finding room in the crowded broadcast spectrum." (*N.Y. Times*, editorial p.24, January 1, 1990.) What is holding back further developments is the probably forlorn hope of yet coming up with a system which would not necessitate the consumer's purchase of another box. It is this issue that attracts the interest of our *marketing colleagues* and I will refer to their research a bit later.

I would like to focus more closely on a theme which underlies much of what I have said before, and this concerns eye movement and thinking. What do we know about such things?

Most of you are probably familiar with eye movement research services which evaluate print advertisements. Elliott Young's *Perception Laboratory, Inc.* in New Jersey has been doing this for a quarter of a century. They expose consumers to print ads at a distance of about eighteen inches (*i.e.*, normal reading distance) while the chin and forehead lean against bars which keep the head motionless. A variant of the Mackworth Optiscan or eye camera then records "direction of gaze" or "line of sight" — not seeing, not perceiving, but looking or *looking at* what.

Meanwhile, the U.S. Government and the Defense Department maintained a similar laboratory at Aberdeen Proving Grounds in Maryland, and there under the direction of Dr. Richard Monty, print materials have been similarly analyzed but unobtrusively. The subject sits in an easy chair and sees no apparatus while his eyes are filmed from behind a one-way screen.

In general, when consumers respond to print ads and other inanimate stimuli, they look the stimuli over in quite an active manner and from one viewer to another there exists quite a variability in what they look at, and in what sequence. The variability of print ad response measured by Starch scores would lead you to expect just such variety of response.

A few years ago another eye movement measurement company in New Jersey began testing TV commercials. They too used intrusive restraining bars to keep the head still, but also used the eighteen or so inch viewing distance which is natural to print but unnatural to television. By having their subjects sit up unnaturally close they so to speak created "eye movements" that would not be present at the normal TV viewing distance.

Since then, Applied Science Laboratories of Waltham, Mass. has come up with a TV commercial testing situation involving some of the unobtrusive features of the U.S. Government laboratory, and a normal TV viewing distance.

When you buy a TV commercial evaluation from ASL you receive a copy of your commercial with the eye movement patterns of 25 viewers all shown at once. This is possible because the individual patterns vary only very slightly. You see a succession of 25 dot clusters upon the screen. They are called a "swarm." That's just what they look like. A swarm of bees or other insects. The technique was developed by Dr. Barbara Flagg, a Harvard psychologist. A client, looking at the "swarm," will realize that one needs only one viewer to show what most people generally tend to look at, but he will also realize that he wouldn't believe such results on only one subject. In short, there isn't very much eye movement, and little individual variation. The movement of the stimulus itself pretty much directs and determines, in a very physical way, what viewers will look at. Again, this is not seeing, perceiving, interpreting or anything but *looking at*!

Now, we come up to 1989 when two marketing directed research tests compared HDTV with conventional TV. Similar footage was shown on a conventional screen and on a screen modified to represent the aspect ratio of HDTV. The finer resolution of HDTV was not involved — only the aspect ratios. The tests were what you would call laboratory tests and subjects were tested in small groups. Both studies showed marked "preference" for the wider screen, and various price premiums would be willingly paid by those having this preference. Since then I have talked with the two study directors Richard Feldman of NBC and Karen Pitts of the David Sarnoff Research Center in Princeton. I found that they were both familiar with the "swarm" technique of Applied Science Laboratories, and I suggested that they test similar TV material on conventional and HDTV aspect ratios to demonstrate (if verified) the hypothesis that on HDTV the swarm will expand and/or break up, *i.e.*, that there will be more eye movement and more individual variability in eye movement. Both responded with interest and said that they would try to do just that.

There is no commercial research on eye movement and thinking, but there is academic research which shows that problem solving is aided and abetted by eye movements. The most startling is research on what happens in the total absence of eye movement. For example, a series of studies by two Russians, V.P. Zinchenko and N. Yu. Vergiles used three different techniques *to eliminate* all eye movement, including saccadic movement.[1] In the absence of movement the object being viewed simply disappears. Thus, eye movement is necessary for seeing itself, much less problem solving. This seems to confirm Piaget's theory that early motor responses in the child become an integral part of perception itself.

Taking these disparate research findings together leads, I suggest, to the view that the greater eye movements associated with the aspect ratio of HDTV will produce, or have the potential (based on the material programmed) to evoke a more thinking or thoughtful response than is the case with conventional television.

For those of you who are familiar with my writings on the subject of low involvement television, you could call HDTV the possible precursor to high involvement television, involvement being defined very much in terms of thoughtful response. Here, rather than view with alarm, I view the consequences of HDTV with pleasure.

In summary and conclusion, we can infer from the new aspect ratio of HDTV that there will be more eye movement. We do not now know how much more but this is readily researchable. We can also infer that the greater eye movement will evoke more subjective response, such as thinking, but again, how much more, and again, this too is researchable. Finally, the whole question of "how much more" would lead to one of two different kinds of expectation for the new medium. Either we would anticipate a new medium of somewhat or modestly more involvement than the old medium, or we would anticipate a medium that could be called *high involvement television* as compared to the present medium of *low involvement television*.

---

[1] Zinchenko, V.P. and Vergiles, N.Y. "*Formation of visual images.*" (Translated by Consultants Bureau, New York, Plenum, 1972). Originally published in Moscow by Moscow Univ. Press. Discussed in pages 331, (especially) 334, 343, 355, 369 in Monty R.A. and Senders J.W. (Eds.) *Eye Movements and Psychological Processes*, Lawrence Erlbaum Associates, Publishers, Hillsdale, New Jersey, 1976.

CHAPTER 47

CONSUMER BEHAVIOR

In recent decades large masses of consumers in the Western world have moved into relatively affluent and secure positions. Their increased purchasing power has given them the opportunity to embroider upon basic needs with a sense of individual taste and creativity, as they search for a style of life rather than for security. Style of life, in this case, refers to the conscious and carefully developed sets or patterns of individual preferences in personal consumer behavior. Increases in disposable income and leisure time have permitted types of personal explorations that have made possible the rise of huge new industries devoted to cultural, recreational, and sports products. At the same time political ideologies based on conflict between the economic classes have all but disappeared,[1] and minority groups are looked at with almost as much interest in their innovations in consumption (for example, how they dress and play) as in their political views.[2] Because the potential variation in consumer behavior is now quite suddenly at a level far over and above that which was once economically dictated, the consumer's search for a personalized style of life becomes mankind's first large-scale nongovernmental, spontaneous, and awkward groping with the problem of economic freedom. The idea of this type of freedom has been appreciated in many lands, even in politically unfree lands where affluence and security do not exist. While it is too early to say what political consequences may emanate from the new consumer ideal, the apparently vast possibilities open to consumer exploration now demand the serious attention of the social sciences in a way that they did not before.

Some social scientists who might otherwise be interested in studying the consumer have been held back by the "silly" effects of initial affluence, an affluence which may permit such strange imbalances in family spending patterns as 'living on beans" in order to afford a Cadillac. Yet in more mature forms affluence permits wiser shopping, for example, the ability to shop at a greater number of supermarkets to take advantage of price cuts and sales without the hindrance of a slavish single-store "loyalty,"[3] the opportunity generally to obtain better and fairer prices,[4] and a lesser susceptibility to advertising.[5] The same selection factors apply to style of life. Here, too, early exploration may produce

Original Publication: *International Encyclopedia of the Social Sciences* (Macmillan/Free Press 1968), pp. 349-354.

bizarre or "silly" effects and combinations, but ultimately, with experience, comes more mature behavior.

Other social scientists who would seriously study the consumer have been held back by a distaste for what seemed to be tendencies toward local conformity in style, not realizing, for example, that the ability to flock together into homogeneous and "conforming" communities may itself be an expression of economic freedom. Furthermore, as changes in style are required by further changes in the cycle of family development, these same consumers flock easily and freely into other but different types of again homogeneous communities. That certain types of life style are now made more visible by the greater freedom for similar people to congregate may suggest an appearance of strong group conformity that persists even in the face of the individual consumer's easy, though less noticed, ability to shift from one style to another.

It is not enough to say that people have more time and more choice. The striking thing is that they are tending not to buy more and more goods as a form of conspicuous consumption, but to buy time to experiment more with their choices. The most conspicuous form of time consumption is the vacation trip. At the same time employees seem eager to receive leisure hours as a substitute for wage dollars. They bid against their employers for their own time, and their time budgets are becoming more important and more worthy of study than their money budgets.

While these tendencies have appeared primarily in those areas of Western affluence which initially made the new consumer innovation possible, their study is also of importance to the less affluent lands of the East. That consumer freedom happened first in the 'rich' West does not make it irrelevant to the East. Hopefully, the spirit of that freedom may be built into economic advances in the East and still newer and equally stimulating styles of life may emerge to compete creatively with those of the West. If anticipated, it may not be necessary to attain Western levels of affluence before the equivalent ideas take hold. For example, it may be possible during the stage of first or early affluence to leapfrog, or at least to inhibit, the consumer tendencies to spend more in terms of class and status considerations and to arrive more quickly at a point where spending reflects the greater freedom of individual style. In the West, it has happened without forethought or warning and even while some poverty remains. The release from serious economic anxiety has permitted many consumers, although not swamped with wealth, to look around for the first time with a sense of real choice about how they might spend their time, what kind of life they would make for themselves, and what kind of people they might be.

CONCEPTIONS OF THE CONSUMER

Professional or official definitions of the study of consumer behavior are somewhat less focused. For example, the division of consumer psychology of the American Psychological Association defines its purpose as the study of human behavior as it relates to the consumption of goods and the uses and acceptance of services. The definition is broad enough to serve as well for a sociological or anthropological association. This breadth may reflect the newness of the concern with professional study of the consumer. That is, behavioral scientists, especially psychologists, have entered into the study of matters related to commerce and industry only in this century, a century which has seen the economy of the United States move from an orientation based primarily on production to one that is based as well on sales and distribution, and finally, and still in the process, to one that is also concerned with consumer needs.

In between the two world wars there developed what might be called the older orientation to consumer psychology, one that was based primarily on an identification with the businessman, the seller of goods and services. With this identification came early emphasis on sales research and studies of advertising effectiveness. To be sure, the latter coincided well with the psychologist's special ability to conduct experimental research on the learning of information, and, by so doing, an enormous research literature developed in advertising psychology.[6] Nevertheless, the new definition of consumer psychology is based not so much on an identification with the manufacturer (as is common in industrial psychology), not so much on an identification with the salesman (as is common in advertising psychology), but more on an identification with the changing consumer himself.

As the consumer begins to innovate in life style, a change is also taking place in how he is viewed by social scientists. The old way was to view him, even define him, predominantly through the eyes of economics. The term "consumer" was not then a social science term, but a focus for concern over efficiency and for a harmonious balance of forces in the free market place. In response to the new affluence the old way of thinking was reflected in a swing from concern with alleged consumer wastefulness to concern with advertising's alleged overpersuasiveness. However, once Packard[7] and similarly inclined critics had clearly and widely raised the alarm that consumers were being made to buy more than they actually needed, the older type of thinking had to be abandoned as a serious approach, that is, it had no further comments to make or questions to ask about what was happening to consumers as people.

While proponents of the older view may acknowledge that the purchase of household appliances saves the time and attention of family members for performance of higher level activities and that consumers spend more on such living aids as they become more affluent, it comes as something of a surprise for them to discover that the proportion of consumer incomes which is spent after taxes, at least in the United States and except for a post-World War buying spree, has remained relatively constant at 92 to 94 percent.[8] Great changes in consumer behavior have occurred, therefore, during a period when, strictly speaking, changes in economic behavior did not. The more serious concern, then, of the social sciences is to chart the social consequences of consumer access to these new living aids and resources.

THEORIES OF CONSUMER BEHAVIOR

Ordinarily, when an area of human behavior is marked off for study by social scientists, one may expect much employment of comparative or experimental analyses to uncover and identify regularities in behavior within the area. These then provide a basis for understanding, as well as for testing the understanding. The tests usually are set up in the form of prediction studies. This testing is efficiently accelerated by a clear outline and definition of the area to be studied. One of the functions of theory is to pose a persistent set of questions and thereby to define what is considered important. However, there is not now a general theory of consumer behavior, although Katona[9] has developed a theory of the role of consumer expectations or confidence upon the levels of spending and saving in the economy. A general theory of consumer behavior has probably not existed since Veblen examined the psychological pressures of social class for their impact on the efficiency of human consumption of goods and resources. From Veblen to Packard, a half century saw no marked change in this economic-psychological approach, except that Packard identifies the cause of consumer inefficiencies not so much in social class pressures per se but in their exploitation and manipulation by advertising and business interests. Both Veblen and Packard are essentially social critics using psychological insights to advance a theory which is basically economic, wherein utility and efficiency are defined as the important qualities.

Any theory based on economics might have deserved to be considered quite seriously in a day when economic indicators were the best predictors of human behavior. Today, this is less so. Income is no longer the best predictor of consumer purchasing; for example, a time series correlation between the data of 17 University of Michigan consumer surveys from 1952 to 1960 and the level of national expenditures for durable goods showed that estimates based on both recent disposable income and attitudes approximate future durable goods expenditures much more closely than the estimates based on disposable income alone. An analysis of variance indicated that consumer demand was more a function of willingness to buy than of ability to buy. In effect, Katona[10] has turned the tables on economics by showing how consumer attitudes of optimism or pessimism initiate changes in economic indicators. The causal flow has been somewhat reversed, therefore, first in observation and then in theoretical formulations. If this is so, if economic predictors are no longer all powerful, what new indicators should we be looking at more closely?

PREDICTORS OF CONSUMER BEHAVIOR

Perhaps stages in the family life cycle are the best predictors of consumer behavior.[11] Is the family a childless couple? Is there a young baby in the family? Have the children grown and left?

In addition there are the many household buying decisions made within one particular stage of the cycle. What predictors seem to work here for the shorter run? One set seems to involve the career roles brought into the marital relationship by the two partners. This is partially a matter of relative buying influence within the pair, as affected by such simple considerations as whether or not the wife earns income outside the home. More important however is the matter of what particular occupations and specific career commitments may be brought together within the pair. Every occupation, especially if it has the life-long involvement of a career, sets forth certain style of life requirements based on where the work is performed, the standards for success, who are the co-workers (clients, colleagues, supervisors), etc. Next to family cycle it is probably industry itself which has the most pervasive, though less direct, influence on style of life. It is important to note, however, that in this sense occupation and profession are not economic but social variables, involving different types of networks of interpersonal relationships much more than different levels of income.

Family and jobs make good starting places for understanding consumers as whole people. Strangely, industry does not yet seek this whole view but tends to spend vast sums on the study of particular consumer functions (for example, food preparation) and closely related products. Yet some sociologists have looked at the new consumer life styles, have asked what products consumers are buying, and have come up with a whole view of the consumer which has relevance to all industry. Riesman and Roseborough, for example, have said that today's young people learn to want a recognizable complex of goods and services which they call "the standard package."[12] This may include a college education, car, gadget-equipped home, and annual travel vacations as base elements. The package may come in a series of standard through de luxe grades, and with the aid of credit progress through those grades can be made easy. Such a view does not, as some have inferred, suggest increased conformity, for obtaining the elements of the package is intimately related to the acquisition of mobility and freedom, that is, greater job choice, reduction of household chores, and increased facilities for and use of transportation. It would seem, however, that as something like a standard package becomes universally wanted, especially for the freedom that is seen in it, then deprivation becomes less tolerable for those without jobs and/or education. On the level of individual protest it may lead to delinquency and crime, but on the level of mass protest it may lead to an insistence on educational and job rights for underprivileged or minority groups. Thus do matters of consumer style shade over into social and political issues.

The matter of social issues raises questions of intensity and amount. For example, to what extent are consumers motivated by the standard package? And how de luxe or how large may this package become? At present we can only cite Chinoy's study of the American automobile worker, which concludes that satisfactions are reported in terms of a small package of independence represented in home and car ownership, with aspirations for further advancement focused on the children and their chances for social mobility through education.[13] While this modest version of the dream may apply only to industrial workers, the emphasis is more on having some of the good things of life and the time to use them and less on the ideologically distant goals. While it is true that in the United States a blue-collar majority is giving way rapidly to a "middle-class" white-collar majority, a similar evaluation has not yet been made for the latter group. This latter group, of course, is exposed to a different side of American industry and is more likely to work in office buildings than in factories. The standards for home ownership and decor of this group may therefore be different and possibly higher than that of the blue-collar group.

The question of what kind of houses people want and what they want in them is a good overall way of assessing the consumer market. For example, the number of new homes for which construction has started each year is the best single indication of whether or not it will be a good year for business. The question of what kinds and numbers of homes to build, and where to build them, becomes a critical determiner of both national economic well-being and of the consumer's physical environment, complete with built-in limitations and opportunities for style development. Thus, the home architects, the appliance designers, the federal housing laws, and the bank credit policies all have significant effects on the potentialities of this environment.

It should also be noted that new houses reflect consumer demand and initiative, or put another way, consumer investment. As Katona[14] emphasizes, the growth and expansion of the economy are dependent on consumer investment as well as business investment, and these are equally important forces in the extent to which they can stimulate or retard the economy.

RESEARCH APPROACHES

With the consumer now seen as so "powerful," it is to be expected that attempts to study him have become intensified. One reviewer has identified six different general approaches:

(1) General studies of consumer behavior: the role of consumers and consumption, consumer spending as investments, consumption in economic development.

(2) Income studies: changes in income distribution, credit, and expenditures by various classes. This category accounts for a large part of past studies.

(3) Population studies: population trends and shifts, life-cycle influences, various demographic classifications.

(4) Life-style factors: studies of factors influencing styles of living, such as purchases, status symbols, social class, images, needs, leisure, convenience. This area is receiving increasing emphasis.

(5) Consumers as decision makers: studies of who makes what decisions, what decisions are planned, who is influential in various situations, the household as a decision unit.

(6) Specific purchase and consumption studies: studies of purchases and determinants of purchases for specific products such as coffee, cleansers, gasoline.[15]

The first three of these approaches are dependent upon availability and analysis of mass data. While the federal and state governments have long made such data available, it is only recently that correspondingly massive tools of analysis have become available (for example, the computer). This means that research in these areas was until recently primarily reportorial. With so much detailed data to comprehend it was all that scholars could do to keep up with descriptive identifications of major historical trends. The computer brings a new type of inquiry to such data — an inquiry that seeks to build dynamic theory and is not daunted by complexities in the manipulation of data. One may expect therefore to hear more in future years, from investigators with a primarily methodological orientation, about the *science* of retailing, of marketing, and of other fields.

The fourth and fifth approaches seem to represent more clearly the opening up of consumer study to sociologists and psychologists. Traditionally, the former have studied the ills of society, such as divorce and unemployment. Psychologists, too, have been involved, if not with society's ills, then with the emotionally ill. However, as the current generation of social scientists has put behind it depression and World War II, and has also participated in the new affluence, there has gradually developed a new curiosity about the nature of the normal personality, a shift away from concern with irrational processes to rational thought, and an interest in theories about how various everyday decisions are made.

All of these areas of research involve a move away from descriptive or reportorial research to inquiry guided by the use of theory and undertaken for the purpose of further theory development. This means that the study of the consumer has now finally linked up with the main body of the behavioral sciences.

As for the consumer himself, we may expect further inroads on his ancient image of himself as a person in want and as one who is preoccupied with the allocation of scarce means to satisfy basic needs. Foote proposes that as the proportion of household expenditures devoted to food continues to fall, today's somewhat obese consumer may well develop wants that do not require production or consumption, such as stimulating conversation or the creation of music.[16]

The constraint on wants such as these will not be income but learning ability. In short, consumers may yet outgrow consumption.

[1] Bell, Daniel , *The End of Ideology* (Glencoe, Ill.: Free Press 1959).

[2] Kluckhohn, C., "Have There Been Discernible Shifts in American Values During the Past Generation?" in Elting E. Morison (ed.), *The American Style: Essays in Value and Performance. A Report on the Dedham Conference of May 23-27, 1957.* (New York: Harper 1958), pp. 145-217; see especially p. 197.

[3] Tate, Russell S., "The Supermarket Battle for Store Loyalty," *Journal of Marketing* vol. 25 (1961), pp. 8-13.

[4] Caplovitz, David, *The Poor Pay More: Consumer Practices of Low-Income Families* (New York: Free Press 1963).

[5] Smith, Stewart A., "Criteria for Media Comparisons: A Critique," *Journal of Marketing Research*, vol. 4 (1965), pp. 364-369.

[6] Lucas, Darrell B.; and Britt, Steuart H., *Advertising Psychology and Research: An Introductory Book* (New York: McGraw-Hill 1950).

[7] Packard, Vance O., *The Hidden Persuaders*, (New York: McKay 1957).

[8] White, Winston, *Beyond Conformity* (New York: Free Press 1960). See especially Chapter 8.

[9] Katona, George, *Psychological Analysis of Economic Behavior* (New York: McGraw-Hill 1951).

[10] Katona, George, *The Powerful Consumer: Psychological Studies of the American Economy* (New York: McGraw-Hill 1960).

[11] Clark, Lincoln H.; and Foote, Nelson N. (eds.) *Consumer Behavior.* 4 vols. (New York Univ. Press 1955-1961). Volume 1: *The Dynamics of Consumer Reaction*, 1955. Volume 2: *The Life Cycle and Consumer Behavior*, 1955. Volume 3: *Research on Consumer Reactions*, 1958. Volume 4: *Household Decision-making*, 1961.

[12] Riesman, David; and Roseborough, Howard, "Careers and Consumer Behavior," in Clark & Foote, *op. cit.*, vol. 2, pp. 1-18.

[13] Chinoy, Ely, *Automobile Workers and the American Dream* (Garden City, N.Y.: Doubleday 1955).

[14] Katona, *op. cit.* note 10.

[15] Halbert, Michael, *The Meaning and Sources of Marketing Theory* (New York: McGraw-Hill 1965).

[16] Foote, Nelson N., "The Image of the Consumer in the Year 2000," in *Boston Conference on Distribution, Thirty-fifth Annual* (Chestnut Hill, Mass.: Boston College 1963), pp. 13-18.

CHAPTER 48

SOCIOLOGY AND CONSUMER BEHAVIOR

In recent decades large masses of consumers in the Western world have moved into relatively affluent and secure positions. Their increased purchasing power has given them the opportunity to embroider upon basic needs with a sense of individual taste and creativity, as they search for a style of life rather than for security. Increases in disposable income and leisure time have permitted types of personal explorations that have made possible the rise of huge new industries devoted to cultural, recreational, and sports products. Because the potential variation in consumer behavior is now quite suddenly at a level far over and above that which was once economically dictated, the consumer's search for a personalized style of life becomes mankind's first large-scale non-governmental, spontaneous, and awkward groping with the problem of economic freedom. The idea of this type of freedom has been appreciated in many lands, even in politically unfree lands where affluence and security do not exist. While it is too early to say what political consequences may emanate from the new consumer ideal, the apparently vast possibilities open to consumer exploration now demand the serious attention of the social sciences in a way that they did not before.

It is not enough to say that people have more time and more choice. The striking thing is that they are tending not to buy more and more goods as a form of conspicuous consumption, but to buy time to experiment more with their choices. The most conspicuous form of time consumption is the vacation trip. At the same time employees seem eager to receive leisure hours as a substitute for wage dollars. They bid against their employers for their own time, and their time budgets are becoming more important and more worthy of study than their money budgets.

While these tendencies have appeared primarily in those areas of Western affluence which initially made the new consumer innovation possible, their study is also of importance to the less affluent lands of the East. That consumer

Originally presented at American Sociological Association Conference on Sociological Issues in Business and Industry, New York City, September 3, 1986.

Editor's note: Much of the theoretical content of this paper is derived from the IESS article (Chapter 46), which appeared 20 years before, but a number of the observations are new.

freedom happened first in the "rich" West does not make it irrelevant to the East. In the West, it has happened without forethought or warning and even while some poverty remains. The release from serious economic anxiety has permitted many consumers, although not swamped with wealth, to look around for the first time with a sense of real choice about how they might spend their time, what kind of life they would make for themselves, and what kind of people they might be.

As the consumer begins to innovate in life style, a change is also taking place in how he is viewed by social scientists. The old way was to view him, even define him, predominantly through the eyes of economics. The term "consumer" was not then a social science term, but a focus for concern over efficiency and for a harmonious balance of forces in the free market place. In response to the new affluence the old way of thinking was reflected in a swing from concern with alleged consumer wastefulness to concern with advertising's alleged over-persuasiveness. However, once Packard[1] and similarly inclined critics had clearly and widely raised the alarm that consumers were being made to buy more than they actually needed, the older type of thinking had to be abandoned as a serious approach, that is, it had no further comments to make or questions to ask about what was happening to consumers as people.

While proponents of the older view may acknowledge that the purchase of household appliances saves the time and attention of family members for performance of higher level activities and that consumers spend more on such living aids as they become more affluent, it comes as something of a surprise for them to discover that the proportion of consumer incomes which is spent after taxes, at least in the United States and except for a post-World War buying spree, has remained relatively constant at 92 to 94 per cent.[2] Great changes in consumer behavior have occurred, therefore, during a period when, strictly speaking, changes in economic behavior did not. The more serious concern, then, of the social sciences is to chart the social consequences of consumer access to these new living aids and resources.

Any theory based on economics might have deserved to be considered quite seriously in a day when economic indicators were the best predictors of human behavior. Today, this is less so. Income is no longer the best predictor of consumer purchasing; for example, a time series correlation between the data of 17 University of Michigan consumer surveys from 1952 to 1960 and the level of national expenditures for durable goods showed that estimates based on both recent disposable income and approximate future durable goods expenditures much more closely than the estimates based on disposable income alone. An analysis of variance indicated that consumer demand was more a function of willingness to buy than of ability to buy.[3] In effect, Katona has turned the tables on economics by showing how consumer attitudes of optimism or pessimism initiate changes in economic indicators. The causal flow has been somewhat reversed, therefore, first in observation and then in theoretical formulations.

With the consumer now seen as so "powerful," it is to be expected that attempts to study him have become intensified. One reviewer has identified six different general approaches:

(1) General studies of consumer behavior: the role of consumers and consumption, consumer spending as investments, consumption in economic development.

(2) Income studies: changes in income distribution, credit, and expenditures by various classes. This category accounts for a large part of past studies.

(3) Population studies: population trends and shifts, life-cycle influences, various demographic classifications.

(4) Life-style factors: studies of factors influencing styles of living, such as purchases, status symbols, social class, images, needs, leisure, convenience. This area is receiving increasing emphasis.

(5) Consumers as decision makers: studies of who makes what decisions, what decisions are planned, who is influential in various situations, the household as a decision unit.

(6) Specific purchase and consumption studies: studies of purchases and determinants of purchases for specific products such as coffee, cleansers, gasoline.[4]

The first three of these approaches are dependent upon availability and analysis of mass data. While the federal and state governments have long made such data available, it is only recently that correspondingly massive tools of analysis have become available (for example, the computer). This means that research in these areas was until recently primarily reportorial. With so much detailed data to comprehend it was all that scholars could do to keep up with descriptive identifications of major historical trends. The computer brings a new type of inquiry to such data -- an inquiry that seeks to build dynamic theory and is not daunted by complexities in the manipulation of data.

The fourth and fifth approaches seem to represent more clearly the opening up of consumer study to sociologists and psychologists. Traditionally, the former have studied the ills of society, such as divorce and unemployment. Psychologists, too, have been involved, if not with society's ills, then with the emotionally ill. However, as the current generation of social scientists has put behind it depression and World War 11, and has also participated in the new affluence, there has gradually developed a new curiosity about the nature of the normal personality, a shift away from concern with irrational processes to rational thought, and an interest in theories about how various everyday decisions are made.

As for the consumer himself, we may expect further inroads on his ancient image of himself as a person in want and as one who is preoccupied with the allocation of scarce means to satisfy basic needs. Foote proposes that as the proportion of household expenditures devoted to food continues to fall, today's somewhat obese consumer may well develop wants that do not require production or consumption, such as stimulating conversation or the creation of music.[5] The constraint on wants such as these will not be income but learning ability. In short, consumers may yet outgrow "consumption".

What are the chances? For this I refer you to the United States Trade Deficit. Not to the budget deficit which is smaller. The Trade Deficit or excess of imports over exports was about $50 billion a year in 1982, and is now about $150 billion. Chairman Paul Volcker of the Federal Reserve Board has written, "For more than two years, growth in the United States has, directly and indirectly, provided the impetus for the world economy. . . . For some countries growth in exports to the United States has become the single most important stimulus."

This worries economists and many other people who rightly fear that as the American consumer buys elsewhere the American worker will lose economic gains. To me it means that America will have to share more of its affluence with the rest of the world, and in so doing will lose more of its own. But, only as defined by the older definitions of consumer behavior. A drop in material affluence perhaps, *i.e.*, a drop in what used to be called "standard of living". But, meanwhile, our materially affluent consumer has been learning non-consumption types of satisfaction in activities and in self-concepts. So the timing may be just right for American consumers to continue innovating and improving their "quality of life," as they share more materially with the rest of the world. This process, these problems, these questions -- are fitting and exciting subjects for sociological study.

---

[1] Packard, Vance O., *The Hidden Persuaders*, (New York: McKay 1957).

[2] White, Winston, *Beyond Conformity* (New York: Free Press 1960). See especially Chapter 8.

[3] Katona, George, *The Powerful Consumer: Psychological Studies of the American Economy* (New York: McGraw-Hill 1960).

[4] Halbert, Michael, *The Meaning and Sources of Marketing Theory* (New York: McGraw-Hill 1965).

[5] Foote, Nelson N., "The Image of the Consumer in the Year 2000," in *Boston Conference on Distribution, Thirty-fifth Annual* (Chestnut Hill, Mass.: Boston College 1963), pp. 13-18.

CHAPTER 49

PAVLOV'S DOG AND THE FUTURE OF CONSUMER PSYCHOLOGY

In late 1957 the Soviet earth satellite Sputnik began whizzing over our heads several times a day. On board was a female dog named Laika, which means "lucky." Half a century earlier another Russian dog, another Laika, was the alleged star of Pavlov's laboratory for the study of the conditioned reflex. Laika's star quality was controversial. Although many dogs were used by Pavlov and his students, Professor Vladimir Bechterev, the leading Russian psychologist of the day (Pavlov was defiantly a physiologist), dismissed much of the findings because "Professor Pavlov bases his conclusions solely on his observations of one lively dog with abundant and spontaneous salivation."[1] And so we had the first public discussion of the single-case controversy — even though there were other dogs used. More important, it is suggested here that misunderstandings in the United States of Pavlov's work inhibited the study of the learning of likes and dislikes. Some new emphases for such studies will therefore be recommended.

Ivan Pavlov, who lived 1849-1936, was a distinguished Nobel prize winner on gastric secretions when, in his fifties, he took up the study of salivation induced by other than food stimuli, e.g., in response to the approaching footsteps of an attendant bringing food, the simultaneous sound of a tuning fork, or the particular beat of a metronome. The precise measurement of the salivation, the rate, number, and size of the drops of the saliva appealed to the American desire for a more "scientific psychology."

Pavlov taught dogs to produce the so-called "conditioned reflex" to the non-food signals because he was interested in then studying the *extinction* of that response. Americans, however, seemed to think that his interest was in the *maintenance* of the response. Pavlov saw conditioned responses as more temporary, the Americans as more permanent. In later years, some American social scientists tended to see all of a national culture as built up and permanently maintained by the conditioning process. The phrase "conditioned by the cul-

Original Publication: *Journal of Advertising Research*, Vol. 34, No. 6 (1994). Originally presented upon receipt of the Award for Distinguished Professional Contribution to Consumer Psychology at the 1993 Annual Meeting of the American Psychological Association.

ture" was another way of putting it. Meanwhile, and in stark contrast, Pavlov and his Russian colleagues emphasized the flexibility of national cultures and of human development. Indeed, V.I. Lenin, the Soviet leader and Pavlov's most important patron, saw the research as verification of the possibilities of the so-called "New Soviet Man," the concept of a new personality emanating from Soviet cultural reforms.

Even the language was translated in error. Pavlov used a Russian word that meant *conditional* suggesting temporary, but the same word in America came out as *conditioned,* suggesting final. As historian Robert Boakes noted, "the Russian word was mis-translated into English as 'conditioned' and it has stayed that way ever since."[2] Now what does this have to do with likes and dis-likes, either those of dogs or of humans?

First, Pavlov's demonstration of the behavioral response role of stimuli other than the true object of desire encouraged a variety of dynamic psychologies that said, in effect, that the appeal of a particular stimulus may not be quite what it seems but may only reflect the appeal of some "hidden," subtle "underlying," more basic stimulus — something "other." And so encouragement was, in effect, given to a half century of excess of dramatic and sensationalistic psychologizing, starting with psychoanalysis but extending to depth interviewing, motivational research, etc. — always wanting to go beyond and, therefore, tending to overlook the appeal of the directly confronted object or subject of study itself: to look over, under, around, but not *at* the stimulus in its own right uninfluenced by other stimuli.

To study the appeal of a particular stimulus directly and without recourse to the influence of other stimuli requires an entirely different approach to the study of likes and dislikes. First to provide such an approach was the French psychologist Pierre Janet who in 1925 coined the term "channelization" and later "canalization" as an alternative to conditioning theory.[3] Canalization suggests that the satisfaction of a broad nonspecific craving (*e.g.,* for food, exercise, color, or tone) progressively narrows down to a craving for that specific object which has repeatedly been the satisfier. For example, not food but pizza; not song but the Rolling Stones. The fixation tends to be permanent as compared to conditioned responses, which require periodic reinforcement.

The evolution of this approach antedates even Janet, for the German philosopher Wilhelm Dilthey, who lived 1833-1911, achieved some fame by asking that more attention be given to what he called the *Ding an sich,* translated as "the thing itself" (and is ultimately derived from Kant).[4] This is one future for consumer psychology: to complement and supplement the study of the influence of one stimulus upon another with more direct study of (the) one stimulus (the thing itself).

An example of direct confrontation of the stimulus is represented in the work of Dr. R.G. Hopkinson, an architect associated with University College in London and with the Building Research Station in Garston, England. Faced

with very special design requirements as, for example, hospital design, he prepared small-scale models of the interiors of various parts of the proposed hospital.[5] The model, about 10' x 10' x 4', permitted a person to enter from beneath
and put his head up in to a glass-enclosed viewing space. With the aid of various lenses the perceptual experience was full scale and "real." The persons invited to have a look were nurses, doctors, and various medical specialists who
would be working in the particular environment shown to them. Their comments began freely and were profuse, without the aid of questionnaires or interviews (in the formal sense). The stimulus took care of all that. It was the
stimulus and not the response measures that needed construction.

Another example: Dr. Milton Blum, past chairman of the psychology department at the CUNY Business School, and former Division 23 president, had
the assignment a number of years ago from the John B. Pierce Housing Foundation to work with a team of architects and designers to design a house that was
"twice as efficient at half the cost." The team first studied what people did in
their own homes, room by room, then abandoned the concept of "rooms" in favor of functional spaces and then built full-scale their new house — this within a
huge loft in one of the buildings that comprise "architect's row," as it is called,
and which is the south side of West 40th Street between Fifth and Sixth Avenues
in Manhattan. The house had many radical features, *e.g.*, a temperature-
controlled "sleeping box" which reduced heating needs in the rest of the house
at night, as well as the need for blankets and pajamas. Bathrooms, dressing areas, and closets all had visible differences from the conventional.

Subjects were invited by appointment to walk through the home but only in
pairs or triads with intervals between each group. Microphones were spaced
regularly along the way to record comment. As in the case of Hutchinson's
model, there was no necessity to prepare interviews or questions, or to accompany the visitors on their tour. Visitors commented to each other freely and at
length.

If the first object of a research approach to the *Ding an sich* is a proper respect for the stimulus, and its presentation, then the second aspect is an appreciation of the fact that the response may somehow change over time, *i.e.*, that
"learning" may take place. Here the canalization hypothesis is approached via
the study of what is sometimes called the effects of "sheer exposure," or more
simply "familiarity."

For example, in one experiment involving classical music and popular music fans, participants listened to the same musical selections each week — classical music fans listened to popular music, and popular music fans listened to
classical.[6] For most of the selections the ratings went steadily upward for six
weeks and then leveled off for both groups of fans. Before-and-after attitudes
toward the type of music showed that each group had changed their minds a bit
about the other type of music. They had learned to like it. While liking for most
of the selections increased over time, there were a few for whom dislike grew at

the same rate as the liked relations. Thus, canalization works both ways, creating likes and dislikes.

Similarly, styles of visual art using five different styles of art and two pictures from each style were also studied (Chapter 1 above). In addition to measuring the liking for each picture and each style, the sense of familiarity with each style was also measured.

"Oriental" paintings were perceived as a particular style but were (predominantly) liked more on a picture-by-picture than on a style basis. Familiarity with the style increased more than any other, perhaps because it is strange to Americans, but no increase in liking for the style took place. "Floral" paintings were especially seen as a particular style but were (predominantly) disliked more on a picture-by-picture than on a style basis. Familiarity with the style increased significantly and apparently produced dislike for the style as such. Modern paintings were seen and liked or disliked style without much item-by-item sensitivity. Familiarity with the style increased moderately, while liking for the style increased significantly. "Landscape" paintings were also seen and liked or disliked as a general style without item-by-item sensitivity. Familiarity with the style increased, but liking did not. "Portraits" were also seen as a special style but were (predominantly) disliked more on an item-by-item than a style basis. Familiarity with the style decreased, *i.e.*, began to be seen as different, and even produced some increase in liking.

One might characterize the Oriental situation as "open"; individual items can be liked, but familiarity with the category still provides room for increase without any shift in liking for the category. Florals, on the other hand, could be characterized as a dead category, where further exposure and familiarity will only broaden the dislike for individual items into a dislike for the category as a whole. Moderns and landscapes are perhaps the most popular categories of those studied here, and further familiarity with the more popular moderns increases their popularity, while further familiarity with landscapes has no further effect on their popularity. Portraits, on the other hand, represent a dead category that apparently can be resurrected or reappreciated. Overall the reaction to each style was measurably different. Thus "learning to like," or dislike, may take different forms.

Another example was a study of sculptured forms, this with 30 different package designs submitted for the Nu-Soft fabric softener product which competed with Downy in the supermarket (Chapter 2 above). The various bottles were shown repeatedly and ratings obtained. Some of the initially liked designs lost appeal over time and some others gained. The final and stable preference ratings had little resemblance to the first set of ratings, so there was a change or learning process taking place here too.

In conclusion, the learning of likes and dislikes is not yet a core topic in any of the subdisciplines of general psychology. But it comes closer to being appropriate as a core topic for consumer psychology. The everyday data of consumer research lends itself very well to being adapted to this topic and, if developed as an ongoing concern of consumer psychology, would give back to general psychology a unique contribution to its concern for the overall science of human behavior. For example, the longer term, even life-long consumer likes and dislikes, based on canalization processes, become part of the personality of the individual in a way that briefly conditioned and easily extinguished conditioned responses do not. It is here that the learning of consumer behavior in general more clearly reflects the human individual, the human personality, and the goals of psychology as an independent science.

---

[1] Boakes, R. *From Darwin to Behaviorism.* (Cambridge, England: Cambridge University Press, 1984).

[2] *Op. cit.*

[3] Janet, P., *Psychological Healing* (New York: Macmillan, 1925).

[4] Dilthey, W. *Einleitung in die Geistewissenschaften* (Leipzig, 1883).

[5] Hopkinson, R.G.; P. Petherbridge; and Longmore, Jr., *Daylighting* (London: Heinemann, 1966).

[6] Krugman, H.E. "Affective Response to Music as a Function of Familiarity," *Journal of Abnormal and Social Psychology*, vol. 38, no. 3 (1943), pp. 338-42.

Printed in the United States
by Baker & Taylor Publisher Services